Industrial Societies after the Stagnation of the 1970s – Taking Stock from an Interdisciplinary Perspective
Editor: Burkhard Strümpel

Industrial Societies after the Stagnation of the 1970s – Taking Stock from an Interdisciplinary Perspective

Editor
Burkhard Strümpel

Walter de Gruyter · Berlin · New York 1989

Editor
Professor Dr. Burkhard Strümpel
Freie Universität Berlin
Forschungsstelle Sozialökonomik
Berlin, FRG

With numerous figures and tables

Library of Congress Cataloging-in-Publication Data

Industrial societies after the stagnation of the 1970s – taking stock from an interdisciplinary perspective / editor, Burkhard Strümpel.
p. cm.
Papers presented at a conference held in Berlin in 1988.
Bibliography: p.
ISBN 0-89925-372-5 (U.S.)
1. Economic history -- 1971– -- Congresses, 2. Economic history -- 1945–1971 -- Congresses. 3. Stagnation (Economics) -- Congresses. I. Strümpel, Burkhard.
HC59.I49337 1989
330.9172'2 -- dc19 89-1116
CIP

CIP-Kurztitelaufnahme der Deutschen Bibliothek

Industrial societies after the stagnation of the 1970s – taking stock from an interdisciplinary perspective / ed. Burkhard Strümpel. – Berlin ; New York – de Gruyter, 1989
ISBN 3-11-011345-7
NE: Strümpel, Burkhard [Hrsg.]

∞ Printed on acid free paper.

 Typesetting and Printing: Tutte GmbH, Salzweg/Passau – Binding: Dieter Mikolai, Berlin. – Cover Design: Hansbernd Lindemann, Berlin. – Printed in Germany.

Preface

The good weather era of post-war prosperity has given way to a period of economic turbulence ushered in by the big bang of the oil embargo in 1973. Subsequently, Western industrial countries were plagued by intolerable rates of unemployment and inflation. Economists disagree about the nature of the disease: Is it acute or chronic, will it take care of itself or are massive doses of therapy needed? The limits of purely economic diagnoses are manifest. New social movements came to the fore, pointing to the role of changing values, aspirations, and life-styles of a new generation accustomed to a degree of material security that their parents and grandparents could only dream of. The authors of this book – economists, sociologists, and political scientists from various countries – have been asked to describe this scenario that has been with us for about 15 years. They do so from the vantage points of their respective disciplines and experiences, often shaped by the specific developments and events in their countries.

This volume is the outcome of an international seminar organized by the editor of this volume and held in Berlin in 1986. The editor owes thanks to David Antal for revising the papers by authors for whom English is not the mother tongue, and to Andreas Bahner, Gerhard Reiter, and Evelyn Stoll for their untiring assistance in organizing the conference and communicating with the authors.

Berlin, September 1988 — Burkhard Strümpel

Contents

B. Macroeconomic Policy Making – An Institutional Perspective

C. Value Change and the Economic Experience of Mass Publics

D. Changing Sources of Sustenance

Authors

Dr. Jacques De Bandt
Laboratoire de Recherche en Économie Appliquée
C.N.R.S. – Université de Paris X Nanterre 200
Avenue de la République
F-92001 Nanterre Cedex

Prof. Michael Bolle
Freie Universität Berlin
Forschungsstelle Sozialökonomik der Arbeit
Albrechtstr. 36A
D-1000 Berlin 41

Prof. Vittorio Capecchi
Universita di Bologna
Faculta magistero
Via Zanboni 43
I-40126 Bologna

Klaus Deimer
International Institute for Empirical
Social Economics (INIFES)
Haldenweg 23
D-8901 Stadtbergen

Dr. Xavier A. Greffe
Université de Nanterre 2
Rue de Rouen
F-92001 Nanterre

Prof. Karl Otto Hondrich
Universität Frankfurt
Arbeitsgruppe Soziale Infrastruktur
Robert Mayer-Str. 5
D-6000 Frankfurt

Prof. Martin Jänicke
Freie Universität Berlin
Fachbereich Politische Wissenschaft
Institut für Innenpolitik und Komparatistik
Ihnestr. 22
D-1000 Berlin 33

Jürgen Kühl
Bundesanstalt für Arbeit
Institut für Arbeitsmarkt- und Berufsforschung
Regensburger Str. 104
D-8500 Nürnberg 30

Ian Miles
The University of Sussex
Science Policy Research Unit
Mantel Building Falmer
Brighton Sussex BN 1 9RF
Great Britain

Prof. Ray E. Pahl
Darwin College
The University of Canterbury
Kent CT2 7NY
UK-Canterbury

Prof. Martin Pfaff
Universität Augsburg und International Institute for Empirical Social Economics (INIFES)
Haldenweg 23
D-8901 Stadtbergen

Prof. Fritz W. Scharpf
Max-Planck-Institut für Gesellschaftsforschung
Lothringer Str. 78
D-5000 Köln 1

Prof. Manfred G. Schmidt
Institut für Politische Wissenschaft an der Universität Heidelberg
Marstallstr. 6
D-6900 Heidelberg 1

Prof. Burkhard Strümpel
Freie Universität Berlin
Forschungsstelle Sozialökonomik der Arbeit
Corrensplatz 2
D-1000 Berlin 33

Prof. Ephraim Yuchtman-Yaar
University of Tel-Aviv
Dept. of Sociology and Anthropology
Ramat-Aviv
Tel Aviv, Israel

Introductory Essay: The Lessons of a Decade

Burkhard Strümpel

At the height of post-war prosperity, after a period of unprecedented economic growth in Western Europe, various theories of development or modernization received considerable attention. We were promised the "tertiary civilization" of the service economy as well as the post-industrial society based on science and planning, the welfare state generating "qualitative growth," the post-materialistic age offering individual self-realization and solidaric belonging. With the onset of the économie problématique of the 1970s, many of these theories became obsolete, although they certainly had drawn attention to important developments. Since then, crisis theories have dominated the public debate of recent historical changes. There is word of a crisis of legitimacy, of an environmental crisis, and of "overloaded" government (Zapf 1986).

The post-war period was full of cross-cultural conformities such as the rapid growth of production and employment, the extension of welfare payments, and income security. All these trends applied to virtually all countries of the West and were explained by common causes of different kinds like the American influence, rising economic interdependence, intensified migration, travel, communication, or deeply rooted processes of secularization.

In the last ten to fifteen years industrial societies have suffered from low economic growth, higher rates of inflation, and a return to levels of mass unemployment unheard of since the Great Depression. And even now, after a dozen years of crisis management, economists have, at best, been able to solve the inflation problem while more than thirty million people remain unemployed in the OECD countries. Whereas the success of the post-war era had been achieved in a lock-step manner, there was now a parting of ways. Differences between countries have increased significantly since the early 1970s. Japan and Austria, for example, have seemed almost unaffected by the general malaise and have done remarkably well overall. Others, like Sweden, Italy, and the United States, have seemed to pursue employment gains at the expense of price stability. Still others, like France, Italy, and West Germany, have seemed willing to accept considerable declines in employment in waging their successful battle against inflation.

But while there is agreement that something has changed for the worse in the early 1970s and that industrial societies have responded rather differently to the worsening economic environment, there is disagreement over the causes of the changes and of the differences in the economic performance of different countries (see Scharpf in this volume).

This book, rather than attempting to present an encompassing system or model of the new environment, is devoted to a theoretically guided inventory of the recent experience, unencumbered by a rigid disciplinary framework. There are at least three perspectives, each of them identified with a particular research tradition. First, the macroeconomic performance of a society is viewed largely as the outcome of endogenous economic forces. Second, economic policies are analyzed as they are institutionally conditioned and impinge on economic performance. Third, the economic behavior and the welfare of mass publics is focused on. The first perspective has traditionally been the domain of economists, the second has more recently been opened up by political scientists, and the third perspective has been developed by a combination of sociologists and behavioral economists.

Economic Approaches

The "endogenous" economic perspective is represented by the contributions by Bolle and Greffe, De Bandt, and Kühl. Bolle and Greffe emphasize the features that structural changes in most Western countries have in common. They examine three qualitative trends: the rise of the service sector; the renaissance of small business, which has recently attracted considerable attention; and the slow, but unmistakable departure from the standard full-time job contract. The central idea of De Bandt's contribution is that new forms of interrelations among economic agents have emerged or have become more apparent. Traditional economic approaches and theories are explicitly based on the assumption that economic agents are mutually independent and linked only through the market mechanism, whose role is thus central both in terms of resource allocation and in terms of distribution. In order to demonstrate the importance of new forms of interrelations between firms, De Bandt points particularly to the vitality of small businesses in the present environment, the remarkable performance of multinational corporations, and the effects of the "recombination" of industrial assets (divestments, mergers, take-overs).

Kühl centers on the differences in the performance between countries. Considering the persistence and pervasive nature of the employment problem, it seems appropriate to supplement his analysis with some references to the long-term changes in the relationship between employment, aggregate work volume, and working-time arrangements.

As Kühl shows, real growth was surprisingly parallel in the major Western countries, the only exceptions being Japan and Britain. However, the employment and productivity statistics differ widely, for instance, between the United States and West Germany. While the United States employed 30% more workers in 1983 than in 1973, West German employment figures stagnated, and her unemployment rate soared. Both countries achieved a growth rate averaging around 3% per year, but the respective productivity performances differ drastically. For the United States, the neoclassical position that wage flexibility downward makes for employment gains seems to have been confirmed. But the misgivings of the Keynesian left about supply-side economics and "laissez-faire" may also be confirmed by these statistics. Many of the jobs that have been created are not good and desirable ones as concerns productivity, buying power, and, presumably, the quality of employment.

The German figures on unemployment are more dramatic, but those on wages and structural change are less so than for the U.S. People who have jobs participate modestly in the – to be sure reduced – growth rate of per-capita income. But an increasing number of people who want to work fail to get jobs.

Wassily W. Leontief (1982) interprets statistics like these as symptoms of the demise of labor as a factor of production.

> Human labor from time immemorial played the role of principal factor of production. There are reasons to believe human labor will not retain this status in the future (1982: 154).

Leontief's position in this time-honored debate does not remain unopposed. Throughout industrial history, so the optimists say, productivity changes have led to frictional unemployment and crises of adjustment. Technological changes, in this view, must not be thought of as displacing workers, they just challenge the economy to generate new, more productive combinations of factors, not the least benefiting those workers displaced (or potentially displaced) from their job through technological change in the first place.

These optimists must be reminded of several historic effects. First, periods of high unemployment have often persisted for considerable periods of time. Rather than being caused by business cycles, they seem to be related to more lasting causes. For instance, in terms of unemployment the Great Depression of the 1930s in the United States lasted far longer than a decade. Second, technological change historically was accompanied by a considerable reduction of working time. The work week in manufacturing industries in the U.S. was shortened from 67 hours in 1860 to about 42 hours in 1950 and has remained almost constant since then. Simple arithmetic points to the overriding importance of working-time arrangements for the explanation of unemployment. As Leontief (1982: 155) also states:

> Such reductions in the average number of working hours per week per employee amount to the withdrawal from work of more than a third of the manufacturing labor force.

The productivity increase must be absorbed by reductions in working time, at least to the extent its effect on the aggregate volume of work is not compensated by additional production. Measured against this yardstick, the Federal Republic was successful only in the 1950s, when millions of unemployed citizens, refugees, and displaced persons from what were formerly the Eastern territories of Germany were integrated into the labor force despite the shrinking volume of work (measured in aggregate hours per annum). In contrast, reduction of working time as an instrument of employment policy was patently neglected after the middle of the 1970s. The gradual diminution of the working time per employee by an average of 22 hours per year in the 1950s and 1960s was slowed down to one third, to less than 15 hours per year, from 1973 to 1985. According to the criterion of securing full employment, an annual reduction of 26 hours would have been needed (Wahl 1985).

Institutional Approaches

Let me restate: Following the oil embargo, economic fortunes varied greatly from one country to the next. After two decades of prosperity, countries with similar economic structures found themselves in very different circumstances. Why did the same deterioration in the international environment affect certain countries differently than others? This puzzle stimulates and emphasizes the institutional perspective that political science contributes to the quest for an explanation of differences in employment and monetary stability.

The disappointing economic performance of the post-post-war era, in particular the dramatic differences in the fate of different countries – all of them enjoying sophisticated economic advice and commanding an array of strategies for macroeconomic intervention – raise the question of economic control. Economics had developed a system of measurements, namely the national accounts, as well as a theoretical paradigm for government intervention: Keynesianism, and finally an armory of instruments known as fiscal and monetary policy. These achievements were to be crowned by an instrumentarium of "fine-tuning," meaning that economic activity, through both quick and gradual adjustments to changing situations, could be held on a steady course of potential growth, high employment, and low inflation. Economists were henceforth even deemed worthy of being awarded Nobel prizes. Yet the 1970s showed that the triumph of economics had been premature. Traditional policies seemed to have no clear positive impact on the most pressing economic problems of our time, notably inflation, unemployment, and the balance of payments. The mediocre performance of this period cannot be interpreted as just a technical problem, as suggested by the "McCracken"-Commission (1977), not just a "sequence of avoidable errors" of economic policy, mainly due to short-sighted interventions by non-expert policy makers when it would have been better to have left action up to the professional technicians. The pervasive, chronic disease of unemployment can hardly be blamed on a wrong choice of conventional economic medicine. After all, the basic condition is roughly the same across all national economic policy styles and strategies, be they inspired by monetarism or Keynesianism, deregulation or neo-corporativism, fiscal discipline or big spending deficits, public generosity vis-à-vis big industry and high technology as opposed to abstinence from intervening in the process of structural change.

Economic doctrines guiding macroeconomic management have traditionally been unequivocal, acultural, and technical. They have combined simple techniques of diagnosis with highly technical policy advice. Examples include the West German post-war anti-trust policies in pursuit of the neo-liberal element of the "social market economy," the attempt of neo-Keynesian economists of the Kennedy-Johnson era to codify procedures for "fine-tuning" the economy on a continuous smooth path of "potential output," and, finally, the monetarist formulas for central banks designed to regulate the quantity of money. Except for cryptic references to the existence of a "market economy" as a boundary condition, these doctrines claim general validity without specifying the premises for their applicability. Yet their emergence, influence, and problem-solving potential are clearly both limited to specific cultures and institutions, and bounded by time and space.

For instance, the success of neo-liberal prescriptions, tempered in post-war Germany by elements of the welfare state, is explainable only against the background of past mismanagement through protracted rationing, an excessive quantity of paper money, and the inefficient use of skills and infrastructure, both industrial and public. Moreover, this success was possible only because popular, government, and business priorities were congruent with the single-minded pursuit of economic reconstruction.

In this volume Scharpf's comparative analysis of economic policies during the great recession of the 1970s is an attempt to combine economic constraints ("feasibility"), economic strategies and doctrines ("strategy choice"), and institutional determinants in a single model. The international comparison is confined to four countries: Sweden, Austria, West Germany, and Britain. Scharpf places particular emphasis on the full-employment goal. He attempts to explain differences in performance by developing a general and rather simple model to diagnose the macroeconomic problem. He assesses the armory of economic policies with respect to their feasibility and effects on goal attainment, and concludes by describing the choices confronting policy makers. However, given the adverse economic environment of the 1970s, these choices become policy dilemmas. Even under the best of circumstances they exact great goal sacrifices from labor, and their range diminishes, particularly in countries ill-suited to consensual institutional arrangements.

A comprehensive quantitative analysis is offered by Manfred G. Schmidt in his contribution. He argues that differences in macroeconomic performance are associated with political variables. High levels of macroeconomic performance and in particular a balanced mix comprising moderately high levels of unemployment have been associated with the extent to which concerted policy formation and economic consensus between capital and labor have prevailed in the OECD countries. There have been two roads to successful management of mixed economics. On the one hand, high levels of macroeconomic performance have resulted from a conservative-reformist approach to economic policy, as in Japan and Switzerland. On the other hand, levels of performance have been achieved by a labor-dominated approach, such as in Austria or Norway.

Returning to the question raised at the beginning of this section, what is known about the validity of the ruling economic doctrines which provide both diagnoses and prescriptions for the present ills? The institutional perspective contributed by political scientists suggests that these doctrines are "good weather theories": they assume a considerable measure of discretion by policy makers regarding the choice of instruments and a high level of efficiency in achieving their goals. Both conditions may have prevailed to a large extent in some historical periods as, for example, in the post-war era of unprecedented growth. Typically these conditions have not been present in the adverse economic environment of the 1970s and 1980s. Rarely do the actions of a single actor bring about better macro performance (Strümpel and Scholz 1987).

Consequently, the politico-institutional analysis of economic processes uncovers a complex picture of multivariate interaction, a picture geared to a "politics" perspective rather than to a technical "policy" approach. Not least important, such research teaches us what policy cannot do. Successful crisis management requires a measure of consensus between different actors, which in turn depends on institutional preconditions (Lindberg and Maier 1985). Times of economic adversity both restrict the range of government discretion and, consequently, emphasize the importance of actors other than government, including employers' associations and micro units (households and enterprises).

The Reaction of Mass Publics

Since World War II, Western democracies have witnessed two basic changes deeply affecting the economic situation of the common man: historically unprecedented increases in real income due to high growth in gross national product and productivity in the wake of technological development, and the emergence of the welfare state, that is, the buildup of a considerable measure of economic security for the old, sick, and disabled. Affluence and economic security tend to cast doubt upon the general validity of two venerable propositions. The first is that the common man's economic behavior is ruled by survival needs, or at least by the overriding goal to increase his command over material resources. The second is that his political preferences and choices are dominated by his pocketbook, or economic self-interest.

With respect to the first proposition, it has been demonstrated that economic affluence and security provide the mass of consumers with a certain extent of latitude, in particular "discretionary income", allowing them to spend or save, to speed up or delay consumer investments (housing, automobiles, household appliances), thus making for aggregate changes in business activity (Katona 1951). Beyond income allocation, these changes have opened up choices in the realm of labor force participation. In many cultures, for example, married women going out to work has become an economically and socially accepted – but not prescribed – course of action. A similar measure of latitude has developed for early retirement or delayed entrance into the lavor market, e.g. for students in institutions of higher learning (Katona, Strümpel, and Zahn 1970).

Also the second proposition has been contested. It is argued that material concerns have become less dominant while non-material goals such as protecting the environment, participation in decision making, social status, and "self-actualization" – all of which are not clearly related to command over material resources – may have increased in importance (Hirsch 1976, Inglehart 1977, Mishan 1969). Questions about a demise of the traditional "work ethic" based on discipline, subordination, and punctuality have been raised (Yankelovich et al. 1985). There has even been talk about a new consumption ethic of "voluntary simplicity." Do mass publics in affluent societies tend to dissociate themselves from the ethics and life-styles of the industrial system of growth, to reduce their identification with the "official" economy based on monetarization, centralization, and division of labor?

The preceding line of argument is at odds with a long and venerable research tradition associated with such diverse authors as Marx, Max Weber, Habermas, Karl Polanyi (1944), and Burkart Lutz (1984). This tradition views the commercial rationality of the mainstream economy as pervading the thoughts and actions of people and institutions, dominating social arrangements, values, and views of the world and shaping the everyday routine of the worker and consumer. Not so the recent disengagement theories. According to them, mass affluence, supported by a strong welfare state, erodes the goals, values, and world views on which industrialization was based. Is it that the very success of this economy has undermined people's loyalty towards the production system and its rationalistic imperatives? For some authors, such as Ronald Inglehart (1977), this possibility assumes an optimistic flair; for other, conservative, authors such as Daniel Bell (1973), Helmut Klages (1985), and Elisabeth Noelle-Neumann (Noelle-Neumann and Strümpel 1984) it is full of pessimistic connotations.

The contributions to sections C and D of this book take up the engagement/disengagement theme on the two levels of values and subjective popular experience on the one hand and behavioral trends on the other. People's reactions to social change cannot be viewed only as a function of the changes in their objective situation, let alone their economic situation as expressed by income or wealth. Rather, they must also be understood as resulting from the changes in people's basic convictions, values, and goals in life, in the way they mentally structure their environment and decode the events and experiences they are confronted with.

Let us first turn to the contributions indebted to the former level of analysis. While Inglehart has analyzed the impact of rising affluence on individual values, Karl Otto Hondrich in this volume presents a more general perspective of the dynamics of value change, based on a broad review of empirical evidence. He draws attention to the proliferation of values. There is not just one freedom to choose from but many. There are contradictions between value domains, for instance between self-actualization and love/belonging. At best, the domains can be reconciled "by abstraction," as evident in the growing importance of values like tolerance, communication, and peace.

Ephraim Yuchtman-Yaar takes on the subjective aspects of the work experience. How does technological change at the workplace affect loyalty and satisfaction to work and employer? The author can take recourse to comparative survey data from several countries. By way of cautious generalization, he documents by and large favorable attitudes toward technological change the workplace. However, there are age differences: the younger, more educated workers are also more articulate, and their skepticism is related to critical attitudes toward economic growth.

Strümpel's contribution deals with changes in perceived well-being of the West German population in the face of stagnating incomes and the aggravation of the employment situation. The author points to continued high levels of satisfaction with income or material well-being. However, while older adults appear – presumably due to the improvement in old-age pensions – to be subjectively better off, the discontent of young, particularly blue-collar, workers has increased. There is a mismatch between the discipline and subordination required by the world of work and the values of independence, autonomy, and self-actualization. However, there is little evidence that the pockets of discontent will resort to political action. On the other hand, solidarity with the unemployed – expressed through wage discipline and preference for a reduction in working time, for example – enjoys a considerable measure of support, particularly in times of rising joblessness.

Ian Miles, whose chapter is based mainly on British data, deals with a most elementary aspect of behavior: time use. The analysis of longitudinal measurements reveals clear-cut, generalizable, plausible trends such as a decrease in paid work among full-time workers and a decrease in time spent on household work by lower-status women. It is intriguing to find that very few changes occuring up to 1976 were extended into the subsequent period. Miles also ponders the impact on time use of information technologies, which he considers powerful motivators for self-service activities.

Sources of Sustenance

In the 1970s the limits of the welfare state became evident, both qualitatively and quantitatively. Roughly constant shares of public budgets spent for transfer payments had to accommodate ever greater numbers of unemployed, old-age pensioners, and welfare recipients. Time and again, the question has been raised as to whether productive efforts outside the market could compensate for the gaps in income left by the stagnation or deterioration in both the employment situation and in government transfers. These questions have been taken up in this book by Pahl and Pfaff/Deimer. The "self-provisioning" efforts within a British semirural community are analyzed by Ray E. Pahl. According to him, the relationship between integration in paid work and the chance to receive non-money incomes is complementary, not compensatory. He suggests that successful integration into the secondary economy nowadays presupposes skills and resources similar to those on which success in the primary economy is contingent. The most important conditions for self-provisioning activities are directly derived from the primary job: skills and their maintenance, contacts with potential suppliers and customers, even materials and tools. This is in contrast to the period of early industrialization, when the traditional family farm offered a livelihood to many an industrial worker who had been laid off temporarily or permanently.

Pfaff and Deimer deal with another form of production outside the official economy, namely, voluntary activity in the field of social services, both through small networks and larger, officially organized arrangements to provide personal care. Like Pahl, the authors emphasize the complementarity rather than the substitutive features of those arrangements. It is the better-off, those who are expected and able to reciprocate, who, in times of need, have the best chance of being helped. There is evidence that one of the obstacles to the evolution of networks of mutual support is the reluctance of the needy to accept help as long as they see little chance to reciprocate. Another kind of complementarity is required. Networks for mutual help can be successful only if they receive support from intermediary or large-scale networks. The authors warn against overburdening small networks with tasks for which they are not suited, tasks such as providing monetary transfers and requiring certain kinds of professional competence and skill. In particular, networks should not be used as an excuse for the retrenchment of social welfare programs.

Vittorio Capecchi's contribution deals with the adjustment to changing work opportunities. He describes the recruitment patterns of entrepreneurs in an Italian region. Ever-increasing numbers of young people, having grown up in working-class or farming families, end up as entrepreneurs in creative crafts. The author links this unusual, or at least overlooked, avenue to mobility to the disengagement from conventional types of paid employment. He also draws attention to the ambiguity in the young entrepreneurs' objective and subjective position squeezed between capital and labor.

Scenarios

The common thread of the contributions by Kühl, Yuchtman-Yaar, Strümpel, and Miles is the pervasive concern over the possibility of society's dualization. The prosperous years of post-war growth and high employment had strengthened the position of the average worker, pensionary, even welfare recipient on both the market and the political arenas. There was more equality and a broader sharing of power. In contrast, the stagnation and post-stagnation years of the 1970s and 1980s have accentuated the inequalities due to differences between people in the command of both physical and human capital and, most of all, in their opportunities for access to employment. There are indications of a segmentation of the working population. Yet it would be pretentious to derive predictions from the large body of analyses presented in this book. It is more appropriate to indicate scenarios of possible developments.

There is the malign scenario of "business as usual" that inevitably will lead to a further segmentation of the working population.

In this scenario, the employers make full and exclusive use of the higher qualified and motivated members of the workforce, relying mainly on standard full-time job contracts supplemented if necessary by overtime and the hiring of marginal workers on temporary, precarious part-time contracts. The reduction of average working time continues to lag behind a reduction of the aggregate work volume and behind the preferences of the labor force. Employment will shrink; unemployment will rise. Employment opportunities will be more polarized than before, and the prospect of utilizing acquired skills will remain dim for many. There is less incentive for the employers to train broad cadres of skilled workers as long as highly motivated and desirable workers, occasionally mockingly referred to as "Olympia teams," are in ample supply. There is "the long arm of the job." One's integration into the money economy tends to be a precondition for successful participation in the non-market economy (Pahl in this volume).

The benign scenario is based on an extended range of choices of working-time arrangements for the employee. As long as women and men are offered attractive opportunities for part-time employment, many more full-time employees and their spouses or partners will be tempted to rethink the most appropriate mix of work in the official economy in accordance with the needs of the family and their preferred leisure pursuits. More working-time options will lead to a differentiation according to the individual variance in life-styles.

A reduction of perceived "overemployment" documented in both Strümpel's and Miles' papers would have an equalizing effect. The range of employment opportunities would be extended for the great majority of workers, not only for the unemployed. The weaker segment, too, those heretofore subject to discrimination and/or relegated to inferior, unstable jobs could look forward to more and better employment opportunities than those available today.

It would be too narrow to consider different scenarios only from the perspective of labor market and employment trends. Martin Jänicke, in his concluding essay, ponders the conditions for adaptive societal responses or innovations on three levels. First technologies relating to "hard" physical production; second social technologies, i.e., the re-organization of human behavior; and intellectual technologies, i.e., the organization of knowledge. A process of societal learning must overcome three myths: the myth of laissez-faire, the myth of high growth rates, and the myth of industry. In his vision of a "scenario of innovation" the author substitutes laissez-faire through cooperative, non-bureaucratic planning linking decentralized modes of decisionmaking to the solution of generally perceived problems. The mobilization of intermediary mechanisms between the centrifugal tendencies of the market and the centripetal power of the state is a theme touched upon by different authors in this volume, namely by De Bandt with regard to the private sector, by Schmidt relating to neo-corporative arrangements, and by Pfaff and Deimer regarding the organization of (non-professional or semiprofessional) social services. Similarly, Jänicke's critique of traditional forms of economic growth builds upon the broad range of empirical findings and interpretations contained in this volume (Kühl, Scharpf, Hondrich, and Strümpel). Indeed, more or less growth – that is not the question. GNP statistics, the foremost indicator of economic performance in the last thirty years, have lost in importance. In contrast to the preceding period, further economic growth is not clearly resulting in improved welfare. There is a demystification of mass consumption, and there are symptoms of satiation among affluent citizens. Most everybody has given up expecting that the employment problem can be solved through economic growth. Growth may create jobs by increasing demand, but it simultaneously destroys jobs by accelerating the substitution of workers by computers or other machines.

Conversely, economic growth will lose its function as a negative symbol, as a bogeyman for the post-materialist opposition. Economic growth in the future, to the extent there is any, will be ecologically less problematic than in the past. The distributional conflict of the future, as Strümpel's contribution suggests, will center less around money and more around non-material resources such as autonomy, participation in decision making, communication, on-the-job maintenance of skills, and chances for self-actualization outside of sphere of work. The capacity of the official, monetarized economy to solve the pressing social problems of our day is overestimated. Whether or not Western industrial societies will be successful in the future will not be decided in the arena of economic growth. The answer to this question will depend on the quality of the technologies adapted, the quality of life, and the handling of social conflict surrounding the distribution of material and non-material resources.

References

Bell, D. (1973): *The coming of post industrial society: A venture in social forecasting*, New York.

Hirsch, F. (1976): *Social limits to growth.* Cambridge/Mass.

Hirschman, A. (1974): *Exit, voice and loyality: Responses to decline in firms, organizations and states*, Cambridge/Mass.

Inglehart, R. (1977): *The silent revolution: Changing values and political styles among western publics*, Princeton.

Katona, G. (1951): *Psychological analysis of economic behavior*, New York.

Katona, G.; Strümpel, B.; and Zahn, E. (1970): *Aspirations and affluence: Comparative studies in the United States and Western Europe*, New York.

Klages, H. (1985): *Wertorientierungen im Wandel: Rückblick, Gegenwartsanalyse, Prognosen*, Frankfurt.

Leontief, W. W. (1982): The distribution of work and income, *Scientific American*, 247, 3, (September): 152–164.

Lindberg, L. N. and Maier, C. S. (1985): *The politics of inflation and economic stagnation*, Washington, D. C.

Lutz, B. (1984): *Der kurze Traum immerwährender Prosperität: Eine Neuinterpretation der industriell-kapitalistischen Entwicklung im Europa des 20. Jahrhunderts*, Frankfurt/Main.

McCracken, P. et al. (1977): *Towards full employment and price stability*, OECD, Paris.

Mishan, E. J. (1969): *Welfare economics: An assessment*, Amsterdam.

Noelle-Neumann, E. and Strümpel, B. (1984): *Macht Arbeit krank? Macht Arbeit glücklich? Eine aktuelle Kontroverse*, München.

Polanyi, K. (1944): *The great transformation*, New York.

Strümpel, B. and Scholz, J. (1987): The comparative study of the economy: dimensions, methods and results. In: Dierkes, M., Weiln, H. N. and Antal, A. B. (eds.): *Comparative Policy Research*, Berlin.

Wahl, S. (1985): Langfristige Trends auf dem Arbeitsmarkt, In: Aus Politik und Zeitgeschichte, Beilage zur Wochenzeitung *Das Parlament*, B 42/85, Bonn.

Yankelovich, D.; Zetterberg, H.; Strümpel, B.; and Shanks, M. (1985): *The world at work – An international report on jobs, productivity and human values*, New York.

Zapf, W. (1986): Wandel und Krisentendenzen in westlichen Industriegesellschaften: Innovationschancen der westlichen Gesellschaftssysteme, In: *Soziale Welt*, Sonderband 4: S. 167–179.

A. Market Structure and Employment Trends

Employment and Productivity in Europe – What are the Perspectives?

*Michael Bolle**) *and Xavier A. Greffe*

Basic Features

In terms of empirical economics, employment patterns are not hard to understand. Growth of output and changes of labor productivity determine the level of employment. This explanation may sound somewhat trivial given the tautological way in which the variables are linked, but it may provide some insights.

Table 1 Civilian Employment (All Activities)

	Average Annual Percentage Changes			
	1953–1961	1961–1973	1973–1979	1980–1984
Austria	1.3	−0.2	0.2	1.3
Belgium	0.6	0.9	0	0.1
Denmark	0.7	1.4	0.8	−0.2
France	−0.1	1.0	0.2	−0.5
Federal Republic of Germany	2.0	0	−0.2	−1.2
Ireland	−1.6	0	1.4	−0.7
Netherlands	1.5	1.0	0.2	−0.5
Norway	0.3	1.4	2.2	0.6
Spain	0.7	0.9	−1.4	−1.2
Sweden	1.0	0.7	1.2	0.2
Switzerland	2.1	1.2	−1.3	−0.1
United Kingdom	3.8	2.2	1.4	−1.3
OECD Europe	0.8	0.4	0.1	
New EC				−0.7
Japan				1.0
United States				1.5

Sources: OECD, various issues.

*) I am indebted to Dipl.-Volkswirt Michael Herr, who not only involved himself in statistical and empirical work but also helped in clarifying ideas.

Table 2 Gross Domestic Product

	Average Annual Percentage Changes 1953–1961	1961–1973	1973–1979	1980–1984
Austria	6.8	4.9	3.1	1.3
Belgium	3.4	5.0	2.3	1.8
Denmark	3.9	4.5	2.1	2.3
France	4.9	5.6	3.0	1.0
Federal Republic of Germany	7.2	4.5	2.4	0.6
Ireland	1.8	4.3	3.6	1.7
Netherland	4.6	5.2	2.5	0
Norway	3.4	4.3	4.4	2.1
Spain	4.7[a)]	6.9	2.8	1.4
Sweden	4.0	3.9	1.8	1.4
Switzerland	5.2	4.1	−0.4	0.9
United Kingdom	5.8	5.1	2.6	1.5
OECD Europe	4.9	4.7	2.4	
New EC				0.9
Japan				4.0
United States				2.7

a) 1954–1961

Sources: OECD, various issues.

European countries experienced a variety of employment patterns in recent decades. In the 1950s and 1960s labor demand was high in Europe, and increased the level of employment considerably (see Table 1). Growth rates of employment slowed somewhat, but even in the 1970s most European countries (remarkably enough, not West Germany) were still able to increase their employment level. It was not until the beginning of the 1980s that the level of employment fell in most European countries, averaging around −0.7% annually from 1980 to 1984 in the EEC member countries, Portugal, and Spain.

It was commonly believed that the diminishing capacity of European countries to create jobs was due to a sharp decrease in the growth rates of output, an argument that seems to be confirmed by empirical evidence documenting the trend in growth rates of real gross domestic product (see Table 2). Annual growth of gross domestic product in real terms averaged around 4.9% from 1953 to 1961 and remained very high until 1973. After the first oil shock, the average annual growth of real GDP declined dramatically, ranging around 2.4% in Europe's OECD countries from 1973 to 1979. The situation was aggravated at the beginning of the 1980s.

For EEC member countries, Portugal, and Spain, the average annual growth of real GDP dropped to 0.9% between 1980 and 1985.

These patterns tend to support the view that the decline of employment can be explained by slower growth. In view of the pure and simple economics mentioned above, however, one might do well to consider labor productivity an even more significant variable. Employment is determined not only by growth of output itself but also by the link between growth of output and changes in productivity. European countries enjoyed high increases in productivity during the 1950s and 1960s. In the 1970s and, even more important, at the beginning of the 1980s productivity trends pointed downwards (see Table 3). Whereas growth of output and productivity gains implied increases in the number of jobs for European countries even in the 1970s, this was not the case at the beginning of the 1980s.

However, the declining capacity of Europe to create jobs is only a partial explanation for the increase in unemployment. The link between

Table 3 Productivity Trends

	Average Annual Percentage Changes			
	1953–1961	1961–1973	1973–1979	1980–1984
Austria	5.5[b)]	5.1	2.9	0
Belgium	2.8	4.1	2.3	1.7
Denmark	3.2[c)]	3.1	1.3	2.5
France	5.0	4.6	2.8	1.5
Federal Republic of Germany	5.2	4.5	3.2	1.8
Ireland	3.4[b)]	4.3	2.2	2.4
Netherlands	3.1	4.2	2.3	0.5
Norway	3.1	2.9	2.2	1.5
Spain	4.0[a)]	6.0	4.2	2.6
Sweden	3.0[c)]	3.2	0.6	1.2
Switzerland	3.1[c)]	2.9	0.9	1.0
United Kingdom	2.0	2.9	1.2	2.8
OECD Europe	4.1	4.3	2.3	
New EC				1.6
Japan				3.0
United States				1.2

a) 1954–1961
b) 1951–1961
c) 1950–1961

Sources: OECD, various issues.

Table 4 Job Deficit, Demand, and Supply

		Average Annual Changes in Percent of			
		Employment	Labor Supply	Job Deficit[1]	Unemployment Rate[2]
Belgium	1971–1980	0.3	0.8	0.5	5.8
	1983–1989	0.0	0.3	0.3	16.1
	1989–1995	0.2	0.0	−0.2	15.2
Denmark	1971–1980	0.7	1.2	0.5	3.8
	1983–1989	0.5	0.3	−0.2	8.4
	1989–1995	0.7	0	−0.7	4.5
France	1971–1980	0.4	0.8	0.4	3.8
	1983–1989	0.0	0.6	0.6	12.2
	1989–1995	0.2	0.4	0.2	13.3
Federal Republic of Germany	1971–1980	−0.1	0.1	0.2	2.8
	1983–1989	−0.2	0.3	0.5	11.1
	1989–1995	−0.0	−0.4	−0.4	6.0
Greece*	1971–1980	0.6	1.3	0.7	*
	1983–1989	1.1	0.4	−0.7	*
	1989–1995	0.9	0.0	−0.9	*
Ireland	1971–1980	1.0	1.0	0.0	7.4
	1983–1989	1.1	1.5	0.4	17.1
	1989–1995	1.1	1.4	0.3	19.0
Italy	1971–1980	0.5	0.9	0.4	6.0
	1983–1989	0.2	0.6	0.4	14.1
	1989–1995	0.2	0.3	0.1	14.5
Luxemburg[3]	1971–1980	1.3	1.3	0.0	0.3
	1983–1989	0.4	0.0	−0.4	*
	1989–1995	0.5	−0.4	−0.9	*
Netherlands	1971–1980	0.2	1.2	1.0	3.4
	1983–1989	0.6	1.0	0.4	16.3
	1989–1995	0.7	0.4	−0.3	14.9
United Kingdom	1971–1980	0.2	0.6	0.4	4.2
	1983–1989	0.2	0.2	0.0	11.9
	1989–1995	0.3	−0.0	−0.3	10.0
EEC – Cold	1971–1980	0.2	0.6	0.4	4.2
	1983–1989	0.1	0.5	0.4	12.2
	1989–1995	0.3	0.1	−0.2	11.0

[1] Annual change of job deficit: Annual change of labor supply minus annual change of employement.

[2] Rate of unemployement: First row: average; second row: end of 1989; third row: end of 1995.

[3] No data available.

Source: Bolle 1986.

growth of output and changes in productivity tells economists something about labor demand. Unemployment is determined by both the demand for and the supply of labor. In order to explain levels of unemployment, one must take the supply of labor into account. The supply of labor did rise in European countries after 1970 up to now and will continue to do so for the next few years. There are two main reasons for this development. The first is a purely demographical one, pointing to high net fertility rates of the 1950s and 1960s. The second reason is a socioeconomical one and is based on the observation that rates of women participating on the labor market have increased considerably. The "job deficit" of European countries, the mismatch between labor demand and labor supply that has resulted in rising unemployment rates, may thus be partly explained by the effects of labor supply and partly by the declining capacity of European countries to create jobs (see Table 4).

The declining capacity of European countries to create jobs is a result of a changing nexus between growth of output and changes in productivity. Policies intended to stimulate future employment must be designed to stabilize the link between growth of output and changes in productivity. Clearly this is not done easily. Policies encouraging growth may end up with a corresponding increase of labor productivity but no positive impact on the labor market, at least not in the medium term, a result known as "jobless growth". Policies stimulating productivity may even depress employment if growth of output does not keep up. On the other hand, following a growth path not based on increases in productivity might ultimately jeopardize growth and employment altogether.

There are many trend-related, cyclical, and structural factors, widely debated by economists, that allow for different interpretations of Western Europe's declining capacity to create jobs. It would be pretentious to ignore these interpretations, for a fragment of truth is contained even in most traditional economic analyses. Instead, we propose to modify the analysis of the changing link between growth and productivity by taking only market phenomena and changing modes of regulation into consideration.

Regulation and Where it Fails

The complexity of the economy is impossible to grasp solely in terms of supply, demand, and equilibrium. Economic processes are regulated by the interdependence of economic, social, institutional, and technical structures. At the heart of the regulatory mechanism is the way in which labor is organized and wages are set, the mechanism of defining and meeting needs, and the way in which the state helps to resolve conflicts while pursuing its tax, expenditure, adjustment, and restructuring policies.

An inefficient regulatory mechanism may be rapidly overcome. But there are also crises of regulation, where new regulatory mechanisms replace old ones. This, in fact, has been taking place in Europe since 1970. Even when the current cyclical recovery of varying strength is taken into account, the performance of the economy indicates mutations in the modes of regulation, which, in turn, are linked to specific types of systems of accumulation.

Two main types of accumulation can be identified: extensive and intensive. In the first case, growth of capital and production occurs in waves, occasionally interrupted by disequilibria to be resolved by a return to more efficient proportions of production, capacity, and demand. There are no basic modifications in the standards of either production or consumption, and productivity gains are slow. With intensive accumulation, production conditions are in a continuous state of change. Productivity gains are high, wages rise rapidly, and patterns of consumption undergo constant modifications. One of the most important characteristics of the intensive accumulation system is that productivity gains do not appear to threaten employment. Instead, they are means of providing a high level of employment. Because they allow wages and production to rise quickly, they lead to a rapid jump in the demand for goods and labor, even rapidly stimulating labor and thereby making it possible to perpetuate growth.

These two modes of accumulation, which can coexist in some cases, tend to occur in succession. The first predominated before 1930, by which time it had run its course. The second mode has prevailed since 1950, though its foundations were shaken at the start of the 1970s. With regard to the organization of labor, personal management, and wage policies, the dissimilar characteristics of both modes of accumulation are easy to identify.

- Taylorism dominated the extensive accumulation system. By putting the organization of labor in the hands of management rather than in the hands of the foreman, Taylorism contributed to the increase in productivity, whereas wage increases were low.
- Intensive accumulation is the time for "triumphant" Fordism. Scientific organization is pushed to an extreme. Productivity grows considerably and implies increases of consumption because of wage policies notably different from those in the scenario of extensive accumulation. This type of labor organization may be efficient, but it is somewhat fragile. The slightest hitch can cause significant interruptions of production, and that at a time when confrontation is becoming a hallmark of industrial labor.

During the 1920s, significant limits on extensive accumulation became evident. After World War I, needs gave rise to a strong expansion in the capital goods sector, for markets for consumer goods were stagnating or sluggish. The continuing importance of rural society, the fact that precapitalistic structures were retained, the suppression of certain foreign markets, and fierce competition between wage earners explain why the system of extensive accumulation could no longer operate efficiently.

The change from extensive to intensive accumulation is best understood by the totally new role of wage policies. The concept rapport salarial, the dual relationship between labor and production and labor and consumption, reflects the new balance in a system of intensive accumulation. This concept is based on three elements: an increase in income related to rising consumption, an increase in income security through a rise in indirect and social remuneration (fringe benefits), and a narrowing of the differences in remuneration between sectors. The rapport salarial bears witness to a much more institutionalized and planning-based management of accumulation.

During the 1970s and at the beginning of the 1980s, however, even the system of intensive accumulation was threatened. Empirical evidence suggests that the prime movers of growth tended to run out of steam:

- Investment sagged in Western European countries. In EEC countries the average rate of investment fell from 21.4% in 1975 to 18.4% of GNP in 1984. The decline of private investment was a common element of the European economies in the 1970s and, even more dramatically, in the beginning of the 1980s (see Table 5).

Table 5 Investment-Quotas (Reported to GDP) (At Current Prices)

	1960	1965	1970	1975	1980	1984
Austria	25.1	27.4	25.9	26.7	25.2	21.7
Belgium	19.2	22.3	22.7	22.1	20.9	15.9
France	20.1	23.2	23.4	23.3	21.7	18.7
Federal Republic of Germany	24.4	26.1	25.5	20.4	22.8	20.3
Italy	22.8	19.3	21.7	20.6	19.8	17.9
Netherlands	24.1	25.3	25.9	20.9	21.0	18.5
Switzerland	25.1	29.1	27.7	24.0	23.8	23.3
United Kingdom	16.9	18.9	19.1	19.4	17.4	16.2
New EC				21.4	20.9	18.5
Japan	31.2	30.1	35.7	32.4	32.0	27.9
United States	17.9	18.8	17.6	17.0	18.5	18.8

Source: Author's computations based on Sachverständigenrat 1985.

Table 6 Change of Real Labor Income Per Employee Compared to Change of Productivity

(1980 = 100)	1960	1965	1970	1975	1980	1984
Austria	84.7	90.3	92.1	103.3	100	87.5
Belgium	80.6	80.7	82.4	95.8	100	95.3
France	94.1	92.5	90.7	98.9	100	98.6
Federal Republic of Germany	84.3	89.2	95.0	101.8	100	92.8
Italy	87.4	93.2	91.6	103.8	100	103.9
Netherlands				101.6	100	90.7
Switzerland	82.5	88.8	90.1	99.6	100	100.4
United Kingdom	91.4	91.7	93.9	107.6	100	96.8
Japan	111.0	99.7	91.4	106.7	100	93.9
United States	95.7	91.9	98.3	97.9	100	97.3

Source: Sachverständigenrat 1985.

- The weakness afflicting the rates of investment was linked to a "profit-squeeze." After about 1970, the change in real labor income per employee was higher than the change in labor productivity. The income position of wage earners, the real wage position, improved. This enhancement of the real wage position was a common feature in Western European countries up to 1975, but in some countries, like France and Belgium, survived even until 1980. It was only after 1980 that the real wage position worsened in all countries except Italy. Improvement of the real wage position led thereafter to a drop in the rate of profit and discouraged private investment (see Table 6).

It should be noted, however, that the drop in the rate of profit is only partly due to the increase in real wages in the 1970s. The prolonged period of full employment in the 1960s brought about wage expectations and rigidities of the labor market unfavorable to the situation in the 1970s. The malfunctioning the labor market in the 1970s was but one source for slow growth and decreasing gains in productivity. Other relevant phenomena are internal structural developments like the diminishing role of intersectorial labor transfers acting as a productivity reserve, the changing relation between the secondary and the tertiary sector of the economy, and the need for a renewal of the capital stock for technologies. These are the most important factors that influenced economic patterns in the 1970s. External factors, too, are partly responsible for slow growth and diminishing gains in productivity: increasingly fierce competition from newly industrialized countries, especially with regard to mass production; the oil shocks; and the transition being made by international monetary system, its highly unstable exchange rates. Given these factors, one might wonder why unemployment did not grow more quickly in the 1970s or why employment did not fall dramatically. The answer is that there were shock absorbers and countertendencies as well.

The rapport salarial was a built-in stabilizer. Even in the 1970s the level of real wages continued to rise. Only after the second oil shock, especially in the beginning of the 1980s, did real wages decrease. The period between the two oil shocks was characterized in particular by slow increases in real wages, which at least stabilized private demand somewhat. Moreover, the importance of indirect remuneration such as unemployment compensation dampened unemployment's first effects on demand. Once the financial mechanisms of the welfare state are jeopardized, however, indirect remuneration can no longer do this.

Beyond built-in stabilizers, there were other tendencies that helped to counter unfavorable shocks. One of the first was generated by changes in financial structures, at least initially: greater use of credit to compensate for the drop in the level of earnings retained by companies, the proportion of public financing, and the generalization of fiscal expenditure allowing companies to postpone some of the necessary reconversion. During the 1970s, however, it became clear that these monetarily based stimuli were only leading to an acceleration of inflation rates without having a lasting effect on self-sustained growth. A second countertendency can be seen in the internationalization of production and investment. At the beginning of the 1970s European countries indeed pursued policies of internationalization by stimulating exports of specific products (automobiles and durable consumer goods) to compensate for the sluggishness of their internal demand. But one might wonder if national economies did not suffer even more severe effects as a result: when world trade stagnates and competition intensifies, taking recourse to internatinal trade seems to be a dubious approach to counteracting unfavorable shocks. This is especially true in an international monetary system that is governed by flexible exchange rates and a growing external debt incurred by developing countries.

Indeed, the system of intensive accumulation, working somewhat efficiently in the 1960s, seemed to be threatened by a major breakdown in the 1970s. In the following section more detailed analysis focusing on the functioning of the labor market will help to identify the structural and trend-related reasons contributing to the crisis of regulation.

Equilibria and Adjustment

The Dynamic Equilibrium of the 1950s and 1960s

From the beginning of the 1950s to the mid-1960s, labor demand was high in Europe. This led to an increase in the number of jobs averaging 1.5 % per year in industry and close to 2 % in services. This demand was satisfied through the interplay of several factors during that period. First, the number of persons between the ages of 14 and 25 years increased, except in West Germany. Second, agricultural productivity rose, doubling the migration rate from rural to urban areas. Third, the immigrant population grew by almost 10 millions and came to account for about 7 % of the EEC population. The participation rate of immigrants in the workforce was above the national average. Fourth, the participation rate of women in the workforce rose. In all countries the rate rose significantly between 1960 and 1975. On the supply side, rising participation rates of women were due to the desire of women for emancipation, to progress made in home technology, to the spread of childcare systems, and to the wider use of contraception resulting in lower birth rates. On the demand side, the rise of service occupations implied the development of more accessible types of jobs. Remarkably enough, when the growth rate began to level off in a number of European countries, female participation rates did not decrease although they had fluctuated cyclically in the past (see Table 7).

Table 7 Proportion of Women in Civilian Employment

	1970	1975	1980	1983
Belgium	32.7	34.4	35.8	37.4
Denmark	39.4	41.6	44.5	46.1
France	35.2	37.0	38.0	39.2
Federal Republic of Germany	36.6	38.0	38.2	38.8
Ireland	26.7	28.0	29.2	31.2
Italia	28.3	29.3	32.1	32.8
Netherlands	26.3	27.5	30.6	33.6
United Kingdom	36.3	38.7	40.2	41.6
EUR 9	34.0	35.6	37.0	38.1
Proportion of Women in Total Employment				
Japan	39.3	37.4	38.7	39.5
United States	36.3	38.7	41.7	42.4

Source: Eurostat, various years.

When unemployment grew at the beginning of the seventies, the supply of labor did not react in a classical way. Even with, or perhaps because of, the increase of unemployment, there was no sign that households were giving up second incomes. In other words, the discouraged-worker effect did not work. Moreover, there was a positive effect on the labor supply because of the extra worker effect. Workers stayed on the labor market because of the measures of job protection implemented during the 1960s. Beyond these labor supply effects are, however, more important factors that were inherited from the full employment of the 1960s and that aggravated the performance of the European economy in the beginning of the 1970s.

Rigidity and Dualism: Consequences of the High Employment Level

There are at least two factors that determined the performance of the labor market in the beginning of the 1970s and that resulted from the high employment level in the 1960s, upward pressure on wages, and dualism of the job market. There are a number of explanations for the pressure on wages to rise even when unemployment is on the rise. Some of them refer to the political and economic power that the unions won in the social struggle at the close of the 1960s; some are based on wage expectations and income policy. Income policies, implemented during the 1960s, might have led to the public misunderstanding that the income rises automatically even in times of slow or negative growth. Quite in line with some ideas of Kalecki, one might argue that, after a long period of full employment, layoffs are no longer interpreted as an incentive to change wage expectations. If declining employment and rising unemployment are regarded as transitory, layoffs are no incentive to adjust wages, at least not in the short run.

The other phenomenon, the dualism or segmentation of the labor market, is the consequence of regulations imposed on employment contracts during times of high employment. In the 1960s measures were taken to protect jobs and to restrain the employer's power to lay off workers. As a result, employers responded to changes of demand by adapting working time instead of the level of employment. When demand and production slowed down in the beginning of the 1970s, firms reacted by reducing overtime, getting rid of workers with a low degree of job protection, and holding on to skilled people with a high degree of job protection. However, during times of recovery in the 1970s, firms would not hire additional workers but again reacted by increasing overtime and resorting to more precarious, low quality types of employment. This process explains why unemployment is unevenly distributed. Primary victims are young and unskilled wage earners as well as older workers lacking protection. Measures taken to protect jobs, perfectly fitted to a high employment level, may have a bias in times of growing unemployment. They protect people who have jobs and discriminate against people who are looking for one.

Structural Trends and the Capacities to Create Jobs

Some structural trends in European economies have already been mentioned, such as the fact that the growing importance of women in the labor force, somewhat persistent rigidities of the labor market, and the role of the rapport salarial no longer serve as built-in stabilizers. But there still are more observable structural phenomena that have determined the performance of European economies in recent decades and that will continue to do so in the foreseeable future. Working time has been reduced, for example. Between 1960 and 1980 average weekly working hours in major European countries decreased by at least 0.7% annually (see Table 8). Working-time reductions occurred in different forms: earlier retirement and the extension of holidays. This process will continue, but issues are probably changing from overall reductions to the flexibilization of working-time arrangements.

The growing importance of new types of jobs was already evident in the 1970s. Whereas full-time employment grew at a slow pace, part-time, short-term, and casual employment developed much more quickly. This is well documented with regard to part-time work. Part-time work has increased considerably for both sexes in the 1970s but was especially important for women. The available data (see Table 9) suggest that the rise of the women's share in part-time employment in the 1970s contributed not only to female employment but also to overall growth in employment. Because of the part-time effects, it certainly is true that

Table 8 Changes in Average Weekley Hours in Manufacturing (Annual Changes in Percent)

	1960–1973	1973–1980
France	−0.5	−0.9
Federal Republic of Germany	−0.8	−0.9
Netherlands	−1.1	−1.0
United Kingdom	−0.7	−0.8
Japan	−0.9	−0.1
United States	0.1	−0.1

Source: Capdevielle and Alvarez 1981.

Table 9 Part-Time Employment

	Ratio of Part-Time Working Both Sexes		Men		Women		Women's Share in Part-Time Employment	
	1973	1981	1973	1981	1973	1981	1973	1983
Belgium	2.8	6.4	0.4	1.3	8.2	16.4	89.8	86.2
Denmark	17.0	20.8	1.9	3.0	40.3	43.6	93.4	92.0
France	5.1	7.4	1.4	1.9	11.2	15.9	82.1	84.6
Federal Republic of Germany	7.7	10.2	1.0	1.0	20.0	25.7	92.4	93.8
Greece[1]		2.1		1.1		4.3		63.0
Ireland[2]	4.0	3.1	1.8	1.3	10.1	8.0	67.5	68.6
Italy	3.9	2.7	2.3	1.4	8.5	5.8	55.4	64.1
Luxembourg[2]	4.5	5.8	1.0	1.0	13.9	17.1	83.3	87.5
Netherlands[3]	4.4	19.4	1.1	8.4	15.5	45.2	80.4	67.6
United Kingdom	15.3	15.4	1.8	1.4	38.3	37.1	92.1	94.3
United States	13.9	14.4	7.2	7.5	24.8	23.7	68.4	70.3
Japan	7.9	10.0	4.8	4.9	17.3	19.6	60.9	67.3

[1] No data available.
[2] 1973 and 1979.
[3] 1981 data are not comparable with 1973 data because of a change in the definition of part-time workers.

Source: OECD 1984.

female employment grew less than official statistics indicate (see Table 7). But even if employment is calculated in full-time equivalence, female employment was higher at the beginning of the 1980s than it was at the beginning of the 1970s.

The growing importance of part-time, casual, and temporary employment is part of the development of more flexible arrangements of working time and employment contracts in the 1970s and will become even more relevant in the future. Closely linked to the expansion of the service sector (in retailing and catering) and the introduction of new technologies, increased flexible use of the workforce was, and remains, an area of experimentation seeking to reduce labor costs and to respond more quickly than in the past to seasonal or cyclical fluctuations of business.

The advantages that firms derive from more flexible types of employment are obvious. This is not the case for labor. The firm's increased control over time coexists with a tendency to channel parts of labor into insecure employment with poor career prospects and low pay.

With regard to productivity it may well be that flexibilization will have positive impacts. On the other hand, it should be clear, too, that a higher degree of flexibility in either working time or employment contracts implies more precarious types of employment than have existed thus far and that the implications for employment statistics are unclear.

The capacity of European countries to create jobs is recent decades is closely linked to other major structural trends, too: sectorial shifts between the secondary and the tertiary sector and the dynamism of small and medium-sized enterprises. In recent decades employment in manufacturing industries has been replaced by employment in the service sector. The proportion of civilian employment in the service sectors has increased continually in European countries, averaging around 57.5 % in 1983 for nine major European countries (see Table 10). Although unable to provide enough jobs to achieve full employment, the service must still be considered to have been the main source of jobs in the 1970s, especially since the number of jobs in manufacturing decreased. One might wonder whether this performance will continue and whether the service sector will stabilize future employment patterns.

First, one should remember that employment and growth in the service industries is not independent from manufacturing. This is especially true for services to producers, which have gained importance in recent years but which are still being linked to the economic performance of goods-

Table 10 Proportion of Services in Civilian Employment

	1970	1975	1980	1983
Belgium	52.5	56.9	62.6	65.8
Denmark	50.7	58.7	63.0	65.6
France	46.4	51.1	55.3	58.0
Federal Republic of Germany	42.1	47.6	50.3	52.4
Ireland	43.1	45.8	49.2	53.2
Italy	40.3	44.2	47.9	51.6
Netherlands	54.6	59.4	63.6	67.1
United Kingdom	52.0	56.7	59.6	63.7
EUR 9	46.1	50.9	54.4	57.5
Proportion of Services in Total Employment				
Japan	46.9	51.5	54.2	56.0
United States	62.6	66.2	66.6	69.0

Source: Eurostat, various years.

producing industries. Second, the creation of jobs by the service industries depends on public policies. Given ongoing efforts to curb public expenditures and to balance the budget, the capacity of public services to create jobs is unlikely to grow. Third, most of the jobs created in certain types of services like personnel services, catering, and retail trades should be described as "bad jobs," meaning low pay and job insecurity. If it is argued that bad jobs are better than no jobs, there remains the fact that unsatisfactory job characteristics still make the creation of bad jobs a second-best solution for future employment.

The intersectorial shifts just mentioned are closely linked to the growing role of small and medium-sized enterprises. Especially well documented for the United States, the reasons for the phenomenon and the consequences it entails for European countries are being debated. There is some evidence that the capacity of small and medium-sized enterprises to create jobs was relatively high and will be relatively high in the future as well. First, the observable increase in the start-ups of new businesses may be explained by a kind of new Schumpeterism. Based on flexible management and being less averse to risk, small and medium-sized firms may adapt to new markets rather quickly and take advantage of new and more flexible methods of production. Second, and partly because flexible technologies have been introduced, the decentralization of production has supported the economic performance of small and medium-sized firms. Often enough, small firms serve as specialized suppliers to large enterprises. This decentralization of production is not only supported by private activities but also promoted by policies designed to help small firms grow and to encourage the creation of new businesses. Third, the evolution of the alternative sector, also launched by public activities, has contributed to the capacity of small firms to create jobs. The impacts of the alternative sector on employment are somewhat difficult to quantify, but there is no doubt that the alternative sector has expanded in recent years. The phenomenon can only partly be explained by economic factors. To a larger extent, the development of the alternative sector must be explained by its aims. Young people in particular are searching for new types of production and work, that are more autonomous and more decentralized than those of the past.

Having already developed in the 1970s, one more feature important to the process of transition from earlier modes of production and regulation to new ones is the diffusion of new technologies. The use of robots, chips, and computers reflects a technological revolution of information technologies and microelectronics that challenges the existing social organization of work and production. However, the application of key technologies even in the 1980s is only just beginning. Computer-aided design, computer-aided quality control, and computer-aided manufacturing have to be considered as the first incremental steps towards computer integrated manufacturing (CIM) of the plant "2000."

The macroeconomic effects of new technologies on the level of employment are subject to debate. But there is no doubt among most economists that new technologies will change production patterns, the structure of qualifications required, and modes of regulation. Standardized mass production, the traditional pattern of production since the industrial revolution, will be replaced by just-in-time-production of specialized products. The flexible, computer-controlled, automated plant allows for highly diversified production processes and products designed to meet specific consumer preferences.

The automated plant, however, is not as empty of people as some futurologists love to think. Research and development as well as programming and systems control require qualified personnel with special skills for new types of work. Even today, demand for skills in systems analysis, systems engineering, electronic engineering, software development, software design, and other areas outstrips supply in EC countries, a barrier to an expansion of employment and growth. In the near future the scale of change in the skills required by new technologies will even increase to a level that can hardly be underestimated. The need for new skills or new combinations of skills typifies all kinds of occupations, even well-established ones like maintenance, for which both electromechanical and electronic skills will be required.

The dramatic change of skills, brought about by the accelerating diffusion of new technologies, can be made possible only by a large investment in training and education. However, the qualitative aspects are even more important. The need for new institutional arrangements adequate to new technologies relates not only to new training and educational systems but also to a vast scope of institutional settings like working-time arrangements, industrial relations, and management systems, even to political and social priorities. The mismatch between new technologies and institutional arrangements is indeed the most crucial problem to be solved if the performance of EC economies is to be improved.

Do Models Exist to Solve the Employment Problem?

The Worsening of Unemployment: A Look Ahead

In many ways the upsurge in unemployment is the most characteristic element of current developments. The question of how to eliminate unemployment constitutes the main concern of almost all governments, although the debate is simply over the issue of whether the fight against inflation or the fight against unemployment takes precedence. But even in the light of the current recovery, the situation stands a great chance of getting worse.

- Demographic patterns will continue to complicate the employment situation throughout the 1980s. According to the OECD, demographic data indicate that unemployment can be expected to increase 0.5 to 1 % annually. The rate of school attendance has stabilized, and given the current drop in birth rates and the need for households to have additional income, there is no reason to believe that the rate of women's participation in the labor force will come down.
- Changes in productivity and growth of output are linked in an unfavorable way. When in the course of the 1960s the process of intensive accumulation was in full swing, jobs were created by gains in productivity which resulted in even higher growth rates. Scenarios of the next ten years or so are based on the idea that changes in productivity and growth of output will, at the most, stabilize the employment level. Productivity increases will fail to generate enough growth to raise the level of employment. The demand for labor will decline, and the supply of labor will increase.

Given the patterns of labor supply and labor demand based on a moderate scenario of the future (see Table 4), it is more than likely that unemployment will remain high. This statement is based on a kind of status-quo prognosis. But if it is true that the system of intensive accumulation has come to an end, and if it is also true that the modes of regulation will adapt to new accumulation sites, the outlook for employment might improve.

Employment Patterns and Economic Policies

Several strategies have been developed for overcoming unemployment: monetarism, supply-side economics, and demand management by fiscal policy. In the following passages we deal only with these strategies as possible solutions to increase employment.

The core of monetarist policy is the controlled and steady growth of the money supply. The central objective is to keep inflation down. As far as this goal is concerned, policies indeed proved to be efficient in the 1970s. In many countries inflation was slowed by a tight monetary policy, reduction of wage increases, and cuts in public expenditures. However, the major risk of monetarist policy soon became evident. At least in the short and medium term, monetarist policies had do pay a high price in terms of slow growth and sharp reductions of employment.

Supply-side economics differ from monetarism. The basic idea is to provide new incentives for economic activity by lowering taxes, stimulating saving and investment, and deregulating business and industry. However, a clear distinction must be made between theory and practice. The recovery in the United States after 1982 has been more of a Keynesian type than one of supply-side economics. Given the effect of public expenditures and tax cuts, the public deficit rose from 2 % in 1981 to 5.4 % of the GNP in 1983 while overall demand was stimulated remarkably. It should be obvious, however, that the position of the dollar as an international reserve currency made it much easier for the United States to finance her budget and current account deficit than it would have been for any other country. Policies after 1982 in the United States must be considered a strange mixture of demand stimuli, supply incentives, and efforts to redistribute wealth and income. The recipe cannot be applied to European countries.

Keynesian demand management is the classical type of policy on which most European countries relied in the 1970s. When unemployment began to rise in the beginning of the 1970s and again from 1978 to 1979, most European countries reacted by increasing government expenditures. Some stimulation of demand did carry through to employment.

Keynesian demand management may be linked to the social management of unemployment. The approach's goal is threefold. To keep workers on the job, to provide opportunities for work in the public sector by creating short-term jobs through appropriate measures, and to increase public investment to match public needs. Nowadays, Keynesian demand management is somewhat outdated, because multiplier and accelerator effects are not working efficiently enough to bring unemployment down considerably and to induce self-sustained growth. Although it seems doubtful that Keynesian demand management is responsible for accelerated inflation, demand management clearly relies on winning a bet: that the economy can be revived rapidly – before the burden of public debt and the possible supplanting of private economic activities become intolerable.

But there is no doubt, too, that some social management of unemployment à la Keynes is needed to lower the burden of unemployment in the short run. All EC countries have an especially high and above-average level of youth unemployment. Contrary to monetarist or neoclassical trust in self-stabilizing mechanisms of the economy in the long run, young people cannot be put off with hopes for better days to come. Instead, policy measures have to be implemented rather quickly to increase the level of employment. In that respect, short-term job-creation programs are suitable, especially, if they are linked to training and qualification measures and aimed to match public needs. The British and German cases show that conservative governments are more convinced than ever that job-creation programs are useful short-term responses to excessively high levels of unemployment.

In almost all European countries public investment fell during the 1970s. Given tight financial constraints on public budgets, public investment was reduced from the desired level. In keeping with initiatives of the Commission of the European Communities, however, in recent years there has been a growing understanding that reductions in public investment are harmful to future growth and employment, one of the reasons being that such action discourages private investment. In a recent study (Bolle et al. 1984) it is shown that there are specific needs for public investment, especially investment aimed to improve the infrastructure. Adequate public investment policies are required, too, if the efficiency of conservation and energy production is to be improved and if the mounting threat to the biological balance of the environment is to be met. The creation of socially desirable jobs for the purpose of bringing down social costs and increasing social benefits require public investment as well. Because of its labor intensiveness, public investment in these areas will have a considerable impact on employment.

For all the differences between their theories, all economists stress the highly sensitive role of private investment in the performance of the economy. Evidently, there is no easy way to stimulate private investment in times of serious slack. Even with the low interest rates and increasing profits in EC countries, private firms still hesitate to invest in real capital because of great uncertainty and risk with regard to the future patterns of the economies. Institutional barriers and the mismatch between economic and technological possibilities constrain private investment to a large extent. There is an urgent need for new institutional arrangements that are appropriate to technological and social priorities. The issue becomes even more important with regard to the integrated European Market planned for 1992 and international cooperation in economic policy.

European countries cannot be regarded as being in a state of short-term disequilibrium. Instead, EC economies find themselves in a period of transition from old modes of production and regulation to new ones. Today, it is by no means clear what kinds of new modes of production or regulation – and hopefully new equilibrium – the future holds. But it is evident that the developing new technological and institutional paradigms challenge economic theory and policy.

References

Bolle, M.; Brancati, R.; Cowie, H.; and Greffe, X. (1984): *Investment policy and employment in the Federal Republic of Germany, France, Italy, and the United Kingdom*, Brussels: Commission of the European Communities.

Bolle, M. (1986): *Vocational training and job creation in EC countries*. Berlin: European Centre for the Development of Vocational Training (CEDEFOP).

Capdevielle, P. and Alvarez, D. (1981): *International comparisons of trends in productivity and labour costs*, Monthly Labour Review, (December): Vol. 104, Nr. 12, pp. 14–20.

EUROSTAT (1985): Statistical Office of the European Communities, Brussels 1985.

EUROSTAT (various dates): Statistical Office of the European Communities, Brussels.

OECD (1950–1979): *National accounts of OECD countries*, Paris.

OECD (1984): *Employment outlook 1983*, Paris.

Sachverständigenrat zur Begutachtung der gesamtwirtschaftlichen Entwicklung (Council of Economic Advisors) (1985): *Jahresgutachten 1985/86*, Bonn.

Cooperative Behavior among Economic Agents within the Production System

Jacques De Bandt

Over the last fifteen to twenty years, the production systems of the developed countries have undergone profound structural changes, some of which have been of an organizational nature. These changes have brought to the fore various forms of cooperative behavior between economic agents within the production system. The purpose of the following pages is to describe specific types of such behavior and, on that basis, to advance the hypothesis that such schemes of cooperation are important to industrial performance and are not merely marginal or exceptional phenomena. Moreover, the following questions will be raised:

1) How do these cooperative behaviors relate to traditional views on the functioning of the production system in developed countries?
2) Are these cooperation schemes a new phenomenon? If so, are they transitory or long-term?
3) To what extent do these cooperative behaviors alter the functioning of the production system?

Contrary to standard economic theory, which holds that efficiency is a function of the intensity of the competitive process, it is argued here that cooperation is an important organizational category that is complementary, rather than opposed, to competition. Indeed, for both the static and dynamic performance of the production system, cooperation is just as important as efficiency. The importance of cooperation in this regard, however, may vary according to the circumstances involved. Cooperation seems to have been developing along with the internationalization of economies and the resulting intensification of international competition, it appears to be an important and sometimes even decisive determinant of performance in the present economic crisis or transition period being experienced in Western industrialized countries. But one can only speculate about the importance of cooperation as a relevant organizational category within what is supposed to be the technological and industrial system of the future.

Structural Changes within the Production System

Ever since the crisis enveloped the world's developed economies at the end of the 1960s, deep structural changes have affected their production systems. Although these changes can be interpreted in different ways, each can be classified into one of three different areas:

1) The most obvious structural changes have been the shifts in the sectoral composition of the production system. The relative importance of the various sectors as a proportion of total industrial value added has been substantially altered.
2) The structural relations between strategic variables of the industrial-growth model – i.e., the model's structural equations – have been somewhat modified. Before the crisis, for instance, exports of manufactured goods were growing more quickly than industrial value added, which, in turn, was growing more quickly than GNP. These relationships no longer seem to hold. Another example of such altered structural relations is the rate of increase in labor productivity. It used to be equal to a certain percentage of the rate of increase in production (the Verdoorn law), but since the onset of the crisis labor productivity's rate of increase has been higher than that of production.
3) In a still more general sense, the specific patterns and interrelationships of production, consumption, and finance underlying the technical and industrial "system" within whose framework the process of industrial growth took place in the 1950s and 1960s have become obsolete. A transition toward a new system is underway.

Structural change can also be viewed in the spatial sense. Of course, no world production system exists yet, but the trend towards building up such a system has been gaining momentum. Global subsystems of production do appear to exist in some industries.

Since the onset of the economic crisis, structural changes have also occurred in quite another sense – the way in which the production system is organized. Consider just three recent and typical examples:

1) In advanced industrial countries small business organizations have generally been faring much better than large ones.
2) Having now gone through a period of adjustment, large multinational corporations are experiencing above-average industrial performances.
3) Processes of transfer and recombination of industrial assets have been accelerated by divestments, mergers, take-overs, and similar moves, a process that has altered the configurations of many firms.

To highlight other organizational aspects of the changes occurring within the production system of advanced industrial societies, the following section focuses on the various forms of cooperation developing among production agents.

Forms of Cooperative Behavior

This section is not intended as an exhaustive list or taxonomy of observable forms of cooperation. The purpose is to give a few examples of cooperative behavior that has developed within the production system not only among firms but, more generally, among the various other economic agents participating in the functioning of that system.

Forms of Cooperation between Manufacturing Firms

Probably the most important category of cooperation schemes concerns various forms of cooperation between manufacturing firms. It thus includes various combinations of competition and cooperation. As for the latter, several forms must be distinguished:
- cooperative subcontracting;
- de facto cooperation among firms, usually small ones;
- clusters of small firms;
- collective entrepreneurship;
- cooperation schemes between large and small firms;
- cooperative research activities of firms;
- interfirm agreements;

Cooperative Subcontracting

Subcontracting, a specific model of interfirm relationship in which autonomous firms in a market relationship also have close contractual links, is a well-known category of industrial organization. Through a precise division of labor and functions, the subcontracting firm is only a "reduced form" enterprise, concentrating its activities on production while the contracting firm concentrates on design, assembly, and marketing.

Depending on the circumstances, the subcontracting relations vary from one extreme (just short of purely seller-buyer relations between autonomous firms) to the other (just short of a complete integration of both firms). Traditionally, the accent has been on maintaining the autonomy of and competition between a large number of subcontracting firms, which are linked with the contracting firm only through short-term contracts. Exceptions justifying more durable relationships exist only in some fields involving sophisticated technical specialization.

Recent empirical studies show that subcontracting relationships, particularly those in the automotive industry, have been shifting away from the autonomy/competition model to the other extreme for about the last fifteen years. Subcontracting relations have become more durable, the number of subcontractors per contractor has dwindled, and the cooperative nature of the relations has increased steadily. Both subcontractor and contractor are cooperating in building up their mutual capabilities in terms of production efficiency and long-term innovative capacity.

Today it is generally accepted that the competitiveness of the Japanese automotive industry is largely due to such forms of cooperative subcontracting. The fact that other automotive firms trying to imitate the Japanese model find it difficult to establish such a system of cooperative relations seems to indicate that this move represents a major organizational change.

De Facto Cooperation Among Small Firms

Under this scheme many firms pool their complementary resources, opportunities, experience, and expertise in pursuit of a common goal, with each firm's share of the responsibility and results being contractually defined. As in traditional joint ventures, two or more firms undertake a specific activity together because such common effort is in their interest (for reasons relating to economies of scale, market share, barriers to entry, and elimination of competition, for example).

There are also several forms of non-contractual cooperation, relationships in which no explicit contract defines the relative shares of responsibilities and results. Acting out of complex motivations, the firms involved merely exchange some of their knowledge, experience, and resources. It can often be supposed that the direct and indirect advantages are considered to be ample compensation for the costs involved. Other reasons for entering into such relationships are solidarity, mutual exchange of services, and sociological ties.

Many studies thus show that there is often a de facto cooperation between firms engaged in interindustrial relations or between firms active on the same market. In the first case two or more firms having a seller-buyer relationship (market relationship) exchange upstream and downstream information in a more or less systematic or organized way and pursue mutual interest by pooling their resources in the design, use, quality control, and adaptation of intermediate products and equipment. (The case of services is treated in a later section of this chapter.) In other words, these firms adopt cooperative behavior to enhance the seller-buyer relationship while retaining their autonomy (see Valla 1982).

In cases of cooperation between firms active on the same market, two aspects must be distinguished. First, it is well known that many large projects, particularly in the export of engineering services, draw on the expertise of firms that remain autonomous in their respective areas of activity. Beyond their involvement in a specific project, firms are taking steps to organize these complementary activities and resources to make their joint operations more efficient and competitive. Second, competing firms (usually small ones) are actually cooperating as well. Such activity appears to be a means to share relevant market and technical information and to enhance the firms' access to new production techniques. A typical example is that of a number of small subcontracting firms competing in the Paris region. They have been cooperating with each other in the collection of required information and the use of numerically controlled machine tools.

Clusters of Small Firms

Empirical studies show that totally independent small firms have been decreasing as a proportion of all firms in Western Europe while the clustering of small firms is becoming increasingly important. These clusters are composed of small firms that do not necessarily have legal or financial links; the firms do not constitute a "group." Their clustering is based primarily on financial links with one person or, in some cases, a few closely related people.[1)]

Collective Entrepreneurship

Collective entrepreneurship, as it is sometimes called, goes one step further towards the cooperation or integration of autonomous, competing firms. It is an arrangement whereby firms with complementary areas of specialization cooperate closely with each other but remain autonomous in the organization and management of their production process, which determines their profitability. The firms not only exchange information and other resources but, to a certain extent, organize collective production, with each firm focusing on a different part of the process and/or product range. This framework allows for an increase in efficiency and flexibility. Combining their efforts, the firms involved cover the entire production process for a large range of products.

The system constituted by the participating firms is based on simplified rules of exchange (barter). Other functions are performed collectively like the purchase of materials, distribution and/or export, and the purchase and maintenance of equipment, including the decisions about, and management of, the production process's horizontal division of labor into specialized tasks. This approach does not preclude the autonomous management of the production unit, however. Perhaps even more important is that it does not eliminate the firms' competitive behavior, as demonstrated by their specialized contributions to the whole, their

---

1) According to one authorized estimate, 17% of all small firms in France belonged to a group in 1980, but the figure rose to 32% when account was taken of the personal financial stake that managers had in other small firms in the country. See Huppert (1981).

mortality rates, and the performance of the production subsystem at large.

There are many examples of collective entrepreneurship in Italy, the best-known being the Italian textile and clothing industry (the Prato case in particular). Outside Italy there is the Portuguese plastics industry and, in Savoy, the French industry for automotive manufacturing. (The latter case falls somewhere between de facto cooperation and collective entrepreneurship.)

Although this scheme for cooperation is similar to the well-known concept of the cooperative, the two approaches are not to be confused. They both involve strong links of cooperation, but the cooperative is an organizational structure in which all units are integrated into a collective organization and divested of their individual economic responsibilities. In the collective entrepreneurship, however, the main focus remains on individual responsibility. The system and some of the functions to be performed in it are organized on a collective basis for the sake of performance.

Cooperation Schemes Between Large and Small Firms

Several forms of cooperation between large and small firms are apparent in present production systems:

- cooperation between one large sponsoring firm and two or more small firms;
- an organized network of small firms cooperating with one large firm;
- joint technological and industrial projects;
- creation of small autonomous units by large firms.

Each of these arrangements is described in the following paragraphs.

For various reasons still to be explored (such as social and regional responsibilities, especially for providing employment, developing unexploited technological knowledge, testing other applications, and conducting trial-and-error experiments), large firms have been developing organized systems for sponsoring small firms, which benefit from the sponsor's various resources and services. The only visible direct benefit of this kind of cooperation is the access to other applications and information.

Several of these cases are well documented (see Conseil et Développement 1982). One of them is the French Compagnie Saint Gobain, whose affiliate, Saint Gobain Développement, is using loans, subsidies, and technical and administrative assistance to sponsor approximately one hundred small firms accounting for some 3,000 new jobs in many different activities such as textiles, plastics, food, electronics, information technology, and pharmaceuticals. A similar example of the sponsorship scheme is the situation in which a large firm forsakes the usual seller-buyer relations with a series of small suppliers and takes steps to develop cooperative relationships within a more or less explicitly organized network. The objective is not only to improve mutual relations to the benefit of both partners but to enhance the production efficiency of the small firms, whose products or services are used by the large firm. The relationship can be viewed as a type of quasi-integration in which the small firms remain autonomous and continue to have relations with other firms. No information is available on the process by which these small firms are selected; the networks seem to have been based on existing relations.[2] As with the sponsorship model, there are several examples of the network scheme. In fact, it seems to be growing in popularity among many of Western Europe's dynamic firms that work with a number of smaller firms for various kinds of goods and services.

The situation is one in which a large firm is engaged in a technological and industrial cooperation project in a developing country. In order to increase the chances of success in this project, the large firm is trying to convince some small firms (usually of their own country) to engage – simultaneously but parallel – in a project which is complementary to their first (big) project.[3] The French firm Pechiney, for example, is known to seek the systematic cooperation of small firms in its international cooperative activities.

Cooperation is also dominant in the fourth type of arrangement, the creation of small autonomous units by large firms. The difference is that such cooperation transpires between firms that are not legally independent. Many new firms have been created in most developed countries in recent years, but relatively few of them are active in areas such as new technologies, products, or services. It appears that large enterprises have created many of the new firms to serve as closely cooperating affiliates, granting them a high degree of autonomy in order to place them outside the logic and structure of the parent company and to keep them free from its rigidities.

Cooperative Research Programs

It would be idle to expound on the importance that research and development, training, marketing, software, and a host of other activities have assumed within firms. What may be important to add is, however,

---

[2] Some studies have been devoted to the "dependence" relationship that small firms develop through their almost exclusive ties to one large firm. It remains to be seen whether integration in an organized network compensates the costs or other disadvantages of such dependence.

[3] A large firm sometimes uses a small one for the sole purpose of being the main actor in such a cooperative venture.

that R & D investments of single firms are often not (or are not felt to be) highly profitable. This perception stems in part from uncertainties about prospects for future growth and likely technological developments, stiff competition in promising fields, and economies of scale. More and more research programs are, therefore, being developed on a cooperative basis between two or more firms with or without support from the government or international agencies.[4] Clearly, then, autonomous firms that are competing with each other, at least in some fields or markets, are also cooperating in order to improve their technological capabilities and innovative capacity.

Interfirm Technological Agreements

There are similar reasons for the recent increase in the number of interfirm agreements for cooperation in the development and exploitation of new technologies and techniques. Technological agreements between firms thus complement cooperative research programs. The distinction between the two types of relationships is that firms cooperating in research do so with no guarantee of results; under interfirm technological agreements firms share in results that already exist. The nature of the cooperation is thus quite different. Evidently it is also increasingly attractive, for the already large numbers of technological agreements, particularly in the high-tech fields, like robotics, information technology, and telecommunications, are rising rapidly.

Cooperative Relations between Producers and Users of Services

Much of the recent literature on service, or tertiary, activities suggests that the nature of the relations between producer and user of services is undergoing fundamental change, at least in some of the expanding services performed for firms (see De Bandt 1985a and 1985c). Traditionally, the distinction between producer and user (or consumer), between supply and demand, has been clear-cut. The producer is solely responsible for the design, production, and marketing of the product or service in question; the relations between producer and user are limited to the delivery of the product and the payment of the price. It is a typical seller-buyer, or market, relationship.

Of course, the relations between producer and user sometimes change when the user orders a custom-made product, thereby interfering, for

---

[4] Because research cooperation (like public intervention in the field of research) does not affect static price competition, it is not usually seen as an obstacle to the free play of market mechanisms. It is clear, however, that research cooperation is changing the conditions that will affect markets and competition in the future.

example, with the producer's design functions. This interference may be minimal if the user's specifications affect only a few technically non-critical dimensions of the product like size or color. As long as the user confines those specifications to the range defined by the producer and as long as the producer remains solely responsible for the conformity and reliability of the product, the relationship does not really change.

The user's interference in the functions usually performed by the producer can be much greater if, beyond respect for professional standards and adherence to administrative rules, the producer is held responsible only for ensuring that the product conforms to the user's specifications and not for guaranteeing that it is reliable or appropriate. In such an extreme and rare situation the producer is not really producing and selling a product but rather selling his productive capabilities and capacities on a time basis. Perhaps this description will help to explain what happens in some service activities.

In certain kinds of services the distinction between producer and user is disappearing to varying degrees because the users participate in the production process. This is the case primarily with non-material and informational services such as engineering, design, consulting, software, marketing, training, and other areas representing a non-material investment by the users. The service per se is only a type of activity performed on a real time basis. The users do not ask for a "product" but rather specify their needs. Since these needs become clear only in due course, the specifications are progressively defined in an iterative way, and the service, which can be performed only while it is being used, is integrated into the production process as a production factor, not as intermediate consumption.[5)]

To the extent that these services are rendered primarily for firms, they represent forms of cooperation between autonomous firms. Service firms are not responsible for an intermediate "product" that does not exist. They are usually paid on a "cost-plus" basis and are responsible only for the quality of the participation of qualified people in the production process. And to be performed, the services require the effective cooperation of the user.

Technological and Industrial Cooperation on an International Level

One of the effects ensuing from the internationalization process is the international transfer of services and technology on a large scale both

[5)] The service is bought from and paid to an independent firm and is thus registered as intermediate consumption. Within the production process, the service contributes to the creation of value added.

within the north and from north to south. This movement, and the flow of payment from south to north, usually corresponds to market relations, which are characterized by supply-demand and power-dependency relations. These relations are organized on a contractual basis between firms, with or without various types of state intervention on both sides. The relations are normally called "cooperation" in the broad sense of the word.

Many firms and countries have mostly been quite disappointed with international transfers of services and technology, however. Although equipment, services, and even complete plants have been sold and paid for, effective transfer of industrial and technological capabilities has been limited. The definition of technology transfer and the technical support it entails is usually restricted in terms of the duration and specific type of tasks to be performed. Responsibility for the effective transfer of technological capabilities is not usually involved.

These experiences and, in some cases, changing power relations have led host countries to call for other arrangements. Through new types of contracts, attempts have been made to extend the seller's responsibilities beyond the sale of equipment, services, or plants to the production – even the sale – of the product. (In France a distinction is made between usine clef en main (projects), produit en main (production capacity), and marché en main (sold products).) But such contracts, too, fail to guarantee the effective transfer of technological capabilities and have usually been just as unsatisfactory as previous agreements.

The search for a different modus operandi has continued nevertheless. One of the objectives of transcending the buyer-seller relationships is not simply to improve the conditions under which technology is bought and sold, but to forge new types of cooperation between firms belonging to very different economic environments and possessing very different levels of industrial and technological capabilities. In short, the aim is to develop cooperative relations in various fields in order to enhance technological and industrial capabilities in the host country. The firm in the north transfers resources and know-how to the legally autonomous firm in the south, which is supposed to develop its own capabilities and gradually to become independent.

What is the difference between this concept and previous arrangements? After all, the transfer of technology involves not only the sale of equipment but the provision of technical support, i.e., "services" to be paid for as agreed, and it has already been pointed out in this chapter that appropriately defined technical support can imply cooperative relations between the producer of the service and the user. The difference is that the firm in the north not only provides services on a commercial basis but engages in real cooperation and becomes jointly responsible for the results. Instead of merely selling services that are more or less efficiently used as inputs by the firm in the south, the firm in the north participates more consistently in the effective transfer of technology and industrial know-how while ensuring the efficient operation of the production plant (or of facilities for such things as research and distribution) and the development of technological and industrial capabilities.

Several examples of this arrangement have been documented by recent case studies of technological and industrial cooperation contracts (see Ministère de la Recherche et de la Technologie 1984). A typical one is the intervention of the French telecommunications firm CIT-ALCATEL in India.[6)] Long-term contracts regulate the cooperative activities of business firms, research, and training units in various complementary fields such as the sale of equipment, sale of plants, operation of plants, development of products, technological research, and training at different levels. In another case, a somewhat more complex scheme of cooperation has been established to develop this kind of close technological and industrial cooperation. A large firm in the north has relations with a small firm that is acting as the main direct cooperator. This set-up combines two of the cooperation schemes analyzed above: the contractual, or even de facto, relationship between a large and a small firm in the north and the agreement between a firm in the north and a firm in the south for the transfer of industrial capabilities. A typical instance of such an arrangement is the link between Renault Vehicules Industries and COFIM (Compagnie Française de Matériel Industriel) in its cooperation activities in Tunisia within the Société Tunisienne de matériaux composites. A similar scheme has been developed in Algeria, Angola, and other countries for the production of truck parts.

The Central Role of Competition in Traditional Approaches

Whereas a company's maximization of profit in a competitive framework has always been one of the central topics of microeconomic theory, it is "industrial organization" – the various ways of organizing production – that has traditionally been the main concern of industrial economics. (These production structures determine how profits are maximized. The

---

6) CIT-Alcatel is an affiliate of C.G.E. and is becoming, through merger with ITT telecommunications activities, the second telecommunication firm in the world (under the name Alcatel-ITT, as of January 1987).

outcome of the "structure – conduct – performance" paradigm varies with the structures, or organizational forms, of production, with organization in this context having essentially to do with the numbers and relative sizes of competing firms.)

Three aspects must be stressed: first, the firms are autonomous units, "autonomy" being understood to refer to such corporate dimensions as production, organization, decision-making, finance, and marketing. In order to maximize their profits, the firms can act on strategic variables corresponding to the "degrees of freedom" that exist within the given market structure. Beyond trying to maintain static equilibrium or to adapt themselves for the short-term, the firms can, of course, also try either to change the existing structure or to withdraw from it, through vertical integration or diversification. Fundamentally, the firms are autonomous: their performance is basically the result of their own capabilities within the competitive framework. Second, the relations between firms are only interindustrial, or seller-buyer, relationships between firms engaging in dissimilar productive activities.[7] Third, industrial organization, or market structure, is characterized mainly, or almost exclusively, by the degree of competition; both the static and dynamic performances of the industrial system are primarily a function of the competitive process. The characterization of the industrial organization can thus be said to be unidimensional.

In that context cooperation does not exist as a possible organizational category; it is usually ignored. When cooperation is recognized as such, it is considered to be either a type of quasi integration (when the ties are strong and durable) or a case of collusion (when the autonomy of the firms is strong). The question is thus whether and how – contrary to traditional theory – cooperation can be considered relevant to an understanding of how the production system functions. Recent literature contains three bodies of thought in which cooperation indeed seems to be precisely such a relevant organizational category.

The Traditional Craft Paradigm

The Second Industrial Divide: Possibilities for Prosperity, by Michael J. Piore and Charles F. Sabel (1984), contains much material about the type

[7] Between firms operating on markets that are the same or similar, "competitive" relations actually refer to the absence of relations. Of course, these competing firms can also develop a form of collusion, but collusion is only the opposite of competition and is thus to be treated as a reduction of competition.

of industrial organization they call flexible specialization as opposed to mass production. In essence, their thesis is that the traditional craft paradigm has been superseded by the mass production paradigm without any decisive economic superiority or advantage being gained. As the authors point out, however, mass production has always necessitated its "mirror image" – craft production. A "residual craft element" has thus been nurtured everywhere to varying degrees, and it is being revived, as the crisis of the mass production economy deepens. Success stories cited by Piore and Sabel assert that "flexible specialization" is likely to be generally applicable (in other circumstances of time and space). In other words, flexible specialization, which used to be the general (and efficient) system of production, has survived despite the circumstances that have been imposing mass production and is now reemerging because of the crisis.

Does Piore and Sabel's theory accurately account for the cooperation schemes that have been observed? The scheme described above as "collective entrepreneurship" clearly has much in common with the industrial districts and "fabriques collectives" that Piore and Sabel describe as typical examples of flexible specialization. It seems, however, that their theory lumps various distinctions together into a central polarity between flexible specialization and mass production. Specifically, these are the distinctions between (1) organizational forms (large or centralized versus small or decentralized), (2) alternative technological or technical production processes, (3) large runs of less expensive products and short runs of expensive products, (4) independent workers and wage earners, and (5) private autonomous production units and collective organization. In other words, Piore and Sabel concentrate on the organizational aspects while ignoring all the complex relations involving the compatibility between and consistency of production, consumption, and organizational modes and patterns.

Even if Piore and Sabel's theory is accepted, it focuses more on flexible specialization than on cooperation. Although the authors' examples do relate essentially to crafts and highly-organized systems, cooperation is seen to be a characteristic feature in only one of the three possible institutional frameworks, namely "municipalism:" municipalism was a form of territorially dispersed production centered on and coordinated by an urban seat. It was up to the municipality in these small unit systems to guarantee the mobility of resources (Piore and Sabel 1984: 31–32).

The "filière de production"

In French industrial economics the emphasis in recent years has been on the filières de production, which are production subsystems, or industries in the broad sense of the word (see Adefi 1985, De Bandt 1982, De Bandt and Humbert 1985, and Morvan 1983). These subsystems include not only the various production stages and the corresponding interindustrial relations but also all of the economic agents having anything to do with the functioning and performance of the subsystem. All of these agents handle the same type of material, depend upon the same technological system, are conditioned by the same changes in the market, and are subject to the same intersectoral competitive pressures.

Generally speaking, these subsystems have three important aspects in the present context:

1) The various components of a subsystem are interdependent in terms of their performance. Beyond their own functioning and performance, the components are dependent on the performance of that subsystem as a whole.
2) This is true in both the static and dynamic sense because of the synergetic forces that can be generated within the subsystem.
3) Both the static and the dynamic performances of a subsystem are largely dependent on the way the interrelations between the various participating agents are organized. Very schematically, the distinction is between a pure market relationship, through which firms aim at a maximization of short-term profits, and a cooperative relationship, through which they aim at collective development of their technological and industrial capabilities, on the basis of which they compete on an equal footing among themselves and on a "higher footing" against outside firms.

Cooperation thus appears to be one way of organizing the relations between firms whose performances are interdependent within a production system. Cooperation in this sense does not eliminate competition but rather changes the competitive conditions, essentially increasing the ability of the participating firms to compete effectively against other firms.

Developmental Industrial Policies

It is well known that state intervention in industrial affairs – be it under the term industrial policy or something other – has been increasing steadily over the years in almost all advanced industrial countries. Aside from the variety of instruments used in industrial policy, there are many different categories of industrial policies or policy measures described in the literature on the subject. Unless these industrial policies involve nothing more than a transfer of resources to the firms, the organization of the production system or of specific production subsystems is affected by the state in one way or another.

Research on organizational approaches has been moving primarily in two distinct directions. The first approach is called the "political economy" of trade or industrial policies, the main idea of which is that firms develop collective action in order to influence public policies, which are then superimposed upon market mechanisms. The basic interpretation of collective action by business interests relates to profit maximization. That is, one way to maximize profitability is to influence discriminatory public decision-making. From this point of view, of course, it is clear that collective action is more collusion than a form of cooperation, for its aim is to solicit income transfers rather than to increase industrial capabilities.

In the second approach it is shown that some countries have been defining and implementing what Chalmers Johnson (1982) calls "developmental" industrial policies: "As opposed to regulatory policies, which are essentially market-rational and which are concerned mainly with forms and procedures, the developmental policies are plan-rational". Such developmental policies or better strategies imply (1) the necessity of setting specific targets, (2) the importance of "effectiveness" as the main decision-making criterion,[8] and (3) the implementation of an organizational model.

As concerns the last point, the literature usually claims that industrial policies are structural, that the state is primarily concerned with the "structures" of the production system. In the present context, however, "structures" mean several things: first, the relative importance of the various industries; second, absolute and relative sizes of firms; and third, the organization of the system.

Cooperation as a Determinant of Industrial Performance

Empirical facts and the foregoing interpretations tend to suggest that cooperation schemes of various kinds do exist and that they may be an important category of industrial performance. As pointed out in the

[8] "The most important evaluative standard in market rationality is 'efficiency'. But in plan rationality this takes lower precedence than 'effectiveness'" (Johnson 1982: 21).

preceding sections, the production system is no longer regarded unidimensionally in terms of the degree of competition but rather in the light of a second dimension as well, the degree and type of cooperation between the participating agents. Whereas cooperation was once considered to be, at best, a departure from pure competition, which is supposed to maximize efficiency and optimize the allocation of resources, it is now seen as another means to enhance efficiency.

Cooperation and competition thus appear to be two distinct dimensions of the way in which a production system or subsystem is organized. They are not contradictory; indeed, they seem to be compatible to a certain as-yet-unknown extent. Cooperation does not mean less competition per se. Competing firms, be they few or many, can also cooperate with one another in some more or less well-defined areas, either temporarily or continuously, and can thereby mutually improve their capabilities and efficiency within the overall competitive framework. Their static and dynamic performances are thus likely to benefit from both competition and cooperation.

We have to accept this idea of a combination of competitive and cooperative behaviors. But research is needed in order to highlight how they combine in real life. We can only indicate some aspects: first, the combination in particular cases of interaction may be as important, or even more important, than the overall, systemwide degree of cooperation and competition. Second, although the aim of cooperation is to increase the industrial capabilities of the participating firms, their objective may well be to better satisfy consumer needs. Often, however, the objective appears to be to gain an industrial advantage over competitors outside the cooperation scheme. Third, cooperation can develop spontaneously among the participants. The emergence of such spontaneous cooperation schemes seems to be greatly influenced by various sociocultural, religious, and political factors.[9] In some countries or regions and in some periods or circumstances (such as strong external pressures) cooperative behavior does appear to be much more frequent than in others. Such cooperation schemes can be organized from outside the production system as well, however, and can then be superimposed upon it, the consequence being a change in the original characteristics of the production subsystem. (See Johnson 1982 on the well-known role of MITI in Japan. In the United States the role of the defense department has been highlighted by several authors. See also De Bandt (1987) on the substantial role that the state has been playing in the organization of some subsystems in France.) Lastly, cooperation is not limited to production firms. It can, and often does,

---

9) It has been shown, for example, that cooperation schemes in Italy have been developing in subregions that had once been politically homogeneous.

include many other agents such as banks, training and research units, and the transport and distribution sectors and can be organized in a variety of institutional frameworks.

Is Cooperation Likely to Gain or Lose Importance?

The main question is obviously whether these kinds of cooperative behavior are a transitory reaction to the crisis that has affected the economies of Western industrialized countries over the last fifteen to twenty years or whether it is a longer-lasting structural phenomenon heralding the new technical and industrial system that is expected to emerge in the near future. Numerous indications suggest that many existing cooperation schemes are typical reactions to the crisis. It is largely responsible for the birth of large numbers of small firms (see De Bandt 1985b), the development of industrial policies (see De Bandt 1983), and the extension of the black economy, and it has been shown to be the reason that many cooperation schemes are essentially defensive.

If Piore and Sabel (1984) present the reemergence of the craft paradigm mainly as a response to the crisis of the mass production economy, it must be remembered that their portrait relates to only some of the cooperation schemes observed. Indeed, the authors try to demonstrate the permanent viability of flexible specialization as an alternative organization model.

However, some of the factors that are supposed to explain the development of cooperative behavior are, in fact, of a structural nature and thus not limited to the crisis of mass production. Among those factors are:

- the internationalization process, which makes it necessary for local subsystems to improve their efficiency;
- the tertiarization process;
- the progressive development and rationalization of research and development activities and research and technology policies.

More generally, there is evidence of the structural development of networks, which are essentially organized subsystems (see Banville 1984 and Bressand 1986). The emphasis on networks might be only another way of focusing on the new organizational forms that are emerging.

Given the technological and organizational transformations that are likely to occur, no one knows what the technical and industrial system of the future will look like. On the basis of current technological evolution, it cannot be said whether the trend is towards centralization or decentralization of production processes (for contradictory assessments, see De Bandt 1985d). Thus, the future of cooperation within the production system is not predictable.

References

ADEFI (1985): *L'analyse de filière*, Paris: Economica.

De Bandt, J. (1982): La filière de production: mythe ou réalité? *Economie et P.M.E.*, 3, (Decembre): 4–12.

De Bandt, J. (1983): La politique industrielle: réponse de l'etat-nation à la crise? *Revue d'Economie Industrielle*, 23, (January–April).

De Bandt, J. (1985a): La productivité dans les services: sens et nonsens, *La productivité dans les services, Cahier "Service,"* 1, (June): 9–32.

De Bandt, J. (1985b): Le ressort de la PME est-il cassé? *Economie et Humanisme*, 286, (November–December).

De Bandt, J. (Ed.) (1985c): *Les activités de service dans les societés industrielles avancées*, Paris: Economica.

De Bandt, J. (Ed.) (1985d): *Long-run growth prospects for industrial countries: conference proceedings*, Washington, D.C.: The World Bank.

De Bandt, J. (1987): French industrial policy: Successes and failures, In: P.R. Beise, J.P. Groenewegen, J.H.P. Paelinck and C.W.M. van Paridon (Eds.): *A competitive future for Europe*, London: Croom Helm LTD.

De Bandt, J. and Humbert, M. (1985): Les filières de production ou la méso-dynamique industrielle dans l'analyse des relations Nord/Sud, *Cahiers du CERNEA*, no. 16, the whole volume, Paris.

de Banville, E. (1984): L'entreprise entre la PMI-sation et l'évolution des réseaux de solidarité, *CRESAL*, (July): St. Etienne.

Bressand, A. (1986): International division of labor in the emerging global information economy: The need for a new Paradigm. Paper delivered at the FAST Seminar on the Internationalization of services, Brussels, 26 June.

Conseil et Développement (1982): Etude des actions d'accompagnement des P.M.E. par les grands groupes et les institutions nationales et régionales, Ministère du Plan, September 1982, Paris.

Huppert, R. (1981): Stratégies de développement des PMI francaises, *Revue d'Economie Industrielle*, 17, 3° trimestre: 26–41.

Johnson, C. (1982): *MITI and the Japanese miracle: The growth of industrial policy, 1925–1975*, Stanford: Stanford University Press.

Ministère de la Recherche et de la Technologie (1984): Cooperation technologique et industrielle France-Tiers Monde, Actes du Colloque de Marseille (1983), La Documentation Francaise.

Morvan, Y. (1983): Reflexions sur le contenu et le destin d'un concept, In: *Entreprise et organisation: Mélanges en hommage à Madame le Professeur Jane AUBERT-KRIER*, Paris, Economica, pp. 131–146.

Piore, J. and Sabel, C.F. (1984): *The second industrial divide: Possibilities for prosperity*, New York: Basic Books.

Valla, J.O. (1982): Eléments d'une approche marketing du concept de filière, *Revue d'Economie Industrielle*, 21: (3° trimestre): 76–92.

On the Predictability of Labor-Force Participation and Employment

Jürgen Kühl

Since full employment was lost in 1974, unemployment in the Federal Republic of Germany has hit more than 15 million people at least once (Karr 1986). In fact, many European countries have been suffering from comparable figures of joblessness, and labor market slack is expected to remain until the late 1990s.

In its recent Euro-Report '86 the Prognos Institute (Prognos 1986a) states that the EEC could reduce its level of unemployment by up to 5 million in the 1990s if an annual economic growth rate of 2.4% is achieved and if Europe strengthens its economic potential. Employment, which has remained constant at 120 million for the twelve EEC countries since 1972, will increase by 2 million by 1990 and by 5 million to a total of 127 million by the year 2000. The employment gap could reach about 15 million jobs in 1990. A constant labor-force thereafter and increasing employment will reduce unemployment by about 5 million people during the 1990s.

If researchers or politicians in the 1970s had projected this threat for the last quarter of the century, there had been a general consensus that high and persistent unemployment would destabilize the political, social, and economic system of Western European countries and of Western Europe as a whole. It is now known, however, that slack labor markets did not fundamentally change the climate of relative political and social calm (Kühl 1981, Kühl forthcoming). But the politics of unemployment, especially the reactions of the unemployed to the discrepancies between the rhetoric and reality of policies towards full employment, do influence the predictability of labor market developments.

One important cornerstone of the projections is the concept of full employment, i.e., a high and productive use of the potential labor-force in decent jobs with commensurate pay and working conditions. This post-war goal is still alive and widely embraced, although there are some serious doubts about its attainability. The discussion centers on the following issues: how realistic is the term "jobless growth", and which effects on employment follow from the fiscal crisis and from budget constraints? Does the panacea: high tech creates economic growth, low tech and no tech create employment, work sufficiently? Does the aim of employer-oriented flexibility of work contracts and working time transform labor back into a commodity, especially during times of weak corporatist models of power sharing and income policies accompanied by diminished union power and deunionization? Why do we observe insufficient sharing of jobs and working hours, and so many obstacles to more and better worker-oriented flexibility? In fact, labor market flexibility is neither a panacea, nor a goal in itself; instead, criteria for an optimal flexibility of job contracts and working hours are necessary. Segmentations of the labor market, the instability of many new jobs, the reduction of full-time employment offering commensurate pay and social security, the reappearence of poverty, and the combination of youth unemployment and long-term unemployment pose additional challenges to the concept of full employment and thus to its predictability.

These considerations have brought some analysts to argue that the goal of full employment is no longer valid. In my view, though, the "new social consensus" (Guy Standing) called "basic income" can be introduced after full employment has been restored. Now we need answers to the questions: who fears full employment? Why do we not pursue the existing full employment strategies (Federal Employment Institute 1980, Therborn 1985, Krupp, Rothschild and Rohwer 1986)?

Given these political influences and recent developments on the labor market, the present chapter centers on four issues.

1) Major obstacles to the medium-term and long-term predictability of the labor-force and employment:
   a) cyclical dynamics of employment, the labor-force, and both registered and hidden unemployment (analysis of the business cycles from 1966 to 1987);
   b) stability of employment and the recent expansion of less stable employment contracts (analysis of turnover);
   c) labor market flows between employment and unemployment (accounting system analysis);
   d) working hours, including overtime and part-time work, and the detachment of working hours from business hours (analysis of working hours and firm operating hours);
   e) gains in autonomous vs. induced employment in periods of recovery and sufficient economic growth (policy analysis).
2) Statistical "megatrends" of the German labor market.
3) Details of predictability.
4) Differences between the employment histories of the United States, Japan, and Europe.

Major Obstacles to Prediction

The first obstacle to prediction is the pronounced influence of the business cycle from 1966 to 1987 in the Federal Republic of Germany (Kühl 1987). Table 1 offers a basic framework to analyze the cyclical dynamics of employment, registered and hidden unemployment, and the potential labor force, i.e., labor supply under conditions of full employment. The annual absolute changes in employment are taken to define the periods of recovery and recession. The analysis may be improved by determining peaks and troughs by quarterly, seasonally adjusted data. The entire base period of the projections spans three complete business cycles. The most recent lower turning point of employment was in the first quarter of 1984. The ongoing upswing of employment is predicted to end during 1987.

The well-known sequence of accelerated economic growth, increased utilization of capacity, reduced short-time work, and increased overtime work in advance of gains in employment applies in all three recovery periods. The interaction between economic growth, productivity performance, working hours, and employment on one hand, and the forces of final demand inducing the cyclical changes on the labor market on the other cannot be discussed here.

The most important findings presented in Table 1 are:

a) The absolute gains in employment during recovery periods A 1 (1969–73 plus 1.023 million), A 2 (1978–80 plus 788,000), and A 3 (1984–87 plus 674,000) are decreasing because of ever slower average economic growth underlying the recovery. The FRG lost 800,000 jobs between 1966 and 1987, suggesting a long-term downward trend in employment.

b) Although there are pronounced cyclical changes in female employment, the gains in the employment of women in A 1 and A 3 were greater than the losses during the preceding recessions. The total employment gain of 178,000 from 1966 to 1987 reflects increases in the more stable employment in the service sector, part-time work and short-term contracts for women, and the consequences of deindustrialization for men, who lost full-time jobs mainly in manufacturing and construction industries. The relatively better employment records for women, especially since 1980, are shown by increasing shares of women in total employment, i.e., from 36.2 % in 1966 to 38.3 % in 1987, in dependent employment, and annual hours (not shown in the table).

c) All three recovery periods brought about very small reductions of registered unemployment: – 50,000 in R 1, – 14,000 in R 2, and – 110,000 in R 3. However, there have been remarkable gains in employment during the recoveries. Hidden unemployment even grew slightly in A 2 and A 3. Registered unemployment among women increased in the ongoing recovery of A 3, while its hidden forms fell a little. Seen against the secular trend of rising rates of female labor-force participation since 1970, the reported gains in female employment were comparatively too small to avoid increases of unemployment among women.

A fourth finding, which is not included in Table 1, shows that the share of foreign workers in employment losses and unemployment increases has always been greater than their share in employment.

In total, the well-known addition of 2.34 million people to the potential labor-force due to the baby boom and female workers was accompanied by an overall loss of 0.8 million jobs, an increase in registered unemployment by 2 million, and an increase in hidden unemployment by 1.1 million from 1966 to 1987, a period of three complete business cycles.[1)]

There is no analysis of the stability and the future of the downward trend in employment, which may be seen from Table 1.

The second obstacle to the predictability of the labor market is the large annual turnover of about 6 million people hired and slightly fewer than 6 million people leaving or loosing their jobs (see Table 2). In addition, Table 2 gives the corresponding figures for placements and new registrations of unemployed workers. There is some evidence that labor market turnover declined over the years of an overall employment deficit.

Cramer's (1986) analysis of the same data source has shown that three out of four jobs were stable (uninterrupted employment with the same employer) during a single year from 1976 to 1981. Over six years, half of the jobs were stable in that sense. They contributed 65 % of labor's volume, and they account for 71 % of all wages and salaries. Stable jobs are held by male (30 years and older) and female (50 years and older)

---

1) Actual figures of registered unemployment in A 3 are:

	1983	1984	1985	1986	1987
Average stock (in millions)	2,26	2,27	2,30	2,23	2,23
New registrations (in millions)	3,70	3,67	3,75	3,64	3,73
Total (in millions)	5,07	5,17	5,21	5,12	5,29
Duration (in months)	6.3	6.9	6.8	6.7	6.7
Long-term unemployment above 1 year (in percentages)					
taken from average stock	24.9	28.8	30.9	32.0	31.8
taken from outflows	12.7	16.5	15.8	13.9	13.6

Source: Federal Employment Institute (internal information).

Table 1 Cyclical Changes of Employment, Registered and Hidden Unemployment, and Potential Labor Force 1966–1987 in the Federal Republic of Germany (in Thousands)

Period	R_iA	ΔE	ΔEF	ΔAL	ΔALF	ΔST	ΔSF	ΔPOT	$\Delta POTF$
1966/68	R_1	− 929	−391	+ 176	+ 46	+ 138	+111	− 615	− 234
1969/73	A_1	+1.023	+512	− 50	+ 35	− 48	− 50	+ 925	+ 497
1974/77	R_2	−1.359	−428	+ 757	+389	+ 517	+275	− 85	+ 236
1978/80	A_2	+ 788	+353	− 141	− 50	+ 15	− 10	+ 662	+ 293
1981/83	R_3	−1.006	−236	+1.369	+523	+ 495	+280	+ 858	+ 567
1984/87[1]	A_3	+ 674	+368	− 108	+ 22	+ 24	− 6	+ 590	+ 384
1966/87	–	−809	+178	+2.003	+965	+1.141	+600	+2.335	+1.743

[1] 1987 preliminary forecast

Definitions:

R_i = Recession period i

A_i = Recovery period i

F = Women

	1986 Total	Women	%
E = Employment	25.746	9.311	36.2
AL = Registered unemployment	2.230	929	41.7
ST = Hidden unemployment	1.131	479	42.4
POT = Potential labor force	29.107	10.719	36.8

Source: Institute of Employment Research, Nürnberg. Kühl (1987): 10

Table 2 Number of People Hired and Number of People Leaving or Losing Their Jobs, Placements and New Registrations of Unemployed Workers 1973-1986 *(in millions)*

Year	Hired	Jobs Left or Lost	Placements	New Registrations
1973	7,7	7,4	2,7	1,9
1975	5,4	6,1	2,1	1,9
1977	6,1	6,3	2,3	3,3
1979	6,7	6,6	2,1	2,8
1980	6,6	6,9	1,9	3,0
1981	6,4	6,8	1,6	3,5
1982	5,7	5,9	1,4	3,7
1983	5,7	5,4	1,6	3,7
1984	6,1	5,5	1,8	3,7
1985	6,4	5,6	1,9	3,8
1986	6,3	5,6	2,0	3,9

Source: Federal Employment Institute, preliminary figures taken from the statistics on dependent employment underlying contributions to social security.

German employees, and in general by employees with sound vocational training in a technical or administrative field. Unstable employment is typical for young, foreign, and unskilled workers. The relationship between stable and unstable jobs did not change much in the late 1970s and in the early 1980s or during recovery periods. In recent years, however, less stable forms of employment in some sectors, occupations, and specific groups of workers have been increasing because of a slack labor market and flexibilization (Klau and Mittelstädt 1986, OECD 1986: September). The huge, although slightly declining turnover per year and the growing numbers of unstable jobs may deteriorate the usual concepts of employment, which contains decreasing shares of standard full-time and unlimited job contracts, and labor-force participation rates as well.

The third obstacle to predictions may be seen from the "labor-force account" analysing the large movements between labor-force, employment, and unemployment per year (Reyher and Bach 1986). About 70% of the new unemployed come out of employment, and the same percentage holds for the outflow of unemployment back to jobs. If we consider the group of unskilled, handicapped, and older (above 55 years) unemployed being out of work for more than one year, nevertheless about 10% of the unemployment outflow of persons with these characteristics are reemployed. Thus, the labor-force account offers deep insights into the nature and magnitudes of labor market flows. So far it has not been used for medium-term projection purposes. But we can expect major improvements in predictability from this new tool. Up to now, only the major stocks of the labor market are projected.

The fourth obstacle may be seen in the fact that the total volume of hours worked in the FRG is decreasing due to the long-run loss of jobs

Table 3 The Development of Annual Hours Worked in the FRG 1973-1985 (Billions of hours, %)

Year	Annual hours of total employment	Females percentage	Annual hours of employees	Females percentage
1973	50,103	34.0	41,200	32.7
1975	46,321	34.5	38,117	33.5
1980	45,914	34.5	38,762	34.6
1981	45,147	34.7	38,151	34.9
1982	44,557	34.9	37,538	35.5
1983	43,774	35.1	36,764	35.5
1984	43,652	35.2	36,600	35.6
1985	43,390	35.3	36,390	35.7

Source: Autorengemeinschaft (1986): 382

mentioned above and due to the following working time arrangements:

a) agreements offering a reduction of weekly working hours to 38.5 hours in major manufacturing, printing, and furniture industries, and retail trade, offering 42% of all workers in the FRG exactly 38.5 hours and 45% fewer than 40 hours per week in 1986 (Bosch 1986);
b) an increase of paid holidays and vacations;
c) a reduction of overtime to 1.5 billion hours, i.e., 4% of all hours worked and 67 hours of paid overtime work per employee and per annum (Bundesminister für Arbeit und Sozialordnung 1986);
d) an increase in voluntary part-time work to 1.88 million workers, most of them women, in 1985. 21.6% of female employees work part-time (Brinkmann, Kohler, Reyher 1986, Table 6), and
e) the shortening of working life by earlier retirement, by pre-retirement pay, arrangements for unemployed persons older than 58 years who receive unemployment insurance benefits without being registered as jobless, and by the possibility offered to the unemployed 59 years and older to leave the labor market if the last employer pays for unemployment insurance and social security up to regular retirement.

According to the discussion at the conference a comment should be given concerning the development of annual hours worked (see Table 3). After 1973 the volume of hours worked decreased by 13.4% until 1985 – about 1% annually. The reductions of working hours mentioned above recently helped to close the gap between the actual development of annual hours and its long run trend. Due to the recovery A 3, hours worked increased slightly in 1986 by 0.5% and 0.3% in 1987.

The share of hours worked by women increased steadily from 34% in 1973 to 35.3% in 1985. Dependent workers contributed 82.2% of the hours worked in 1973 and 83.9% of them in 1985. Womens' share of the hours worked by the dependent work-force increased by 3 points during that time. Today, about 15% of the hours worked by women stems from part-time work. Contrary to the overall reduction in annual hours worked, women in dependent employment have contributed a relatively constant 13 billion hours per year over the last twenty years.

The final obstacle to the predictability of the labor market stems from varying political influences, because about half of the gains in employment during all three recovery periods (A 1 – A 3) were brought about by expansionary employment policies, labor market policies, and working time arrangements (Kühl 1986). Market and business cycle forces accounted for the other half. Whereas in A 1 traditional Keynesian policies in West Germany reinforced an upswing based on exports and private investment that soon restored the full employment that the country enjoyed in the golden 1960s, the post-OPEC I recovery A 2 was based on a quite modern combination of supply-side and demand-side measures aiming at better conditions for economic growth and employment, investment programs, regional activities, and active labor market policies, mainly occupational training and retraining, and job creation. Between 1974 and 1982 there were 14 programs – ten expenditure programs of DM 64 billion and four tax and investment programs of DM 16 billion. Spurred by these activities, annual economic growth reached 3.6 % from 1976 to 1980, real gross investment grew annually by 6.8 %, the share of investments in the GNP increased to 24 %, and employment expanded by about 800,000 persons. But because the German potential labor-force had increased by 400,000 since 1975 and because the number of foreign workers by 1980 had matched its previous peak, these additional jobs were accompanied by only a small reduction in unemployment. As a consequence of the explosion of unemployment during R 2, enormous deficits in the unemployment insurance emerged (DM 7.3 billion in 1975 and DM 3 billion in 1976). By law, they were financed from the federal budget. In 1977 and 1978 small budget surpluses followed, and the Federal Employment Institute brought about reasonable results in 1979. Furthermore, 90 % of the young people in the FRG received vocational education. Although it is difficult to make an exact assessment of the effects that all these programs had on employment, the famous German Institute of Economic Research concluded that these expansionary policies accounted, by cautious calculation, for half of the gains in employment in the late 1970s.

The ongoing recovery A 3, which started in the beginning of 1984, is expected to increase employment by a total of 675,000 including 1987. From the lower turning point until the end of 1986 employment grew by about 600,000. The average rate of real-GNP-growth is a little more than 2.0 % per annum for the five years of economic recovery. It has been shown that the weak performance of private consumption due to moderate wages, increased flexibility of earnings and less unemployment compensation on the one hand, and the retardation of public investments due to tight fiscal policies on the other account for the result that the path and job content of economic growth is insufficient to achieve a faster reduction of unemployment than is brought about at present (Süsser 1985). The recent switch from exports to domestic demand is believed to work out neutral in terms of employment. It is uncertain whether private consumption and public investments will back A 3 for the remainder of the recovery in a way which leads to stable and sustained growth of employment.

In A 3, again, half of the employment increases stem from policy measures: increases of public job creation by more than 50,000, work-start wage and training subsidies account for 20,000 jobs, the reduction of weekly hours of work to 38.5 hours for 42 % of the employees had a total employment effect of 150,000 (Seifert 1987), regional investment programs created 20,000 jobs, the increase of short-term contracts and of part-time employment account for 50,000 jobs, vocational education in the "dual, i. e., apprenticeship system", which is calculated statistically like employment, was expanded by about 60,000 young people. Additional employment effects are attributed to the promotion of self-employment, to the continued payment of unemployment benefits for three months if an unemployed person enters self-employment, and to the expansion of the self-help, solidaristic sector to about 4,000 enterprises and projects containing roughly 100,000 jobs.

Labor supply was reduced by three policy measures:

a) a terminated remigration subsidy which induced 100,000 foreigners to leave the FRG;
b) paid parental leave for 10 months beginning in 1986 in which about 270,000 to 300,000 working mothers and some fathers will participate; most of them will remain on the employment registers for social security reasons even if their work-place has been refilled by a terminated contract; this effect leads to double counting of about 50,000 employees;
c) collective agreements assisted by law concerning the earlier retirement for workers of the age 58, offering a public contribution of 35 % to pre-pension pay if the work-place is refilled by unemployed or by young persons who finished their vocational education, but who are not employed further. There are about 70,000 participants.

The registers of unemployment were decreased by two effects:

a) the participation in vocational training and retraining of unemployed persons increased by about 50,000 in 1986;
b) roughly 50,000 older unemployed persons are allowed to leave the registers although they still may receive benefits.

To conclude, the employment gains in recoveries were brought about to one half by policy measures of different mix and structures. If there is no strategic commitment to full employment policies, these measures are very difficult to predict.

Megatrends

The long-term developments on the West German labor market are shown in Figure 1, which is based on three different sets of assumptions about crucial determinants of the labor supply and demand up to the year 2000.

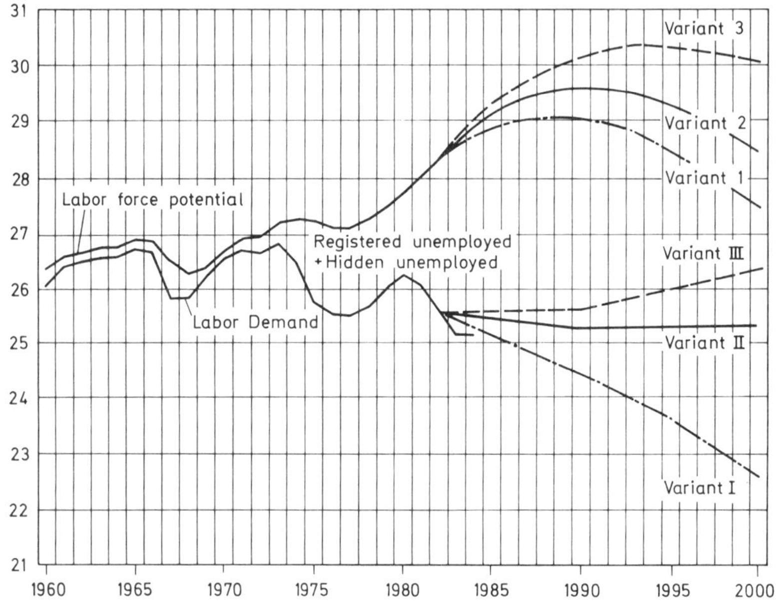

Labor Market Balance 1960-2000
-without the effect of the "pre-retirement regulation"-
(in million persons)

Assumptions concerning the development of labor force

	Variant 1	*Variant 2*	*Variant 3*
Germans	Weakening of the long-term trend of participation rates	Continuation of the long-term trend of participation rates	Intensified rise of female participation rates
Foreigners	Moderate trend extrapolation of the participation rates		
Migration	till 1988 −450000 1989/1995 ± 0 1996/2000 + 75000	± 0	+55000 per year (1988/1992+85000)

Assumptions concerning the development of labor demand

		Variant I	*Variant II*	*Variant III*
Growth rate (per year)	1982/2000	+1,2%	+2,5%	+3,0%
Productivity increase (GDP per employed person – per year)	1982/2000	+1,9%	+2,5%	+2,8%

Source: Federal Employment Institute (internal information).

Figure 1 The German Labor Market 1960–2000

According to the projections for the Federal Republic, long-term annual economic growth of 2.5% would allow the employment level of 1984 to be maintained until 2000. Annual economic growth of only 1% would entail a reduction of about 2.5 million jobs by 2000, while 3% annual growth would create 1 million additional jobs. The annual increase in productivity amounts to approximately 2.5% per employed person in the middle-range variation, to 1.9% in the low variation, and to 2.8% in the high one. The calculations already take into account annual reductions in working hours ranging from 1% to 1.3%.

By contrast, the potential West German labor-force expands by 1990 in all three projections, which include three variations of the German labor-force behavior, particularly that of women, and three migration alternatives for foreigners. Even if the continuing trend towards women's employment slows, and despite a net loss of 450,000 foreigners due to migration, the potential labor-force will increase by 300,000 persons. The measures used so far to reduce the potential labor-force – financial aid for remigration, for early retirement, and for paid parental leave, for example – could restrain this increase temporarily.

The Prognos and the IAB projections show that there is a risk of high registered and hidden unemployment in the EEC as a whole and in the FRG specifically, though some improvements for the end of the century are conceivable, if optimistic assumptions are made (Prognos 1985, 1986b). All these projections are based on stable basic trends expected to continue in the FRG in the future:

a) The rate of women's participation in the labor-force continues to increase, even when the labor market remains slack, even in single-parent families with dependent children, even if family incomes grow in real terms. Past projections underestimated that long-run trend.
b) The employment system demands higher or better qualified manpower in two ways. First, activities that need qualified or highly educated manpower (such as research and development, management, decision-making, quality control, supervision, monitoring and maintenance, and business services) are increasing. Second, the available jobs within a given activity are filled with better qualified manpower than they were previously. On the other hand, activities that demand little or no vocational training or formal education are decreasing.
c) Services continue to increase in two ways. First, service sectors keep growing, especially private services are doing so more rapidly because of constraints on the public budget. Second, the service content of industrial activities is increasing. Growth in the number of jobs means growth in the range and number of services. But there are some doubts whether the unemployment figures expected will disappear completely in services (Scharpf 1984).

d) The reduction of working hours per week and per working life, and the increase in voluntary part-time work are leading to fewer hours worked per year. The volume of annual hours continues to diminish. Due to the flexi-concept, working hours are detached from a firm's operating hours, an arrangement that may lead to more appropriate work schedules and more economical utilization of expensive capacities (Reyher et al. 1985).

The projections combine the well-known manpower requirement approach, which is calculated from different demand-side assumptions about economic growth, productivity, and hours of work, with supply-side calculations of developments in the potential labor-force by age, sex, and family status and in the corresponding rates of labor-force participation in each population group. These projections do not forecast the likely development. They can only serve as indicators or policy advisory instruments. Even the most recent projections confirmed the challenges to employment policy, reduction of working hours, creation of public jobs, and manpower policy that were predicted in the mid-1970s. Thus the ongoing labor market slack was the crisis projected best by labor market research.

The improvement in the reliability of those projections has been largely due to better data, more research, more sophisticated methods, and more acute analysis of results. Predictability may be improved further if appropriate indicators of labor market flexibility are introduced into the projections. Although the existence of a widening employment gap in comparison to a growing female labor-force and the baby-boom generations has been wellknown for all EEC countries for ten years, no use has been made of policy instruments and institutions to avoid the unemployment figures projected.

There are some fundamental objections to the methods of the projections. First, they use "pure" economics: the projections of the demand for qualified manpower depend to a large degree upon economic assumptions concerning economic growth, productivity, technology, working hours, and structural change. Little influence is given to the educational system, changes in society, and social qualifications which gain importance. Social qualifications mean behavioral attitudes beside and above educational and vocational attainments and skills of workers. If numbers of years of schooling and vocational training increase and if about 90% of an age cohort has corresponding certificates, employer's screening methods use other criteria during persistent labor market slack (Blaschke 1986).

Secondly, the projections assume "optimal conditions" during the base period of the projections: it is unknown whether the actual structure of employment reflects the true demand for labor. If there was underutilization of qualified manpower in the past, i.e., employment below the individual's qualifications and capacity to work, this kind of "misemployment" would be prolonged into the future.

Thirdly, there are margins of occupational flexibility which offer more or less alternatives to fill a given job with different qualifications or to perform many different jobs out of one occupation/qualification. If these potential or actual margins are added to the projections by occupation, activity, or qualification, the self-adaptability of the labor market is taken into consideration as it works in reality.

Fourth, there are "feed backs" out of the individual or political actions and reactions of demand and supply on the projections, making them more or less different from the probable development.

A rather controversial critique of the projections, especially of the variation 2/II is made by Schäfer (1986). The results are called "optimistic" because future unemployment is underestimated. Risks concerning female participation rates and part-time jobs may be greater than assumed. The major components of final demand are seen as extremely fragile because of international competition, reluctant state intervention, and insufficient private consumption. Productivity increases in the manufacturing sector due to increased rationalization may be stronger, and the corresponding loss of industrial jobs may not be compensated for by the service sectors. The 1% reduction of yearly working hours, which is assumed in the projections leading to a 33-hour-working week in the year 2000 or even less, is called insufficient to fill the gap between economic and productivity growth.

There are some detailed objections to the concept of potential labor-force: the concept refers to rates of labor-force participation under conditions of or near to full employment. It works pretty well during the business cycle, because at peak levels of employment potential and actual labor-force are near to each other. But during long-term periods of labor market slack, there is no period of full employment to make corrections of the potential participation rates by age, sex, and family status. Moreover, the relationship between labor market slack and participation rates is not well known. The ongoing trend of increasing rates by women has already been mentioned. But what is the balance between additional workers and discouragement due to long-term unemployment?

Many EEC countries tried to diminish their potential labor-force by early retirement, financial aid for remigration of foreign workers, and extension of youth and adult education (such as school attendance, vocational education, apprenticeship system, retraining, recurrent education). Although early retirement and remigration lead, at least temporarily, to less supply of labor, the extension of educational measures may lead to higher participation rates in the coming years.

The expansion of temporary work, fixed job contracts, part-time work for economic reasons, job sharing, temporary help on the one hand, and the flexibilization of working hours on the other may erode the basic concept of labor-force participation. This holds true for the expansion of non-conventional work, too.

Beside the well-known objections to the traditional manpower requirement approach, there are some controversial issues concerning the demand side of the projections.

There is some evidence, that the relationship between economic growth, productivity, and employment is still fairly close after corrections are made for the usual changes in short-time work, i.e., involuntary part-time work for economic reasons, overtime work, and hires. There is no link to the issue of wages and wage differentials (Bombach 1986).

The basic assumption of an employment threshold, i.e., a rate of economic growth equalling out productivity gains to keep employment constant, may be questioned on the following grounds: the threshold was decreasing for years, it may have reached its trough turning point now. Some negative influences on productivity are overcome, new products and techniques, a better educated work-force, large new vintages of very productive capital, and international competition will improve productivity growth, as further reductions of working hours do.

The detaching of working hours from firm operating hours enables a large and elastic increase of the current number of jobs without additional investment when final demand grows. A survey in the German manufacturing industries (Reyher et al. 1985) showed that:

- two thirds of all establishments would extend their operating hours in case of sufficient demand;
- the average extension of operating hours could be 15 hours per week;
- for the manufacturing industry as a whole, the operating hours could be extended by 10% from 61 to 67 hours per week.

Therefore, the employment elasticity of the total production potential at given capacities exceeds by far the existing estimates.

The most crucial part of the projections is the medium- and long-term development of labor productivity. In order to consolidate and add to existing quantitative projections, surveys have been made in the manufacturing sector, trade, and banking industries. The major findings are:

in the future the following influential factors for labor productivity in firms will be most important: mechanization and automation, use of data processing and microelectronics, job planning, improvements in qualifications, production of higher quality products as well as utilization of new material- and energy technoligies. Except for the increased usage of newer material- and energy technologies, these measures were already preferentially employed in the years 1980–84, in addition to the reduction in labor-force surpluses. The relatively high accuracy of the quantitative predictions of labor productivity and its main factors in influence became evident in the first evaluation of the survey methods.

The increasing turnover of firms, i.e., births and deaths of establishments of conventional and non-conventional type, influences the concept of demand for labor and jobs. Jobs are created and rearranged more rapidly, and they are disappearing faster than under full employment conditions. Firm turnover leads to decreased stability of branches and jobs. Less stable forms of employment are expanding. A permanent job offering full-time work year by year, decent pay, and human conditions of work may not reflect anymore the usual standards of employment under conditions of labor market and firm flexibility with increasing detachment of working hours and operating hours. The balance between a productive employment stability and necessary structural change by hiring and firing may be lost if "employment at will" expands further. Does the notion of participation rates still hold in case of the new ways of employment or in case of rapid flows between employment and unemployment? Thus, many forms of destandardization of employment influence predictability, making it more difficult to foresee basic trends on the labor market. Union efforts to control flexibility have just started, they cannot be predicted so far.

International Differences

There are large international differences in the basic relationship between output, employment, and productivity, and the corresponding performance of real labor costs per employed person. Figure 2 gives the development (1973 = 100) of these factors of the labor market in the United States, Japan, and four major European countries: France, the Federal Republic of Germany, Italy, and the United Kingdom from 1974 to 1986 (Klau and Mittelstädt 1986).

In the United States the well-known low level of productivity growth was completely in line with growth in real labor costs. Accordingly, output growth was closely related to gains in employment. The strong recovery since the 1982 recession, which was overcome by stimulation of public demand, made the GNP grow more rapidly than employment. Seven of the ten sectors having the most expansive absolute gains in employment offered below-average wages in 1984. The loss of international U.S. competitiveness, the risks of the huge private, public, and foreign debt, and too rapid deindustrialization in favor of service jobs

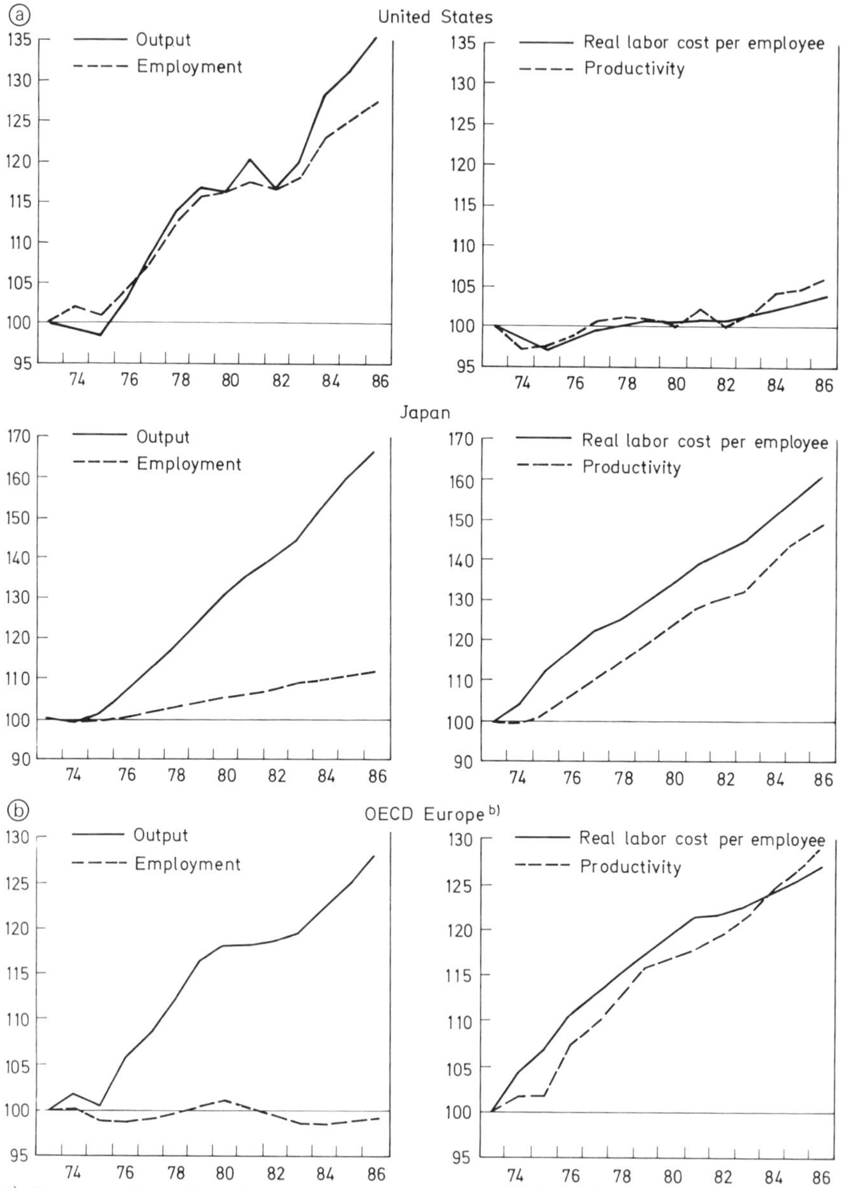

a) Compensation of employees per employed person deflated by GDP deflator.
b) France, Germany, Italy, United Kingdom.

Figure 2 Output, Employment, Productivity and Real Labor Costs per Employed Person [a)], 1973 = 100

Source: Klau and Mittelstädt 1986: 23.

were the major disadvantages of the U.S. solution (Bundesanstalt für Arbeit 1986).

Japan had relatively steady increases of output and employment, with increases in real labor costs keeping up with remarkable gains in productivity.

Europe's economic growth between 1974 and 1986 was comparable to that in the United States, but employment stagnated in the long run. Until 1983, the end of profit squeeze, productivity ran below real labor costs. But in the last three years, when productivity exceeded labor costs, demand restrictions allowed very little gain in employment.

Europe's four largest economies had the least growth performance and the lowest job content of GNP growth. Between 1974 and 1986, employment in manufacturing declined. The difference between the size of the increasing labor force and the viable capital stock, which determines the potential number of jobs, is particularly large in Europe. In the 1970s, the United States and Japan witnessed an improvement of youth's relative position on the labor market, while Europe experienced the same shift in the mid-1980s. Demographic developments may ease the situation in some countries, but less so in Europe than they have in the United States.

In Europe, unemployment rates for young people (15–24 years of age) increased drastically in the 1980s and have now leveled out at an unacceptable figure above 21 % as compared to 12 % in the United States and 6 % in Japan. In Europe, there has been no improvement in youth employment during this upswing, a significant change from previous recoveries.

Europe had significantly higher shares of employment-reducing sectors in manufacturing. Major job losses in steel, ship building, construction, and basic industries had no corresponding compensation. If there were employment gains at all in manufacturing, they amounted to less than 1 % between 1973 and 1983.

The expansion of service jobs was slower in Europe than in the United States and Japan. In Europe, there were serious attempts to increase the employment content of economic growth through adjustments in working hours. The subsequent reduction in hours worked per person in European countries was due in part to voluntary cuts and economic factors.

In the United States and Japan, it is seriously discussed to provide employment for an aging population while Europe, operating in the opposite direction, offers early retirement, preretirement pay, and part-time work to older workers to vacate jobs for the baby-boom generation.

The highly controversial issue of labor market flexibility may offer some explanations for the different paths being taken to stimulate

Table 4 Indicators of Labor Market Flexibility (1970s and early 1980s) Synoptic Table

	United States	Japan	Germany	France	United Kingdom	Italy
1. Short-run real wage rigidity[a)]	low	low	low	high	high	inter-mediate
2. Intersectoral labor cost differentials[b)]	average	average	low	high	low	high
3. Change in (2)	rising	stable	rising	falling	falling	falling
4. Inter-industry wage differentials[c)]	high	high	low	low	low	average
5. Change in (4)	rising	rising	rising	falling	falling	falling
6. Change in dispersion of intersectoral productivity differentials[d)]	falling	stable	rising	rising		falling
7. Change in ratio of female to male wages[e)]		falling	rising	stable	rising	rising
8. Change in ratio of female to male unemployment rate	falling	rising	rising	falling	rising	falling
9. change in ratio of youth to adult wages	falling	stable		stable	rising	
10. Change in ratio of youth to adult unemployment rates	falling	falling	rising	rising	rising	
11. Unemployment replacement rates[f)]	low	low	high	high	low	low
12. Change in part-time employment relative to full-time employment	small increase	small indrease	strong rise	strong rise	small absolute	small fall

a) Short-run price coefficient divided by cyclical coefficient (money wage equations for private non-farm business sector).

b) Coefficient of variation of sectoral labor cost differentials (compensation per employed person).

c) Coefficient of variation of inter-industry hourly wage differentials (pay for time worked).

d) Coefficient of variation of sectoral output per employed person.

e) Hourly adult wages.

f) Unemployment benefits per unemployed person as a percentage of net income of average production worker.

Source: Klau and Mittelstädt 1986: 41.

Table 4 (continued)

	United States	Japan	Germany	France	United Kingdom	Italy
13. Change in annual hours worked per employment person	small fall	small rise	average fall	strong decline	strong decline	small decline
14. Earnings exempt from employers' social security contributions	zero	intermediate	inter mediate	zero	high	high
15. Rise in unemployment relative to high acapacity use (shift in "Okun curve")	small	small	moderate	strong	strong	strong

employment. But without better theories and without a clear way to distinguish the indicators of flexibility in the behavior of employers from the employees' interests in flexibility, little improvement is likely. Klau and Mittelstädt (1986) offer fifteen indicators of labor market flexibility and their tentative magnitudes in the countries considered in this section (see Table 4), and give some tentative explanations of their findings. Since there are such important differences between European countries, the table seems to reveal little or no systematic relationship explaining Europe's lack of ability to create jobs. The analysis may be improved if indicators of final demand and of potential labor-force are added to those of labor market flexibility.

Flexibility on the labor market is no panacea and no goal in itself. The completely different employment records of the countries considered here cannot be explained sufficiently by national differences in labor market regulations. But there are differences in the existing balances between the internal capacities of firms to adapt to new tasks, techniques, products, and employment stability; differences that link labor market flexibility, and on-the-job mobility to productivity. Workers work better and they accept internal job rotation more readily if their jobs are stable.

Conclusions

The predictability of participation in the labor force and of employment has increased with improvement of data and research methods, and through the practice of combining traditional projections with surveys in industry or labor markets. Predictability is also influenced by new developments on the supply side (reactions to slack labor markets, reduced and more flexible working hours, the expansion of educational attainment, and new forms of non-conventional work, for example) and on the demand side (such as instability of the employment threshold, the detachment of working and operating hours, and a deeper analysis of productivity). Whereas the concept of occupational flexibility improved the traditional manpower requirement approach by introducing actual and potential degrees of occupational mobility and substitution at the work place, further gains in predictability stem from the replacement of the concept of occupation with the concept of the main activity on the job. Modern demand projections are divided into categories according to on-the-job activity and level of qualification (Prognos 1986b).

Unrelieved labor market slack has been the most precisely predicted crisis in the post-war period. Persistent mass unemployment was foreseen more than a decade ago. Most projections do not see a substantial change by the early 1990s. What made governments, institutions, and pressure groups sure that the unemployed would not take political action to change their situation? Why was there such little commitment to full employment in most of the industrialized countries?

The improvements in economic projections did not lead to adequate action to ensure full employment by 1990. Is the social consensus of full employment and public welfare being supplanted by a new consensus of persistent unemployment or basic income? Is a decent standard of living thereby being detached from employment?

References

Abbrevations:
MittAB = Mitteilungen aus der Arbeitsmarkt- und Berufsforschung, published by W. Kohlhammer, Stuttgart
BeitrAB = Beiträge zur Arbeitsmarkt- und Berufsforschung, published by Institut für Arbeitsmarkt- und Berufsforschung der Bundesanstalt für Arbeit, Nürnberg

Autorengemeinschaft (1986): Zur Arbeitsmarktentwicklung 1986/87: Entwicklungstendenzen und Strukturen, *MittAB*, 3: 351–384.

Blaschke, D. (1986): Soziale Qualifikationen am Arbeitsmarkt und im Beruf, *MittAB*, 4: 536–552.

Bombach, G. (1986): Lohnniveau, Lohnstrukturen und Beschäftigung, *List Forum*, 13, 1985/86, no. 5.

Bosch, G. (1986): The dispute over the reduction of the working week in West Germany, *Cambridge Journal of Economics*, 10: 271–290.

Brinkmann, Ch., Kohler, H. and Reyher, L. (1986): Teilzeitarbeit und Arbeitsvolumen, *MittAB*, 3: 362–365.

Bundesanstalt für Arbeit (Ed.) (1986): Wirtschafts- und Arbeitsmarktentwicklung in den USA und in der Bundesrepublik Deutschland, *BeitrAB*, 96, Nürnberg.

Bundesministerium für Arbeit und Sozialordnung (BMA) (1986): Überstundenbericht 1986, Bonn, BMA; cf. Überstunden, Entwicklung, Strukturen und Bestimmungsgrößen, *BeitrAB*, 98, Nürnberg.

Buttler, F., Kühl, J. and Rahmann, B. (Eds.) (1985): Staat und Beschäftigung. Angebots- und Nachfragepolitik in Theorie und Praxis, *BeitrAB*, 88.

Cramer, U. (1986): Zur Stabilität von Beschäftigung: Erste Ergebnisse aus der IAB-Stichprobe aus der Beschäftigtenstatistik, *MittAB*, 2: 243–256.

Federal Employment Institute (BA) (1980): *Employment policy in Germany – Challenges and concepts for the 1980s*, Nürnberg: BA.

Karr, W. (1986): Die Arbeitslosigkeit von 1974–1985 – Eine globale Übersicht, *BeitrAB*, 42.8: 56–57.

Klau, F. and Mittelstädt, A. (1986): Labour market flexibility, *OECD Economic Studies*, 6 (Spring): 7–44.

Krupp, H.-J., Rothschild, K. and Rohwer, J. (Eds.) (1986): *Wege zur Vollbeschäftigung: Grundlinien eines wirtschaftspolitischen Gesamtkonzepts zum raschen Abbau der Arbeitslosigkeit*, Freiburg: Rombach.

Kühl, J. (1981): Labour markets and industrial relations in the recession in Germany 1973–1978; in: *The management of industrial conflict during the recession of the 1970s*, E. Tarantelli and G. Willke (Eds.), 123–156, Stuttgart, Firence, Brussels; Klett-Cotta, Le Monnier, Bruylant.

Kühl, J. (1986): Labour policy in the Federal Republic of Germany: Challenges and concepts, paper presented to the International Conference on "The Employment Problem: Strategies for European Countries", Rome, 17–18 October, in: *Review of Labour Economics and Industrial Relations* Vol. 1, No. 3, Winter 1987, 25–56.

Kühl, J. (1987): Drei komplette Zyklen 1966–1987, *Arbeit und Beruf*, 1: 9–11.

Kühl, J. (forthcoming): *Arbeitsmarktpolitik ohne Vollbeschäftigung: Reaktionsweisen und Strategieoptionen öffentlicher Arbeitsmarktpolitik*, Arbeitskreis Sozialwissenschaftliche Arbeitsmarktforschung (SAMF).

OECD (1986 September): *Employment outlook*, Paris: OECD.

OECD (1986): *Labour market flexibility: Report by a high level group of experts to the Secretary General*, Paris: OECD.

Prognos AG (1985): Die Zukunft der Arbeitslandschaft: Zum Arbeitskräftebedarf nach Umfang und Tätigkeiten bis zum Jahr 2000, *BeitrAB*, 94 nos. 1 (report) and 2 (tables), Nürnberg.

Prognos AG (1986a): *Euro-Report '86*, Basel: Prognos.

Prognos AG (1986b): Zum Arbeitskräftebedarf nach Qualifikationen bis zum Jahr 2000, *BeitrAB*, 95, Nürnberg.

Reyher, L. and Bach, H.-U. (1986): AGR: Arbeitskräfte-Gesamtrechnung Bundesrepublik Deutschland, *BeitrAB*, 100, Nürnberg.

Reyher, L., Spitznagel, E., Streck, W. R., Teriet, B. and Vogler-Ludwig, K. (1985): Zu den Beschäftigungspotentialen einer Entkoppelung von Arbeits- und Betriebszeit, *MittAB*, 1: 30–40.

Schäfer, C. (1986): Auch bei Wachstum bleibt die Bekämpfung der Arbeitslosigkeit bis zum Jahre 2000 eine politische Aufgabe – Szenarien zur Entwicklung des Arbeitsmarktes bis 2000, *WSI-Mitteilungen*, 3: 145–162.

Scharpf, F. W. (1984): Strukturen der post-industriellen Gesellschaft oder: Verschwindet die Massenarbeitslosigkeit in der Dienstleistungs- und Informationsgesellschaft?, Wissenschaftszentrum Berlin, discussion paper IIM/ LMP 84-23, Berlin.

Seifert, H. (1987): Was hat die 38,5-Stunden-Woche gebracht? Beschäftigungseffekte und Formen der Arbeitszeitverkürzung, *Sozialer Fortschritt*, 5: 102–107.

Süsser, H.-G. (1985): Lehren aus den Konjunkturzyklen der Vergangenheit, *Wirtschaftsdienst* 1985/III.

Therborn, G. (1985): *Arbeitslosigkeit: Strategien und Politikansätze in den OECD-Ländern*, Hamburg: VSA-Verlag.

IAB-Kurzbericht 8.12.1987 and Kühl 1986: 34–35.

B. Macroeconomic Policy Making – An Institutional Perspective

Antagonism and Cooperation in Four Countries: Economic Policies and Performance

Fritz W. Scharpf

Economic Performance: The End of Convergence

The overall theme of this conference – "Industrial Societies After the Stagnation of the 1970s" – may yet prove to have been prematurely optimistic. But while our difficulties may not yet be over, there is, indeed, general agreement with the proposition that we have been in a period of relative economic stagnation since the early 1970s – at least when compared with the quarter of a century that went before. On the average, industrial societies suffered from lower economic growth, higher rates of inflation, and a return to levels of mass unemployment unheard of since the Great Depression of the 1930s. And even now, after a dozen years of crisis management, we have – at best – been able to solve the inflation problem while mass unemployment persists at the level of more than 30 millions in the OECD countries.

There is also agreement – or at least there should be – over the second proposition that differences between countries have increased significantly after the early 1970s. While the indicators of economic performance of most industrial societies had become reasonably similar after the period of post-war reconstruction, they began to diverge once more in the 1970s. Some countries – like Japan, Norway or Austria – seemed almost unaffected by the general malaise and did remarkably well overall. Others – like Sweden, Italy, and the United States – seemed to pursue employment gains at the expense of price stability, and still others – like Switzerland and West Germany – seemed willing to accept considerable employment losses in their successful battle against inflation. The data are all there in the papers presented by Bolle/Greffe and by Manfred Schmidt in this volume.

But while there is agreement that something has generally changed for the worse in the early 1970s, and that industrial societies have responded rather differently to the worsening economic environment, there is almost complete disagreement over what it is that has changed and over the factors which might explain the differences in the economic performance of different countries. The second issue is very well covered in Manfred Schmidt's excellent contribution to this conference. I fully agree with his incisive criticism of the literature – and I almost agree with the explanation that he himself proposes.

Schmidt suggests, essentially, that the successful management of the economic difficulties of the 1970s depended critically upon the institutional capability of some countries to rely upon "a high degree of concerted policy formation and high levels of stable consensus between capital and labour" – and he associates this capability with the presence of one or the other of two political conditions: either "labour commanded a dominant or hegemonic position" or "pronounced non-socialist, conservative-reformist tendencies have been in power". Countries were less successful, it would follow, when political forces were more nearly balanced or deadlocked – so that no single "camp" could coordinate all efforts from a position of accepted hegemonic leadership or, at least, with an effective preponderance of power.

In the context of the existing literature this is a highly sophisticated explanation, and it goes about as far as quantitative comparisons in political science could go. If I nevertheless suggest that it may not go far enough, it is because of the self-conscious limitation of its scope to the concerns of the professional political scientist. Yes indeed, institutional capabilities and the balance of political power are among the most important determinants of the responses of various countries to the economic crises of the 1970s and 1980s. But institutional capabilities are not general-purpose instruments, and neither are political power constellations. Both have their specific selectivity, permitting them to respond to some types of problem situations more effectively than to others. Thus, in order to adequately explain success or failure, we need to assess the "goodness of fit" between political and institutional capabilities on the one hand, and the specific requirements of the economic crises of the last decade on the other hand. Unless we are able to do so, our quantitative correlations may well be spurious, or at least unstable over time when the underlying economic problem changes its nature – which happened in 1979/80 (with the consequence that, in the 1980s, Austria was less successful and the United States were more successful than Schmidt's hypothesis would have predicted) and which may well be happening again right now.

Short-Term Vs. Structuralist Explanations

That means, of course, that even in political science studies we ultimately cannot dodge the questions of what was and is the nature of the underlying economic problems and which strategies of national economic policy might or might not succeed under such conditions. Yet a mere glance at the state of this discussion among economists might be enough to drive us back to our own concerns. Shortly after the beginning of the crisis, it is true, mainstream economists were at least able to agree on a common diagnosis which is neatly summarised in the following quote from the McCracken-Report to the OECD in 1977 (14):

> ... our reading of recent history is that the most important feature was an unusual bunching of unfortunate disturbances unlikely to be repeated on the same scale, the impact of which was compounded by some avoidable errors in economic policy.

The "unfortunate disturbances" were, of course, the first oil price shock of 1973/74 and the more general food and raw materials shortages preceding and accompanying it. Equally unsurprising, the "avoidable errors in economic policy" in the eyes of the McCracken group were, in the first place, the inflationary financing of the Vietnam war by the United States, and then the lack of determination of major countries in their fight against inflation in the early 1970s and, perhaps, the continuation of deflationary policies in some countries after the onset of the crisis. There was nothing, in short, that more intelligent and energetic macroeconomic management could not have avoided, or could not now correct. But these were happy days, theoretically speaking.

In the meantime the technocratic optimism of such ad hoc explanations has long been replaced either by the deep gloom of secular theories of stagnation or by the flagellantism of structuralist explanations of the crisis. The first tend to emphasise the utterly exceptional conditions of the post-war decades, and to interpret the difficulties of the 1970s and 1980s not as a temporary crisis but, rather, as the long-delayed return to capitalist "normalcy" (Borchardt 1982, Lutz 1984), or they tend to revive Kondratieff-Schumpeterian speculations about the "long waves of capitalist development" which also would support expectations of an inexorable economic decline during the present decades (Eklund 1980). In either case there is very little that economic policy could do to avoid or alleviate the crisis.

Structuralist explanations, on the other hand, tend to emphasise either the "institutional sclerosis" of over-organised and over-regulated economies (Olson 1982), or to lament the disastrous consequences of union power and of the tax burden of the welfare state for the vitality of capitalist economies. Even Michael Bolle and Xavier Greffe seem to subscribe to this type of structuralist analysis when they interpret present difficulties as a "crisis of regulation" in which "investment quotas have sagged in Western European countries" because of the "profit squeeze" exerted by improvements of the real wage position and because of "rigidities of the labour market". Again, there is not much that conventional economic policy could do about the problem – except to reduce the tax burden of the welfare state, to deregulate the economy and the labour market, and to weaken the organisational strength and the conflict potential of unions through appropriate industrial-relations legislation – all in the hope of revitalising the "animal spirits" of investors and entrepreneurs. This is, of course, the strategy adopted in Britain and other European countries after 1979, and in Germany after 1982. While it may have helped to increase profits and to reduce the rate of inflation, it certainly has not yet demonstrated its effectiveness in combatting mass unemployment.

So where does that leave us in our effort to understand the nature of the economic problems of the past decade – and to identify those economic-policy measures which could have explained the relative success of some countries? It seems to me that we would do well to return to the more short-term and ad hoc analysis of the McCracken Report. Such a world view does not ignore the possibility of longer-run structural problems – indeed it will be shown that the mismanagement of short-term problems is likely to create all the long-term problems that the structuralists have focused upon. I further assume, without being able to demonstrate it in this paper, that the necessary longer-term structural change would have been more easily accomplished if the short-term (random or cyclical) "disturbances", of which the McCracken report was speaking, had been managed better. In short, I suggest that the failures of short- and medium-term macroeconomic management ought to be taken more seriously than is currently fashionable in the search for explanations of our economic woes.

The early 1970s were undoubtedly a period in which several things had gone wrong at the same time in terms of short-term macroeconomic management. There was, first, a good deal of demand-pull inflation, much of it generated by an oversupply of US dollars which central banks were obliged to buy at fixed exchange rates. And just when the transition to a regime of floating exchange rates in 1973 provided national governments with a new freedom to pursue their own stablisation goals, inflation received an enormous cost push from exogenous increases of food, raw materials and, above all, oil prices. Thus, the battle against inflation became even more urgent.

At the same time, however, the three- or four-fold increase of oil prices within a few months meant that purchasing power was being transferred to the OPEC countries on a massive scale. Even if they had been able to immediately "recycle" their additional income into additional demand for consumer and capital goods, the result would have been major problems of structural adjustment among the industrialised countries. As it turned out, however, it took about two or three years before the OPEC countries were able to fully absorb their new wealth. In the meantime the accumulation of OPEC surpluses in the amount of 55 billion US dollars in 1974 created a demand gap of similar proportions in the industrialised world. If nothing was done about it, the predictable result was an increase in demand-deficient unemployment.

Economic-policy makers, in 1974/75, were thus confronted with the double-barrelled threat of cost-push inflation and demand-gap unemployment just at the time when they were beginning to succeed in their battle against the previous problem of demand-pull inflation. If they found themselves limited to macroeconomic demand management with the conventional armatorium of expansionary or restrictive fiscal and monetary policy, they were in serious trouble. Should they choose to fight unemployment with expansionary measures, they would allow firms to pass on cost increases and they might rekindle demand-pull inflation as well. But if they chose to fight inflation instead, restricting aggregate demand could not directly influence the exogenous cost increases themselves. The best that could be achieved was either a profit squeeze (if firms were prevented from recovering their higher costs through higher prices) or a reduction of output (if firms were able to pursue a mark-up-pricing policy in the face of inadequate aggregate demand). In either case the consequence would be increasing unemployment and a reduction of investment which would reduce future employment opportunities.

From this dilemma there was one – and only one – escape in the 1970s: if a country was able to rely upon effective incomes policies in addition to the conventional instruments of expansionary and restrictive fiscal and monetary policy, its economic policy would gain additional degrees of freedom which might be used to fight inflation and unemployment simultaneously. The crucial element was wage restraint. If increases in unit labour costs could be kept below the rate of inflation, the cost-push pressure on prices could be significantly reduced, leaving the government free to defend full employment by stabilising aggregate demand through expansionary fiscal and monetary policy measures.

This, then, was the "Keynesian" economic hypothesis underlying the imputed success of labour-dominated consensual strategies during the crisis of the 1970s: if there was an implicit or explicit understanding between the government and the labour unions under which the unions would exercise wage restraint while the government was reflating the economy, the unions would assume the responsibility for combatting cost-push inflation while the government could pursue full employment without having to pay the price of accelerating inflation. Yet, if the economics of success were so essentially simple – why was it that so few countries were actually able to pursue the concerted strategies necessary to their realisation? The answer lies, I suggest, in the institutional difficulties of the potentially successful economic strategy.

The Difficulties of a Keynesian Solution

In order to appreciate the difficulties of the Keynesian solution, we need to look more closely at the constellation of interests which is involved. Let us begin with the point of view of a "labour-dominated government." It must be concerned with both problems, inflation and unemployment. But – given its dependence upon the labour vote and upon the political support of organised labour, it also must have a clear political priority for avoiding open unemployment at almost any cost. From the perspective of such a government, then, the strategic "concertation" of wage restraint with demand reflation (the upper right cell of Figure 1) is clearly the preferred solution.

When viewed from the union perspective, however, the interest constellation is much more ambiguous. For unions, unemployment – or the threat of rising unemployment – is even more of a problem than it is for labour-dominated governments, but inflation as such is less of a union concern. Instead, unions have a strong interest in increasing the real income of their members, and inflation matters only to the extent that nominal wage increases are wiped out by it. Thus, if they could be sure that the government will in fact maintain full employment, they would always be tempted to shift from wage restraint to an expansionary wage

			union wage policy	
			expansionary	restrictive
government policy	expansionary	unemployment inflation	low very high	low low
	restrictive	unemployment inflation	very high low	high very low

Figure 1 Payoff Matrix of a Labour-Dominated Government

policy. This temptation is strongest for very small unions or in company-level bargaining, where inflation appears as a "collective evil" that could not be much reduced by one's own wage restraint, while one's own real incomes would suffer very much from the inflation generated by wage increases elsewhere. Thus it would be entirely rational for all small unions to push for the highest nominal wage increases which they could obtain.

Very large unions on the other hand (or the union movement as a whole) would at least have to consider the impact of high nominal wage increases upon inflation and, hence, upon real wages – and they might also take into account the difficulties which aggressive wage policies might entail for the continuing political viability of government full-employment policies (which for small unions is also a collective good that would not be much influenced by their own strategies).

			union wage policy	
			expansionary	restrictive
government policy	expansionary	unemployment	low	low
		real wages	high	low
	restrictive	unemployment	very high	high
		real wages	high	low

Figure 2 Payoff Matrix of a Small Labour Union

The reason for this concern arises from the fact that even labour-dominated governments must be politically sensitive to the demand for price stability. Thus, if the unions would not offer sufficient protection against inflation, the government might eventually have to shift to a more restrictive policy stance, or it might be displaced by a conservative government that was willing to realise aggregate demand in order to fight inflation. In either case the payoff of union wage strategies would change radically. As a consequence, unemployment would rise – and the unions would be defenseless against it. Once the money supply was effectively reduced, raising real wages could not increase effective demand – but it would surely create a profit squeeze that would push up "classical" unemployment. Thus, in order to minimise employment losses, the unions would now be pushed back, willy-nilly, towards the wage moderation from which full-employment policies had tempted them away.

Ironically, it is the small unions and company-level bargaining units that would have the greatest incentive to "cooperate" with a severely restrictive government policy. Unlike inflation, unemployment is not a "collective" but a "private evil" which is directly affected, to some degree by the wage costs of individual firms. Thus, the smaller the bargaining unit the greater would be the willingness of workers to save their own jobs through wage concessions – even if that kind of competition would push wages down for everybody.

It is obvious, therefore, that the ideal "Keynesian concertation" of government and union strategies does not represent a stable game-theoretical equilibrium. If the government is in effect "labour dominated" (meaning that it is politically committed to the full-employment priority), then the unions will be strongly tempted to pursue wage goals which are incompatible with their explicit or implicit responsibility for price stability. As a consequence, inflation may increase to politically intolerable levels – meaning that even a labour-dominated government may have to shift its priorities, or that it will be replaced by a conservative government committed to the fight against inflation as its topmost political priority.

When that happens, however, the unions have no choice but to restrain their wage demands while unemployment remains high. And unemployment is likely to remain high: if restrictive policies are pursued for any length of time, investment will have suffered, and the number of available working places will have been reduced below the level needed for full employment. Once that has happened, unemployment will have become "structural" – meaning that demand reflation could not eliminate it without inflationary overheating. Thus, the intersection of restrictive demand management and wage restraint may in fact represent a game-theoretical equilibrium – or a trap: government could not reflate the economy back into full employment even if it wanted to do so, and the unions would be forced by high levels of unemployment to maintain their general wage restraint.

Objectively speaking, the union movement as a whole would surely have every reason to avoid this least-favoured scenario. But in order to do so, it would have to solve two equally difficult strategic problems: it would need to forego certain short-term wage gains in anticipation of uncertain medium- or longer-term dangers, and it would need to discipline the rational egotism of its subunits in the interest of solidaristic strategies. The enormous difficulties of both tasks become obvious when one begins to examine the concrete historical experiences of four countries, Austria, Britain, Sweden, and the Federal Republic of Germany – all of which were led by "labour-dominated governments" at the beginning of the economic crisis.

Austria, Britain, Sweden, West Germany: Four Cases in Point

Of the four countries only one, Austria, was in fact able to consistently pursue the concerted strategies discussed above at least until the end of the 1970s. As in most other countries, the first response of government fiscal policy to the crisis was expansionary – with a significant increase of the public deficit. As wage settlements were also undesirably high in 1974/75, the rate of inflation reached 10% in 1974. Nevertheless, the government continued on its expansionary course, relying upon a combination of hard currency policy and union assurances of future wage restraint to deal with the problem of inflation. And, indeed, unit labor costs were reduced after 1975, and inflation came down to around 4% by 1978 – even though registered unemployment never increased above the full-employment level of 2% until the end of the decade.

If the Austrian experience demonstrates the economic potential of Keynesian concertation strategies during the 1970s, the rise and fall of the "Social Contract" in *Great Britain* illustrates their institutional difficulties. In principle, the early responses to the crisis were similar in both countries – except that British wage settlements were much more exorbitant in 1974 and 1975, so that the rate of inflation reached 24% by 1975. But after they realised the difficulties which this implied for the survival of the Labour government, the Trades Union Congress and individual unions agreed to a policy of wage restraint in order to curtail runaway inflation – and to allow the Labour government to continue its moderately expansionary anti-unemployment policy. And like in Austria, the policy was successful. By 1978 inflation had been dramatically reduced from 24% to 8.3% while employment continued to increase and unemployment, though higher than in Austria and Sweden, remained quite low.

But here the similarity ends: the Austrians with their highly concentrated structure of 16 industrial unions and with their highly centralised patterns of wage bargaining were able to implement wage restraint in an entirely business-as-usual fashion. Union leaders and employers associations were of one mind about the need for a determined but gradual reduction of wage pressures, and they simply planned their annual settlements accordingly. By contrast, Britain with her highly fragmented union structure of over 100 separate unions, many of them quite small and often competing with each other, and with decentralised patterns of shopfloor bargaining, had no chance whatever of treating wage restraint in the manner of ordinary business. Instead, the Social Contract could only succeed if the greatest possible publicity was employed to generate a maximum of moral, ideological, and political pressure upon individual unions and their shop stewards. The appeal was to "give a year for Britain," and the reference was to the "spirit of Dunkirk." Furthermore, in order to emphasise the solidaristic morality of the Social Contract (and also to discourage evasions through a simple and highly visible rule), the agreement was for a fixed-sum wage increase of 6 pounds per week for everybody during the first year, and for an even lower flat-rate settlement during the second year.

In the light of later events, it needs to be emphasised that the Social Contract was a dramatic success in its own terms, observed almost without exception during its first two years – and reducing the increase of unit labour costs from 29.4% in 1975 to 9.4% in 1976. But moral fervor could not substitute indefinitely for the institutional weaknesses of an extremely fragmented union organisation, and flat-rate wage settlements were beginning to seriously distort a highly differentiated wage structure as well. In short: when the Callaghan government asked for a fourth year of the Social Contract in the Summer of 1978, union leaders were no longer able to offer their support – and a series of wildcat strikes escalated into official strikes of ever-increasing scope and bitterness, until the country came virtually to a standstill in the "winter of discontent" of 1978–79. The rest is modern history: Margaret Thatcher's resounding election victory in May of 1979 marked the end of any concerted government-union strategies in Britain, and as British unions learned the hard way to accept the non-negotiable discipline of monetarist demand management, British rates of inflation were coming down slowly while unemployment moved up much faster and has steadfastly remained above the 3-million level ever since.

The *Swedish* experience illustrates yet another variation of the same story. Again, the government's first response to the crisis was expansionary, and again wage settlements in 1974–75 were pushing up the rate of inflation. But when an agreement on wage restraint might have had a chance in 1976, the Social Democratic government lost the election (for reasons having less to do with economic management than with the dispute over nuclear energy). The bourgeois coalition, which came into power after 44 years of Social Democratic rule, had only one priority on which they could agree: they would continue to prevent open unemployment at almost any cost. And so they did. Being not close enough to the unions to negotiate any kind of concerted strategy, they combined repeated devaluations with the all-out subsidisation of employment in crisis-ridden industries – and with a continuation of Social Democratic policies increasing public sector employment and the employment-substituting measures of active labour market policy.

As a result, open unemployment in Sweden remained as low as it was in Austria, and the number of persons employed increased more than in any other European country. This is a remarkable achievement by any standards – even if one acknowledges that most of the additional employment was in part-time jobs for women in the local public and social services. The price which the bourgeois coalition governments were willing to pay was an escalation of public deficits – with interest payments of the national government exceeding one fifth of total expenditures in the early 1980s.

But what about the unions? Surely not much love was lost between them and the bourgeois governments. Yet, on the other hand, Swedish union leaders in the 1950s and 1960s had developed a statesman-like sense of responsibility for the welfare of the national economy, and they were unlikely to abandon this self image merely because they did not agree politically with the government of the day. Apparently, something more serious must have happened to explain the inflationary push of Swedish wages in the late 1970s and early 1980s. Again, the best explanation that I have is institutional. Sweden is usually listed together with Austria as having the most concentrated and the most centralised union organisation. But, strictly speaking, that description holds only for blue-collar industrial unions united in the powerful "LO" which, until recently, was indeed able to conduct central wage negotiations across all sectors of industry. White-collar unions, on the other hand, had always been organised according to different principles, cutting across the jurisdictional demarkations of LO industrial unions.

For a long time these organisational anomalies had not mattered much as white-collar unions had been willing to accept the hegemonic leadership of LO in their own wage settlements. But with the increase of white-collar employment and with the increasing organisational strength of white-collar unions, that pattern changed. Aquiescence gave way to competition, and in some years the white-collar unions even usurped the wage leadership which LO unions had always claimed as their birthright. No wonder, therefore, that inter-union competition (and the effect of ubiquitous compensation clauses in wage settlements) prevented a return to the Swedish tradition of macroeconomically "reasonable" wage settlements during the time of the bourgeois coalition governments. Instead, Swedish inflation rates remained above average, and the profitability and international competitiveness of Swedish industry never recovered – despite a seemingly endless succession of devaluations of the Swedish krona.

Thus, when the Social Democrats returned to power in the Fall of 1982, unemployment was still very low, but the rest of the Swedish economy and, above all, the public budget were in a rather bad shape. Confronted with the urgent need to consolidate the budget, the new government virtually ended the expansion of public-sector employment as well as the subsidisation of employment in declining industries. Instead, it attempted to combine a once-for-all massive devaluation of the krona to stimulate exports and profits in the export industries with "social-contract"-like appeals for union wage restraint. By a lucky coincidence, this strategy profited from the export boom generated by the strong US dollar and American economic expansion after 1982. The closer political ties between unions and government and the moral pressure exerted by the government have also helped to dampen the effects of inter-union competition for the time being. But whether that will be enough to assure continuing success for the management of the Swedish economy remains to be seen.

The Federal Republic of Germany, finally, introduces an entirely new element into our account of the successes and failures of "labour-dominated governments". The initial fiscal response of the federal government, to be sure, and of the Länder as well, was quite as expansionary as the fiscal policies which Austria had adopted. And increases in unit labour costs, while also inflationary in 1974, were far more moderate in 1975 and thereafter than those in Austria – or in any other OECD country, for that matter. Nevertheless, German economic policy did not achieve a successful concertation between government fiscal and monetary policy on the one hand, and union wage policy on the other hand, except for a brief period between 1977 and 1979.

But in contrast to Britain and Sweden, the problem in Germany could not be located on the union side. While their wage bargaining is not quite as centralised as it was in Sweden and still is in Austria, the organisational structure of the sixteen industrial unions in Germany shows the same degree of concentration as in Austria – and much less inter-union competition than was true in Sweden during the last decade. On the whole, those of the German unions which are capable of exercising wage leadership are also large enough (and economically sophisticated enough) to consider the macroeconomic consequences of their own wage settlements – which, of course, does not mean that these settlements should always please economic-policy makers in government or in the central bank. Thus, if concertation failed in Germany, the reason was not organisational problems of the unions – it was the very special role of the central bank.

In order to appreciate this point, we must first reexamine the notion of a "government fiscal and monetary policy" which we have used so far. This assumes an identity of the policy priorities and of the perceptions of policy makers in both fields – which may, or may not, exist in reality. If they had an entirely free choice, at least, one should expect that monetary policy makers would prefer policy priorities which are different from those of a "labour-dominated government". In general, it seems reasonable to assume that price stability will be their topmost priority and that unemployment, if it is considered a problem at all, will be a rather secondary concern of theirs. Thus, if a politically independent central bank were to consider its strategy choices vis-à-vis the choices of union wage policy, its payoff matrix might look as follows:

			union wage policy	
			expansionary	restrictive
monetary policy	expansionary	(unemployment) inflation	very high	low (?)
	restrictive	(unemployment) inflation	low	very low

Figure 3 Payoff Matrix of an Independent Central Bank

Even if the unions might be trusted to exercise wage restraint when the government was committed to reflating the economy (which, from the bank's point of view must appear as a rather doubtful proposition), monetary policy makers would still have an unconditional preference for restrictive policies. Not only would that put them on the safe side in case the unions would not deliver on their promises, but it would improve the outlook for price stability even if they did. And like virtue, price stability is never firmly assured and always in need of greater commitment and effort. Even now, with the annual rate of inflation below 1%, the Deutsche Bundesbank will not relax its monetary vigilance – and the 1970s had never provided it with that degree of comfort.

The point would not be worth belabouring if monetary restraint were not such a terribly effective policy instrument with the capability of completely overwhelming the effects of fiscal expansion. By limiting the supply of money, it is able to constrain aggregate demand regardless of the size of the government deficit. At the same time, rising interest rates will increase the exchecker costs of public borrowing as well as the costs of private investment. They may also raise the exchange rate and discourage export demand. But that is not all.

The most important consequence of rising interest rates is an increase in the opportunity costs of investment capital. Household savings and the accumulated profits of enterprises need no longer seek productive investments in order to earn satisfactory rates of return. At high interest rates, government bonds and other financial assets may offer even more attractive opportunities to realise the potential "surplus value" of accumulated capital – and without the risk that is inevitably associated with productive investment. In order to compete, therefore, productive investments must offer higher rates of expected profits – which, of course, could only be achieved by reducing the competing claims of labour and of the state. As a result, rising interest rates will either reduce the comparative attractiveness of real investments – with the predictable result of an investment gap and a subsequent increase of "classical unemployment". Or they will require a compensatory redistribution in favour of the profits accruing to the capital factor – and at the expense of the shares going to labour and to government. In other words: when interest rates are increased, the "terms of trade" between capital, labour, and the state are changed in the favour of capital.

If that is so, the effective coordination between fiscal policy and monetary policy must be a second crucial precondition for the success of Keynesian full-employment strategies – certainly equal in importance with the "cooperative" capabilities of labour unions. Institutionally, that coordination was no problem at all in three of the four countries:

The Österreichische Nationalbank is a private-law corporation whose stocks are jointly owned by the government and by the "social partners", unions, and employers associations, which not only have seats on its governing board but also control appointments to the directorate. Thus, close personal and political ties among decision makers in all three areas may have been even more important for the uncomplicated concertation between fiscal, monetary, and wage policy than the formal controls exercised by government over the bank's policy decisions. The Bank of England, on the other hand, has no formal and few informal ties to the unions. But its formal position is that of a department of the Treasury – completely subordinate to government directives. And while – under the watchful eyes of a highly articulate and influential financial press – its professional authority is usually respected, there is no question at all that monetary policy could ever conflict with the economic-policy priorities of the government. The same is true in Sweden, where the governors of the Riksbank are directly elected by the Parliament – assuring a political majority for the government of the day during each election period.

By contrast, the Deutsche Bundesbank (like the equally independent Federal Reserve in the United States) is a federal institution whose decision-making body is only partly appointed by the national government. In its monetary policy decisions, furthermore, it is entirely independent from any directives – the most the government could ask for is that a decision should be delayed for a few weeks to allow for further consultation. Thus, while the bank is by law requested to cooperate with the economic policy of the federal government, it is free to define the terms of such cooperation by its own lights. And since the fall of 1974, it has chosen to define cooperation in "monetarist" terms – meaning that the bank would announce its own targets for monetary expansion each year, inviting the government and the social partners to adjust their own policy choices accordingly. In a country whose political sensitivity to inflation problems is exceptionally high, and in a government coalition whose survival depended upon the continuing support of a "bourgeois" party, the Social Democrats in the federal government probably had good political reasons to avoid an open clash with the bank's anti-inflation policy, even if they should have disapproved of it.

The unfortunate result was that twice, in 1974 and in 1980–81, a relatively vigorous fiscal expansion was neutralised in its economic effectiveness by a sharply restrictive monetary policy. As a consequence, West Germany was among the two or three OECD countries with the lowest rates of inflation throughout the crisis period. But she was also among the countries which suffered the greatest losses of employment – exceeded only by Switzerland after 1974 and by the United Kingdom after 1980. Thus, the fact that registered unemployment in West Germany remained below the OECD average in the 1974–79 period had little to do with a successful full-employment economic policy. It was mainly the result of policies reducing the supply of labour – mainly trough preventing further immigration and encouraging the emigration of foreign workers and through the effects of various forms of early retirement for older workers. Without these supply-side measures, registered unemployment would have risen much faster, crossing the two-million mark already between 1975 and 1977 – rather than in 1982.

Concerted Action and its Institutional Preconditions

To summarise: in the 1973–79 period, labour-dominated governments in highly-industrialised Western societies did indeed have a chance to maintain full employment and reasonable price stability. The economic precondition was a concerted strategy combining expansionary fiscal and monetary policy with union wage restraint. The institutional preconditions of success were a union structure capable of adopting and maintaining wage policies that would not fully exploit the opportunities for wage increases provided by full-employment conditions, and institutional arrangements within government that assured the subordination of monetary policy to the full-employment priorities of the government.

As it turned out, governments in all four countries did in fact attempt to achieve the economically optimal concertation of fiscal, monetary, and wage policy. But only in Austria were both of the institutional preconditions of success fulfilled to the same degree.

In the United Kingdom, and to a lesser degree in Sweden as well, the organisational structure of the union movement and the institutional arrangements for collective bargaining made wage restraint difficult to achieve. In Britain the attempt to use the ideological commitment of the "Social Contract" as a substitute for the inadequate institutional capabilities of the union movement was dramatically successful for a few short years – but then it failed even more dramatically in the "winter of discontent" of 1978/79. In Sweden the unions – because of wage competition within their own ranks and perhaps also because of a lack of political rapport with the bourgeois coalition governments – also contributed to wage-push inflation which the government was unable to control. But the government was willing and able to maintain extremely high levels of employment through subsidies to industry, through a very high volume of active-labour-market measures and, above all, through a rapid expansion of public-service employment. The price was an even more rapid increase of public deficits.

In the Federal Republic of Germany, finally, the institutional conditions on the union side did facilitate a consistent policy of wage restraint after 1974, and the federal government also pursued an expansionary fiscal policy at the beginning of the crisis. The German central bank, however, was institutionally capable of pursuing its own policy priorities regardless of the government's political commitment to full employment – and, economically, monetary restraint turned out to be more effective than fiscal expansion. The result was an extremely high degree of price stability and very high employment losses.

This, then, seems to be the combined economic and political explanation of the relative success or failure of the economic policies of four labour-dominated governments in the 1973–79 period. But why was it that the solution which worked so well for Austria in the 1970s seemed to run into ever increasing difficulties even in Austria in the 1980s, and seemed to fail completely when the French Socialists attempted to adopt it in 1981/82? And why is it that decidedly non-socialist regimes seemed to do remarkably well politically and reasonably well economically in the 1980s? The explanation which I propose is, again, economic and institutional at the same time – with the one qualification that in contrast to the 1970s there was now no plausible economic strategy which could have satisfied the policy priorities of labour-dominated governments.

Yet, what was it that changed so fundamentally in 1979? First, there was the second oil-price shock which, again, increased cost-push inflation and created a demand gap in the industrialised countries of over 100 billion US dollars in 1980. But, while the policy response of most industrialised countries to the first oil crisis had been Keynesian expansion, it now was monetarist restraint not only in the United Kingdom but, much more importantly, also in the United States. There, the Federal Reserve under its new chairman Paul Volcker had finally converted from a Keynesian to a monetarist perspective, and had decided even before the second oil crisis to squeeze out inflationary expectations through restricting the supply of money. The price push of the Iranian oil shock only helped to increase their determination. But as dollar interest rates increased, the debt burden of second- and third-world countries, which had rapidly built up during the recession of the 1970s, reached crisis proportions as well. Loans which could not be repaid had to be replaced by new and even more uncertain loans – whose interest rates did, of course, include a considerable risk premium over and above the rates in the United States.

As a consequence, the international level of interest rates increased to exorbitant heights after 1979. This, in turn, created an extremely hostile economic environment for all countries whose political priorities would have called for expansionary fiscal and monetary policies. If they insisted upon increasing their own money supply and lowering their internal interest rates, the international capital and money markets, whose responsiveness to differences in expected rates of return had become almost instantaneous during the 1970s, would immediately respond with a withdrawal of funds from that country. The result would be a devaluation of the currency and an increase in the rate of inflation – which, before long, would compel even governments with an unambigous priority for full-employment to switch to more restrictive policies. This, at any rate, is what happened when the newly elected Socialist government in France attempted to implement the full-employment strategy which had been successful in Austria during the 1970s.

While in the 1973–79 period, individual countries had still been free to pursue either expansionary ("Keynesian") or restrictive ("monetarist") policies, the rising dollar interest rates, combined with a steadily rising exchange rate of the US dollar, eliminated the choice of an expansionary monetary policy. Whether it fitted their political priorities or not, all governments were forced to "import" the monetarism of the United States. But, as the German example had already demonstrated in the 1970s, that also increased the price, and reduced the effectiveness, of expansionary fiscal policy. And if government policy was restrictive, neither an expansionary nor a restrictive wage policy of the unions could hope to defend or recover full employment. In short: the worldwide switch to a monetarist monetary policy effectively eliminated the possibility of successful Keynesian solutions at the national level.

Of the four countries whose performance in the 1970s were discussed before, the United Kingdom had ceased to be "labour dominated" in 1979 and the Federal Republic in 1982 – or perhaps already in the Fall of 1980, when elections had increased the political weight of the Free Democrats in the Social-Liberal coalition. Under their new governments, both countries chose to embrace, rather than to fight, the monetarist discipline of international capital markets, and to accept rising unemployment as the inevitable cost of greater stability and of better opportunities for future economic growth.

Of the remaining two countries, Austria tried to stay on the course that had been successful in the 1970s. But with the effective loss of national control over the conduct of monetary policy, the burden which had to be carried by fiscal policy, by incomes policy, and by public-sector industries became much heavier, while unemployment nevertheless increased to levels that would have been politically unacceptable in the 1970s. Even though Austria, like everybody else, began to profit from the American economic recovery after 1982, the need became ever more compelling to reduce the public deficit and to salvage publicly-owned firms that had been asked to operate more like employment agencies than like profit-seeking enterprises. As a consequence, the "Austrian model" has lost much of its former appeal abroad.

The Swedish Social Democrats, after their return to power in the Fall of 1982, did not have the option of staying on the previous course. The catastrophic deficits of the external balances and of the public budgets did require dramatically new policy departures. The new government chose to devaluate the krona by a rate which was larger than expected – and which provided protection against further capital flight. If it was possible to reestablish the conditions for wage restraint, the strategy might improve the profitability and international competitiveness of Swedish industry – but even under the best of circumstances, it would not quickly reduce the pressure on the labour market and, hence, it would not allow the government to reduce its financial commitment to active labour market policy without accepting increases in registered unemployment.

Finally, even if it would succeed in Sweden, the Swedish strategy – unlike the Austrian model in the 1970s – could not be generalised without becoming economically self-defeating. Not all countries could at the same time devaluate their currencies to create an export boom. Thus it seems reasonable to conclude that neither Austria nor Sweden have been able to come up with a generally plausible strategy that could have assured full-employment under the new conditions of the international economic environment of the 1980s. The reasons for that conclusion seem to follow directly from the analysis of the German difficulties in the 1970s:

If the international level of interest rates rises, the "terms of trade" between capital and all other claimants for shares of the gross national product are altered in favour of capital. As a consequence, there is an increase in the minimal level of profitablity which productive investments must achieve in order to compete with other opportunities for capital use. Devaluation combined with wage restraint in Sweden was one way of increasing the profitablity of investments in the export industries; Austrian-type subsidisation of investments, also combined with continuing wage restraint, was another. Any other form of increasing the profitability of productive investments over and above the minimum profitability defined by the level of international interest rates would also do. But in all cases, what was required was a purposeful redistribution of national income in favour of profits from productive investment. Or, to put the same conclusion in different words: during the 1970s, the interests of wage earners and capital owners (which, of course, might be the same persons) still converged in most countries in a joint interest in economic growth. After 1980, that coalition fell apart when capital was able to collect higher returns in the international financial markets than could be offered by reasonably profitable productive investments.

The Dilemma of Labour-Dominated Governments

Once that coalition of interests had fallen apart, labour-dominated governments also lost their comparative advantage over other political constellations. If the only chance of economic success did in fact depend upon the ability to increase the profitablity of investments sufficiently to catch up with the rising rates of return offered in the international capital markets, then any government that was politically bound to labour interests was at a disadvantage. The same was true, of course, of unions which were institutionally capable of solidaristic action. In either case, the greater degree of power would enable labour interests to resist attempts at forced redistribution in favour of capital interests. But the political battles which they might win were likely to be economically pyrrhic victories when the international environment provided more attractive alternative opportunities for capital. And no matter what degree of "encompassing" rationality might be achieved by a powerful labour movement and its political representatives: their capability for organised self-exploitation would always lag behind the degree of exploitation achievable in countries with weak or nonexistent labour unions and with "capital-dominated" governments. This, together with the massive expansionary impulses of huge public deficits, explains the phenomenal employment gains of the United States in the last few years.

One might, of course, reasonably ask the author of such dismal conclusions for suggestions of a more promising strategy which might allow labour-dominated governments to evade the unattractive choice between mass unemployment and voluntary submission to greater degrees of exploitation. Obviously, there are such suggestions – ranging from a single-minded pursuit of technological innovation in order to increase labour productivity (and, hence, the profitability of investments without the need to reduce wage incomes) to the uncoupling of employment opportunities from profits through an increase of publicly financed employment or through the solidaristic redistribution of working time (and incomes) between those who have jobs and the unemployed. But all of these solidaristic solutions could be described as "socialism within one class," because they would have to respect the greater distributive claims of capital owners. For that reason, they would all be less satisfactory, from a labour-dominated perspective, than the solutions which could have worked in the 1970s and before.

To end on a speculative note: could it be that the international economic situation was undergoing yet another fundamental change right now – and a change for the better, at that? The present fall of oil prices could indeed be interpreted as an "oil crisis in reverse" – with a reduction of cost-push inflation and an increase of effective demand within the industrialized world. At the same time, the falling exchange rate of the US dollar seems to create opportunities for lowering the interest rates of all other countries which had been foreclosed since 1980. Thus, at least for the time being, national Keynesianism might indeed work again.

And so it might – provided that the debt crisis of the Third World will remain in abeyance, and provided that OPEC will not be revived by the rapid fall of oil incomes. But even then, we should not expect that a return to the concerted strategies that were (or would have been) successful in the 1970s would now suffice. At least in those countries which were not able to prevent mass unemployment from building up, we now have a large stock of structural unemployment which mere demand reflation, even if combined with wage restraint, could not eliminate. If governments tried to reflate the economy beyond the production potential of existing capacity, demand-pull inflation would reappear. And if governments and unions would try to stimulate additional productive investments to such a degree that the structural job deficit could be eliminated, they would again be compelled to attempt a massive redistribution in favour of capital interests. Thus, even if we were (temporarily – because the internationalisation of capital markets is likely to be irreversible) again in a situation in which national Keynesian strategies had a chance of success, we would still need to rely upon solidaristic strategies of publicly-financed employment, and of work sharing, in order to eliminate unemployment.

The present essay, therefore, does not end on a happy note: the hope of the 1960s, that national governments might be able to achieve full employment and price stability and all other goals of economic policy at the same time, was disappointed by the worldwide economic crises beginning in the early 1970s. And while the economic environment then would have allowed Keynesian strategies to succeed, the institutional requirements of the necessary coordination between government fiscal and monetary policy, and union wage policy, were so demanding that only very few societies could have succeeded. In the 1980s, however, even that slender hope was destroyed by another change in the economic environment which transformed the terms of trade between capital, labour, and governments in favour of capital interests. In purely economic terms (i.e., without regard to issues of distribution), countries which offered the least institutional resistance against being exploited by capital interests were now at an advantage. Whether that situation is now changing again is still uncertain. But even if it is, the reduction of high levels of structural unemployment could not be accomplished without the institutional capability for solidaristic strategies which is so difficult to achieve.

References

Borchardt, K. (1982): *Wachstum, Krisen, Handlungsspielräume der Wirtschaft*, Göttingen.

McCracken, P. et al. (1977): *Towards full employment and price stability*, Paris: OECD.

Eklund, Klas (1980): Long waves in the development of capitalism, *Kyklos*, 33: 383–419.

Lutz, B. (1984): *Der kurze Traum immerwährender Prosperität: eine Neuinterpretation der industriell-kapitalistischen Entwicklung im Europa des 20. Jahrhunderts*, Frankfurt/Main.

Olson, M. (1982): *The rise and decline of nations: Economic growth, stagflation and social rigidities*, New Haven.

The Political Management of Mixed Economies: Political Aspects of Macroeconomic Performance in OECD Nations (1960–1984)

Manfred G. Schmidt

Introduction

In comparison to earlier phases of economic development, the level of economic performance that was achieved in the OECD nations in the 1960s and early 1970s was high. Rates of economic growth were high, and rates of unemployment remained at a historically low level (Maddison 1982). The benefits of the new prosperity were widely diffused. The new system was remarkably productive, and it was also remarkably stable (Shonfield 1969). In a sense, almost all OECD economies were success stories in this period in terms of historical growth and employment records. However, some OECD economies were more successful than others. For example, the economies in Germany, Japan, and France, among others, performed better than the economy of the United States or the United Kingdom. To what extent did the level of aggregate performance vary with political aspects of the OECD economies in the 1960s and early 1970s? This is one of the questions that will be addressed in this essay.

Signs of underlying economic weakness, such as increases in inflation rates, began to emerge in the late 1960s, but it was not before the mid-1970s that the Western nations found themselves fully confronted with an economic malaise. In the period following the first oil price shock in 1973, all OECD nations were plagued by economic problems such as reduced rates of GDP growth, increases in inflation rates, unemployment rates, and balance of payment difficulties. However, the first basic question on which attention will be focused in this paper, is why some nations suffered less than others and why some countries managed to recover earlier than others? The second basic question is on the extent to which differences in levels of performance after 1973 mirror differences in political conditions.

Why do levels of macroeconomic performance vary as much as they do? A vast body of literature on economic history and economic policy in Western nations suggests that differences in levels of performance depend upon a wide range of structural and economic factors such as trading positions, sectoral composition of national economies, differences in capital stock and labor supply, and differences in policy stances, to mention just a few examples.[1] While much of this literature investigates the impact of "proximate causes" (A. O. Hirschman) and structural and economic background factors on levels of performance, recent contributions from the literature on the comparative politics of economic policy focus on some of the major "deeper" social and political causes of successful or unsuccessful management of the economy. It is on the latter approach to the study of economic performance that attention will center in this essay.

In comparative studies on the political economy of Western nations, a number of genuinely political variables have been identified as major determinants of economic performance, among them the organizational structure and power of labor, the distribution of political power between labor and capital and between socialist and nonsocialist tendencies, the duration of uninterrupted democracy, the existence or absence of corporatist linkages between producer groups and the state, and the intelligence inherent in institutions deserve to be mentioned first.

Broadly speaking, three different views have dominated the field of studies on comparative political economy: (1) the "rise-and-decline-of-nations" hypothesis, (2) the "power-of-labor" hypothesis, and (3) the "policy-concertation" hypothesis. According to the first school of thought, the strength of organized interest groups, itself associated with the duration of democratic experience, and, in particular, the strength of trade unions and Social Democratic governments have created institutional rigidities such as sticky wages, minimum-wage legislation, legal protection of job security that prevent the labor market from clearing and that undermine the national economies' capability of fully mobilizing the potential strength inherent in market economies. Thus, for example, following Mancur Olson's book entitled *The Rise and Decline of Nations* (1982), it has been argued that rates of economic growth are inversely related to a wide variety of variables that are indicative of the extent to which the OECD economies have been plagued by institutional sclerosis such as the strength of particularistic distributional coalitions, the size and growth of government in general, and the size and growth of the welfare state in particular, and the extent to which political arenas were occupied by the labor movement and Social Democratic parties (see, for

[1] See, for example, Altvater, Hübner, and Stanger (1983), Boltho (1982), Lindbeck (1983), Maddison (1982), and in particular for the pre-1973 period, Denison (1967), Kindleberger (1967), Maddison (1964).

example, Bernholz 1982, Cohen 1985, Sloan and Tedin 1985: 35, Weede 1984, and Weede 1986).

By contrast, a second group of scholars has followed a paradigm of class politics in arguing that successful economic performance in Western democracies is associated with, and by inference depends upon, the existence of relationships between centralized capital and labor and, in particular, centralized and organizationally powerful labor movements. According to this view, powerful trade unions, acting in conjunction with governments of leftish complexion and centralized systems of industrial relations, have been conducive to the achievement of higher rates of economic growth and lower levels of unemployment, frequently, though not necessarily, at the cost of higher rates of inflation (see, for example, Cameron 1984, Hibbs 1977, Lange and Garrett 1985, Martin 1973, Stephens 1979, Whiteley 1983).

According to a third school of thought, differences in levels of economic performance may be partly attributable to differences in political ideologies and distribution of power between collective actors. However, the bulk of differences would reflect differences in politico-institutional conditions, such as coherence in economic planning, and the degree to which policy formation and interest intermediation are characterized by corporatist arrangements (see, for example, Cox 1982, Czada 1983 and 1984, Katzenstein 1984 and 1985, Keman 1984, Lehner 1986, Scharpf 1984, Schmidt 1982, Wilensky 1981). The explanations that the latter school of thought advance are at least partly derived from Andrew Shonfield's seminal study entitled Modern Capitalism (1969). Shonfield argued that the economic success stories of the post-war period were each based on their own formula for coping with economic problems. While the political and institutional conditions in these countries differed widely, the management of the institutional apparatus that guided the economy was similar in nature. Shonfield argued that there were many indicators of relative success in nations that had the basic bits of apparatus required for systematic economic planning, the requisite forms of collaboration by interest groups, and the "appropriate habits of mind". In the post-war period, for example, countries such as France, Austria, the Federal Republic of Germany, and Sweden were institutionally better equipped for coping with economic problems than were other countries such as Italy, the United States, and the United Kingdom. Disorganized processes of policy formation (Italy), the separation of powers and its concomittant, the competitive theory of government (United States), or other potent traditions ingrained in the political system, such as "an abiding prejudice which sees it as the natural business of government to react – not to act" (Shonfield 1969: 386) (United Kingdom) impeded the development of active, interventionist governments. Thus, the formulation of coherent economic policy was seriously impaired in these countries.

The extent to which Shonfield's hypothesis fits the data on macro-economic performance after 1965 has been a matter of controversy. Critics of Shonfield's study have argued that the period of supergrowth ended in the late 1960s and that there was nothing that planning could do to restore it (Kindleberger 1967). Shonfield himself pointed out "that there is no reason to suppose that the patterns of the past ... will reassert themselves in the future" (1969: 62). Continuing prosperity on the scale of the period before 1965 would have been possible. However, the interesting question is whether success would have been probable. The answer to this, in Shonfield's words, "depends very largely on political will and skill: specifically on the management of the institutional apparatus which guides Western economic life" (1969: 63).

Each of the three views of the relationship between political circumstances and macroeconomic performance lends itself to an empirical test. According to the "rise-and-decline-of-nations" hypothesis, the level of macroeconomic performance is higher in countries characterized by a more limited role of the state and, in particular, a short history of uninterrupted democracy, and lower in older democracies and countries in which labor commands a dominant position. By contrast, the "power-of-labor" hypothesis predicts that the management of mixed economies in countries characterized by dominant labor movements results in levels of performance higher than those in countries in which nonsocialist tendencies dominate. Finally, the "policy-concertation" hypothesis predicts a positive relationship between levels of aggregate performance and the coherence of economic planning, in conjunction with strong linkages between the state and the economy.

In the following sections of this essay, attention will be focused on the extent to which these alternative hypotheses are compatible or incompatible with data on several major aspects of macroeconomic performance in twenty-one Western nations in the period from the early 1960s to the mid-1980s. Attention will be centered on a few politically important macro-economic indicators[2] such as economic growth (measured by the average annual percentage change in real GDP), rates of unemployment (measured by the total number of unemployment as a percentage of the total labor force), and rates of inflation (measured as the annual average

[2] Thus, a full analysis of economic performance, including dimensions such as international competitiveness, trends in productivity, and viability of economic structures, not to mention indicators of distributive and redistributive policies, is beyond the scope of this essay.

percentage changes in consumer price indices).[3] Indicators of economic performance show a marked break in the period immediately after the first oil price shock. For this reason, the analysis is conducted separately for two subperiods, 1960–1973 and 1974–1984.[4] In what follows, my major interest is in accounting for long-term associations between political factors and economic outcomes. It follows from this that the analysis presented here is not presumed to be an explanation of why economic growth, rates of inflation, and rates of unemployment have varied in individual countries by subperiods. Moreover, the analysis needs to be complemented by a comparative study of genuinely economic determinants of macroeconomic performances.

1960–1973

Among the group of countries in which high levels of economic performance were achieved in the period from 1960 to 1973, Germany, Japan, Austria, Switzerland, and the Netherlands deserve to be mentioned first, but it also needs to be stressed that levels of performance were high in Australia and, mainly because of extremely high economic growth rates and low levels of inflation, in Greece. Relative to the average of OECD economies in this period, the level of aggregate performance in the United Kingdom and Ireland was low, while the Scandinavian countries and the Southern European nations, except Greece, rank between these extremes (see Table 1).

Success or, conversely, relative failure in one area of intervention did not spill over into all the other aspects of macroeconomic performance, however. Indeed, there seems to be an empirically identifiable tendency for the existence of a trade-off by which success in one area or, at the extreme, in two areas necessarily limits successful control elsewhere. Some countries such as Japan were successful in maintaining very high rates of economic growth, but in doing so, they encountered difficulties in their effort to control inflationary pressure. In a second group of countries, comprising mainly the German-speaking nations and the

---

[3] Economic data was taken from OECD official statistics. Political data was mainly taken from Beyme (1984), Cameron (1984), ILO (1985), Keesing's Contemporary Archives, and Schmidt (1982).

[4] The analysis covers the OECD member countries except Yugoslavia, Turkey, Iceland, and Luxemburg. The latter two countries were dropped from the sample for reasons of small size. Turkey and Yugoslavia were excluded from the analysis, because their economic systems are dissimilar to the economies of other OECD nations.

Benelux countries, policymakers were successful in maintaining low levels of inflation and unemployment, while rates of economic growth were below those achieved in countries such as Japan, Greece, Portugal, and Spain. In several countries, successful policy was confined to one dimension of performance. Economic policymakers in the United States, for example, long accepted a less pro-inflationary trade-off between price stability and unemployment than the majority of the OECD member countries and acquiesced in higher unemployment. Unlike the "social Keynesianism" that emerged in the Scandinavian and in the majority of the continental European countries, the type of Keynesianism that was adopted in the United States was of a "commercial" nature (Weir and Skocpol 1983). This involved a policy stance that tended to be too deflationary in character relative to the nature of the electorate's political demand (Hibbs 1985).

The relative success and the relative failures of the 1960s all varied by economic policy area. Economic growth was highest in Japan and in a group of countries comprising Greece, Portugal, and Spain, in which authoritarian regimes were in power. By contrast, growth rates in older democracies were much lower. Empirical analysis conducted for the purpose of this essay revealed a strong inverse relationship between rates of economic growth on the one hand and age of democracy and size of government on the other in the period from 1960 up to 1973 ($R^2 = .69$).[5]

[5] The regression of age of democracy (measured by the number of years of uninterrupted democracy up to 1960) and the average size of government (measured by the average of the total outlays of general government as a percentage of GDP in the period from 1960 to 1973) on rates of economic growth (measured by average annual percentage change in real GDP in 1960–1973) yields:

$$\begin{aligned} Y' = 10.9 &- \underset{(.008)}{.033(X_1)} - \underset{(.029),}{.148(X_2)}, \quad R^2 = .6944 \end{aligned}$$

with Y = rates of economic growth,
X_1 = age of democracy,
X_2 = size of government.

Data was taken from Weede (1984: 413 and 423), complemented by Cook and Paxton (1975), Furtak (1981), and OECD (1981, 1985a and b).

The results of the data analysis reported here are compatible with the findings in Weede (1986) only with respect to the pre-1973 period. By contrast, the estimate of the regression equation for the data on 1974–1984 results in insignificant relationships. The regression equation for 1974–84 is

$$Y' = 3.08 - \underset{(.007)}{.007(X_1)} - \underset{(.02),}{.013(X_2)}, \quad R^2 = .0678$$

with X_1 measured by the number of years of uninterrupted democracy up to 1974. Thus, Weede's revised "rise-and-decline-of-nations" hypothesis does not adequately explain the period following the first oil price shock. For a more detailed discussion, see further below in this chapter and Schmidt (1987).

Moreover, GDP growth rates in the 1960s and early 1970s were inversely related to the power of labor[6] and the political complexion of governments.[7] Overall, growth rates tended to be lower in countries in which trade unions were powerful and in which governments were center-left or leftish.

Thus, the data on economic growth in 1960–73 are compatible with the view that powerful distributional coalitions and "creeping socialism" negatively affect the level of macroeconomic performance,[8] although exceptionally high levels of economic growth in countries such as Japan, Greece, Portugal, and Spain may be attributable more plausibly to differences in labor supply, economic backwardness, size of the agricultural sector, and technological catch-up processes (see, for example, Friedland and Sanders 1985, Kindleberger 1967, Merigo 1982).

While the "rise-and-decline-of-nations" hypothesis is supported by comparative data on economic growth in the 1960s and early 1970s, rates of economic growth do not necessarily covary with success or failure in other aspects of performance. While the achievement of high rates of economic growth significantly contributed to high total employment growth, real GDP growth has no one-to-one relationship with full employment and relative price stability. High-growth countries were plagued by higher levels of inflation (see, for example, Japan) or persistently higher levels of unemployment (Greece), while a second group of countries, comprising mainly of Germany, Austria, Switzerland,

---

[6] The average annual rate of growth of real GDP, 1960–1973 is inversely associated with Cameron's index of organizational power of labor (Cameron 1984: 165–167). Cameron's index comprises the sum of the product of an index of the collective bargaining power of the labor confederations multiplied by the percentage of the labor force that is unionized and an indicator of organizational unity of labor. The classification of Greece, Portugal, and Spain was based on Mielke (1983).

[7] The political composition of national governments was measured by a left-right rank-order scale based on regime type and shares of cabinet seats held by parties of different ideological complexion: 1 = authoritarian regimes (such as Greece from 1967 to 1974, Portugal, and Spain); 2 = democratic governments of the right (such as the United States, Japan, France, Canada); 3 = democratic government of the center-right such as Belgium, the Netherlands, and Italy), 4 = democratic government of the center-left (comprising countries in which Social Democratic-liberal coalitions and Grand Coalitions between Christian Democratic parties and Social Democratic parties have participated in government between 1960 and 1973, and countries with frequent changes in the political complexion of government from Labor to Conservatives or from Conservatives to Labor. Representative examples include Austria, Germany, Denmark, and the UK); 5 = democratic government of the left (dominant or hegemonic position held by Social Democratic party, as was the case in Sweden). The statistical association between rates of economic growth and political composition of government is strongly negative.

[8] See also Saunders (1985) and Weede (1986). See also note 5 in this chapter.

and the Benelux countries, achieved a more balanced pattern of economic development. In these countries, rates of inflation and rates of unemployment remained low, whereas economic growth was just at the average level of the OECD economies (see Table 1 and Figure 1). The experience of the latter group of countries does not readily lend itself to the generalizations derivable from the "rise-and-decline-of-nations" hypothesis, the major merit of which is an explanation of why growth rates have differed. However, an explanation of differences in the growth-

Table 1 Economic Growth, Inflation, and Unemployment (1960–1973)

	Economic growth[1)]	Rate of inflation[2)]	Rate of unemployment[3)]
Austria	4.9	4.1	1.7
Australia	5.2	3.6	1.8
Belgium	4.9	3.6	2.3
Canada	5.6	3.3	4.8
Denmark	4.4	6.3	1.3
Finnland	4.8	5.9	2.3
France	5.7	4.6	2.2
Germany	4.5	3.5	0.8
Greece	7.6	3.3	4.6
Ireland	4.6	11.5	5.2
Italy	5.4	4.5	5.5
Japan	9.6	6.2	1.2
Netherlands	5.1	4.8	1.2
New Zealand	4.1	4.9	0.3
Norway	4.2	5.0	1.7
Portugal	7.0	5.3	2.4
Spain	7.2	6.7	2.8
Sweden	4.1	4.5	2.0
Switzerland	4.3	4.2	0.1
United Kingdom	3.1	5.2	3.1
United States	4.0	3.2	4.4
Arithmetic Mean	5.2	5.0	2.5

1) Average rate of growth (annual percentage changes) of real GDP 1960–73.
2) Consumer price indices, average annual percentage changes, 1960–73.
3) Average rate of unemployment (as a percentage of total labor force) 1960–73. Standardized rates of unemployment, except Denmark, Greece, Ireland, New Zealand, Portugal, and Switzerland.

Sources: OECD (1982), OECD (1985a), OECD (1985b).

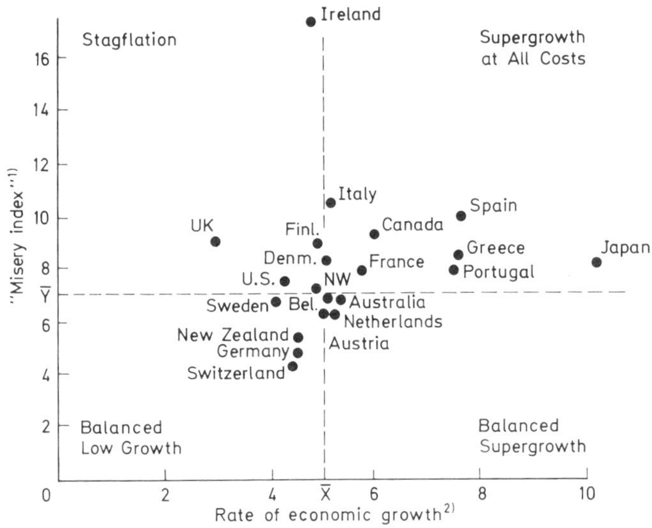

[1] Sum of rate of inflation and rate of unemployment. For a breakdown of the index see data in Table 1.

[2] Average annual changes in percentages, real GDP.

Figure 1 Economic Growth, Inflation, and Unemployment (1960–73)

Sources: OECD (1982), OECD (1985a), OECD (1985b).

inflation-unemployment mix seems to be beyond the scope of the "rise-and-decline-of-nations" hypothesis.

A pattern of balanced economic development, which has been characteristic of countries such as Germany, Austria, Switzerland, and Japan, to mention just a few examples, more readily lends itself to an explanation that follows discussions on politico-institutional aspects of managing modern capitalism. For example, Shonfield's study from the 1960s marks one of the roads that led to economic success in the 1960s and early 1970s. Coherent guidance of the economy, in conjunction with low levels of industrial dispute between labor and capital, may be regarded as a sufficient, though not necessary, condition of high levels of performance.

Within the group of countries characterized by coherent economic policy and industrial consensus, one can discern a variety of political formulae.

- A technocratic-paternalistic approach was adopted in Japan and France. In both countries political control of the economy depended upon the "partnerships between state technocrats and industrial constituencies" (Maier and Lindberg 1985: 586), while labor found itself excluded at the national level but included at the enterprise level (Pempel and Tsunekawa 1979, Yamamura 1985, and Zysman 1985).

- By contrast, a conservative-reformist mode of regulating the economy, in conjunction with cooptation of labor, and a system of social partnership primarily favoring national labor, have prevailed in Switzerland.
- While economic policy in France, Japan, and Switzerland has been shaped by the political weakness of labor and the political dominance of nonsocialist tendencies, the pattern of balanced economic development that was characteristic of West Germany and the Netherlands prior to 1973 was based upon a policy process in which trade unions, Social Democratic parties, and, in particular, Christian Democratic parties have played a major role.

The growth-inflation-unemployment mix differed considerably in the period from 1960 to 1973. Moreover, a wide range of variation marked the political conditions that were conducive to maintaining high levels of performance. However, widely shared political explanations of economic outcomes, such as the "rise-and-decline" hypothesis and the "power-of-labor" hypothesis, have not been consistently supported by analysis of the relevant data. By contrast, the extent to which economic growth was compatible with full employment and price stability had a fairly strong association with the extent to which the policy process was marked by coherent economic planning and economic consensus between capital or labor. In this sense, the thrust of Shonfield's message in Modern Capitalism has continued to be compatible with the macroeconomic performance in the Western democracies in the period from 1960 to 1973 (although the relatively high levels of performance that were achieved in Australia and Greece do not lend themselves to the generalizations that can be derived from Shonfield's study). Two success stories of the 1960s, Switzerland and Japan, were not extensively covered in Shonfield's studies. However, economic policy in Japan and Switzerland have broadly been in line with the prescriptions derivable from Shonfield's study (see, for example, Lehner 1987). In these countries, collaboration between interest groups (in conjunction with the inclusion of national labor in Switzerland and the exclusion of labor in Japan) and the appropriate habits of mind have been defining characteristics of the policy-making process.

1974–1984

For a variety of reasons, the analysis of which is beyond the scope of this essay, governments in Western nations were confronted with an unprecedented challenge in the 1970s and early 1980s (see, for example, Boltho 1982, Maddison 1982). The setback to economic growth, rapidly accumulating inflationary pressure, balance of payments difficulties, cost-push factors, and deflationary tendencies produced serious problems for the management of mixed economies after the first oil price shock in 1973. The task of pursuing policy without causing pain became much more difficult than in the post-war period up to the mid-1970s.

In almost all respects, the level of macroeconomic performance registered by OECD economies in the 1970s and early 1980s was far lower than that which had been the norm for over two decades. All nations were plagued by the economic malaise of the 1970s and early 1980s, but some countries suffered far less than others. For example, most of the success stories of the pre-1973 period, in particular Japan, Austria, Switzerland and, albeit with weaker labor-market performance, West-Germany, managed to maintain levels of performance that were above average in the OECD area as a whole. In addition, Norway ranked highest in performance, mainly because she maintained levels of employment and high levels of economic growth, the latter being at least partly due to revenues from North Sea oil.[9] At the bottom of the performance ranking in the post-1973 period came nations that have had lower levels of performance in the 1960s – the United Kingdom, Belgium, Italy, Spain, and Portugal.

Just as levels of performance in OECD economies varied considerably from one policy area to the next in the 1960s, so, too, did levels of aggregate performance in the period following the world-wide recession of the mid-1970s.[10] After 1973, the highest rates of economic growth

---

[9] With respect to the changes in levels of performance from the period 1960–73 to the period 1974–1984, two other countries ranked at the top: Sweden and Ireland. In Ireland's case, however, levels of performance in the pre-1973 period were relatively low, so the overall level of performance in the period following the first oil price shock remained relatively low. Analysis of changes in levels of performance from one period to another may result in new insights in the politics of economic policy (see, for example, Lange and Garrett 1985). Broadly speaking, the results of the present study are also valid in the context of a research design focused on changes across periods, except for changes in the economic growth rates. The decline in growth rates is inversely related to the power of labor. On this, see Lange and Garrett (1985).

[10] The correlation between rates of economic growth and rates of inflation is low and insignificant ($r = .15$) and so, too, is the correlation between economic growth and rates of unemployment ($r = -.04$). By contrast, average rates of inflation are weakly associated with average rates of unemployment ($r = .34$).

were achieved in Japan, Norway, and Ireland, while average annual rates of real GDP growth were very low in Switzerland largely because of the extremely restrictive stabilization policy of the mid-1970s. With the exception of 1974/75, the Japanese authorities were also successful in mitigating inflationary pressure, while inflation rates in the two other high-growth countries were moderately high (Norway) or very high (Ireland). In the majority of countries in which inflationary tendencies were successfully controlled in the 1960s, however, in particular in

Table 2 Economic Growth, Inflation, and Unemployment, 1974–1984

	Economic growth[1)]	Rate of inflation[2)]	Rate of un-employment[3)]
Austria	2.4	5.9	2.4
Australia	2.7	10.7	6.2
Belgium	1.7	8.0	8.9
Canada	2.7	8.9	8.4
Denmark	1.7	10.2	7.8
Finland	2.8	11.4	4.9
France	2.2	10.9	6.2
Germany	1.7	4.6	4.5
Greece	2.5	18.8	3.6
Ireland	3.5	15.0	8.8
Italy	2.0	16.2	7.6
Japan	3.9	7.4	2.1
Netherlands	1.6	6.2	7.6
New Zealand	1.7	13.2	2.2
Norway	3.9	9.3	2.1
Portugal	2.3	23.1	7.2
Spain	2.1	16.2	10.0
Sweden	1.7	10.0	2.3
Switzerland	0.5	4.2	0.4
United Kingdom	1.1	12.9	8.0
United States	2.4	8.1	7.4
Arithmetic mean	2.2	10.5	5.6

[1)] Average annual growth rate (annual percentage changes) of real GDP, 1974–84.

[2)] Consumer Price Indices, average annual percentage changes, 1974–84.

[3)] Average rate of unemployment (as a percentage of total labor force), 1974–84, standardized rates of unemployment, with the exception of Denmark, Greece, Ireland, New Zealand, Portugal, and Switzerland.

Sources: OECD (1985a), OECD (1985b).

Switzerland, Germany, and Austria, levels of price instability remained low throughout the post-1973 period. Unlike the period of post-war prosperity, the 1970s and 1980s were a time when most OECD nations were plagued by high levels of unemployment and large increases in the rate of unemployment, in particular in the Benelux countries, the United Kingdom, Portugal, and Spain, whereas a second group of countries (Austria, Japan, Norway, Sweden, and Switzerland) managed to maintain full employment or, at least, low levels of open unemployment (see Table 2).

Of course, high economic growth rates such as those in Japan and Norway facilitated the maintenance of full employment, while governments faced with low rates of economic growth found it far more difficult to control unemployment. However, the precise nature of the relationship between economic growth and outcomes in other areas of economic management such as inflation rates and levels of unemployment have varied considerably from country to country.

One of the most intriguing findings of the data analysis conducted for the purpose of this essay is that there were nations in which low or moderately low rates of economic growth were reconciled with low or moderate rates of inflation and low or moderately low rates of unemployment. Plots of the rate of economic growth against the "misery index," which comprises average rates of inflation (or changes in the rate of inflation above the level of the "core inflation rate" of the 1960s) and average rates of unemployment (or changes in the average rate of unemployment relative to the "core rate of unemployment" in the 1960s), indicate the extent to which the OECD nations have been successful in generating balanced economic development.

Three findings that emerge from Figures 2 and 3 deserve attention.

- The lower left-hand cell and the lower right-hand cell in Figures 2 and 3 represent nations that, on the whole, have been more successful than others in coping with the twin problems of inflation and unemployment at given levels of economic growth. These are Japan, Norway, Austria, Switzerland, West Germany, and Sweden.
- The Japanese case and the Norwegian case can be explained straightforwardly. High rates of economic growth are conducive to the maintenance of high employment levels, and, depending on the capacity to control inflationary expectations, they also facilitate the maintenance of low or moderately high inflation rates. Consequently, high rates of economic growth tend to vary with low scores on the "misery index." By contrast, low rates of economic growth tend to be associated with high levels of unemployment or high levels of inflation, or, at the extreme, with a stagflationary situation. Consequently, low rates of economic growth rates tend to be associated with high scores

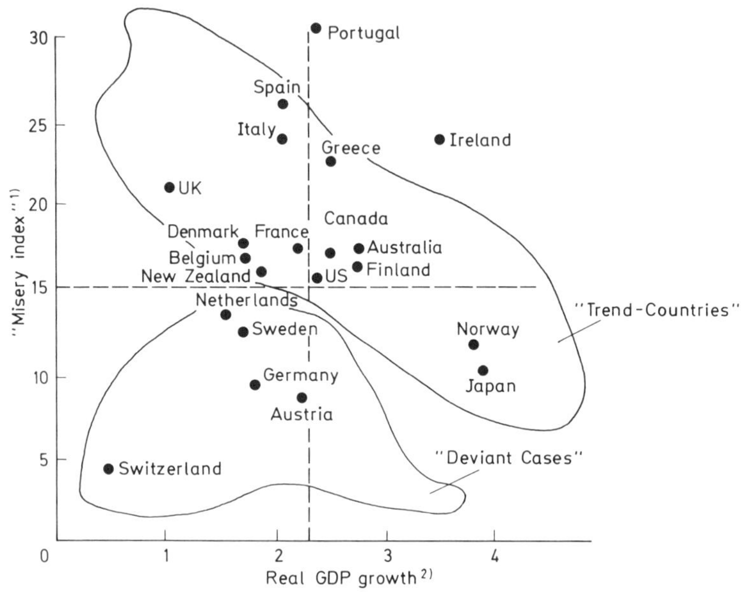

[1] Average rate of unemployment plus average rate of inflation, 1974–84.
[2] Average annual growth rates.

Figure 2 Economic Growth, Inflation, and Unemployment (1974–84)

Sources: see Table 2.

on the "misery index." Statistically speaking, the trend in the data on GDP growth and the "misery index" explains much of the high economic performance in Japan and Norway.

- The most intriguing finding in the data arrayed in Figures 2 and 3 concerns the countries that fall below the trend curve. In this group of nations, in particular in Austria, Switzerland, West Germany, and Sweden, the scores on the "misery index" are "too low," relative to the trend in the OECD nations as a whole. In other words, these nations have managed to sustain "too much full employment" (Sweden and Austria) or "too low rates of inflation" (Germany, for example) or a combination of both, despite the impact that adverse economic circumstances have had on the economy.

Why did these economies perform better than other OECD economies in terms of the general trend that exists between economic growth and the "misery index"? And why is it that Japan and Norway have been capable of reconciling growth with full employment and moderately high levels of

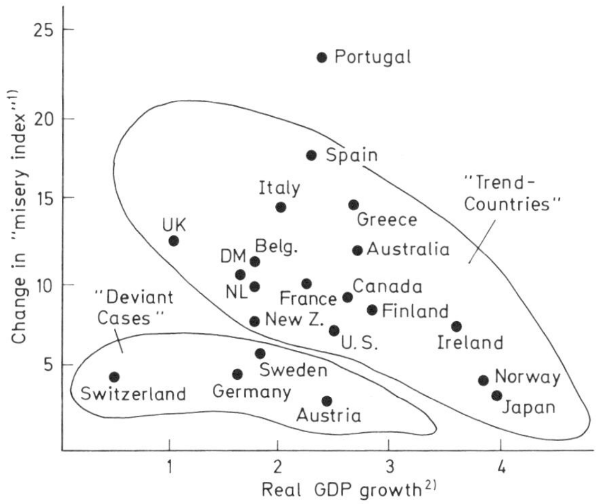

1) Sum of average rate of unemployment and average rate of inflation in 1974–84 minus sum of average rate of unemployment and average rate of inflation in 1960–73.

2) Average annual growth rates, 1974–84.

Figure 3 Economic Growth and Changes in Inflation and in Unemployment

Sources: see Table 2.

inflation? And how is the low level of performance in other OECD economies to be accounted for? In seeking to answer these questions, I will focus attention on the political hypotheses that were introduced in the first section of this essay. Unlike economic performance in the period from 1960–73, that from 1974–84 is not explained by the "rise-and-decline of nations" hypothesis. There is no clear-cut relationship between the indicators of economic performance in 1974–84 that were used in this essay and the age of a country's democracy. Nor is there much evidence supporting the view that leftish or rightish governments have produced levels of performance higher or lower than their respective counterparts. Furthermore, there is nothing in the data that is compatible with the hypothesis that the power of labor consistently varies with economic outcomes (although the interaction of powerful labor and leftish government may be regarded as a sufficient, though not necessary, condition for maintaining full employment).[11]

---

[11] The correlation between these variables and indicators of economic outcome are all low and insignificant.

By contrast, the explanatory variables that Shonfield's study on modern capitalism and the literature on comparative corporatism suggest to be of importance match remarkably well with indicators of performance, especially levels of unemployment and rates of inflation (and changes thereof). Our empirical results tend to converge with the results that are to be derived from several comparative studies on the political economy of Western democracies (see, for example, Blaas and Guger 1985, Cameron 1985, Crouch 1985, Lindberg 1985, McCallum 1985, Paloheimo 1984, Schmidt 1982, Tarantelli 1983). In overall terms, high levels of macroeconomic performance were achieved in countries such as Japan, Switzerland, Germany, Austria and Norway, which experienced a high degree of concerted policy formation and high levels of stable consensus between capital and labor. Low levels of macroeconomic performance and, in particular, high levels of unemployment and high levels of inflation were characteristic of countries in which the formation of coherent economic policy was impeded by highly fragmented policy processes and high levels of unstructured class conflicts. Representative examples include the United Kingdom and the United States.[12)] In a third group of countries – Sweden, Finland, Denmark, Belgium, the Netherlands, France, and Ireland – the degree of policy concertation is high or moderately high, but unlike the first group of countries mentioned, this group also had high or moderately high levels of class conflicts after the first oil price shock.[13)] Depending on the precise nature of power distributions that prevailed, the authorities in these countries opted for full employment at all costs (as in Sweden) or for a policy stance that placed major emphasis on the control of inflationary pressure (as in Germany) (see Figures 4 and 5).

In overall terms, then, differences in macroeconomic performance after the first oil price shock in 1973 are compatible with a hypothesis that focuses attention on the association between concertation and consensus on the one hand and macroeconomic performance on the other.

---

12) The measure of concerted policy formation was mainly based on Lehmbruch's (1984) scale of corporatist concertation (medium corporatism and strong corporatism) and on the concept of "concertation without labor" (France and Japan). Economic consensus or, conversely, unstructured class conflicts, were empirically measured by average annual strike volumes from 1974 to 1984. Strike volumes below the threshold of 100 strike days lost per 1000 workers were classified as "economic consensus" (Japan, West Germany, Austria, Norway, and Switzerland). Data was taken from the *ILO Yearbook of Labour Statistics (1984)*.

13) It must be emphasized that our approach centers attention on highly aggregated data. Studies on disaggregated levels of analysis reveal considerable variation in the degree of policy concertation. For the United States, see Hollingsworth and Lindberg (1985).

The Politics of Concerted Policy Formation

I have contented myself with pointing out the existence of a statistical association between economic outcomes and political variables. The approach that has been chosen in this essay shares a weakness with most studies on political and social correlates of economic outcomes, namely, that structures and instruments which intervene in the complex relationship between political factors and outcomes tend to be regarded as representing a black box (for exceptions to this rule, however, see several comparative studies on unemployment rates, such as Scharpf 1984, Schmidt 1987). While a full analysis of causal links between political factors and economic outcomes is beyond the scope of this essay, it can be argued that a detailed investigation would benefit from consideration of certain mechanisms that intervene in the relationship between economic consensus and policy concertation on the one hand and high levels of macroeconomic performance on the other.

The first such mechanism is the fact that economic consensus between capital and labor involves a type of structured, stable, and predictable class conflict associated with low levels of industrial dispute. Thus, the political, social, and economic costs, that open class conflicts involve, are low in consensus cum concertation countries. Moreover, and more important from the point of view of macroeconomic policy, institutionalized class conflicts involve greater stability and predictability of behavior on the part of the major producer groups, and this, in turn, improves conditions that are required for effective macroeconomic policy.

The second intervening mechanism is the fact that economic consensus in conjunction with a highly concerted process of policy formation involves increased systemic responsibility on the part of the trade unions and increased social responsibility on the part of government. Under these circumstances, the probability of successful and stable political exchange between collective actors will be enhanced. The political exchange between systemic responsibility, social peace, and even trade union acceptance of prolonged wage restraint, and compensation in terms of guaranteed claims to consultation, influence, and material benefits such as social wages or full employment reduces uncertainty about potential gains of a cooperative strategy on the part of labor. Uncertainty will be reduced further by governments that are stable and credible in their commitment to combat stagflationary tendencies.

Given Mancur Olson's theory on the impact that special interest organizations have exerted on policy outputs and policy outcomes, it needs to be stressed that highly encompassing interest organizations have

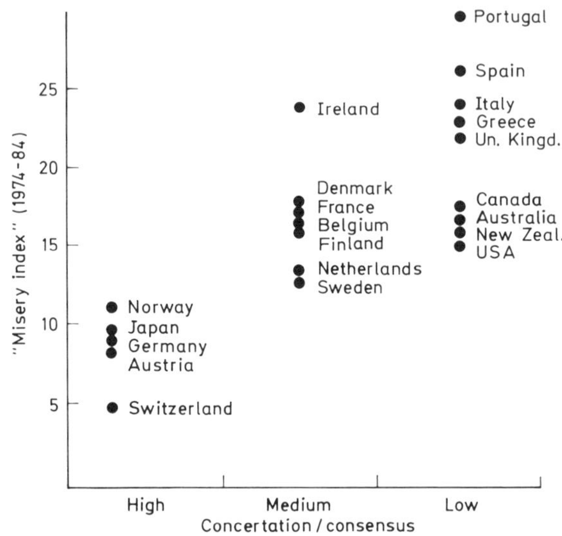

Figure 4 Concertation, Consensus, and the "Misery Index", (1974–84)
Sources: see Tables 1 and 2, Figures 1, 2, and 3.

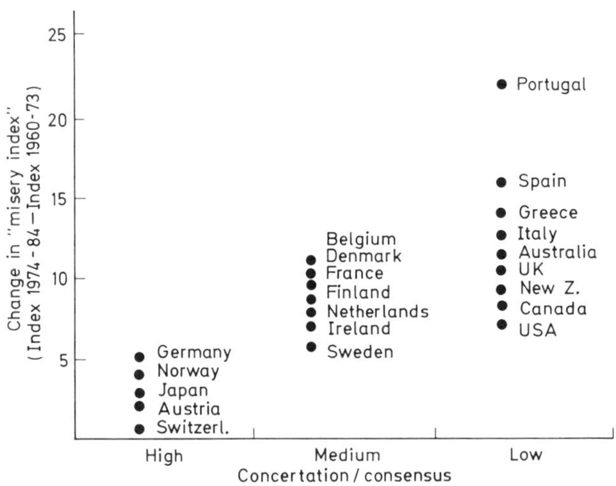

Figure 5 Concertation, Consensus, and Change in the "Misery Index"
Sources: see Tables 1 and 2; Figures 1, 2, and 3.

very different incentives than do narrow special-interest organizations. Olson (1982) has argued that

> sufficiently encompassing or inclusive special-interest organizations will internalize much of the cost of inefficient policies and accordingly have an incentive to redistribute income to themselves with the least possible social cost, and to give some weight to economic growth and to the interests of society as a whole (90).

It can be argued that policy-formation processes that are marked by a high degree of concertation between powerful producer groups and the state and high levels of economic consensus between labor and capital will also internalize much of the cost of reduced levels of macroeconomic performance and will thus give considerable weight to the interests of society as a whole, particularly to the maintenance of a balanced mix of growth, relative price stability, and lower levels of unemployment. The very conditions that have nurtured incentives serving the interests of society as a whole have facilitated the design and implementation of well-coordinated policies across different policy areas.

Moreover, economic consensus between capital and labor and a high degree of concerted policy formation across policy areas may be regarded as factors that maintain low levels of inflationary expectations. Furthermore, they tend to improve the degree of coordination between fiscal policy, wage policy, and monetary policy (Tarantelli 1984a and b). Thus, concertation and economic consensus tend to create a "virtuous circle" of government economic policy; a result that promotes, and is promoted by, cooperative strategies between social classes. Where this virtuous circle is fully established, it results ideally in more efficient and more effective macroeconomic policy.

By contrast, the economic policy process in countries characterized by unstructured class confrontation and high levels of institutional fragmentation tends to result in a vicious circle of economic policy, one that both promotes, and is promoted by, short-term, particularistic, and volatile policy stances on the part of the government and the collective organizations of labor and capital. In periods of escalating inflationary expectation, policymakers in these countries tend to be confronted with a troublesome dilemma. To bring inflation down when labor has a strong, or moderately strong, bargaining position means having to lower the expected rate of inflation. But this can be done only by lowering the inflation rate itself. Given the absence of policy concertation and consensus policymakers have found that the way to break out of this circle is to create a recession of sufficient length and severity.

There is no reason to suppose that concerted and consensual practices in the management of mixed economies result in the best of all macroeconomic worlds. Moreover, concertation and consensus should not be conceived of as institutional insurances against policy failure. In fact, numerous policy failures were reported by countries that can justifiably pride themselves on their being equipped with high levels of concertation (on Germany, see Kloten et al. 1985 and Scharpf 1984, for instance; on Sweden, Martin (1985);[14)] and on the Netherlands, Braun and Keman 1986). In the long run, however, policy failures seem to have been less numerous and less extreme in this group of countries than in countries in which policy formation was fragmented and class conflicts were unstructured. At least in some important areas of economic policy, concertation and consensus have facilitated efforts geared to maintaining high levels of performance.

The precise nature of the successes in the 1970s varied from country to country, depending upon a wide range of conditions such as the availability of policy instruments, the willingness to use or create instruments, economic feasibility, political ideology, and political imperatives and constraints. In terms of policy instruments, the successful management of the Japanese economy in the 1970s and early 1980s mainly reflects a determined policy stance in demand management, a wide variety of public and private labor market policy measures, supply-side-oriented interventions, and efforts that were geared to actively restructuring the Japanese economy (see, for example, Boltho 1985 and OECD 1984). In political terms, the active policy stance adopted by the government is partly attributable to the tradition of technocratic-paternalistic policy-making. In addition, political pressure on the Liberal Democratic Party has been important, in particular the decline in the share of votes going to the Liberal Democratic Party in the 1970s and early 1980s (Yamamura 1985). Demand management, subsidies given to industry, and capitalist growth strategies have also been influential in Austria and Norway. By contrast, Switzerland's major success was the control of inflationary pressure through extremely restrictive monetary policy in the mid-1970s and the maintenance of full employment for nationals. As a result of markedly restrictive monetary policy and of wage restraint by the trade unions, West German policymakers were successful in maintaining relative price stability. Moreover, the rate of unemployment in Germany remained at a level below the OECD average in the 1970s (but they increased dramatically in the early 1980s). However, while the West German policy mix proved to be reasonably successful in terms of standard performance indicators such as GDP growth, rates of growth in productivity, balance of current accounts, and levels of international

---

14) See for the Scandinavian countries in general Andersson (1985), Esping-Andersen (1985) and Mjøset (1985), and, in particular for Sweden, Bengtsson, Eriksson, and Sederblad (1984) and Martin (1985).

competitiveness (Gahlen et al. 1985), the employment content of economic development in West Germany was weaker than that of policy mixes, which comprised the less restrictive stances on monetary policy adopted in such countries as Sweden, Norway, and Japan.

Thus, the case of West Germany in the 1970s and early 1980s points to an important qualification of the view that concertation and consensus improve a country's economic performance. The potential inherent in high levels of concertation and consensus seems to have been fully used in two groups of countries: first, those like Austria and Norway, in which labor commanded a dominant or hegemonic position; and second, those like Japan and Switzerland, in which nonsocialist, conservative-reformist tendencies have been in power. Partly because the distribution of political power has been less clear-cut in the Federal Republic, West German policymakers do not seem to have fully used the potential inherent in the country's institutional apparatus.

In particular, experience with the labor market and employment policy has remained unsatisfactory. Trade unions and the Social Democratic Party have been strong enough to successfully demand a higher social wage. Moreover, trade unions and the Social Democratic Party are too strong to allow employment to grow along Japanese and North American lines, for to do so would entail a far higher level of wage flexibility and mobility than is politically and culturally acceptable in West Germany. However, trade unions and the Social Democratic Party have not been strong enough to establish a real "balance of class forces" in the economy and in the policy process along Austrian or Norwegian or Swedish lines. In political terms, the coexistence of relative price stability, high levels of competitiveness, and weak labor market performance in Germany is thus largely attributable to a balance of political power that comprises both the achievements and the relative weakness of the labor movement.

As pointed out earlier, the highest levels of macroeconomic performance after 1973 and, in particular, the most balanced pattern of economic development have been achieved in the context of a labor-dominated policy process such as that in Austria and Norway and in a policy process dominated by conservative-reformist forces such as those in Japan and Switzerland. In other words, there have been two major roads to economic success in the 1970s and in the 1980s.

On the labor-dominated road to economic success, the content of policy is mainly of a public and active-interventionist nature. In these countries, the responsibility for providing social and economic welfare falls largely to the state. In contrast to this, the conservative-reformist road to macroeconomic success rests upon a private-public policy mix. In terms of the size of government and in terms of subsidies granted to crisis industries, conservative-reformist governments are much more restrictive than their labor-dominated counterparts, but in both groups of countries the extent and intensity of state intervention is large when it comes to righting the imbalance created by economic change and economic recessions. The Keynesian function and the social policy function of the state is more muted in the conservative-reformist countries. However, in sectors of strategic importances, such as monetary policy, regional and agricultural policy, industrial policy, and, particularly in Switzerland, control of the foreign-labor supply, the role of the state is by every conceivable standard interventionist par excellence. It is certainly not the market alone that has been the single driving force behind the success stories of Japan and Switzerland. The roots of success are to be found in the interaction of the "invisible hand" in the market economy and the "visible hand" of the state.

Conclusion

The relative autonomy of the private sector vis-à-vis the political system remains considerable in all Western nations. Thus, the policymaker's room to maneuver is rather limited. Efforts geared to controlling the economy politically are confronted with fundamental difficulties. In overall terms, there has been no country in the OECD area in which policymakers managed to maintain stable economic growth, relative price stability, and full employment over a prolonged period. Governments must necessarily order their priorities in the field of economic policy. At best, a partial control over the economy was achieved in the Western nations between 1960 and 1984.

However, the degree of partial political control over the economy has varied considerably from nation to nation. For example, countries such as Japan, Switzerland, Austria, West Germany (especially in the 1960s), and Norway (especially in the 1970s and early 1980s) have been among the relative "success stories" of the industrial nations. Analysis of economic and political data reveals that the level of macroeconomic performance is associated with, and – by inference – is influenced by, political structures and processes. Thus, studies that have focused on the links between politics, policy, and economic outcomes receive support from this essay.

Nevertheless, the relationships between political variables and economic outcomes do not seem to be of the kind suggested by the "rise-and-decline-of-nations" paradigm and the "power of labor" paradigm. While there is evidence to support these views with respect to economic growth in the 1960s (which is inversely related to the age of democracy and to power of labor), there is nothing in these approaches to account for the difference in levels of overall performance and, in particular, the growth-inflation-unemployment mix. By contrast, the success stories in the OECD area before and after 1973 largely consisted of countries characterized by coherent policy, concerted policy-formation processes and economic consensus between capital and labor. In a sense, Andrew Shonfield's seminal study on modern capitalism thus continues to be one of the most valuable contributions to the comparative study of macroeconomic performance.

It is yet in another respect that this chapter has departed from the majority of studies on the political economy of Western democracies. The central assumption in most of the studies in this field of research is that linear, unifunctional relationships exist between macroeconomic outcomes and political variables such as the political complexion of governments, the power of organized labor, corporatism, and the age of a country's democracy. As has been pointed out in this chapter, however, there are many roads that lead to Rome. In particular, relatively successful management of mixed economies has been the result of two very different approaches. A labor-dominated approach to macroeconomic management has generated outcomes that are similar to the outcomes of pronounced nonsocialist, conservative-reformist regimes in economic policy.[15]

Thus, one of the messages that are to be derived from this chapter points to a theme that has not yet been sufficiently explored in the literature of comparative political economy: there have been many roads that lead to Rome and, in political terms, there have been several roads that lead to big government and reduced state budgets, high levels of social welfare and low levels of social welfare, high levels of redistribution or, conversely, low levels of redistribution. Moreover, there have also been two different roads to relative macroeconomic success in the period of economic stagnation in the 1970s and early 1980s – a labor-dominated road to economic success, such as in Austria and Norway, and a bourgeois, conservative-reformist road to success, such as in Japan and Switzerland.[16]

---

15) See also the results reported in Friedland and Sanders (1985) and Schmidt (1983).

16) See, for example, the results of recent comparative studies on environmental policy (Jänicke, Mönch, and Ranneberg 1986, Vogel 1987), social policy (Castles 1985), labor market policy (Schmidt 1984, 1985, 1987), tax policy (Przeworski and Wallerstein 1985), economic policy (Lehner 1987), and economic regulation (Schubert 1987).

References

Altvater, E.; Hübner, K.; and Stanger, M. (1983): *Alternative Wirtschaftspolitik jenseits des Keynesianismus*, Opladen.

Andersson, J. O. (1985): The Nordic countries challenged. Summary of the work of a research group on the economic policies in the Nordic countries in the 1970s and 1980s, Joint Sessions of the ECPR, Barcelona, March 1985.

Bengtsson, L.; Eriksson, A.-C.; and Sederblad, P. (1984): The associative action of Swedish business interests – The Swedish employer's confederation and centralized collective bargaining in 1980, 1981, and 1983, Discussion Paper IIM/LMP 84–24, Wissenschaftszentrum Berlin.

Bernholz, P. (1982): Expanding welfare state, democracy and free market economy: Are they compatible? *Zeitschrift für die gesamte Staatswissenschaft*, 138: 583–98.

Beyme, K. von (1984): *Parteien in den westlichen Demokratien*, Munich and Zürich.

Blaas, W. and Guger, A. (1985): Arbeitsbeziehungen und makroökonomische Stabilität im internationalen Vergleich. In: *Sozialpartnerschaft in der Krise: Leistungen und Grenzen des Neokorporatismus in Österreich*, pp. 255–78, (Eds.): P. Gerlich, E. Grande, and W. C. Müller, Vienna, Cologne, Graz.

Boltho, A. (Ed.) (1982): *The European economy: Growth & crisis*, Oxford.

Boltho, A. (1985). Was Japan's industrial policy successful? *Cambridge Journal of Economics*, 9: 187–01.

Braun, D. and Keman, H. (1986): Politikstrategien und Konfliktregulierung in den Niederlanden, *Politische Vierteljahresschrift*, 27: 78–99.

Cameron, D. R. (1984): Social democracy, corporatism, labour quiescence and the representation of economic interest in advanced capitalist society, In: *Order and conflict in contemporary capitalism*, pp. 143–78. (Ed.) J. H. Goldthorpe, Oxford, England.

Cameron, D. R. (1985): Does government cause inflation? Taxes, spending, and deficits, In: *The politics of inflation and economic stagnation*, pp. 224–79, (Eds.): L. N. Lindberg and C. S. Maier, Washington, D. C.

Castles, F. G. (1985): *The working class and welfare: Reflections on the political development of the welfare state in Australia and New Zealand, 1890–1980*, Wellington, Sydney, London, and Boston.

Cohen, Y. (1985): The impact of bureaucratic-authoritarian rule on economic growth, *Comparative Political Studies*, 18: 123–136.

Cook, C. and Paxton, J. (1975): *European political facts 1918–73*, London and Basingstoke.

Cox, A. (Ed.) (1982): *Politics, policy and the European recession*, London and Basingstoke.

Crouch, C. (1985): Conditions for trade union wage restraint, In: *The politics of inflation and economic stagnation*, pp. 105–139, (Eds.): L. N. Lindberg and C. S. Maier, Washington, D. C.

Czada, R. (1983): Konsensbedingungen und Auswirkungen neokorporatistischer Politikentwicklung, *Journal für Sozialforschung*, 23: 421–40.

Czada, R. (1984): Zwischen Arbeitsplatzinteresse und Modernisierungszwang: Industriepolitische Performanz und gewerkschaftliche Orientierung im inter-

nationalen Vergleich, In: *Wirtschafts- und Sozialpartnerschaft in Österreich*, pp. 135–83, (Ed.) H. Wimmer, Vienna: VGWO.
Denison, E. F. (1967): *Why growth rates differ*, Washington, D.C.
Esping-Andersen, G. (1985): *Politics against markets: The social democratic road to power*, Princeton, N.Y.
Friedland, R. and Sanders, J. (1985): The public economy and economic growth in Western market economies, *American Sociological Review*, 50: 421–37.
Furtak, R.K. (Ed.) (1981): *Politisches Lexikon Europa*, 2 vols., Munich.
Gahlen, B.; Rahmeyer, F.; and Stadler, M. (1985): Zur internationalen Wettbewerbsfähigkeit der Deutschen Wirtschaft, Discussion Paper IIM/IP 85–19, Wissenschaftszentrum Berlin.
Hibbs, D.A., Jr. (1977): Political parties and macroeconomic policy, *American Political Science Review*, 71: 1467–87.
Hibbs, D.A., Jr. (1985): Inflation, political support, and macroeconomic policy, In: *The politics of inflation and economic stagnation*, pp. 175–195, (Eds.): L.N. Lindberg and C.S. Maier, Washington, D.C.
Hollingsworth, J. and Lindberg, N. (1985): The governance of the American economy: The role of markets, clans, hierarchies, and associative behavior, Discussion Paper IIM/LMP 85–8, Wissenschaftszentrum Berlin.
International Labour Office (ILO) (1985): *Yearbook of labour statistics 1984*, Geneva: ILO.
Jänicke, M.; Mönch, H.; and Ranneberg, T. (1986): Umweltschutz durch Strukturwandel: Eine Vorstudie über 31 Industrieländer, Discussion Paper IIUG dp 86–1, Wissenschaftszentrum Berlin.
Katzenstein, P.J. (1984): *Corporatism and change: Austria, Switzerland, and the politics of industry*, Ithaca and London.
Katzenstein, P.J. (1985): *Small states in world markets: Industrial policy in Europe*, Ithaca and London.
Keman, H. (1984): Politics, policies and consequences: A cross-national analysis of policy-formation in advanced capitalist democracies (1967–1981), *European Journal of Political Research*, 12: 147–70.
Kindleberger, C. (1967): *Europe's postwar growth: The role of labor supply*, Cambridge, Mass.
Kloten, N.; Ketterer, K. H.; Vollmer, R. (1985): West Germany's stabilization performance, In: *The politics of inflation and economic stagnation*, pp. 353–402, (Eds.): L.N. Lindberg and C.S. Maier, Washington, D.C.
Lange, P. and Garrett, G. (1985): The politics of growth: Strategic interaction and economic performance in the advanced industrial democracies, 1974–1980, *The Journal of Politics*, 47: 792–827.
Lehner, F. (1987): The political economy of distributive conflict, In: *Managing mixed economies*, (Eds.) G. Castles, F. Lehner, and M.G. Schmidt, Berlin and New York, 54–96.
Lindbeck, A. (1983): The recent slowdown of productivity growth, *The Economic Journal*, 93: 13–34.
Lindberg, L.N. (1985): Models of the inflation-disinflation process, In: *The politics of inflation and economic stagnation*, pp. 25–50, (Eds.): L.N. Lindberg and C.S. Maier, Washington, D.C.: The Brookings Institution.

Lehmbruch, G. (1984): Concertation and the structure of corporatist networks, In: *Order and conflict in contemporary capitalism*, (Ed.): John H. Goldthorpe Oxford University Press, pp. 60–80.
Maddison, A. (1964): *Economic growth in the West*, London.
Maddison, A. (1982): *Phases of capitalist development*, Oxford.
Maier, C.S. and Lindberg, L.N. (1985): Alternatives for future crises, In: *The politics of inflation and economic stagnation*, pp. 567–88, (Eds.): L.N. Lindberg and C.S. Maier, Washington, D.C.
Martin, A. (1973): The politics of economic policy in the United States: A tentative view from a comparative perspective, *Sage Professional Papers in Comparative Politics*, 1: 01–040.
Martin, A. (1985): Wages, profits, and investment in Sweden, In: *The politics of inflation and economic stagnation*, pp. 403–66, (Eds.): L.N. Lindberg and C.S. Maier, Washington, D.C.
McCallum, J. (1985): Inflation and social consensus, *The Economic Journal*, 93: 784–805.
Merigó, E. (1982): Spain, In: *The European economy*, pp. 554–80, (Ed.) A. Boltho, Oxford.
Mielke, S., (Ed.) (1982): *Internationales Gewerkschaftshandbuch*, Leverkusen.
Mjøset, L. (1985): *Nordic economic policies in the 1970s and 1980s*, Oslo.
OECD (Organization for Economic Co-operation and Development) (1982): *OECD economic outlook – Historical statistics 1960–1981*, Paris: OECD.
OECD (1984): Japan: Then ... and now, *OECD Observer*, No. 127: pp. 3–15.
OECD (1985a): *OECD economic outlook – Historical statistics 1960–1983*, Paris: OECD.
OECD (1985b): *OECD economic outlook*, No. 38, Paris: OECD.
Olson, M. (1982): *The rise and decline of nations: Economic growth, stagflation, and social rigidities*, New Haven and London.
Paloheimo, H. (1984): Distributive struggle and economic development in the 1970s in developed capitalist countries, *European Journal of Political Research*, 12: 171–90.
Pempel, T.J. and Tsunekawa, K. (1979): Corporatism without labour? The Japanese anomaly, In: *Trends towards corporatist intermediation*, pp. 231–70, (Eds.): P.C. Schmitter and G. Lehmbruch, London.
Przeworski, A. and Wallerstein, M. (1985): Comment on Katz, Mahler, & Franz, *American Political Science Review*, 79: 508–10.
Saunders, P. (1985): Public expenditure and economic performance in OECD countries, *Journal of Public Policy*, 5: 1–21.
Saunders, P. and Klau, F. (1985): *The role of the public sector: Causes and consequences of the growth of government*, OECD Economic Studies No. 4, Special Issue, Paris: OECD.
Scharpf, F.W. (1984): Economic and institutional constraints of full-employment strategies: Sweden, Austria, and West Germany, In: *Order and conflict in contemporary capitalism*, pp. 257–90, (Ed.) by J.H. Goldthorpe, Oxford.
Schmidt, M.G. (1982): The role of parties in shaping macroeconomic policy, In: *The impact of parties*, pp. 97–176, (Ed.) by F.G. Castles, London, Beverly Hills.
Schmidt, M.G. (1983): The welfare state and the economy in periods of economic

crisis: A comparative study of twenty-three OECD nations, *European Journal of Political Research*, 11: 1–26.

Schmidt, M. G. (1984): The politics of unemployment: Rates of unemployment and labour market policy, *West European Politics*, Vol. 7, No. 3: pp. 5–24.

Schmidt, M. G. (1985): *Der Schweizerische Weg zur Vollbeschäftigung*, Frankfurt and New York.

Schmidt, M. G. (1987): The politics of labour market policy, In: *Managing mixed economies*, pp. 4–53, (Eds.): F. G. Castles, F. Lehner, and M. G. Schmidt, Berlin and New York.

Schubert, K. (1987): Politics and economic regulation, In: *Managing mixed economies*, pp. 169–196, (Eds.): G. Castles, F. Lehner, and M. G. Schmidt, Berlin (forthcoming).

Shonfield, A. (1969): *Modern capitalism: The changing balance of private and public power*, Oxford.

Sloan, J. W. and Tedin, K. L. (1985): Regime type and public policy in Latin America, 13th IPSA World Congress, Paris, July 1985.

Stephens, J. D. (1979): *The transition from capitalism to socialism*, London and Basingstoke.

Tarantelli, E. (1984 a): The regulation of inflation and unemployment in Western countries and the degree of neocorporatism, Rome (Unpublished manuscript).

Tarantelli, E. (1984 b): The credibility of monetary policy and the regulation of inflation and unemployment in Western countries, Paper prepared for the conference on "Unemployment," University of Toronto, November 1984.

Vogel, D. with the assistance of V. Kuhn (1983): The comparative study of environmental policy: A review of the literature, In: *Comparative Policy Research*, pp. 99–170, (Eds.): M. Dierkes, H. N. Weiler, and A. B. Antal, Aldershot.

Weede, E. (1984): Demokratie, schleichender Sozialismus and ideologischer Sozialismus als Determinanten des Wirtschaftswachstums, *Zeitschrift für Politik*, 31: 408–424.

Weede, E. (1986): Verteilungskoalitionen, Staatstätigkeit und Stagnation, *Politische Vierteljahresschrift*, 27: 222–236.

Weir, M. and Skocpol, T. (1983): State structures and social Keynesianism: Responses to the Great Depression in Sweden and the United States, *International Journal of Comparative Sociology*, 24: 4–29.

Whiteley, P. F. (1983): The political economy of growth, *European Journal of Political Research*, 11: 197–214.

Wilensky, H. L. (1981): Democratic corporatism, consensus and social policy: Reflections on changing values and the "crisis" of the welfare state, In: *The welfare state in crisis: An account of the conference on social policies in the 1980s, OECD, Paris, 20–23 October 1980*, Paris: OECD, pp. 185–195.

Yamamura, K. (1985): The cost of rapid growth and capitalist democracy in Japan, In: *The politics of inflation and economic stagnation*, pp. 467–508, (Eds.): L. N. Lindberg and C. S. Maier, Washington, D. C.

Zysman, J. (1985): Inflation and the politics of supply, In: *The politics of inflation and economic stagnation*, pp. 140–172, (Eds.): L. N. Lindberg and C. S. Maier, Washington, D. C.

C. Value Change and the Economic Experience of Mass Publics

Value Changes in Western Societies – The Last Thirty Years

Karl Otto Hondrich

Aims, Concepts and Methodological Questions of Research on Values

Conducting research for purely scientific reasons needs no justification; everything is interesting or can be legitimately declared to be so. The political impact that research can have is another matter, however, a fact that may prompt policymakers and politically-minded people to want to know about value trends in contemporary societies. First, values may indicate the directions toward which human activity is heading. Knowledge of changing value trends could provide means of predicting trends of human action. Moreover, a theory that spells out and interrelates the factors contributing to value change may be a useful prerequisite for political action aimed at influencing values and behavior. Second, even if not translated into social action, values are important in their own right. The value level of social reality is no less important than the action level. For individuals, values have an expressive function; they tell people what they should be aiming for and why. For society, values provide a common understanding and thus have an integrative function. It is from the system of values that political goals and activities are derived. Those goals and activities that are not consistent with a society's value reality bring about conflicts that might be much stronger than, for instance, distributive conflicts.

Values are ideas of desirable states, shared by collectivities or majorities within a collectivity. They orient human activities towards realizing desirable states. It should be emphasized that there is a difference between "desirable" and "desired" states.

> Mere desiring does not instate a value; the desires have as it were to be criticized and compared. The existence of the value-element may transform the desired into the not-desired or the ambivalently desired (Kluckhohn 1961: 19).

If one defines needs as conscious or unconscious desires of an individual, then values bring in social judgements and thus transform mere desires into distinctive desirable and undesirable states. This social element is what allows for the distinction between needs and values. The social character of values is decidedly mixed; it introduces alternatives, preferences, in short, choice or freedom while imposing social constraints on biological necessities. Value as a concept of desirability contains both aspects: free choice and constraints. Desirable states cannot be conceived of without implicit reference to what is necessary. There is always a combination of freedom and obligation in the concept of value.

Not only values, but also needs are socially determined. They are products of the social fabric, at least to a certain degree. But there is still an additional social aspect that is particular to values. Although values have their place in the minds of individuals, they do not refer to desirable states of individuals alone but to desirable states of social systems or collectivities as well. They provide for a normative concept of social systems and their regulative principles. To the degree that those concepts are shared, passed down, and supported within the collectivity, values are deeply anchored, relatively stable, and more difficult to change than normative concepts that refer to states of the individual only.

Since it is appropriate not to confound values and needs as two different levels of social reality, it is also useful to distinguish both from action as a third level. Although we may tend to try to make those levels of social reality consistent, the latter stubbornly maintain or even increase their contradictory and partly independent character. I think it is desirable for people to go to the theater; I myself desire to go to the movies, but then I actually stay at home watching television.

This shows that neither observed activity nor personal need can be taken, as is often postulated, as indicators of value preferences. Since people cannot and will not always comply with their own values, it would be wrong to deduce their values from their actions alone. In the following analysis, which relies heavily on aggregated survey data and which, unfortunately, neglects value statements from organizations, parties, governments, legal documents, and other sources, I take expressed attitudes of values as indicators for "real" values. Sometimes I must resort to questions that measure needs or activities more than values, for it is not always possible to make the distinctions clear given the few time series that are available for longitudinal studies.

The following analysis has other regrettable limitations as well. Since lack of time prevented me from gaining access to data pools from most European countries, I deal mainly with value trends in West Germany and, to a lesser degree, in the United States. Nevertheless, a few comparative studies on other countries were available for the analysis. Attempted generalizations will have to be examined in the light of other data. I have not broken the data down into subgroups. The challenge of writing this paper was not so much to give a complete picture of the data but to give a very different interpretation of the same data treated by other analysts of value change (Inglehart 1977, Klages 1983, Kmieciak 1976, Meulemann 1982, Noelle-Neumann 1978, Opaschowski and Raddatz 1982). I start with a discussion of the changing values of domains of life: religion, politics, family, work, and leisure. I continue by discussing values as regulative principles of social life, but confine myself to the examination of two popular theses: first, the erosion or "proletarization" of bourgeois values, particularly the value of achievement; and second, the transformation of bourgeois values into post-bourgeois values. I conclude by pointing to different and hitherto neglected dimensions of value change and by reflecting on the impact that value change has on technological, economic, and societal performance.

The Value of Life Domains

As imperfect as it is, Table 1 is intended to provide a first impression of the relative subjective "importance" that life domains had for the decade from 1973 to 1982. The ranking is completely consistent with data that "one's own family and children" were ranked highest, ahead of "occupation and work," and "leisure time and recreation." Moreover, it should not be surprising that the ranking of the values listed in Table 1 changed little in just ten years. Which changes these were, however, is surprising. Quite contrary to the thesis that the value of "leisure time" is continuing to increase (see Opaschowski and Raddatz 1982), this domain falls from second to third place on the value ladder, with "work" climbing from fourth to second place. Even in 1983, when the question was not about "importance" but rather about "how much space" the different domains occupied in the respondent's life, the rank order was the same as that obtained in the 1976 survey, "work" coming after "family life" but before "leisure time" (Hondrich and Schumacher 1988).

Unexpectedly, "religion" was upgraded and "politics" was downgraded at the bottom of the hierarchy. Data on political interest and church attendance continuously suggest the opposite movement (Meulemann 1982). This is but one indication of the often contradictory character of data on value change. The contradictions of long- and short-term change are dealt with later in this chapter.

Because the original 4-point scale used up to 1976 was changed to a 7-point scale in the later surveys, the percentages for 1973 and 1976 should not be compared with those of 1980 and 1982. Where comparisons are admissible, however, it is remarkable that the percentages of the "very important" statements continuously decreased between 1973 and 1976, as well as between 1980 and 1982. This suggests that value change not only involves shifts in rank orders, but also that all domains of life can be devaluated at the same time. Both interpretations seemed to be vindicated between 1973 and 1982, a decade in which economic recession and growing concerns about ecological problems were reflected as decreasing optimism. The "value climate" as a whole changed from the heated euphoria of the 1960s to the cooler, more pessimistic outlook of the 1970s.

The Decreasing Value of Religion

Perhaps the most striking loss of value that has become apparent for a domain of life over the last thirty years has been documented in the realm of religion. In West Germany church attendance was still high in 1953; only 13 % of the people questioned about the matter at that time said they never went to church. This percentage slowly increased for a decade and then jumped to over 30 % in 1965, exceeding 40 % by the mid-seventies (Meulemann 1982). (It is understandable that this development is not reflected in Table 1, which covers only the years from 1973 to 1982.) In the

Table 1 Importance of Life Domains in West Germany. Percentage of Responses "Very Important" on a 4-Point (1973 and 1976) and 7-Point (1980 and 1982) Likert-Scale

Life Domain	1973	1976	1980	1982
One's own family and children	A 72.7	A 70.1	A 66.5	A 66.0
Leisure time and recreation	C 54.2	B 47.3	B 44.3	B 38.1
Friends and acquaintances	D 52.9	C 36.4	C 41.8	C 35.8
Occupation and work	B 46.8	D 31.3	D 30.7	D 27.1
Politics and public life	G 29.2	G 20.0	E 18.1	E 15.9
Relatives	E 25.2	F 13.6	F 14.6	F 14.6
Religion and church	F 18.3	...	G 13.5	G 10.8

Source: for the 1973 and 1976 data, see Bargel (1979); Porst (1980); For the 1980 and 1982 data see ZUMA (unpublished information).

United States church attendance was much higher and increased slightly between 1952 and 1964. But that country, too, experienced a change, with the percentage of non-attendants in the population almost doubling from around 6% to over 11% and creeping to 15% in 1978 (Converse et al. 1980: 144–146).

The different levels and developments of church attendance in two similarly industrialized and dynamic societies make it very difficult to uphold the general and popular thesis that correlates industrialization and secularization. From a European perspective, secularization might be taking place as a result of a historical heritage in which almost the entire population was born into one of the two big religious confessions, which are closely related to state organizations. It might well be that the decreasing attendance and adherence to religious practices in Europe, particularly in Germany, are due primarily to the decreasing acceptance of elements of big organizations and even of power that, in the European context, are associated with institutionalized religion. If longitudinal indicators of a genuine interest in religious questions and unconventional religious communities were available, they would very likely show much less devaluation of religion than the statistics on church attendance do.

Nevertheless, it seems obvious that religion has lost the central focus it had as a moral authority in medieval life. The formulating of morally binding standards, the defining of values and norms, functions that had been all but monopolized by religious communities and churches, has been scattered among many different institutions and social systems throughout society, such as the state, legal authorities, scientists, intellectuals, the educational establishment, mass media, and the family. It is impossible today to maintain that the function of establishing modern society's moral code lies in any one domain of life. The fact that moral authority has become diffuse, has sometimes been interpreted as a loss of moral cohesion in general.

It has been said that social activity is less and less guided by values and norms and more and more by cognitive standards and practicality. This is a highly speculative and, I believe, false statement. We will never be able to prove that society today is less – or more – pervaded by moral regulations than it was earlier. But it can be stated empirically that there is increasing participation of institutions and individuals in the discussion and reformulation of those regulations. We may call this the democratization of morals. (And one should keep in mind that only a very small part of the value system changes at any one time.) This democratization of morals can be seen in the decreasing impact of norms and values officially stated by the church on economic, family, and sexual life. Thus, the declining value of religion is expressed in its declining impact on society's value system. Religion is losing its moral function for the whole of society. By confining itself to religious belief (and not to the moral structuring of worldly affairs), the church may be constituting and stabilizing religion as a value in itself. During the twenty years of dramatically reduced church attendance between 1956 and 1975, the percentage of West Germans who expressed a "belief in a life after death" declined only slightly from 42% to 36% (Meulemann 1982).

The Increasing Value of Politics

Decreasing authority of the church and increasing value of politics are contrary, clearly documented tendencies in the West German public between 1953 and 1979. The share of respondents who said they would switch off news broadcasts concerning church matters increased from 17% to 31%; those who were used to switching off statements by political parties or political commentaries decreased (from 42% to 26% and from 34% to 21%, respectively Noelle-Neumann and Piel 1983a: 175). This confirms what is known about the amazing increase in political interest, political participation, confidence in the different aspects of the political system, and approval of basic democratic institutions that has been noted in the Federal Republic of Germany during the last three decades (Arzberger 1982, Baker et al. 1981, Conradt 1980).

Table 2 National Subjective Competence (1959/1960 and 1974): Percentage of Survey Respondents Who Consider Unconventional Political Action Like Demonstrations a Legitimate Means of Protesting National Laws onsidered Unjust or Harmful (A); Total Percentage of Responses (B); Total Number of Respondents N (C)

	Britain			United States			Germany			The Netherlands	Austria
	1959	1974	1974 1959 Difference	1960	1974	1974 1960 Difference	1950	1974	1974 1959 Difference	1974	1974
A		4.3	+4.3	0.3	3.6	+3.3	1.9	9.5	+7.6	16.5	5.9
B	110.9	117.9	+7.0	124.9	147.2	+22.3	106.8	124.4	+17.6	122.0	111.7
C	(903)	(1244)		(926)	(1570)		(890)	(2151)		(939)	(1244)

Source: Barnes and Kaase (Eds.) (1979): 144. For data on 1959 and 1960, see Almond and Verba (1963).

In the course of this process, Germany's positive valuation of political activity and democratic institutions has caught up with that of older democracies. In some respects, West Germans now trust and value their political system even more than the British and Americans do. The upward movement of "politics and political life" in te ranking of life domains in the F.R.G. starkly contrasts "The Decline of the Civic Culture" in Great Britain (Kavanagh 1980), the "Political Culture under Stress" (Abramovitz 1980) and "The Confidence Gap" (Lipset and Schneider 1983) in the United States.

Is the positive attitude that Germans now show towards their political system only a resurgence of the proverbial German loyalty to their state (Staatsgläubigkeit), a loyalty akin perhaps to the "authoritarian personality" of the old days? As Table 2 shows, this does not seem to be the case. West German citizens, more than other Europeans (except the Dutch) and more than Americans, consider taking unconventional political action like demonstrations if they want to protest national laws that seem to be unjust or harmful.

Table 3 National Subjective Competence (1959/1960 and 1974). Percentage of Respondents Who Said that They Can Do Something About an Unjust or Harmful Local Regulation or National Law

	Local Regulation						National Law					
	1956–60		1974		1974 1959–60		1959–60		1974		1974 1959–60	
Country	(%)	%	(%)	%	% Differences		(%)	%	(%)	%	% Differences	
The Netherlands	(–)	–	(62)	71	(–)	–	(–)	–	(43)	53	(–)	–
Britain	(78)	81	(64)	74	(–14)	–7	(62)	66	(57)	66	(–5)	0
United States	(77)	82	(71)	77	(–6)	–5	(75)	78	(78)	82	(+3)	+4
Germany	(62)	67	(67)	70	(+5)	+3	(38)	40	(56)	59	(+18)	+19
Austria	(–)	–	(43)	48	–	–	(–)	–	(33)	41	(–)	–

Source: Barnes and Kaase (Eds.) (1979): 141. For data on 1959 and 1960, see Almond and Verba (1963).

As for combining conventional and unconventional political actions, Germans did not judge the idea to be as successful as Americans and British did, but between 1959 and 1974 the increase in the perceived

Table 4 Responses to a Question About Basic Attitude Towards Social Change (in Percentages[1])

Question: "On this card are three basic kinds of attitudes vis-à-vis the society we live in. Please choose the one that best describes your own opinion.
1. The entire way our society is organized must be radically changed by revolutionary action.
2. Our society must be gradually improved by reforms.
3. Our present society must be valiantly defended against all subversive forces."

	1970 (Febr.–March)[2]			1976 (November)			1977–1979 (six polls)[3]			1981 (October)			1982 (October)		
	Revolutionary action	Reforms	Defence against subversion	Revolutionary action	Reforms	Defence against subversion	Revolutionary action	Reforms	Defence against subversion	Revolutionary action	Reforms	Defence against subversion	Revolutionary action	Reforms	Defence against subversion
Belgium	4 %	80 %	16 %	6 %	73 %	21 %	6 %	72 %	22 %	10 %	70 %	20 %	10 %	68 %	22 %
Denmark	:	:	:	4	55	41	3	59	38	2	58	40	2	60	38
Germany	2	76	22	2	56	42	2	49	49	5	55	40	3	52	45
France	5	82	13	14	67	19	11	70	19	5	67	28	5	68	27
Ireland	:	:	:	8	67	25	7	67	26	4	65	31	9	59	32
Italy	8	80	12	13	68	19	9	63	28	6	64	30	8	69	23
Luxembourg	1	70	29	2	59	39	4	68	28	5	70	25	3	63	34
Netherlands	6	78	16	5	60	35	5	62	33	6	58	36	5	59	36
United Kingdom	:	:	:	8	65	27	7	64	29	10	62	28	6	58	36
Greece	:	:	:	:	:	:	10	60	30	9	66	25	7	30	33
Community[4]	(5)	(79)	(16)	8	64	28	7	61	32	7	62	31	5	62	33

[1] Meaning those who explicitly choose one of the three options. Don't knows average 7 % for all countries and over the whole period, with a maximum of 15 % in Belgium.
[2] The 1970 survey was made only in the original six countries and the reformist option was worded slightly differently ("by intelligent reforms").
[3] Average of two polls for Greece: October 1980 and April 1981.
[4] Weighted average.

Source: Euro Barometer 1982, no. 18: 48.

impact of political action in general was most pronounced in West Germany (see Table 3).

In the United States, Britain, and West Germany – three countries for which there are comparative data for 1959 and 1974 –

> the overall political repertory had broadened considerably by 1974, and unconventional, direct action types of political influence had found their way into the repertory of a wider segment of the population (Barnes and Kaase 1979: 163).

It also becomes very clear that

> a considerable portion of the public in five advanced industrial societies has already accepted direct action techniques without abandoning conventional types of political involvement.

Conventional and unconventional political participation are not mutually exclusive but rather complementary.

Church attendance which in the previous section was taken as an indicator for the decreasing value attached to religious participation, is a highly conventional type of action. If there were time series data for unconventional religious action, they might reveal an increasing number and value of those activities, say, in sectarian or worldwide youth movements or an increasing amount of superstition. In any case, the portion of the population taking part in unconventional activities seems to be much smaller in religion than in politics.

Altogether, one may conclude that in recent decades Western societies have developed a fairly stable, positive attitude towards their democratic political systems and the social system as a whole; that the direction of change in these attitudes was the same in all countries (see Table 4); that West Germany and Italy, which started the post-war period with a collapse of their political structures, went through greater changes in political values than other countries did; and that unconventional political action in the 1960s and 1970s did not undermine the positive valuation of the democratic system but rather strengthened it by incorporating new added elements and forms of commitment.

The Value of Family Life

Although the family ranks highest in the value hierarchy of life domains listed in Table 1, objective and subjective data seem to suggest that its value is declining (Allerbeck and Hoag 1985, Meulemann 1982, Schumacher and Vollmer 1982). Housewives increasingly want to leave, and really do leave, the family part-time for a job outside the home. The increasing incidence of divorce, legal and other ways to facilitate the decision by couples to get divorced, and the increasing desire "to make divorce easier" indicate that keeping the family together is not as important as it once was. Marriage is considered less important for happiness than it used to be. The percentage of 16-to-18-year-olds who responded in the survey that they want to get married eventually decreased from 97% to 87% between 1962 and 1983, the same two decades during which the importance of marriage for having children leveled off. In 1962 90% of the young respondents thought it was important for a woman to be married when she has a child; twenty years later the percentage had fallen to 52% (Allerbeck and Hoag 1985: 97). The number of children per family has plummeted, and although data indicate a certain stability of the widespread preference for the two-child-family, a recent study in West Germany (von Rosenstiel et al. 1984) suggests that there is a tendency to desire only one child.

This evidence seems to contradict data showing the high importance of, and satisfaction with, family life. It also seems to challenge the results of our own research (Hondrich and Schumacher, 1988, and Vollmer 1986), which indicates that people want to spend much more time with their children and their partner than they do spend. The marginal utility of time spent with family members is higher than that of every other use of time except "leisure time." A possible explanation to the contradiction lies in the fact that the tendency to withdraw time and relevance from the family does not mean the forsaking of intimate life-styles. There is an increasing tendency to substitute for and complement the family by living together with a partner or a group without being married, by contacting friends, and by becoming a member of voluntary, especially athletic, associations (Allerbeck and Hoag 1985, Noelle-Neumann and Piel 1983a). Instead of competing with other realms of life, the family appears to be losing out to quasi-family private life-styles. There is a slight devaluation of the family as an institution, but not of family life. Deinstitutionalization of family life should not be misunderstood as a movement against institutions as such. The underlying unintended tendency is towards acknowledgement and reinstitutionalization of quasi-family life-styles.

In the long run, the devaluation of the institutionalized family may be explained in terms of the functions that it has gradually lost: providing for joint welfare through a large multigenerational group of family members, for secure and stable social relations within the family framework, for monogamous sexual relations, and for a sharing of the responsibilities of childrearing; as we have seen, it is becoming less and less important for wives to share the task of childrearing with their husbands. What has remained as a "pure," very specialized family function has become all the more important and attractive: providing emotional support and harmony between at least two persons, say, as partners or in a father/mother-child relationship. In this respect, the functions of the family have not been lost but rather strengthened. Between 1953 and 1979 confidential and intimate exchange increased between family members, particularly between parents and children. It is much higher than that between family members and people outside the family (Hondrich and Schumacher, 1988, Noelle-Neumann and Piel 1983a: 96–97).

Today, the family is a paradox. Its attractiveness vis-à-vis the realm of work is based on the fact, that it has abandoned many of its obligatory functions, and has thus moved even closer to the realm of freedom. But compared to quasi-family life-styles and leisure outside the family, the institutionalized family, in the eyes of a small but increasing portion of the population, still embraces too many constraints and obligations. Nevertheless, it seems premature to conclude that the process of devaluating social obligations and revaluating individual freedom will go on.

The Value of Work and Leisure

At first glance there seems to be a striking parallel between the realm of work and the family: people who are occupied in the work system want to spend less time in it. Not only has the number of real working hours declined considerably, several time series of survey questions, including one survey question on the reduced readiness for job induced mobility (Schlie 1984), indicate that many people who are employed full-time want a reduction of working hours and increasingly seem to prefer the time outside of work.

A second look at the survey results pertaining to the decade from 1973 to 1982 reveals the differences between the spheres of work and family. Whereas the percentage of people who wanted to end their marriages or who did not want to get married increased (on a low level), the percentage of people who would have completely abandoned work if they could have afforded it decreased from 30% to 22% (Vollmer 1986: 324). Comparable figures for the United States show the same trend, though it is spread over two decades. US women's commitment to work increased considerably, whereas US men's commitment to work remained stable (see Table 5). Young people, when asked which kind of needs are especially important to them, ranked "an occupation that I like" higher than "much leisure time" (see Table 6). The edge of the former over the latter actually increased between 1973 and 1979. The slightly diminished importance of "good income" may be interpreted as a value change from extrinsic (work as an instrument for the realization of other values) to intrinsic (work as a value in itself) motives.

This data leads to the conclusion that the value of additional or extended working time is decreasing for the majority of people in industrial societies. Nevertheless, the value of participation in the working system, the value of work as such, is increasing. As Behrens

Table 5 Responses to A Survey on Work Commitment Among Working Men and Women in the United States in 1957 and 1976 (in Percentages)

Work Commitment	Men 1957 (%)	Men 1976 (%)	Women 1957 (%)	Women 1976 (%)
Would not go on working If Money Not Needed	15	16	42	23
Would go on Working If Money Not Needed	85	84	58	77
Reasons for Going on Working:				
Achievement Commitment (Working gives feeling of accomplishment, makes you feel successful)	4	12	1	10
Affiliative Commitment: (Likes chance to be with people, friendships, helping people)	2	3	8	10
Work as Habit: (Only way of life R knows, easier to keep on what yor're doing)	2	3	2	2
Moralistic Commitment: (Work keeps you healthy, prevents feeling useless or immoral, "good to work")	9	8	3	4
Time Use Commitment: (Avoids boredom, upset if didn't work, go crazy if no work)	55	43	27	24
Escape from Home Commitment: (Better than house-work, being with family, staying at home)	1	1	3	8
General Like: (Like to work, like the work I'm doing)	10	9	14	13
Total Number	924	763	301	612

Source: Veroff, Douvan, and Kulka 1981: 258.

Table 6 Responses to a Survey on the Ranking of Needs (in Percentages). What is Important to Young West Germans?

	1973	1979
Personal freedom	85	85
An occupation that I like	68	80
Free choice of a job	63	67
Good earnings	70	67
A nice apartment	68	66
Much leisure time	56	64
Clean air, clear water	61	63

Source: Jugendwerk der Deutschen Shell 1981: 47.

(1984) has elaborated, this is particularly true for those people who cherish the value of self-actualization: there is no alternative to the value of participation in the work system. True, additional leisure time is valued more highly than additional working time (Hondrich and Schumacher, 1988), but this does not indicate a declining commitment to the work system. On the contrary the growing attraction of the work system means that adults in a couple or a family with children ultimately work outside the home, making the modern family's collective involvement in the work system higher than it was for the traditional family. The demand for more leisure time and free time for the family thus does not mean that people are turning away from work but that their attraction to the professional work system is greater than ever before. The higher value of leisure results from the higher value of work. Similarly, the higher value of reduced working time results from the higher and expanding value of participation in work. Values that initially seem to be contradictory are really complementary.

Additionally, there seems to be a change in the value attached to the characteristics of work. Physically hard and demanding work that subjects the worker to the discipline of superiors and machines and that makes up the identity of the "classical" blue-collar worker, lost value, while the value of intellectually demanding work that encourages self-reliance and responsibility increased. This can be considered a result of the educational explosion and of the changing technological and organizational character of work. Not just any kind of job was highly valued; the value of "modern" jobs increased – even among members of the young generation, who are often and superficially accused of preferring leisure time over work.

This information corroborates the observation that people who are outside the occupational system, particularly the unemployed and housewives, have a continuous drive to enter it, particularly if working time is reduced. It is also in line with the result that "occupation and work" are considered increasingly important (see Table 1).

On the other hand, employed people prefer a reduction of their working time. Per saldo and, amazingly enough, in society in general, there is a preference for an increase in the number of working hours, although individuals, particularly those in full-time jobs, prefer to work fewer hours (Hondrich and Schumacher, 1988, Vollmer 1986: 325).

The US data (which extends from 1958 to 1974 only) show a most noteworthy advance of intrinsic values as measured by the responses to the criterion "work is important, gives a feeling of accomplishment." The opposite, downward trend is in the extrinsic value ("steadiness of income") of a job. On the other hand, the less frequently cited extrinsic criterion of a "high and increasing income" registered some gains

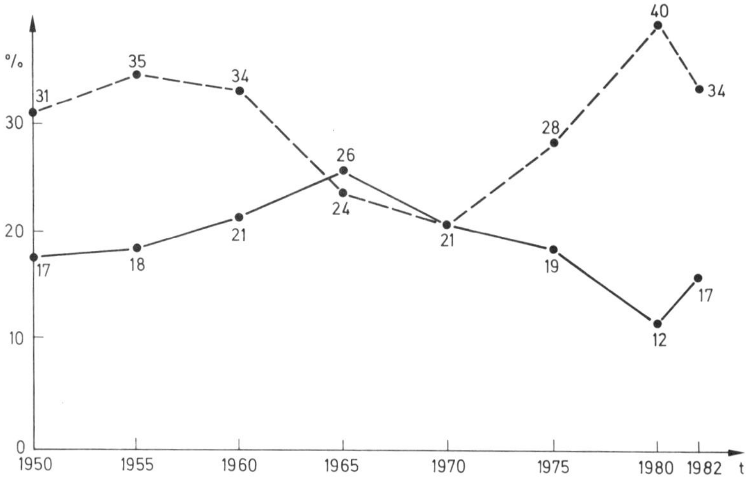

work as a task: ————
work for money: - - - - - - -

Figure 1 Work as a Task or as a Means for Making Money? Question (to employed West Germans only): "Do you feel your work to be fulfillment of a task or as a means to earn money?"

Source: Pawlowsky 1986.

(Converse et al. 1980: 159–161). The declining importance of secure income (and the parallel decline in the importance of job security) can be explained largely by the economic boom in the 1960s and 1970s. In Europe there does not seem to have been such a demise of security values (see Noelle-Neumann and Piel 1983 b: 426). The problem of identifying a long-term trend for the extrinsic and intrinsic meaning of work is well illustrated in Figure 1.

From 1950 to the mid-1960s work was increasingly considered a "fulfillment of a task" and less a means to earn money. This trend reversed until approximately 1980, when the trend swung back. The percentages in 1980 are exactly the same as those recorded thirty years ago! I draw three conclusions from this fact. First, there often turns out to be no value change in the long run, although short-term shifts may suggest one. Second, extrinsic and intrinsic values of work do not trade off as if value change were a zero-sum game. Instead, values diversify; many new, flexible, and equally acceptable meanings of work emerge. Third, it is quite logical and plausible that intrinsic as well as extrinsic rewards of work eventually increase in value. This conclusion is consistent with the fact that participation in the work system (not increasing working time!) is becoming even more important for establishing a "complete," socially recognized individual identity and that income is a decisive instrument with which to enjoy increased amounts of free time and all the hedonistic opportunities it offers.

Summing up the results of the analysis so far, one can say that, in modern, highly industrialized societies the value of extended working time and of hard, physical work is decreasing, as is the value of income security and job security as characteristic rewards of work – in the United States more so than in Europe. At the same time, the value of paid work is increasing as is the value of the intrinsic (identity-forming) and extrinsic (income) aspects of work. The value change in favor of those aspects of work does not contradict but rather complements the increasing value of leisure time and recreation.

Changes in the Value of Regulative Principles

From Puritan "Calling" to a General Achievement Orientation

In his book, *The First New Nation*, Seymour Martin Lipset (1963) emphasized achievement and equality as key American values. This idea seems to be supported in a recent comparative study on "Work and Human Values" (Yankelovich et al. 1985), in which a survey comparing industrialized nations showed the United States to have one of the highest percentages of people who indicate a "strong work ethic" as measured by their positive response to the statement "I have an inner need to do the best I can regardless of pay." Only Israeli had a higher percentage of such responses (see Table 7).

In Milton Rokeach's (1973: 57–58) well-known famous rank orders for "terminal" and "instrumental" values, however, achievement ("a sense of

Table 7 Perceived Work Ethik in Various Countries

	U.S. %	Israel %	F.R.G. %	U.K. %	Sweden %	Japan %
Work ethic is:						
Strong	52	57	26	17	45	50
Moderate	21	33	54	48	44	52
Weak	27	7	15	31	7	26

Source: Yankelovich et al. 1985.

Table 8 Terminal Value Medians and Composite Rank Orders of Needs for American Men and Women

	Male	Female	
N =	665	744	p
A comfortable life	7.8 (4)	10.0 (13)	.001
An exciting life	14.6 (18)	15.8 (18)	.001
A sense of accomplishment	8.3 (7)	9.4 (10)	.01
A world at peace	3.8 (1)	3.0 (1)	.001
A world of beauty	13.6 (15)	13.5 (15)	–
Equality	8.9 (9)	8.3 (8)	–
Family security	3.8 (2)	3.8 (2)	–
Freedom	4.9 (3)	6.1 (3)	.01
Happiness	7.9 (5)	7.4 (5)	.05
Inner harmony	11.1 (13)	9.8 (12)	.001
Mature love	12.6 (14)	12.3 (14)	–
National security	9.2 (10)	9.8 (11)	–
Pleasure	14.1 (17)	15.0 (16)	.01
Salvation	9.9 (12)	7.3 (4)	.001
Self-respect	8.2 (6)	7.4 (6)	.01
Social recognition	13.8 (16)	15.0 (17)	.001
True friendship	9.6 (11)	9.1 (9)	–
Wisdom	8.5 (8)	7.7 (7)	.05

Figures shown are median rankings and, in parentheses, composite rank orders.

Source: Rokeach 1973: 58.

accomplishment") is ranked only seventh by American men (tenth by women), with equality being ninth (see Tables 8 and 9).

The data are not contradictory in a strict sense, but they do stimulate questions. For example, are achievement and equality really prominent in the American value system? Have those two values in the course of history perhaps lost their rank at the top? What would happen to the value hierarchy if other values like job security, environmental protection, and tolerance were introduced? To which degree does the rank order of values correspond to actual problems mentioned in the mass media?

Those questions make it evident that only one aspect of value systems and value change has been considered, no matter what kind of value is discussed on an empirical basis. The next question, then, is whether that aspect is important or at least interesting. By dealing with the value of achievement, I am entering into an ongoing discussion that seems interesting enough. The latent "leitmotiv" thereof is the idea of

Table 9 Instrumental Value Medians and Composite Rank Orders of Needs for American Men and Women

	Male	Female	
N =	665	744	p
Ambitious	5.6 (2)	7.4 (4)	.001
Broadminded	7.2 (4)	7.7 (5)	–
Capable	8.9 (8)	10.1 (12)	.001
Cheerful	10.4 (12)	9.4 (10)	.05
Clean	9.4 (9)	8.1 (8)	.01
Courageous	7.5 (5)	8.1 (6)	–
Forgiving	8.2 (6)	6.4 (2)	.001
Helpful	8.3 (7)	8.1 (7)	–
Honest	3.4 (1)	3.2 (1)	–
Imaginative	14.3 (18)	16.1 (18)	.001
Independent	10.2 (11)	10.7 (14)	–
Intellectual	12.8 (15)	13.2 (16)	–
Logical	13.5 (16)	14.7 (17)	.001
Loving	10.9 (14)	8.6 (9)	.001
Obedient	13.5 (17)	13.1 (15)	–
Polite	10.9 (13)	10.7 (13)	–
Responsible	6.6 (3)	6.8 (3)	–
Self-controlled	9.7 (10)	9.5 (11)	–

Figures shown are median rankings and, in parentheses, composite rank orders.

Source: Rokeach 1973: 58.

decadence, of cultural decline. Western societies are seen as being caught in a self-destructive process eroding the values on which their dynamism and world-wide supremacy was founded. It appears to me, however, that the main problems of value change lie elsewhere.

It was Max Weber (1965) who opened the discussion by pointing to a connection between the rise of capitalism and protestant calling (Beruf). The idea of "calling" is a precursor of the value of accomplishment or achievement. It embraces a methodical organization of human efforts, an orientation of organized energies toward a goal of "inner-worldly" work and success, and a general meaning, a chance for the Calvinist to prove himself to be a predestined instrument of God's purpose. (For extensive interpretation, see Poggi 1983: 62–64). Weber was aware at the time he was writing that the religious meaning of calling had already faded away. To him, that fact was no reason to be pessimistic about capitalism's future. As he stated, capitalism no longer needs the religious spirit – the same spirit that had helped to bring it into existence. But was there anything to fill the vacuum of values? Weber mentioned three possibilities: competitive acquisitiveness (Erwerbsstreben, das sich mit rein agonalen Leidenschaften assoziiert), specialization without spirit (Fachmenschen ohne Geist), and hedonism without compassion (Genußmenschen ohne Herz) (1965: 188–89).

All three possibilities reveal Weber's cultural pessimism – a pessimism held today by those who believe that the bourgeois work ethic is disappearing in a sea of hedonism, egalitarianism, and purely instrumental attitudes towards work. Is this what is happening to the puritan value of "calling"? Originally, "calling" as a value underlying the methodical organization of energy must have been sectarian, bourgeois, and elitist in character, namely, (a) shared by few people only, (b) accepted consciously and voluntarily (Weber: „Der Puritaner wollte Berufsmensch sein – wir müssen es sein"), (c) guided by a religious meaning, (d) oriented towards work and success, and (e) made dominant in all life spheres. In the process of expanding capitalism the value of a methodical organization of life was extended to more and more people, came to be imposed by economic and technological constraints, lost its religious meaning, extended the idea of accomplishment from work to other life spheres, and thus became linked to goal-orientations other than those developed in the work system.

This account may give an idea, in simplistic terms, of the transformation of "calling" into "achievement." The process can also be understood as a democratization of the idea of methodical organization of effort. The further the idea extends to ever more people and realms of life, the more it loses its emphatic character and the more it is weakened in the process. It shares this fate with all ideas and activities that undergo democratization. They do not seem to be what they were when they were ennobled by belonging to quasi heroic minorities. A value like "calling" trickles down and is transformed when it is shared by many people. At the same time, however, the number of people sharing the value increases, and this, in turn, stimulates the representation of the value by charismatic personalities or folk heroes.

One of the most striking conflicts and paradoxes produced by the transformation of "calling" into "achievement", is that external constraints of Vergesellschaftung, mediated by education, increasingly force upon people a concept of voluntary, and self-accountable innerdirected action: achievement. Achievement and freedom belong together as values. Self-responsibility, which has been promoted by the protestant idea of calling, has gone a long way and goes much further nowadays. Its meanings cannot be based solely on religious teaching or on goals prescribed in the work system. One must select its meanings from a variety of life domains and goals. In this context, achievement is a more abstract and general value than calling. Achievement encompasses actions based on many different values. It may also become a higher value than more specifically defined values to which it may be directed: scientific discovery, superior athletic performance, or harmony within the family, for example. The act of accomplishment, the feeling of doing one's very best, independently from own goal-orientation, may become a value in itself, supported by no other rewards than by the feeling of self-actualization.

On the one hand, this value orientation is extremely individualistic, an advance in individualism, so to speak. On the other hand, accomplishment can be felt in a collective effort, or it can be given a collective meaning.

This brings me back to the data. Does it point to an erosion of the achievement value? First, since achievement orientation has become decamped from religious meaning and the traditional protestant work ethic, it is not threatened by a relative devaluation of religion and, possibly, of work. It is not known to which degree achievement

Table 10 Value Concerns of Europeans: Responses to a Survey (in Percentages).

Question: "In your opinion, which are the great causes of this list for which it is worthwhile nowadays to take risks and make sacrifices?"

	B	DK	D	F	IRL	I	L	NL	UK	GR	CE[1]
Peace	65	61	57	77	45	76	79	68	58	85	67
Human rights	43	48	38	53	41	40	59	54	44	59	44
Fighting poverty	37	34	29	56	38	43	52	34	37	54	40
Freedom of the individual	34	29	31	55	26	34	46	34	42	60	40
Protection of the natural environment	33	33	39	37	20	26	46	40	36	48	35
National defense	13	18	17	28	11	23	28	9	28	44	23
My religious beliefs	10	8	13	12	35	21	21	15	15	41	16
Equality between men and women	14	22	17	16	9	12	40	19	14	34	16
A united Europe	14	7	13	14	4	9	33	9	5	21	11
Revolution	3	3	3	3	1	3	3	3	2	7	3
None of the above, don't know.	11	14	14	3	15	3	2	6	6	5	7
Total[2]	277	277	271	354	245	290	409	291	287	458	302

[1] Weighted.
[2] Sum exceeds 100% due 40 rounding.
Source: Euro-Barometer 1982.

Table 11 Educational Goals for Life in Germany: Responses to a Survey (in Percentages)

Question: "We' ve put together a list of what children should be provided with for their later life, things they should learn in the home. Which points do you consider especially important?"

	1967 Oct.	1977 Dec.	1979 Oct.	1982 Jan.	1983 Feb.
Politeness and good behavior	85	76	80	75	76
To do their work properly and conscientiously	76	70	71	70	75
To respect different opinions, be tolerant	59	64	72	65	72
To assert, themselves, not be easily discourage	59	68	66	63	68
To be frugal with money	75	65	65	66	65
To be a good judge of human nature, choose their friends wisely;	53	60	57	61	62
A healthy way of life	58	57	59	58	60
Love of knowledge, the desire to keep widening their horizons	47	49	49	46	49
To fit into the order of things, to adjust	61	51	52	45	46
To enjoy books and reading	36	28	33	36	36
Interest in politics, an understanding of political affairs	30	29	37	30	33
To be modest and reticent	37	28	29	27	31
A firm belief, firm religious commitment	39	24	29	25	27
Technical knowledge, to the able to deal with modern technology	29	24	26	25	24
To enjoy art	21	17	19	19	21

Source: Noelle-Neumann 1981: 35; Noelle-Neumann and Piel 1983b: 93.

orientation can, or actually does, exist without the support of a deeper meaning provided by other values.

But it may well be that values like "peace" and newly emerging ecological concerns substitute for the religious meaning of calling and indicate a deeper reorientation in our attitudes towards the world. By this I mean a reorientation that may be functionally equivalent to the emergence of puritan ethics four-hundred years ago. It is starting as a minority movement connected with a conscious reorganization of values and life-styles, but no one can know what its long-term consequences will be. The data in Table 10 does not indicate which values will be the most influential in shaping future values in the long run. Nevertheless, there are some clues to an answer to this question. For example, in a country like

Ireland, where "religious belief" is still very highly valued, it is interesting that "peace" and "protection of nature" rank relatively low on the scale. This result suggests that in other countries with reversed value-relationship, the "new" values at least partially supplant religion in its function of giving meaning and orientation to people's lives.

Second, the devaluation of regulative principles like industriousness, politeness, subordination, and thrift, which are traditionally considered important to the domain of work, fails to indicate a depreciation either of work or of achievement. As the hierarchy of educational goals in Table 11 shows, "to work properly and conscientiously" only temporarily lost ground and is considered particularly important.

Moreover, the decreasing importance of "disciplinary" other-directed values and a corresponding upgrading of self-reliance and responsibility, particularly among younger and educated people, reflect changing demands made by the occupational system. Lastly, self-reliance and responsibility are principles directly linked to the value of achievement, as has been shown above. They indicate not a waning but rather a waxing of the achievement value.

Third, just as the values of achievement and freedom are related, so, too, are achievement and equality. Rising levels of achievement in a society presupposes equality of opportunity for ever more people. Beyond that, the achievement principle as a distributive norm leads to demands for "equal pay for equal performance," including equal pay for men and women. But to which degree is the principle of unequal rewards for unequal performances accepted? The Allensbach Institute has constructed the case of a father who has two sons and can afford a trip to England for one of them only. After thinking about it, he tells them that the grades in the next school report card will decide which of the two sons may make the trip. In 1962 62% of the German workers surveyed approved of this decision; ten years later the percentage dropped to 49 percent. This finding does not necessarily mean that norms of achievement and competition are losing support; rather the data from the survey reveals increasing awareness of the different meanings of achievement in the contexts of work and family. "To do one's very best" in the family does not always mean to work hard at the office and to get high grades in school. It could be to give love, support, and help to other family members regardless of their achievements outside the family.

Fourth, the extension of the achievement value from work to other life domains should not be misinterpreted as an exportation of criteria and goals from the working system to other systems. On the contrary, in accepting the abstract value of achievement, the family must also reject those achievement goals and rewards that are alien to it. If reward for good performance rather than the achievement value itself is rejected in family life, then reward for good performance is unlikely to be transferred as a value from one life sphere into another. Actually, each sphere may have its own, different norms of achievement.

From Material to Post-material Values?

In the preceding section I argued that values related to freedom of choice and values related to equality are advancing in step with the value of achievement. This hypothesis seems to fit well with Ronald Inglehart's thesis of a "silent revolution" (1977) as a change from material or bourgeois value priorities ("maintaining order in the nation," "fighting rising prices") to post-bourgeois preferences ("giving the people more say in political decisions," "protecting freedom of speech"). Inglehart's thesis is plausibly based on Abraham Maslow's psychological theory of a hierarchy of needs (1954) and on the assumption that people who, like the post-war generation in Western Europe, grew up when economic security and political stability was relatively great, will take the satisfaction of those needs for granted and will turn to "higher" needs such as those of belonging, aesthetic and intellectual development, and participation.

Unfortunately, the reexamination and recent discussion of Inglehart's data do not support the thesis and the theory behind it (Hondrich and Vollmer 1983, Böltken and Jagodzinski 1983, Lafferty 1976, Mohr 1984,

Table 12 The Changing from Materialist to Post-materialist Value-Orientation in Europe, in Percent of Total Adult Population

		1970	1973	1976	1978	1980
Belgium	P[1)]	14	14	14	12	
	M[2)]	32	25	30	31	
Federal Republic of Germany	P	10	8	11	11	12
	M	43	42	41	38	41
France	P	11	12	12	16	
	M	38	35	41	31	
Great Britain	P	8	8	8	8	
	M	36	32	37	34	
Italy	P	13	9	11	10	
	M	35	40	41	44	
Netherlands	P	17	13	14	22	
	M	30	31	32	28	

1) p = post-materialists
2) m = materialists
Source: Inglehart 1981: 880–900; 1984.

Murck 1980). As Table 12 shows, the percentage of post-materialists remained low and almost stable in six European countries during the seventies.

Additional examination of data shows that "post-bourgeois" value choices are just as prevalent among a generation born and raised during great economic difficulties as they are among a generation born and raised during the "age of affluence" (Lafferty 1976: 134).

How can one explain the contradiction between the statement that values of self-determination as expressed in educational goals are advancing, and the statement that Inglehart's theory of post-bourgeois value change is not confirmed? There is a combination of three convincing solutions. First, Inglehart's indicators (freedom of speech and political participation) are formulated too narrowly. As has been demonstrated in this chapter, other questions concerning political participation and professional and educational goals indicate that post-materialist values are becoming more pronounced than they have been.

Second, this trend is not necessarily accompanied by a relative devaluation of material and security aspects of life. Particularly in Europe, as Marsh (1975: 169) has argued for Great Britain and Hondrich and Vollmer (1983: 90) have for West Germany, security and material values do not have a zero-sum relationship with values of self-actualization; the importance of both sets of values is rising. (Security values are less important in the United States than in Europe.) What is wrong is not so much Inglehart's thesis of post-materialism, but rather the notion that the values in the value hierarchy behind it simply change positions.

Third, new values like ecological equilibrium or women's self-actualization do not follow from older security values in a predictable rank order. They are not so much a consequence of the satisfaction of other needs or of the realization of other values, but rather of their non-realization or of unintended consequences (Hondrich 1983). Since unintended consequences are unforeseeable, the same is true for new values that react to them by recombining elements of old values. Thus

the value choices in question are more the result of a combination of current interests and cognitive-symbolic set (education, local traditions, level of political awareness, etc.), than they are of "deeper," childhood-induced needs (Lafferty 1976: 134).

Explanations, Trends, and Implications of Value Change

Value change may be explained in very general terms by adaptation or by saturation. The concept of adaptation suggests that persons and collectivities adapt their ideas of what is desirable to social, economic, and technological processes, which are considered stronger than the world of values and, hence, are thought of as being inevitable and necessary. The change in the character of work from physically hard, other-directed, and day- and life-long activity to intellectually and emotionally demanding, responsible, and achievement-oriented activity that must be done within limited time is an example of structural inevitability: who would be able to stop or reverse the process? Thus, the value attached to work changes according to structural necessities and limited personal opportunities. The influence of those outside constraints and opportunities can be clearly studied in the differing orientations that unskilled, skilled, and professional labor has towards work. (I have not dealt with the ample empirical evidence of value differences in subgroups.)

Paradoxically, reducing work's character as a necessity is itself a developmental necessity that calls for the adaptation of values, requires, for instance, a higher degree of acceptance of unemployment. Nevertheless, what is necessary and inevitable is defined in a social process. There are social limits to necessity where adaptation fails. The destruction of nature is no longer accepted as inevitable. The value change in favor of preserving ecological processes cannot be understood as an adaptation to what the human race has, but as a reminder and warning of what it has lost and of what it should have. Value change can be explained, in this respect, as negative adaptation, as resistance to negative consequences of developments that are no longer considered inevitable.

The saturation model of value change neglects the aspect of necessity and deprivation in value change and points to the elements of opportunity and free choice that arise when society has reached necessary levels of value attainment. But what happens then? According to the model, one possibility is that there is a developmental logic, that there are inherent dynamics, with one level of values following logically from earlier levels, as Maslow and Inglehart assume. Evidence for this kind of historical determinism is lacking. The other possibility assumed in the model is that new values develop in an unforeseeable situational context as reactions to the strains, deprivation, and unintended consequences of earlier developments. This alternative point of view leads back to the explanatory model of negative adaptation.

The main dimensions of value change may be misconceived as long as attention is directed towards hierarchies of values. As I have demonstrated, contradictory value movements – functional gains and functional losses – make it difficult to assess upward and downward changes in values within life domains and regulative principles. What really changes are aspects of value and frontiers within domains of life (concerning qualified versus unqualified work, for instance) and within general principles (such as the equality of reward versus the equality of opportunities). In addition, frontiers shift between domains of life and between regulative principles.

These processes of functional social differentiation and recombination are reflected in value changes as –

1) A proliferation of values. Today, one must differentiate (and sometimes choose) between many freedoms and equalities. Whereas people used to think in terms of only a few realms of life, one now has access to many different realms. "Leisure time" alone covers many recreational, educational, athletic, and travel activities. It is their abundance and their inherent character of free choice that makes for their increasing value.
2) An increasing separation and contradiction between the various value domains and between regulative principles, including love, achievement, and social justice.
3) A reconciliation of proliferating and contradictory values by abstraction. This explains the growing importance of values like tolerance, communication, and peace (see Tables 11 and 12). The process by which emerging value abstractions can become solutions for increasing conflict between values has not received due attention yet.
4) A redefinition of the value of participation, a new meaning that refers not to upward participation in decision-making hierarchies but to horizontal participation in different life domains such as the participation of women in higher education and work. This meaning of participation is linked to values of self-actualization and self-determination inasmuch as participation in many realms frees the individual from hitherto dominating realms like work and housework.
5) An equalization of values, particularly between men and women and between social strata (an empirically well-documented aspect that I have had to neglect in this chapter). Such equalization is not to be confounded with a uniformization of values. On the contrary, it promotes opportunities to choose and combine individual value preferences relatively independent of class or status.
6) Contradictions between the mainstream of value change and value systems, subcultures, and countercultures constructed by minorities.

As some observers have emphasized (Klages 1983, Meulemann 1982), European countries, particularly West Germany, witnessed a "shift" of attitudes from the mid-1960s to the late 1970s, one that reflected increased interest in politics, leisure activities, and new life-styles. It was ended and even reversed by a slight revival of traditional values in the 1980s. The period of accelerated value change paralleled a period of economic prosperity, at times of overemployment, a period in which few people had to worry about finding and holding a job. What was felt as a change in secular values at that time was largely an extraordinary stimulation of social activity and the feeling that things can be changed. Being typical for boomtimes, the feeling has gradually abated since 1973.

Lastly, these considerations call attention to values that, because they do not change, are not usually dealt with by value research. Two kinds of values can be identified in this respect. The first includes such values as material security and political order, which are thought to change but which, as the data show, do not change at all or much less than expected. The second kind of value neglected by value research encompasses values that have deep evolutionary roots in all societies and mental structures – the abstract regulative principles of reciprocity, solidarity, and order, for instance. They could be labeled metavalues and are associated essentially with the realm of preconsciousness. This does not mean that they are necessarily precluded from consciousness, if this were so, then humans could not know and argue about them. They become part of conscious debates only when people make the effort to reflect upon them, whereas values become values by everyday discussion. When talking about values, one should keep in mind that change in some values is accompanied by, and even presupposes stability in, a large universe of elementary or metavalues.

References

Abramovitz, A. L. (1980): The United States – Political culture under stress, In: *The civic culture reconsidered*, (Eds): G. A. Almond and S. Verba, Boston and Toronto.

Allerbeck, K. R. and Hoag, W. J. (1985): *Jugend ohne Zukunft?* Munich and Zürich.

Almond, G. A. and Verba, S. (1963): *The civic culture*, Princeton.

Arzberger, K. (1982): Ausdifferenzierung des Staates und Differenzierungsprozesse im politischen System heute, In: *Soziale Differenzierung: Langzeitanalysen zum Wandel von Politik, Arbeit und Familie*, Frankfurt am Main.

Arzberger, K. (1983): Stabilität und Wandel im Verhältnis zwischen den Generationen, In: Hondrich und Vollmer, (Eds.).

Baker, K. L.; Dalton, J.; and Hildebrandt, K. (1981): *Germany transformed: Political culture and the new politics*, Cambridge, Mass. and London.

Bargel, T. (1979): Überlegungen und Materialien zu Wertdisparitäten und Wertwandel in der BRD, In: Klages and Kmieciak, (Eds.).

Barnes, S. H.; Kaase, M. (Eds.) (1979): *Political action: Mass participation in five Western countries*, Beverly Hills and London.

Behrens, J. (1982): Die Ausdifferenzierung der Arbeit, In: *Soziale Differenzierung: Langzeitanalysen zum Wandel von Politik, Arbeit und Familie*, Frankfurt am Main.

Behrens, J. (1984): "Selbstverwirklichung" – oder: Vom Verblassen aller Alternativen zur Berufsarbeit, In: *Ansprüche an die Arbeit – Soziale Indikatoren XI*, (Eds.): H.-J. Hoffmann-Novotny and F. Gehrmann, Frankfurt am Main.

Böltken, F.; Jagodzinski, W. (1983): In an environment of insecurity: Postmaterialism in the European Community 1970–1980: *Comparative Political Studies*, 17, 4, (January): 453–484.

Conradt, D.P. (1980): Changing German political culture, In: *The civic culture reconsidered*, (Eds.): G.A. Almond and S. Verba, Boston and Toronto.

Converse, P.E. (1980): *American social attitudes data sourcebook*, Cambridge, Mass.

Euro-Barometer (1982): No. 18, Commission of the european communities, Brussels.

Hondrich, K.O. (1983): How do needs change? In: *Consumer behaviour and environmental quality*, (Ed.): L. Uusitalo, Aldershot.

Hondrich, K.O. and Vollmer, R. (Eds.) (1983): *Bedürfnisse – Stabilität und Wandel*, Frankfurt.

Hondrich, K.O. and Schumacher, J. 1988: *Krise der Leistungsgesellschaft?* Opladen.

Inglehart, R. (1977): *The silent revolution: Changing values and political styles among Western publics*, Princeton.

Inglehart, R. (1981): Postmaterialism in an environment of insecurity, *American Political Science Review*, 75: 880–900.

Jugendwerk der Deutschen Shell (1981): *Die Einstellung der jungen Generation zur Arbeitswelt und Wirtschaftsordnung*, Hamburg.

Kavanagh, D. (1980): Political culture in Great Britain – The decline of the civic culture, In: *The civic culture reconsidered*, (Eds.): A. Almond and S. Verba, Boston and Toronto.

Klages, H. (1983): Wertwandel: Chancen der Synthese von Pflicht- und Selbstentfaltungswerten, In: *Zukunftsperspektiven gesellschaftlicher Entwicklungen*, pp. 38–45, Prepared for the government of the Land of Baden-Württemberg, Stuttgart.

Klages, H. and Kmieciak, P. (Eds.) (1979): *Wertwandel und gesellschaftlicher Wandel*, Frankfurt am Main and New York.

Kluckhohn, C. (1961): The study of values, In: (Ed.) D.N. Barrett.

Kmieciak, P. (1976): *Wertstrukturen und Wertwandel in der Bundesrepublik Deutschland*, Berlin.

Lafferty, W.M. (1976): Basic needs and political values: Some perspectives from Norway on Europe's "silent revolution," *Acta Sociologica*, 19.

Lipset, S.M. (1963): *The first new nation*, New York.

Lipset, S.M. and Schneider, W. (1983): *The confidence gap: Business, labor and government in the public mind*, New York and London.

Marsh, A. (1975): "The silent revolution": Value priorities and the quality of life in britain, *The American Political Science Review*, 69: 21–30.

Maslow, A.H. (1954): *Motivation and personality*, New York.

Meulemann, H. (1982): Value change in West Germany 1950–1980: Integrating the empirical evidence, Paper presented at the 10th World Congress of Sociology, Mexico City, 16–21 August.

Mohr, H.-M. (1984): Postmaterialismus in der Bundesrepublik? Working paper nr. 141, Sonderforschungsbereich 3, Frankfurt and Mannheim.

Murck, M. (1980): *Soziologie der öffentlichen Sicherheit*, Frankfurt.

Noelle-Neumann, E. (1978): *Werden wir alle Proletarier? Wertwandel in unserer Gesellschaft*, Zürich and Osnabrück.

Noelle-Neumann, E. (1981): *The Germans: Public opinion polls 1967–1980*. Westport, Conn.

Noelle-Neumann, E. and Piel, E. (Eds.) (1983a): *Eine Generation später: Bundesrepublik Deutschland 1953–1979*, Munich, New York, London, and Paris.

Noelle-Neumann, E. and Piel, E. (Eds.) (1983b): *Allensbacher Jahrbuch der Demoskopie 1978–1983*, Band 8, Munich, New York, London, and Paris.

Opaschowski, H.W. and Raddatz, G. (1982): *Freizeit im Wertewandel*, BAT-Freizeit-Forschungsinstitut, Hamburg.

Pawlowsky, P. (1986): *Arbeitseinstellungen im Wandel*, München.

Poggi, G. (1983): *Calvinism and the capitalist spirit: Max Weber's protestant ethic*, London.

Porst, R. (1980): Nationaler Sozialer Survey: Deskriptiver Vergleich mit ausgewählten Zeitreihen, ZUMA, Mannheim (Manuscript).

Rokeach, M. (1973): *The nature of human values*, New York.

Rosenstiel, L. von et al. (1984): Lust auf Kinder? Höchstens 1..., *psychologie heute*, 5: 20–31.

Schlie, F. (1984): *Informationstechnik als Herausforderung: Zur Gestaltung von Leistungssystemen*, Dissertation, Frankfurt am Main.

Schumacher, J. and Vollmer, R. (1982): Differenzierungs- und Entdifferenzierungsprozesse im Familiensystem, In: *Soziale Differenzierung: Langzeitanalysen zum Wandel von Politik, Arbeit und Familie*, (Ed.): K.O. Hondrich, Frankfurt am Main.

Veroff, J.; Duvan, E.; and Kulka, R.A. (1981): *The inner American: A self-portrait from 1957 to 1976*, New York.

Vollmer, R. (1986): *Die Entmythologisierung der Berufsarbeit*, Opladen.

Weber, M. (1965): *Die protestantische Ethik*, Munich and Hamburg.

Yankelovich, D.; Zetterberg, H.; Strümpel, B.; and Shanks, M. (1985): *The world at work: An international report on jobs, productivity, and human values*, New York.

Economic Culture in Post-Industrial Society: Orientations Toward Growth, Technology and Work[1)]

Ephraim Yuchtman-Yaar

Introduction

The post World War II era of spectacular success of Western societies in the achievement of economic growth and material affluence has widely influenced the intellectual perspectives on the nature of these societies and the course of their development. Probably the most important concept which has been employed analytically and historically in order to capture the main processes underlying this development is that of "Industrial society" (Aron 1967a, b, Bell 1961, 1976, Bendix 1956, Dahrendorf 1967, Kerr et al. 1973, Lipset 1960, Moore 1963). For some scholars the logic of industrialism prevails in Western and non-Western nations as a universal and inevitable process. Accordingly,

> The world is entering a new age – the age of total industrialization. Some countries are far along the road; many are just beginning the journey. But erverywhere, at a faster or slower pace, the peoples of the world are on the march towards industrialism (Kerr et al. 1973: 29).

Despite the fact that such an extreme deterministic statement is not shared by all proponents of the industrial society, and despite differences about its consequences, universality, and determination, there is general agreement first, that there exists a core of techno-economic characteristics which define different levels, or stages, of industrialization and, second, that this core is essential for understanding the social, political, and cultural patterns which emerge in each of these stages (i.e., the pre-industrial, industrialy, and post-industrial).

1) Financial support from the Pinhas Sapir Center for Development is gratefully acknowledged. This paper is a product of a larger study on Work and Human Values, reported upon in D. Yankelovich et al. (1983). We wish to thank Ilan Talmud for his assistance in the preparation of the manuscript.

Our purpose in this paper is to present data and discuss some of the emerging cultural patterns that have been associated with advanced industrial societies. More specifically, we are concerned with popular economic culture and its congruity with the core features of industrialism – technological progress, economic growth, and centrality of work. Popular economic culture refers to the patterns of economically related values, cognitions, and behavioral dispositions of individual members of society. Following Strümpel and Yuchtman-Yaar (1983), we distinguish between two levels of economic culture according to the object of orientation: individual (i.e., level of "economic man") or society (i.e., level of "economic citizen"). As our discussion is unfolded below, it will become evident that both levels of economic orientation are reflected in the debate over the cultural expressions of advanced industrialism.

Cultural Contradictions of Post-Industrialism?

During the 1960s proponents of the logic of industrialism wrote extensively about the coming of the "post-industrial" society, representing the next, and the most advanced stage of industrialism. Some of these proponents described this stage in an euphoric aura of optimism, based on the premise that its productive capacity would suffice to solve the ancient problem of material scarcity (Kahn and Weiner 1967). The most explicit prognosis expressing this view is given by the statement of the Ad Hoc Committee on the Triple Revolution (1966, quoted by Bell 1976: 462). According to this, the era of cybernetic technology which has just begun would result "in a system of almost unlimited productive capacity which requires progressively less labor," and, "It is necessary to recognize that the traditional link between jobs and income is broken. The economy of abundance can sustain all citizens in comfort and economic security whether or not they engage in what is commonly reckoned as work."

Recent observations of the post-industrial era have adopted a more sober view about its consequences for man and society. The realities of economic slowdown, coupled with chronic problems of inflation and unemployment, proved the forecasts of "an end to scarcity" to be premature and futile. And yet, despite the economic crises of the 1970s and 1980s, the advanced industrial nations have shown a remarkable ability to sustain the affluence of their citizens. This capacity derives from the persistence of productive efficiency as well as from the institutionalization of welfare policies which guarantee a significant share in the material pie for the weaker strata of society.

These socioeconomic developments have given rise to new issues and concerns about the post-industrial society. Bell, one of the first theorists of this type of society, has been apprehensive about the "revolution of rising expectations" and "rising entitlements" (Bell 1975). The first type of revolution derives from the rising standards of living and the promise of material progress, while the second phenomenon is due mainly to the emergence of the welfare state and its promise of equality. Both processes are detrimental to the economy, because they express absorption in hedonistic behavior and weaken the traditional values of work and social responsibility.

A related portrayal of the post-industrial society has been presented by Yankelovich (1981), who contrasts the normative climate of the American public during the early post-war era with the values and attitudes developed in the last two decades. The first period was characterized by a high degree of harmony between the imperatives of the economic system and the nature of individual goals:

> Economically, what Americans wanted for themselves as individuals also served society's goal of economic growth, and that growth, in turn, gave Americans the material goods and improved social standing that motivated them to work hard (1981: 171).

The dominant work ethic of that period – "self denial" – was necessary to economic growth, while the fruits of the latter were necessary to "reinforce the discipline imposed by self-denial."

More recently, this spirit of self-denial has given way to growing desires for self-actualization which have been crystallized into a new form of cultural expression. The new culture does not mean that the pursuit of material well-being is weakened or abandoned:

> Most Americans want more material goods and more personal freedom. To the comfort we have, we want more leisure [...] we wish to preserve economic security and also add a dash of adventure, excitement and change (1981: 176).

This hedonistic mood implies, however, that personal desires achieve the status of an ethical norm which replaces the older ethics of hard work and commitment to collective goals.

While Bell is concerned with excessive entitlements for material rewards, and Yankelovich with the craving for the best of both worlds of material and non-material rewards, Inglehart (1975) has further developed the argument of "post materialism". According to him, the socioeconomic characteristics of post-industrial society have bred a new pattern of human concerns which departs drastically from the traditional value hierarchy of industrialism. The new pattern, which encompasses the social, economic, and political spheres, is distinguished by the priority given to such values as freedom, participation, the quality of life, and self-expression. Material rewards in this culture have a low priority, and the idea that economic progress is the solution for the well-being of individuals and society is no longer simply accepted. Consequently, material rewards, careerism, and socioeconomic mobility cannot function as effective incentives in the realm of work, and the post-materialist person is often driven to fulfill his or her desires for self-actualization outside the ordinary setting of the economy. Furthermore, such person does not care much about, and may even oppose, the core values of industrial society – rationality, efficiency, and mastery over the environment – since the realization of such values is destructive for those aspects of the quality of life that he or she cares about.

Inglehart acknowledges that the post-materialistic outlook is still confined largely to the younger and more educated cohorts whose formative years had been deeply influenced by realized expectations as well as by disillusionment with economic growth. Nevertheless, his argument implies that as post-industrial society becomes more fully established, so will the culture of post-materialism.

Notwithstanding the differences in emphasis and interpretation, these three perspectives on the post-industrial society have in common a view which is widely shared among contemporary scholars. This view maintains that the transformation of society from an industrial to a post-industrial stage is inevitably followed by fundamental changes in the value-hierarchy of its members. The essential element of these changes is the underminding of identification with and loyalty to the imperatives of industrialism at both the level of "economic man" and that of "economic citizen." Whether because of excessive levels of entitlements or the search for new life-styles, commitment to work has been weakened, and the idea of economic progress is no longer considered by many as a collective goal to be cherished.

A key element in the determination of the attachement to work and its reward value for individual workers is the nature of its underlying technology. Concern with this factor has a long history among students of industrialization, particularly as regards its negative effects in terms of alienation. However, the prospects of the post-industrial society seem, for some writers, quite promising in shifting the trend and overcoming the alienating effects of technology. This optimistic view is based on the continuing transition from a machine technology of fabrication – the dominant technology of industrial society – to an automated technology of processing, which dominates post-industrial society (Blauner 1964, Faunce 1968). The new "intellectual technology" (Bell 1976), exemplified by the processing involved in telecommunication and computer systems, will bring along fundamental changes in the occupational structure and the nature of work which will be increasingly composed of professional and technical jobs. Such a trend is likely to reduce alienation at the workplace and provide greater opportunities for self-actualization.

But this optimistic view is not shared by all analysts of technology and its progression. For some, there exists an inherent contradiction between cultural values of social bonds and of human freedom and the imperatives of modern technology (Ackerman 1981, Freeman and Cain 1974, Habermas 1972, Touraine 1974). The new technologies have also been accused of having been introduced with little regard for workers' welfare and interests, thus creating displacement and dislocation, particularly in times of recession (Weltz and Schmidt 1976). Moreover, although the new technologies tend to free the worker from physically harsh and mentally boring tasks, they leave him with little to do and with limited opportunities to apply available skills, or to develop new ones (Cooley 1980). This line of criticism has also been directed against some of the more recent and sophisticated technologies (e. g., the "micro-chips"). The main argument here is that such new developments are so pervasive in their effects and so rapidly introduced that they threaten to create high levels of unemployment and allow little time for readjustment (Rothwell and Zegfeld 1979).

Put more generally, these gloomy views about the impact of technology seem to reinforce the argument that the techno-economic features of post-industrial society facilitate the emergence of response patterns which contradict its industrial foundations. Aside from the question of validity of this view, any attempt to assess its implications must bear in mind Bell's (1976) observations that the techno-economic and occupational structure of society does not completely determine its cultural and political realms. In fact, these three domains were more closely linked by a common value system during the earlier phase of industrialism, while in our times there has been an increasing "disjunction" among them. The implication of this observation is that despite their common core of techno-economic and occupational attributes, post-industrial societies may not respond uniformly in terms of values, meanings, and other aspects of economic culture. As important as the industrial characteristics may be, it is possible that the cultural and political contexts of each nation mediate the effects of technology as well as of other attributes of post-industrial society (Lane 1976).

However, the assessment of such trends has suffered from the paucity of empirical studies in general, and of comparative research in particular. To be sure, there have been a few cross-national studies concerned with these issues, especially with the impact of technology (e. g., Archibald et al. 1981, Armer and Isaac 1978, Form 1971, Reimanis 1978, Shepard et al. 1978). But most of these studies, as noted by Schweitzer (1981), are only "quasi-comparative" in the sense that an analytic sample survey conducted within one society is simply replicated, often many years later, in another society. The lack of systematic and explicitly comparative work on the similarities and differences between various societies [...] represents another neglected area.

In the present study we have attempted to come closer to the prerequisites of a meaningful comparative research. The data represent the responses of individuals in six industrialized countries – the U.S., Britain, Germany, Sweden, Japan, and Israel. Obviously, these nations vary considerably with respect to a number of demographic, cultural, political, and socioeconomic characteristics. Yet, and despite such differences, these nations also share a relatively advanced stage of industrialism, especially when compared to developing or third-world countries. In fact, we would argue that the data-base of this comparative research involves a fairly representative, albeit incomplete, group of post-industrial Western democracies. The questionnaire items were jointly formulated by teams of social scientists from each of these countries, and the surveys were conducted simultaneously during the period of June to December 1982. Representative stratified samples were drawn in each of the six populations, involving a toal of 5,957, although the technology-related items represent the responses of only those 2,344 individuals who had experienced some technological change in the past 10 years (by self-report).[2)]

Results

We begin with a set of empirical findings concerning the issue of economic growth. Two related questions were addressed on this issue. First, we deal with the extent to which growth can be regarded as a collective goal supported by individual members of society. Given the recent debate about the consequences of growth for society, the question of its popular legitimacy seems particularly relevant. Second, we examine the public view on the influence of growth on one of the most troublesome trends on the socioeconomic scene of Western democracies – the rising levels of unemployment.

The public views on these questions are given in Table 1 and Table 2.

It is evident from the first column of Table 1 that the idea of economic growth is thought of positively by the large majority of the public. This

---

2) For a detailed description of the research design, instrumentation and analysis, see Yankelovich et al. 1983.

tendency is fairly consistent in the four countries for which data are available, though to varying degrees: whereas in Israel the support of growth is practically unanimous, a significant minority of Germans apparently have some doubts about it.

Table 1 Evaluations of Economic Growth*)

	Total[a)]	U.S.A.	F.R.G.	U.K.[b)]	Sweden	Japan[b)]	Israel
1) good	74	73	60	–	69	–	92
2) bad	10	17	10	–	10	–	4
3) don't know	16	10	30	–	21	–	4
	100	100	100		100		100

*) Stimulus question: "On balance, do you think economic growth is good or bad?"
1) good,
2) bad,
3) don't know.

a) Weighted average percent.

b) Item not included in that country.

Table 2 Perceived Effects of Growth on Employment*)

	Total[a)]	U.S.A.	F.R.G.	U.K.[b)]	Sweden	Japan[b)]	Israel
1) good	58	64	54	55	66	41	66
2) bad	34	19	30	43	24	58	28
3) don't know	9	16	17	2	10	1	6
	101	99	101	100	100	100	100

*) Stimulus question: "Here are two persons talking about economic growth:
A says: If the economy continues to grow, there will be more unemployment because more jobs will be replaced by machines.
B says: If the economy continues to grow, new jobs will be created because more will be produced.
Which one of these two persons do you agree with?"
1) A,
2) B,
3) Don't know.

a) Weighted average percent.

b) Item not included in that country.

Table 3 Evaluations of Economic Growth: By Sex, Occupation, and Age*)

	Total[a)]			U.S.A.			F.R.G.			U.K.[b)]			Sweden			Japan[a)]			Israel		
I. Sex Differences	M[c)]	F		M	F		M	F		M	F		M	F		M	F		M	F	
1) good	77	69		76	69		63	56		–	–		77	60		–	–		92	92	
2) bad	9	12		17	18		9	11		–	–		7	14		–	–		4	5	
3) don't know	14	19		8	13		28	33		–	–		16	26		–	–		4	3	
	100	100		101	100		100	100					100	100					100	100	
II. White Blue-Collar Differences	W[d)]	B		W	B		W	B		W	B		W	B		W	B		W	B	
1) good	70	63		75	69		62	57		–	–		75	61		–	–		94	90	
2) bad	12	13		16	18		11	8		–	–		10	11		–	–		4	6	
3) don't know	17	24		9	12		27	34		–	–		15	28		–	–		2	4	
	99	100		100	99		100	99					100	100					100	100	
III. Age Differences	Y[e)]	M	O	Y	M	O	Y	M	O	Y	M	O	Y	M	O	Y	M	O	Y	M	O
1) good	67	76	75	69	75	71	55	61	68	–	–	–	58	70	80	–		–	91	3	88
2) bad	13	9	10	21	15	18	12	10	8	–		–	15	9	8	–		–	6	3	6
3) don't know	20	15	15	10	10	11	33	29	24	–		–	27	21	12	–		–	4	3	7
	100	100	100	100	100	100	100	100	100				100	100	100				101	99	101

*) Stimulus question: See Table 1
a) Weighted average percent
b) Item not included in that country
c) M 3 = Male; F = Female
d) W = white-collar; B = blue-collar
e) Y = Up to 29; M = 30–54; O = 55+

The generally favorable climate for economic growth is indicated by the results of Table 2 as well. Overall, the public tends to attribute to growth positive rather than negative effects on employment opportunities. This perception is common, although in different degrees, to all nations, with the notable exception of Japan (to which we shall come back later in the discussion). Yet, it should be noticed that, unlike the general attitude to growth (Table 1), there is a substantial minority in each country which regards growth as detrimental for employment. In order to examine which parts of the public are more apprehensive about the relationship between growth and employment, we present in Table 3 the distribution of responses according to sex, occupational status, and age.

Table 3.I reveals the existence of sometimes small but consistent sex differences according to which women are less inclined to think that economic growth facilitates employment. This trend is maintained also in Japan, where over 70% of females, as compared with 55% of males, adopt a negative view on this relationship.

The comparison between white and blue-collar workers (see Table 3.II) shows a similar pattern across all nations, whereby the attribution of positive influence to growth on employment is more prevalent among white-collar occupations.

Finally on this question, we may notice from Table 3.III that younger workers (up to 29 years of age) have less confidence in the growth-employment connection than their older peers. This distinction is fairly uniform in all countries, although the clearest differences are obtained in Germany and in Sweden.

The reservations that are held about the consequences of growth by woman, blue-collar, and younger workers are reflected also in the attitudes of these groups to the more general question of whether growth is "good" or "bad." As can be seen from Table 4, positive evaluations are consistently less frequent among them, with the exception of Israel, where the advocacy of growth reaches over 90%, so that there is little room left for any significant intergroup variations. At the same time it must be acknowledged that the general support for growth is remarkably high even in these groups, and it seems as if the apprehensions about the risk of unemployment is not a decisive factor in the formation of general attitudes toward economic growth.

Going beyond the level of empirical description, we suggest that the systematic inter-group variations reported in Tables 3 and 4 can be parsimoniously explained in socioeconomic terms. Those groups which have an advantageous position in the economic system adopt more favorable attitudes toward its functioning. Such an advantage is generally more typical of men vis-à-vis women, of white-collar as compared with blue-collar workers, and of older as against younger workers. Put

Table 4 Perceived Effects of Growth on Employment: By Sex, Occupation, and Age*)

	Total[a]			U.S.A.			F.R.G.			U.K.			Sweden			Japan			Israel		
I. Differences[b]	M	F		M	F		M	F		M	F		M	F		M	F		M	F	
1) good	60	54		68	59		56	49		57	52		75	55		44	27		67	65	
2) bad	33	35		17	22		29	31		42	48		17	32		55	71		27	69	
3) don't know	7	11		15	18		15	19		1	1		8	13		1	2		5	6	
	100	100		100	99		100	99		100	101		100	100		99	100		99	100	
II. White Blue-Collar Differences[d]	W	B		W	B		W	B		W	B		W	B		W	B		W	B	
1) good	60	50		69	58		52	55		64	46		70	60		46	35		68	63	
2) bad	30	41		16	23		30	28		34	51		19	31		52	64		29	34	
3) don't know	10	9		15	19		17	16		1	2		11	9		2	1		3	3	
	100	100		100	100		99	99		99	99		100	100		100	100		100	100	
III. Age Differences[d]	Y	M	O	Y	M	O	Y	M	O	Y	M	O	Y	M	O	Y	M	O	Y	M	O
1) good	52	59	61	61	66	67	47	54	65	50	56	59	55	66	75	34	41	45	63	68	62
2) bad	38	33	31	23	18	18	33	31	22	49	42	39	36	22	18	65	58	52	34	27	27
3) don't know	10	8	8	17	16	16	20	15	14	1	2	3	9	11	6	1	1	3	3	6	11
	100	100	100	101	100	101	100	100	101	100	100	101	99	99	101	100	100	100	100	101	100

*) Stimulus question: See Table 2
a) Weighted average percent
b) M = Male; F = Female
c) W = white-collar; B = blue-collar
d) Y up to 29; M = 30–54; O = 55 +

somewhat differently, the more vulnerable strata in the economy respond more skeptically about the benefits associated with its growth. Nevertheless, the overall picture suggests that the majority of workers in these advanced industrial nations, with the sole exception of Japan, can be characterized, to the extent that support of economic growth can be taken as a valid indicator, as loyal economic citizens. Furthermore, since the minority view about the negative consequences of growth is more typical of the weaker strata in the economic system, it can probably be more easily tolerated or controlled.

Work Commitment and Goals

In this section we concentrate on workers' attitudes and preferences in the realm of their own working life. Specifically we present data about two related issues. First, we deal with the nature of commitment to work in order to assess whether it promotes or hinders productivity at the job level. Second, we probe into the nature of work-goals in order to examine the kind of rewards that workers look for in their jobs. Both aspects of commitment and goals may inform us about the extent to which the labor-force in these nations is psychologically in accord with the imperatives of work in the formal economy.

The nature of work commitment is indicated by the response distribution presented in Table 5.

Table 5 Commitment to Work*)

	Total[a)]	U.S.A.	F.R.G.	U.K.	Sweden	Japan[b)]	Israel
1. High	62	68	42	66	56	–	79
2. Low	30	24	41	30	36	–	18
3. Don't know	8	9	17	4	9	–	3
	100	101	100	100	101		100

*) Stimulus question: "Here are two persons talking about their jobs.
A says: I am fully committed to my work and often do more than I am required to do. My job is so important to me that I sacrifice a lot for it.
B says: In my job I do what I am asked to do: Nobody can complain about me. But I don't see the point of extra exertions. After all, my job is not that important to me."

a) Weighted average percent.

b) Item not included for that country.

Table 6 Most Desired Outcomes of Working Life*)

	Total[a)]		U.S.A.		F.R.G.		U.K.		Sweden		Japan		Israel[b)]	
	Parents	Self	Parents	Self	Parents	Self	Parents	Self	Parents	Self	Parents	Self	Parents	Self
1. a living	45	31	50	38	29	11	45	22	53	27	47	35	–	54
2. S.o.L.	44	48	40	43	56	62	48	65	39	46	38	48	–	26
3. self-develop.	7	17	6	17	6	19	4	11	5	23	14	16	–	17
4. don't know	4	3	5	2	10	8	3	2	3	5	2	0	–	3
	100	99	101	100	101	100	100	100	100	101	101	99	–	100

*) Stimulus questions: Perceived parental attitudes: How do you think your parents regarded their work? Did they mostly...
1. Work to make a living and survive?
2. Work to improve their standard of living and advance?
3. Work to develop themselves as persons?
4. Don't know.
For the interviewee – What about you? Do you mostly...
1. Work to make a living and survive?
2. Work to improve your standard of living and advance?
3. Work to develop yourself as a person?
4. Don't know.

a) Weighted average percent.

b) Item not inclicued in that country.

It is apparent from this table that the clear majorities in all countries, except for Germany, express high commitment to their work and acknowledge its centrality in their lives. The finding with respect to Germany is apparently not incidental, and therefore deserves attention. We may recall, going back to Table 1, that German workers were found to be least keen on the idea of economic growth and, along with British and Japanese workers, less confident in the positive impact of growth on employment. It appears, then, that both as economic men and economic citizens, a significant minority of German workers do not identify with the core values of industrialism.

The German example may be contrasted with the case of Israel. The latter stands out as the nation whose workers are committed to their own jobs more than in any other country, and whose support for growth is also unsurpassed. This contrast in popular econimic culture is discussed by Strümpel and Yuchtman-Yaar (1983).

Table 6 presents the ultimate goals that workers attempt to achieve in their jobs. The three alternative goals, of which respondents were asked to select only one, presumably correspond to levels of industrialization and affluence. It is therefore interesting to compare the goal hierarchy of the respondents with the work-goals they attribute to their parents.

The results show, first, that raising the standard of living is the most popular work-goal for the present generation of workers. The only exception to this tendency is Israel, where the majority of respondents claim that they work mostly in order to make a living. The explanation of the Israeli case seems straightforward. This is the one least advanced industrially among the six nations, and its workers have not reached the standard of living which prevails in those countries.

The argument relating the changes in work-goal priorities to changing economic and social circumstances is further strengthened by the inter-generational comparison shown in Table 6. This comparison demonstrates that respondents in all countries tend to attribute to their parents a much greater preoccupation with the problem of survival. Complementarily, whereas nearly one fifth of the present generation maintains that they work primarily in order to develop themselves as persons, they perceive very little of such interest among their parents.

It appears, then, that the impact of advanced industrializations and the affluence associated with it on workers' work-values can be detected on the basis of inter-societal and inter-generational comparisons.

The pattern of results presented in Tables 5 and 6 raises, once more, the question of intrasocietal differences. In the discussion of economic citizenship we have noticed that the more vulnerable groups in society are less supportive of the logic of industrialism. Are the same groups less integrated to the microeconomic level of their own work?

Table 7 Commitment to Work: By Sex, Occupation, and Age*)

	Total[a]			U.S.A.			F.R.G.			U.K.[b]			Sweden			Japan[b]			Israel		
I. Sex Differences	M	F		M	F		M	F		M	F		M	F		M	F		M	F	
1) high	63	61		65	71		43	39		68	64		58	52		–	–		79	79	
2) low	29	31		26	20		39	44		29	31		34	37		–	–		18	19	
3) don't know	8	9		8	9		17	16		3	5		7	10		–	–		3	2	
	100	101		99	100		99	99		100	100		99				99		100	100	
II. White Blue-Collar Differences	W	B		W	B		W	B		W	B		W	B		W	B		W	B	
1) high	65	49		72	61		48	32		80	54		64	43		–	–		87	68	
2) low	24	43		20	29		34	54		17	41		24	51		–	–		12	30	
3) don't know	11	8		8	10		19	14		3	5		12	5		–	–		1	2	
	100	100		100	100		101	100		100	100		100	99					100	100	
III. Age Differences	Y	M	O	Y	M	O	Y	M	O	Y	M	O	Y	M	O	Y	M	O	Y	M	O
1) high	52	66	66	61	70	73	31	43	58	57	69	74	45	58	55	–	–	–	71	81	75
2) low	39	27	25	30	22	18	51	39	28	39	28	19	45	33	38	–	–	–	22	16	24
3) don't know	9	7	9	9	8	9	18	17	15	4	3	6	10	9	8	–	–	–	7	3	1
	100	100	100	100	100	100	100	99	101	100	101	99	100	100	101	–	–	–	100	100	100

*) Stimulus question: See Table 1
a) Weighted average percent
b) Item not included in that country

The figures in Table 7.I indicate only small and inconsistent differences between women and men, as regards the centrality of work. This finding may appear surprising since females, as noted earlier, are generally disadvantaged in the labor market, particularly with respect to hierarchy of positions and levels of earnings. However, several studies (e. g., Crosby 1982, Yuchtman-Yaar 1984) have already shown that working women generally express a high degree of contentment with their jobs and complacency with their paid income. This phenomenon is explained by the tendency of women to scale down the levels of material rewards to which they feel entitled. Correspondingly, it is possible that the hierarchy of work-goals is different for men and women, so that the latter emphasize to a larger extent the realization of post-materialistic values. Some clues about such sex differences are provided in Table 8.I.

The findings in Table 8.I indicate that men are indeed more oriented to economic goals, particularly the improvement of the standard of living, whereas women identify more with the search for self-fulfillment. We suggest the interpretation of these differences in terms of the general shift from the goals of survival to material progress, as pointed out above. Accordingly, working women, most of whom are married to working men, may have a greater freedom about the choice of whether to join the labor force in the first place, and of which kind of job to take, in the second place. To be sure, the relatively recent phenomenon of enhanced participation of females in the labor market is still dominated by economic considerations. But for a significant number of working women the participation in this market is mainly influenced by expectations of self-actualization. In this respect, the traditional division between sex roles in society, according to which responsibility for the economic position of the family and its social status are in the province of men, may have provided greater leeway for married women to decide whether to pursue non-material goals in their working life.

The case of Israel should be noticed once again in this context. We observe here a sharp distinction between men who are still largely immersed in the task of making a living, and a sizable group of women, larger than in any of the other countries in absolute and relative terms, who claim that they work mostly to develop themselves as persons. Since we are not aware of other signs indicating that Israeli women are distinctively post-materialists, it is possible that their emphasis on self-actualization represents a reaction to their husbands' high involvement in working-life. Indeed, in addition to the subjective measure of work commitment which puts Israeli men at the top (Table 7), there exists evidence that they work more hours weekly and have extra jobs in larger proportions than working men in other industrial societies. It should be noted also that the rate of participation of Israeli women in the labor

Table 8 Most Desired Outcomes of Working Life: By Sex, Occupation, and Age*)

	Total[a]			U.S.A.			F.R.G.			U.K.			Sweden			Japan			Israel		
I. Sex Differences	M	F		M	F		M	F		M	F		M	F		M	F		M	F	
1) a living	33	28		39	35		11	12		21	24		25	30		34	38		65	36	
2) S.o.L.	51	44		43	43		65	57		70	58		55	35		50	43		23	31	
3) self-develop	13	24		15	20		15	25		7	15		18	29		16	19		8	31	
4) don't know	3	4		3	2		9	7		2	3		3	6		0	0		4	2	
	100	100		100	100		100	101		100	100		101	100		100	100		100	100	
II. White Blue-Collar Differences	W	B		W	B		W	B		W	B		W	B		W	B		W	B	
1) a living	21	33		30	47		7	17		16	28		23	32		31	40		48	66	
2) S.o.L.	53	52		46	39		59	67		68	62		45	48		51	45		28	25	
3) self-develop	22	11		22	11		26	8		15	7		26	16		18	15		23	8	
4) don't know	4	3		2	2		8	8		1	4		6	4		0	0		1	1	
	99	100		100	99		100	99					100	100					100	100	
III. Age Differences	Y	M	O	Y	M	O	Y	M	O	Y	M	O	Y	M	O	Y	M	O	Y	M	O
1) a linving	29	33	29	41	37	32	11	11	12	28	19	22	32	26	27	32	35	38	42	57	59
2) S.o.L.	49	48	50	39	44	49	61	63	61	62	70	57	42	47	44	44	51	45	33	24	27
3) self-develop	19	16	17	18	16	17	18	19	21	10	9	15	24	22	22	24	14	17	25	16	7
4) don't know	3	3	3	2	3	1	10	7	6	0	2	6	3	5	6	0	0	0	0	4	8
	100	100	99	100	100	99	100	100	100	100	100	100	101	101	99	100	100	100	100	101	101

*) Stimulus question: See Table 6

a) Weighted average percent

market and their socioeconomic basis are typical of such societies, so that our findings cannot be explained in terms of selection effects.

Turning to white- and blue-collar workers, we are informed by Table 7.II that there exist relatively large differences in the work-role commitment of these groups. As implied by our discussion of economic growth, the more advantaged occupants of white-collar jobs express greater devotion to working life – still another indication that this group is better integrated into the economic system. This pattern can also be seen when the goal structures of these two groups are considered (Table 8.II). In all countries more blue-collar (33 %) than white-collar workers (21 %) state that they work mainly to make a living. Conversely, more white-collar (22 %) than blue-collar workers (11 %) are mainly interested in self-fulfillment. These differences are important, because the preferences of the white-collar workers are in accord with the nature of technological changes at the workplace (to be discussed in the next section). Nevertheless, it should be noted that the central tendency in both groups is oriented to the materialistic goal of working in order to improve the standard of living. In this regard, they are well-adapted members of the labor market and the incentive system underlying its operation.

The figures shown in Table 7.III pertain to the distributions of work commitment according to age. These figures reveal a clear trend according to which younger workers are less committed to work than their older cohorts. The age gap on this issue is most salient in Germany, where about 50 % of the younger age group indicate that work is a peripheral domain in their lives.

Relating these findings to the reported age differences with respect to the attitudes toward economic growth, it seems reasonable to suggest that the younger cohorts of post-industrial societies tend to be less loyal to the economy at both levels of economic man and economic citizen. The observation that the young workers in Israel do not conform to this general pattern implies that its interpretation should be conceived in terms of generational rather than age effects; specifically, the younger cohorts in the more advanced industrial societies have been brought up under conditions of economic security and affluence which nurtured the development of post-materialistic preferences. Such an experience has not been fully shared by their Israeli counterparts who continue therefore to express as much commitment to work as their older peers.

The findings with regard to the goal priorities of the three age groups reveal generally small and inconsistent differences with the exception of Israel, where the popularity of self-actualization appears to be inversely related to age (Table 8.III). These results suggest that although the young workers in Israel may be as committed to work as the older generation, their goal-priorities have nevertheless changed in the direction of postmaterialism. The lack of similar generational differences among more advanced countries may be explained on the basis of the previous set of findings: being less loyal to the economy, the young people in these societies search for gratifications outside the realm of ordinary work.

Reactions to Technology

The main question addressed in this section concerns the impact of technological changes at the workplace in terms of workers' alienation. As evident from the introduction to this paper, much of the debate on the functioning of technological progress has centered on the nature of this impact, with views ranging from extreme pessimism to optimism. The data presented below bear on this debate from the viewpoint of the workers' own experience: to what extent have the changes attributed to the technological factor aggravated or extenuated alienating attributes of the job?

Table 9 Perceived Effects of Technological Change*[)]

Perceived Effect	Total[a)]	USA[b)] (N = 2.344)	Germany	Sweden	Japan	Israel
More monotonous	28[c)] (8)[d)]	22 (8)	25 (8)	25 (9)	41 (7)	–
Lonelier	26 (9)	18 (7)	19 (9)	31 (8)	31 (8)	39 (8)
More of a psychological burden	44 (6)	–	35 (7)	40 (7)	62 (3)	56 (5)
More difficult	48 (5)	38 (3–4)	48 (5)	45 (5)	69 (2)	46 (7)
More dependent on others	40 (7)	38 (3–4)	38 (6)	44 (6)	30 (9)	51 (6)
More responsible	67 (1–2)	–	57 (3)	66 (2)	74 (1)	78 (1)
Less physical strain	53 (3)	35 (5)	58 (2)	60 (3)	42 (6)	64 (3)
More interesting	67 (1–2)	74 (1)	61 (1)	74 (1)	59 (4)	72 (2)
Cleaner	51 (4)	42 (2)	52 (4)	53 (4)	51 (5)	61 (4)

*) Stimulus question: "As a result of technological changes my job has become more monotonous, more..."
1. applies or partly applies
2. does not apply

a) Weighted average percent

b) Item not included for that country

c) Figures reflect percent replying "applies" or "partly applies"

d) Figures in parentheses are rank ordered percentages relative to other items.

The findings presented in Table 9 reveal a generally positive public view on the consequences of technology. Thus, the majority of respondents agree that their jobs have become more responsible and more interesting (both 67 %), as well as cleaner (51 %), and entailing less physical strain (53 %). On the other hand, negative effects – such as monotony, loneliness, psychological strain, dependence, and difficulty – are perceived as less applicable (all below 50 %). This positive pattern can be seen more clearly when we examine the rank-order of the percentage rates. Thus, the positive effects of technological change receive generally the top ranks of 1–4, with but a few and slight deviations.

The only significant exception to this trend is Japan where – contrary to respondents in all other nations – a majority of workers feel that technology has made their jobs considerably more difficult (69 %) and more of a psychological burden (62 %). Correspondingly, fewer Japanese workers agree that their jobs have become less taxing physically and more interesting psychologically.

Japan has often been depicted as representing a unique industrial model which combines traditional values of social bonds with modern values of rationality and efficiency. Indeed, the Japanese scene was portrayed a few years ago in *Time Magazine* as "An Industrial Nirvana" (Time 1980). In light of this commonly-held view, we were curious to explore whether the findings about the reactions of Japanese workers to the impact of technology are reflected in their job experiences more generally. And in fact they are. Thus, Japanese workers are particularly liable to regard their jobs as routine (48 % – as compared with Israel – 37 %, Germany – 36 %, and Sweden – 28 %). They also feel they have the least "say about what goes on" at the workplace (51 % vs., for example, 91 % in Sweden, 74 % in the U.S. and Germany); are least likely to say that they "produce something important" (60 % as compared with Israel – 70 %, and the U.S. – 80 %), that they are proud of their jobs (51 % vs. Israel and the U.S. – 72 %), that they feel useful and productive (64 % vs. Sweden – 95 % and Germany – 87 %), or that they work at an organization with fair rules of promotion (33 % vs. Israel – 65 %, Sweden – 63 %).

These findings, which correspond to virtually all the dimensions of alienation – powerlessness, meaningfulness, normlessness, and self-estrangement, as depicted by Seeman (1957, 1972, Mottaz 1981) suggest that the Japanese industrial scene is not as harmonious as commonly perceived. Indeed, our findings indicate that the impressive success of Japanese firms, especially in technological innovation and efficiency, may have been achieved at the cost of the psychological welfare of workers. These processes may also explain the negatively deviant attitude of the Japanese to economic growth (Table 7). It is possible that their relatively

Table 10 Perceived Effects of Technological Change: By Sex*)

Perceived Effects	Total[a)] Male	Female	USA[b)] Male	Female	Germany Male	Female	Sweden Male	Female	Japan Male	Female	Israel[b)] Male	Female
More monotonous	28[c)] (9)[d)]	27 (8)	21 (6)	22 (6)	25 (8)	25 (8)	23 (9)	29 (8)	40 (7)	46 (7)	–	–
Lonelier	29 (8)	20 (9)	19 (7)	15 (7)	20 (9)	17 (9)	36 (8)	21 (9)	32 (8)	25 (8)	41 (8)	30 (8)
More of a psychological burden	48 (6)	37 (7)	–	–	36 (7)	31 (7)	42 (7)	36 (7)	62 (3)	61 (2)	56 (5)	55 (3–4–5)
More difficult	52 (5)	41 (5)	40 (3–4)	33 (5)	49 (5)	44 (5)	50 (5)	38 (6)	70 (2)	60 (3–4)	45 (7)	48 (7)
More dependent on others	40 (7)	38 (6)	40 (3–4)	36 (2)	39 (6)	36 (6)	45 (6)	40 (5)	30 (9)	24 (9)	51 (6)	54 (6)
More responsible	70 (1)	56 (2)	–	–	61 (2)	49 (4)	72 (2)	58 (3)	74 (1)	72 (1)	82 (1)	64 (2)
Less physical strain	52 (4)	51 (3)	35 (5)	35 (3–4)	60 (3)	56 (1–2)	61 (3)	59 (2)	41 (6)	47 (6)	67 (3)	55 (3–4–5)
More interesting	68 (2)	65 (1)	74 (1)	76 (1)	62 (1)	56 (1–2)	78 (1)	68 (1)	59 (4)	60 (3–4)	72 (2)	68 (1)
Cleaner	53 (3)	47 (4)	46 (2)	35 (3–4)	54 (4)	50 (3)	55 (4)	49 (4)	50 (5)	51 (5)	62 (4)	55 (3–4–5)

*) Stimulus question: see Table 9.
a) Weighted average percentage.
b) See Footnote (b), Table 9.
c) See Footnote (c), Table 9.
d) See Footnote (d), Table 9.

Table 11 Perceived Effects to Techological Change: By White Blue-Collar Differences[*)]

Perceived Effects	Total[a)] WC	BC	USA[b)] WC	BC	Germany WC	BC	Sweden WC	BC	Japan WC	BC	Israel[b)] WC	BC
More monotonous	24[c)] (8)[d)]	33 (8)	17 (6–7)	31 (6)	22 (8)	32 (8)	21 (9)	29 (9)	40 (6)	41 (7)	–	–
Lonelier	23 (9)	32 (9)	17 (6–7)	20 (7)	17 (9)	24 (9)	27 (8)	35 (8)	29 (8–9)	34 (8)	35 (8)	55 (7)
More of a psychological burden	45 (6)	45 (5)	–	–	34 (7)	35 (7)	42 (7)	36 (7)	61 (3)	63 (3–4)	56 (5)	58 (5–6)
More difficult	50 (3)	47 (6)	37 (4)	38 (3)	47 (4)	47 (5)	52 (3)	37 (6)	69 (2)	68 (2)	49 (7)	43 (8)
More dependent on others	40 (7)	38 (7)	40 (3)	33 (4–5)	39 (6)	38 (6)	45 (6)	40 (5)	29 (8–9)	31 (9)	51 (6)	58 (5–6)
More responsible	64 (2)	70 (1)	–	–	56 (2)	60 (3)	65 (2)	70 (2)	73 (1)	75 (1)	73 (1)	89 (1)
Less physical strain	48 (4–5)	60 (3)	36 (5)	33 (4–5)	53 (3)	71 (1)	50 (4)	74 (1)	39 (7)	47 (6)	65 (4)	70 (3)
More interesting	69 (1)	63 (2)	80 (1)	62 (1)	64 (1)	51 (4)	77 (1)	72 (3)	57 (4)	63 (3–4)	72 (2)	76 (2)
Cleaner	48 (4–5)	58 (4)	41 (2)	44 (2)	45 (5)	68 (2)	46 (5)	60 (4)	51 (5)	50 (5)	66 (3)	62 (4)

[*)] Stimulus question: see Table 9.
[a)] Weighted average percentage.
[b)] See Footnote (b), Table 9.
[c)] See Footnote (c), Table 9.
[d)] See Footnote (d), Table 9.

unpleasant experiences with the battle for productivity and efficiency at the workplace have been extended to an unfavorable view about economic growth in general. The discussion of the mood among workers in Japan should not obviate the general trend of beneficial outcomes attributed to technological change in all other countries. We now turn to examine if such outcomes are similarly evaluated by different groups within nations.[3)]

The comparison with regard to sex groups indicate that there are only minor overall differences between males and females in the perceived impact of technological change, both in terms of absolute percentages and ranking. Yet, it is perhaps telling that where significant differences do appear, they do not seem to reflect a uniform trend in terms of more or less alienation. Instead, they reveal differentiation in job-related attributes which are closely associated with established patterns of sex roles in the labor market. Thus, men perceive their jobs as having become more responsible (70% vs. 56%), but also more difficult (50% vs. 41%), psychologically stressful (48% vs. 37%), and lonelier (29% vs. 20%).

Perhaps of no lesser importance is the observation that more men than women in all countries indicate that they have experienced effects of technological change – whether positive or negative. This finding, along with the previous one, suggests that technological progress does not attenuate sex differences in the occupational structure; in fact, it may even buttress them, although both men and women seem, on balance, to enjoy its effects in terms of decreased alienation at the workplace.

The comparison between white- and blue-collar workers shows that the generally positive view of the impact of technological change is replicated for both groups, as indicated by the absolute and rank-ordered percentages (Table 11). This trend persists when individual nations are examined, except for Japan where we find once again that respondents, regardless of occupational status, express more negative reactions to technology.

An examination of specific effects, however, reveals some significant differences between white- and blue-collar workers. Perhaps the least surprising finding is that blue-collar workers are more likely to claim that their jobs have become cleaner. Undoubtedly, white-collar jobs had suffered less from pollution in the first place. Equally obvious is the blue-collar workers' feeling that their jobs now involve less physical strain (60% vs. 48%) – probably again a function of the relatively small extent

3) For technical reasons we are unable to present age-group comparisons, and given here are sex and blue-collar – white-collar comparisons only.

of physical exertion involved in white-collar jobs even before recent technological advances.

Blue-collar workers do appear, however, to have paid a price for reduced pollution and decreased physical strain: in all countries they claim in larger proportions that their jobs have become lonelier (32 % vs. 23 %) and more monotonous (33 % vs. 24 %). These findings strike us as confirming the view about the implications of introducing advanced technologies into blue-collar jobs: the stereotype of men and women performing repetitive tasks in the company of machines. Nevertheless, these figures should not obscure the central tendencies of blue-collar workers to testify that their jobs have become more rewarding. In other words, there exists a favorable climate for the introduction of technological changes among white-collar and blue-collar workers alike.

Conclusions

The preceding analysis was aimed at the assessment of certain aspects of economic culture prevailing in post-industrial society. The main issue underlying this analysis has to do with the problem of congruity between the imperatives of industrialism and the economic orientations of the public: to what extent it is valid to maintain that the techno-economic system of industrial society is associated with emerging patterns of human concern and experience which contradict – at least potentially – the functional prerequisites of such a system. This general question was examined here with respect to three different elements of popular economic culture. At the level of economic citizen, we presented data concerning the support given by the public to the pursuit of economic growth. At the level of economic man, the findings pertain, first, to the question of work-goals and commitment and, second, to the subjective appraisal of technological change in terms of alienation.

Although our data represent but a few selected aspects of the complex domain of economic culture, and despite the limited number of nations included, we believe that the results of this analysis permit some meaningful generalizations and conclusions pertinent to the problem of congruity. Let us summarize them briefly:

- It is apparent that the peoples of these nations – with the possible exception of Japan – are characterized by a common pattern of orientation to technology, work, and economic growth. The fact that such a pattern is clearly discernible, regardless of some systematic differences across nations, can be taken as important – albeit limited – evidence for the convergence hypothesis: i.e., Western societies, sharing a similar base of industrial structure, tend to foster similar features of economic culture.

- Substantively, the economic orientations of the public seem to be generally compatible with the credo of industrialism. This tendency is consistently manifested in the widespread support given to economic growth, in the positive evaluations of technological change, and in the centrality of working life for the majority of the labor force. On the basis of such indicators we may conclude, therefore, that the economic culture of post-industrial society is essentially integrated with its techno-economic domain.
- Alongside the central tendency of the public's sentiments we must take notice of a significant minority which appears to be disenchanted with the promises of industrialism at both the level of economic man and that of economic citizen. Thus, while the argument over the cultural contradictions of the post-industrial society has probably been overstated, it is evidently not irrelevant.

However, our data suggest that the expressions of disloyalty to the economy do not necessarily stem from a uniform pattern of human concern. Among blue-collar workers they apparently result from unsatiated material needs and aspirations that the economy of advanced industrialism has promised to fulfill. Among the younger workers, on the other hand, such expressions may indicate an emerging incongruity between the materialistic promises of the post-industrial economy and the post-materialistic orientation of the youth. The observation that this trend is clearer in Germany and Sweden supports the thesis that the combination of advanced affluence and welfare-state predominance may weaken the traditional basis of loyalty toward the economy.

- Considering some of the more salient differences among nations, we comment here only about the case of Japan.[4)] The Japanese public is mostly unsupportive of economic growth and least delighted with the effects of technological change. These findings are consistent with some recent reports about problems of morale and discontent among workers in Japan. Thus, while as noted above, a few years ago the Japanese economic scene was glowingly described, more recently we encounter different popular headings such as "A Paper Tiger?" (*Newsweek* July 1984) and "Cracks in the Japanese Work Ethik" (*Fortune* May 1984). In interpreting these trends we should bear in mind that although Japan holds a prominent place among the small group of post-industrial nations, its socio-cultural heritage sets it apart

4) Germany and Israel, which represent two other instances of notable difference, are discussed in Strümpel and Yuchtman-Yaar (1983).

from the Western members of this group. It is possible, therefore, that the manifestations of malaise in the Japanese public stem from culturally-rooted resistance to the enhanced Westernization of Japan. Such resistance, however, may only reflect a transient phase of readjustment, as Japan converges into the economic culture of the West.

References

Ackerman, W. (1981): Cultural values and social choice of technology, *Int. Soc. Sci. J.*, 23 (3): 447–465.

Archibald, P., Owen, A. and Cartrell, J. (1981): Propertylessness and alienation: Reopening a 'shut' case. In: R.F. Geyer and D. Schweitzer (Eds.), *Alienation: Problems of meaning, theory and method*, London and Boston: Routledge & Kegan Paul.

Armer, M. and Isaac, L. (1978): Behavioral consequences of psychological modernity: Comparative evidence from three societies, Paper Presented at the 9th World Congress of Sociology, Uppsala, Sweden.

Aron, R. (1967a): *Eighteen lectures on industrial society*, London: Weidenfeld & Nicholson.

Aron, R. (1967b): *The industrial society*, London: Weidenfeld & Nicholson.

Bell, D. (1961): *The end of ideology*, New York: Collier.

Bell, D. (1975): *The coming of post-industrial society*, Harmondsworth: Penguin.

Bell, D. (1976): *The cultural contradictions of capitalism*, London: Heinemann.

Bendix, R. (1956): *Work and authority in industry*, Berkeley: University of California Press.

Blauner, R. (1964): *Alienation and freedom: The factory worker and his industry*, Chicago: University of Chicago Press.

Cooley, M. (1980): *Architect or bee?* London: Hand & Brain.

Crosby, F. (1982): *Relative deprivation and working women*, New York: Oxford University Press.

Dahrendorf, R. (1967): *Class and class conflict in industrial society*, London: Routledge & Kegan Paul.

Faunce, W.A. (1968): *Problems of industrial society*, New York: McGraw-Hill.

Freeman, R. and Cain, G. (1974): *Labor market analysis of engineers and technical workers*, Baltimore: Johns Hopkins University Press.

Form, W.H. (1971): The accomodation of rural and urban workers: The industrial discipline and urban living: A four-nation study, *Rural Sociology*, 36: 488–508.

Fortune Magazine, May 1984.

Habermas, J. (1976): *Legitimation crisis*, London: Heinemann.

Inglehart, R. (1975): *The silent revolution*, Princeton, N.J.: Princeton University Press.

Kahn, H. and Wiener, A. (1967): *The year 2000*, New York: MacMillan.

Kerr, C. et al. (1973): *Industrialism and industrial man: The problems of labor and management in economic growth*, Harmondsworth: Penguin.

Lane, D. (1976): *The socialist industrial state*, London: George Allen & Unwin.
Lipset, S.M. (1960): *Political man*, London: Heinemann.
Moore, W.E. (1963): *The impact of industry: Modernization of traditional societies*, Englewood Cliffs, N.J.: Prentice-Hall.
Mottaz, C. (1981): Some determinants of work-alienation, *The Sociological Quarterly*, 22 (4): 515–529.
Newsweek Magazine, July 1984.
Reimanis, G. (1978): Alienation and powerlessness in four cultures, Paper presented at the Ninth World Congress of Sociology, Uppsala, Sweden.
Rothwell, R. and Zegfeld, W. (1979): *Technical change and employment*, London: Frances Pinter.
Schweitzer, D. (1981): Alienation theory and research: Trends, issues and priorities, *Int. Soc. Sci. J.*, 33 (3): 523–556.
Seeman, M. (1959): On the meaning of alienation, *Am. Sociol. Rev.*, 24: 783–91.
Seeman, M. (1972): Alienation and engagement, In: A. Campbell and P.E. Converse (Eds.), *The human meaning of social change*, 467–527, New York: Russell Sage.
Shepard, J.M. and Kim, D.I. (1978): Alienation among factory workers in the U.S. and Korea: A comparative study, Paper presented at the Ninth World Congress of Sociology, Uppsala, Sweden.
Shepard, J.M., Kim, D.I. and Hougland Jr., J.G. (1979): Effects of technology in industrialized and industrializing societies, *Sociology of Work and Occupations*, 6 (4): 457–481.
Strümpel, B. and Yuchtman-Yaar, E. (1983): Germany and Israel: Contrasting cases in popular economic cultures, Paper presented at the Sixth Annual Scientific Meeting of International Society of Political Psychology, July, St. Catherine's College, Oxford University.
Time Magazine, An industrial Nirvana, September 8, 1980.
Touraine, A. (1973): *Production de la société*, Paris: Editions du Seuil.
Weltz, F. and Schmidt, G. (1976): *Introduction of new technologies, employment policies and industrial relations*, London: Anglo-German Foundation.
Yankelovich, D. (1981): *New rules: searching for self-fulfilment in a world turned upside down*, New York: Random House.
Yuchtman-Yaar, E., Moore, D. and Fishelson, G. forthcoming: Deprivation and complacency of working women.

Popular Bases of Conflict and Solidarity – A Review of the Evidence from a Decade Économie Problématique

Burkhard Strümpel

The Problem

Did the economic difficulties of the 1970s and 1980s lead to an aggravation of distributional conflict? A well-known line of argument points in this direction. Daniel Bell (1975) and Lester Thurow (1979) view the declining growth rates in the light of a "revolution of rising expectations" fueled by the historically unprecedented era of post-war expansion. The lower income strata, so the argument goes, had ignored their inferior relative position as long as they enjoyed absolute increments in real income. Before, there had been two avenues toward individual improvement: social mobility, implying an advance in one's own position relative to others in society, and rising general affluence, that is, increasing real incomes per capita in the economy. Whereas social mobility can be experienced only by some, the other avenue for income progress is open to the large majority of the population, including those whose social status remains stable. Their progress depends on the growth of the economy. The 1970s brought income stagnation and deprived the non-mobile worker of the only, and highly cherished, source of participation in material betterment. There is growing discontent.

This view stands in contrast to older but almost forgotten approaches in the Durkheim tradition according to which people tend to react to a crisis or external threat facing the collective through cooperation and solidaristic behavior. It is hard to understand why social researchers have failed to balance their interest in distributional conflict through equally intensive concern for the solidarity theme. A prima facie overview over the past decade problématique of Western industrial societies remains rather inconclusive: on the one hand, democratic governments may have become more shortlived, voters and electoral majorities more volatile, largely due to disappointed economic expectations and unfulfilled promises. On the other hand, ambitious income guarantees and transfer mechanisms generated by the modern welfare state have remained basically intact. This is the first time in history that large-scale economic difficulties do not threaten the physical existence of large segments of the population. Moreover, rates of inflation – often considered the primary economic symptom of distributional conflict – after flaring up during the 1970s, have abated in the first years of the 1980s. In addition, the all but secular increase in unemployment has failed to result in manifest destabilization of public affairs. The last wave of unconventional protest and opposition, the student revolts of the late 1960s, cannot easily be traced to economic origins and happened while the Western economies were still performing in high gear.

These thoughts suggest already that both conflict and solidarity are not mechanistic consequences of some economic condition. Rather, they are the results of an intricate interaction of circumstances and preconditions. It is precisely the failure of the social sciences to deduce the undercurrents of social peace or strife from economic origins that has motivated the author to take up the present topic.

The term "conflict" as used in this paper denotes behavior or attitudes that aim at a change of the rules for the distribution of resources (Yuchtman-Yaar 1976: 542). Examples include the disapproval of unemployment compensation, participation in strikes for higher pay or shorter working hours, or participation in demonstrations against the closing of a plant. "Solidarity" is the other side of the coin: the term describes the inclination to reduce distributional claims and or favor transfers to other groups in the interest of alleviating pressing social problems, e.g., unemployment.

The paper is organized as follows: First, the "objective" material situation and its subjective reflection in the sense of satisfaction or discontent will be at issue. How do people experience their economic situation, how satisfied or dissatisfied are they with their material well-being? Second, attention will be paid to the relative deprivation of different subgroups along occupational status and age lines. Third, we look beyond material resources at the distribution of work quality. The fourth section deals with the potential for unrest by the unemployed and tries to gauge the signs of backlash against the jobless. Fifth and lastly offers a short debate on the preconditions for altruism or solidarity in the context of the employment problem will be offered.

A Revolution of Rising Expectations?

Western industrial societies are on a plateau of historically unprecedented incomes and material assets. In the last 30 years real incomes, measured by the usual statistics, have multiplied. Although high growth rates characteristic for the first two post-war decades have diminished, absolute increments to real average incomes have stayed roughly unchanged, at least in Western Europe (cf. the contribution of M. Bolle and X. Greffe to this volume).

How do people perceive their economic situation? The following presentation will emphasize medium-term changes in conflict/solidarity and its psychological antecedents. Data referring to only one point in time will only be reported if they are available for more than one country. Data collection (especially surveys based on national samples) has become so expensive that longitudinal data even for one country – not to speak of comparative data – are still very rare. This is true in spite of individual or collective efforts (e.g., the bi-annual Eurobarometer surveys sponsored by the European Commission in Brussels, the various National Social Surveys in the US, Britain, and Germany), or individual efforts (such as

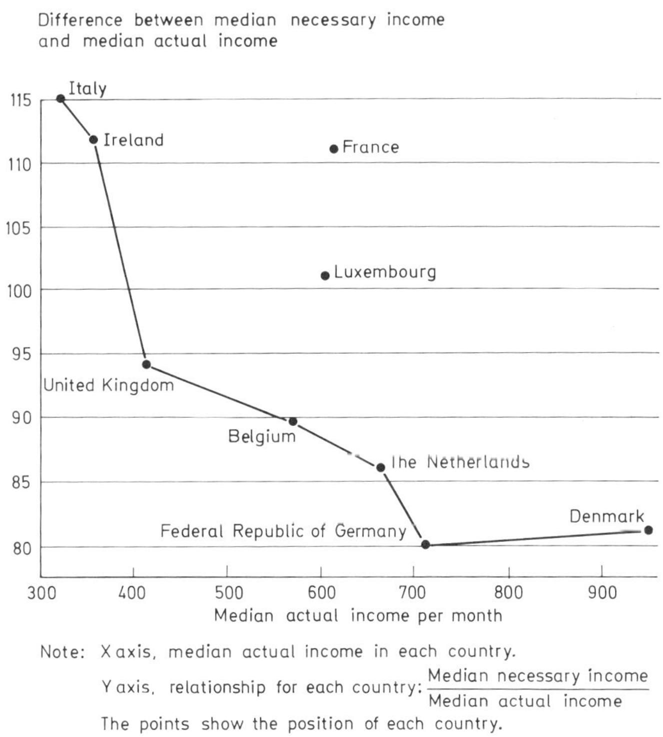

Chart 1 Necessary Income and Actual Income

Source: Eurobarometer, March 1984.

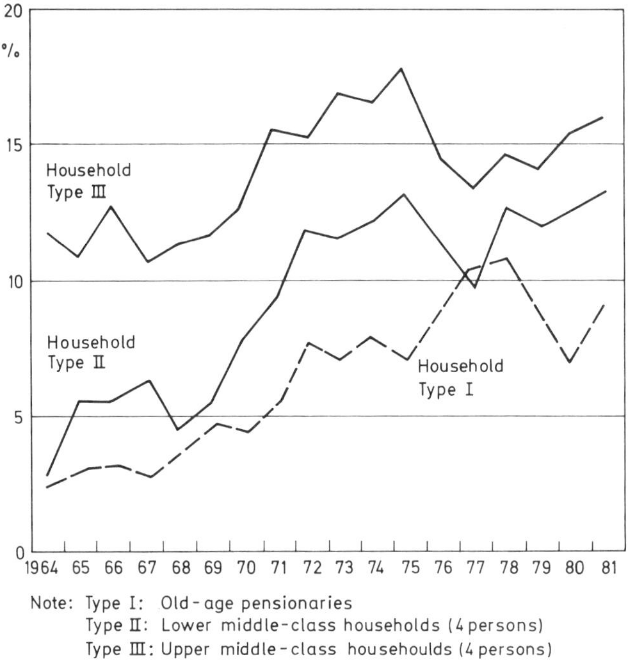

Chart 2 The Rate of Saving of German Households

Source: Statistisches Bundesamt 1980: 8, 1981: 9. Poser 1982.

the project "Jobs in the 80s," coordinated by Yankelovich et al. (1985) or "Aspirations and Affluence" (Katona, Strümpel, and Zahn 1970)). Also, the German Institut für Demoskopie Allensbach has provided a respectable number of time series for monitoring the attitudes of the German population. Unfortunately, few counterparts of these data exist in other countries.

A Eurobarometer publication (1977) compares income aspirations with the real income in the member countries of the EC. Results of the question, "Which level of income is absolutely necessary for meeting your bills and expenses?" are confronted with the household income reported by respondents. Chart 1 exhibits, for the whole of the European community, a remarkable degree of correspondence between average demands and accomplishment. However, there are revealing differences between countries. First, there is a plausible, but by no means trivial, link between affluence and satisfaction. It is in particular West Germany, the largest country in the high real income group, whose citizens seem relatively content with their situation. This finding is in line with a number

Table 1 Satisfaction with Personal Economic Situation: W. Germany, Adults 19 Years or over, in %

Question: "How would you describe your own economic situation? Would you say very good, good, so-so, not too good, poor?"

	All adults										blue-c. workers	
			16–29		30–44		45–59		60 and more		16–29	
	1967	1982	1967	1982	1967	1982	1967	1982	1967	1982	1967	1982
very good/good	39	40	45	43	40	43	39	48	35	41	39	18
so-so	39	39	36	44	44	40	40	36	36	37	36	53
not too good/poor	22	21	19	26	16	17	21	16	21	22	25	29
sum	100	100	100	100	100	100	100	100	100	100	100	100

Source: Institut für Demoskopie Allensbach, Archive.

of time series observations about Germany: high and rising rates of consumer savings, in particular of the lower income strata (Chart 2) and, as suggested by Table 1, a remarkable, persistently favorable evaluation of the own income situation over the last fifteen years. These data, at any rate, do not suggest any sensitivity either to rising real incomes – average incomes in 1982 were higher than in 1967 – or to declining rates of income growth, as characteristic for 1982 compared to 1967. We do, however, observe a larger proportion of young people under 30 complaining about their unsatisfactory situation.

Pockets of Relative Deprivation

Times of economic adversity, at least in modern history, have always stimulated the debate on equality as a maxim of social justice. Is inequality a luxury society can afford only in times of growth, and can maintain in times of stagnation only at its own peril? We are no doubt witnessing an erosion of traditional notions favoring status and reward differention:

1) The norm of equality is increasingly being accepted – albeit not implemented – in some life domains: health care, public safety and protection by the law, universal suffrage, and educational opportunity.

2) It is increasingly recognized that everybody, regardless of input, is entitled to income that ensures a "decent" minimum standard of living.
3) There is more intense social comparison between subgroups of society sensitizing participants in the distributional game.

Although these trends will remain far short of effecting or legitimizing radical redistribution in the near future, there is some evidence that moving toward more equality might meet with popular acceptance. Yuchtman-Yaar (1983) reports a significant negative correlation between income and the sense both of entitlement and of relative deprivation. However, the dynamics of aspirations differ among subcultures within a society.

In the United States professionals have been shown to be more "saturable," that is, they tended to reduce the margin of material aspirations with rising income, in contrast to executives and people in business, who tended to retain high margins of unfulfilled aspirations even in the face of relatively high incomes (Strümpel 1976). This difference seems to be due to a specific value structure of professionals with college degrees who are more frequently oriented toward non-material goals such as self-actualization and satisfying work than are other subgroups with about equal average income whose values and priorities are more strongly linked to monetary income.

These findings remind us that receiving less income than "significant others" in most cases leads to dissatisfaction and a sense of deprivation only to the extent that it is considered inequitable, that is, illegitimate. The standards applied for judging the fairness or equitability of a situation, while tainted by self-interest, express in part a social consensus about the rules of remuneration and their application. Sometimes, particularly during times of war or national emergency, austerity and even sacrifice is accepted as necessary or inevitable. The sense of equity then can be seen as a symptom of social integration as manifested in the distribution of products and resources. If very many people disagree with the rules applied or feel that the rules agreed upon fail to be implemented, the orderly give and take that links individuals in any social system, is jeopardized.

In a setting of intensified social comparison, inequality matters. France may be the one larger nation in the EC that enjoys relatively high levels of prosperity and average income without having reached a degree of income equalization characteristic for other relatively prosperous countries. In France the proportion of the population below the poverty line is higher than in the other larger Western European countries, with the possible exception of Italy (Table 2), and the sense of deprivation is particularly pronounced (Chart 1).

Turning from comparative conjectures about inter-country differences

Table 2 A Relation of "Appreciative Systems" of Different Populations to Social and Economic Conditions

	Average annual growth in private consumption expenditure (%) 1965–1976	Gini-coeffic. of incomes inequality	Incomes maintenance expenditure as per cent of GDP	"Egalitarian," per cent of population	Per cent of population viewing society as "unfair"	Per cent of population below poverty line
	1	2	3	4	5	6
Germany	3.3	0.386(7.1)	12.4	30	10	3
France	4.0	0.417(10.9)	12.4	49	26	16
Netherlands	3.6	0.264(6.6)	14.1	36	13	n.a.
United Kingdom	1.6	0.327(6.1)	7.7	18	17	7.5

1. OECD, *National Accounts*, 1976. The figures refer to per capita private final consumption expenditure.
2. Table 11, M. Sawyer, "Income Distribution in OECD Countries", *OECD Economic Outlook*, Paris, July 1976. The figures refer to post-tax incomes, adjusted for family size. (The figures in brackets refe to the ratio of the unadjusted post-tax income of the top 20 per cent to that of the bottom 20 per cent of the income distribution.)
3. Table 1, *Public Expenditure on Income Maintenance Programmes*, OECD, July 1976. The figures refer to the early seventies.
4. Appendix Table 1, *Euro-Barometre* No. 5, July 1976. The figures refer to the proportion of people who consider it "very important to try to reduce the number of both very rich and very poor people".
5. Table, 18, *Ibid.*
6. Table 29, *Public Expenditure on Income Maintenance Programmes,* op. cit.

Source: Klein 1981: 170.

to comparisons between time points in Germany, Table 3 exhibits a reading of people's sense of equity with regard to their income and asset position for two years, 1969 and 1979. Again, a remarkable stability, even improvement, of the popular sentiment vis-à-vis the prevailing economic conditions emerges. However, there are clearly evolving pockets of relative deprivation: younger workers, primarily from the blue-collar segment, express themselves again more critically. The data from Sweden – a country characterized by high egalitarian distribution of income – fails to exhibit similar differences.

Table 3 Sense of Equity: all adults

Question: "On the whole, do you believe income and assets in the Federal Republic are distributed equitably or not equitably?"

	Unskilled blue-collar workers '69	'79	Skilled blue-collar workers '69	'79	Lower level white-c. workers '69	'79	Upper level white-c. '69	'79	Selfempl. '69	'79	Farmers '69	'79	Total '69	'79
equitably	38 %	42 %	43 %	47 %	48 %	50 %	61 %	56 %	45 %	62 %	43 %	50 %	44 %	50 %
not equitably	42	43	44	40	38	38	25	28	34	20	45	36	40	37
undecided	20	12	13	12	13	11	13	16	21	16	13	14	15	12
n =	156	199	184	271	166	371	47	100	62	101	47	44	657	1086

	Blue-collar workers						White-collar workers					
	16–29 years '69	'79	30–44 years '69	'79	45 and older years '69	'79	16–29 years '69	'79	30–44 years '69	'79	45 and older years '69	'79
equitably	46 %	40 %	44 %	50 %	30 %	46 %	46 %	42 %	48 %	55 %	61 %	60 %
not equitably	37	50	40	34	54	36	43	44	34	32	28	28
undecided	17	8	16	2	16	1	11	12	18	12	10	11
n =	132	193	97	148	102	129	83	166	62	191	67	109

Source: Institut für Demoskopie Allensbach.

Chart 3 Germany, 1958–1982: Satisfaction with Work, with Income, with Life Generally

Source: Yankelovich et al. (1985).

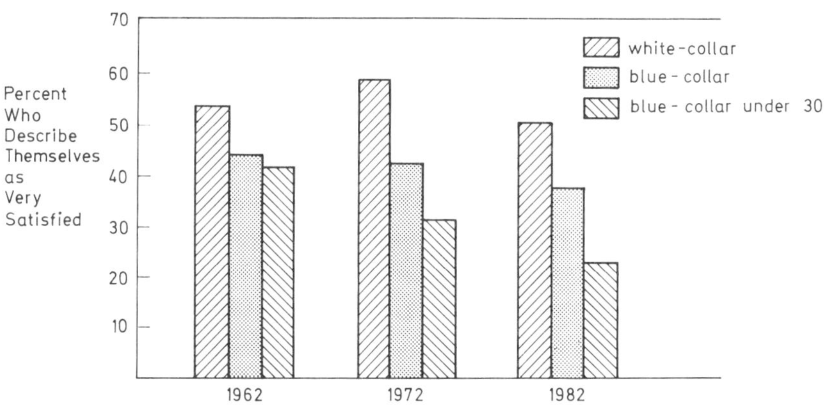

Chart 4 Job Satisfaction in West Germany

Source: Institut für Demoskopie, Archive.

The signs of discontent among younger workers must be seen in the context of situational changes. In the 60s and early 70s the welfare states of Western Europe were relatively kind to their older citizens. Retirement incomes increased more than net wages or salaries. In contrast, younger people have been hit hard by rising unemployment. Unemployment is merely the tip of the iceberg. While middle-aged workers tend to be relatively well settled in their jobs and careers, it is the job entrants who are the main victims of hiring stops or attrition of advancement within the organization. Also, mobility between jobs is jeopardized. Many workers are stuck with unsatisfactory jobs. Chart 3 confronts the severely declining job satisfaction of German workers over the last 20 years with rising levels of satisfaction with income, and Chart 4 locates this decline again primarily in the young blue-collar segment. In the next section I shall try to explore further this disquieting rift between part of the younger generation and the rest of society.

The Non-Monetary Arena for Distributional Conflict

How shall we explain the massive decline in job satisfaction? Should it be true that money and material well-being have become less important criteria according to which people judge their position in the economy, then we have to look for other criteria that may have gained in importance. According to the late British economist Fred Hirsch (1976), rising real incomes have resulted in a certain saturation with mass consumption goods. However, the dynamics of growth aggravate the competition for "positional goods," that unlike mass produced consumption goods cannot be reproduced with diminishing marginal costs, such as jobs commanding high social status, rare works of art, apartments in the West End. And Ronald Inglehart (1977) has pointed to the emergence among the younger generation of "post-materialist" aspirations for environmental protection, citizens' involvement in deciding about their own affairs, and "self-actualization" partly replacing the dominant concerns of older people for values oriented toward achieving and securing command over material resources. The affluence characteristic for the period when the younger generation grew up brought to the fore higher-order needs, whereas the material deprivation that prevailed during the formative years of today's older people left lasting marks on their value structure, despite changed material circumstances (Inglehart 1977; Hondrich in this volume).

Within less than a decade occupational preferences in particular have changed greatly. Whereas in the middle of the 1960s a qualified majority of Germans and a strong simple majority of Americans rated economic security as the most important characteristic of a good job, in 1972–1973 the item "important work, feeling of accomplishment" had gained ground significantly (Katona and Strümpel 1978). Moreover, the traditional virtues of courtesy and subordination, diligence, modesty, and even respect for the employer's private property seem to have lost authority in both countries, particularly among younger people. The number of those who accept "hard work" as desirable and who

Table 4 Commitment to Work: Workers, 18 years and over

Question: "Here are two persons talking about their job.
A says: I am fully committed to my work and often do more than I am required to do. My job is so important to me that I sacrifice a lot for it.
B says: In my job I do what I am asked to do: nobody can complain about me. But I don't see the point of extra exertion. After all, my job is not that important to me.
Which of the two says what you also tend to think, A or B?"

in %	W. Germany 1967		W. Germany 1982	USA 1983			Sweden 1982			Great Britain 1982		
A	54		41	68			56			66		
B	33		41	24			36			30		
Age 1982/3	−29	30–54	55–	−29	30–54	55–	−29	30–54	55–	−29	30–54	55–
A	32	44	58	61	70	73	45	58	55	57	69	74
B	50	39	27	30	22	18	45	33	38	39	28	19
Occupation 1982/3	White-c. worker		Blue-c. worker	White-c. worker		Blue-c. worker	White-c. worker		Blue-c. worker	White-c. worker		Blue-c. worker
A	47		34	72		61	64		43	80		54
B	34		53	20		29	24		51	17		41

Source: Comparative Study "Jobs in the 80s and 90s"; table generated by the author.

subordinate pleasure to duty has diminished. The secular trend indicated by Inglehart appears to hold true even when monitoring changes between relatively short time intervals (Noelle-Neumann 1978, Yankelovich et al. 1985).

Table 4 presents results from the cross-national survey "Jobs in the 80s". The traditional work ethic, encompassing the commitment to sacrifice if need be, seems to have remained stronger in the Anglo-Saxon countries than in West Germany and Sweden – countries characterized by both high affluence and strong welfare states. In all four countries it is the young that defect from traditional values in droves.

Later time series data for Germany suggest a shift in workers' demands towards their jobs away from money to "intrinsic" satisfaction. "High income" seems to have become less important, "interesting, responsible work" and job security appear to have gained in importance. Again, this

Table 5 Demands Towards Work: Workers, 18 years and over, W. Germany 1973–1983

Question: "Several attributes of work are listed here. Please select those you regard to be very important."

Most important demands	Unskilled blue-collar workers		Skilled blue-collar workers		Lower level white-collar		Upper level white-collar		All workers	
in %	1973	1983	1973	1983	1973	1983	1973	1983	1973	1983
High income	69	47	74	55	63	47	57	53	67	50
Interesting/ responsible work	58	67	73	76	78	81	76	89	71	79
Job security	78	83	77	85	77	85	77	75	77	84

Source: Allensbacher Archiv, IfD-Survey 1042, 3072, 4020 / Pawlowsky and Peter (1984).

trend turns out to be particularly pronounced for blue-collar workers (Table 5).

When asked to choose one of the two avenues for improving living standards – wage increases or reduced working time – the majority of workers in the member countries of the European communities (51 %) preferred shorter work hours over higher wages (42 %); in Germany the respective figures were 55 % and 35 % (Eurobarometer 1978). The desire for shorter work hours appears to be particularly strong in countries enjoying a relatively high real income per capita (see Chart 5).

Are the changing demands met by the world of work? The evidence, again confined to West Germany, suggests otherwise. Table 6 summarizes the comparisons between the outcomes of two assessments by German workers of their work in 1964 and 1983, respectively. Complaints about working conditions, physical and psychic, have significantly increased.

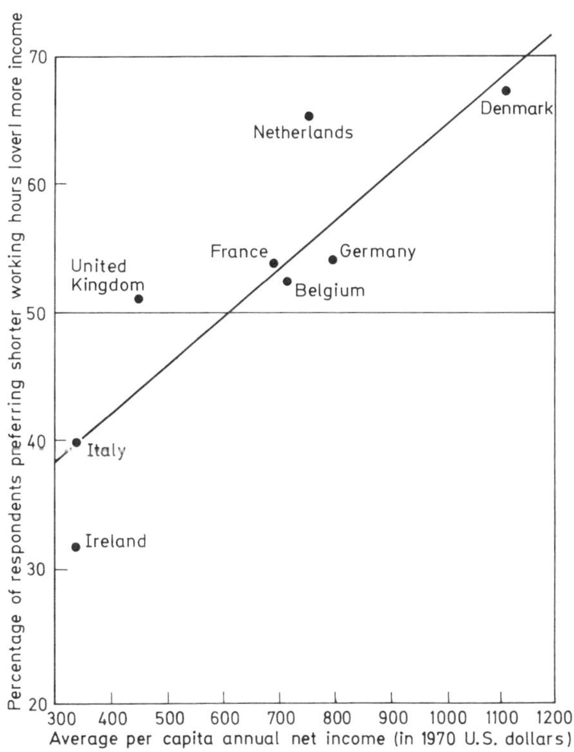

Chart 5 Preference for Shorter Working Hours at Constant Rates of Pay

Source: Eurobarometer (1978).

Table 6 Criticism on Attributes of Own Job (Index): W. Germany, Workers, 18 years and over

Strain Factors	Unskilled blue-collar workers		Skilled blue-collar workers		Lower level white-collar workers		Upper level white-collar workers		Selfempl.	
	1964	1983	1964	1983	1964	1983	1964	1983	1964	1983
Sum of complaints (added percentages)										
1. Physical strain	85	116	74	96	36	52	14	29	49	79
2. Psychic strain	38	47	40	39	41	59	61	67	56	65
3. Work content	71	97	55	67	49	61	40	38	35	38

1. Index: "Too much standing, running around"; "Physically exerting"; "Inconvenient, cramped body posture" (3 Items).
2. Index: "To much work, too much hurry"; "Nervewrecking, mentally exerting, physically straining" (2 Items).
3. Index: "No variety, always the same"; "Too much responsibility ..."; "No chances for promotion" (3 Items).

Source: Pawlowsky and Peter (1984).

Table 7 Discretion on Job: West Germany, Workers, 18 years and over

Question: "Most gainfully employed people can influence some of the conditions involved in their work, while in other matters they are dependent on others and factors beyond their control. Do you think you could describe your own situation with the help of the scale below?" (Scale ranging from O = "no freedom" to 10 = "completely free").

	Unskilled blue-collar workers		Skilled blue-collar workers		Lower level white-collar workers		Upper level white-collar workers		All Workers		
	'73	'82b	'73	'82b	'73	'82b	'73	'82b	'73	'82a	'82b
Low discretion (0–3)	36%	51%	21%	29%	16%	26%	8%	5%	20%	32%	25%
Med. discretion (4–6)	35%	32%	33%	44%	39%	39%	9%	21%	31%	32%	34%
High discretion (7–10)	28%	15%	45%	26%	45%	34%	83%	73%	49%	36%	40%
Don't know	1%	2%	1%	1%	–	1%	–	1%	–	–	1%
	100	100	100	100	100	100	100	100	100	100	100
n =	281	158	254	232	387	389	122	141	1183	1166	1022

Source: Allensbacher Archiv, IfD-surveys 2096, 2223, 4oll ('82a = May 1982; '82b = July 1982).

The increase is particularly conspicuous for lower occupational strata, in particular blue-collar workers. German workers increasingly experience their work as dependent on circumstances outside of their control. The sense of discretion has decreased, particularly for the bulk of the working population (Table 7).

To summarize: there is indeed – to be sure, scattered – evidence that the arena for distributional conflict has shifted from material to non-material resources. In the more prosperous industrial economies a new cleavage seems to have emerged, centering more on the quality of employment than on money. It would be inaccurate to describe these changes as saturation. However, there seems to be a growing mismatch between the output of the economic system and people's aspirations, values, and preferences. There is a lack of feedback between people and both the market and the polity. What the industrial system has to offer in abundance – cars, refrigerators, air travel to the crowded Spanish coastline – has become less attractive, and what would be attractive – an education offering social and economic mobility; a vacation in an unspoiled environment; a job that provides decent pay and a measure of self-determination, meaning, and flexibility – is harder to come by than in the past. This perspective of reality – to which could be added Ralf Dahrendorf's vision of the work society running out of jobs – indicates a need for institutional adaptation rather than GNP growth in order to align popular demands and system output. Yet tradeoffs between material and non-material goal attainment, such as between work, income, consumption, and leisure; between income and quality of employment; between material comfort and resource-saving consumer behavior are largely constrained, often by the well-known roadblocks of oligopolistic interests or sheer administrative inertia.

Attribution and Ressentiment

Our analysis failed to reveal an aggravation of conflict around money. On the other hand, there emerges a considerable ferment of discontent and deprivation in unfamiliar areas of conflict: employment opportunities, quality of work, and working time are at stake. The last big wave of strikes in Germany evolved around the issue of working time. Moreover, unemployment is the focal point. Age differences widen into generational gaps. The old guard jealously defends its privileges against a new generation of workers whose aspirations have been nourished by a secularized zeitgeist, who are being confronted with an unfavorable labor market, and who often must accept second or third choice jobs or careers, interspersed with episodes of joblessness.

Is unemployment a hotbed for social unrest? And those on the other side of the fence who are fully employed, often over-employed: do they mobilize empathy or ressentiment? What are they willing to do or to give up to alleviate unemployment or the plight of the unemployed? Or do they feel threatened by the additional strain millions of unemployed exert on the welfare state and its financial viability? Is there a backlash of the haves against the have-nots?

Available evidence from several countries agrees on one point: the unemployed hold still. According to an ambitious analysis of a large representative cross-section of American unemployed, the latter, to be sure, are less content with their situation than those with jobs. However, there is hardly any intensification of political participation or cynicism against the rules governing the distribution of rewards in society. Quite to the contrary, those who are out of work consistently participate less than their working counterparts in politics, regardless of whether the measure of participation is political interest, voting, or other political activity. However, this lower level of participation appeared to be the result of the social characteristics of the unemployed – their selective recruitment from social groups that are ordinarily not active – rather than of the experience of unemployment per se. With one exception, the authors found no evidence that the experience of joblessness is accompanied by a withdrawal from political or organizational life. That single exception bears mention: the unemployed seem to withdraw from union activity (Schlozman and Verba 1979: 359f.).

The main results of Schlozman and Verba's study are confirmed through analyses from other countries (Daniel 1981, Delauny 1983, Galland and Louis 1981, Hentschel 1979). In sum, political and societal orientations seem relatively impermeable to the effects of personal experience. The political attitudes of unemployed appear to be determined by their lasting characteristics: employment status, political socialization, etc., rather than by their employment situation.

There is then little prospect that the unemployed, through a politicization of discontent, will activate the society into remedial action. But what is the position of the employed majority on the continuum between solidarity and backlash?

There are two hypotheses. The first is that "altruistic" social policies are a function of economic prosperity, and that the middle classes of poor societies will opt against such policies; the second is that support for solidaristic social policies may increase, as the experience of risk in the économie problématique becomes more generalized: income maintenance then becomes the vested interest of a majority. According to Klein (1981: 170),

> Britain is unique not only in terms of the punitive attitude towards the poor but also for the fact that, in the period 1965 to 1976, private consumption expenditure grew at less than half the rate recorded in both Germany and the Netherlands [see above Table 2; B.S.]. Over the past fifteen years, support for altruistic Welfare State policies – such as increased spending on social security benefits – tended to be highest among those voters who felt that they had done well for themselves and were optimistic about their future economic prospects. In contrast, those worse off and not hopeful about the future also tended to be less generous: for example, they tended to attach less importance to policies designed to reduce the level of unemployment. Poor economic performance may thus create a "vicious" circle, in which economic and social policies conflict with each other instead of sustaining each other.

Conversely, the German experience seems to be consistent with the second hypothesis. Chart 6 summarizes the changing attitude of the

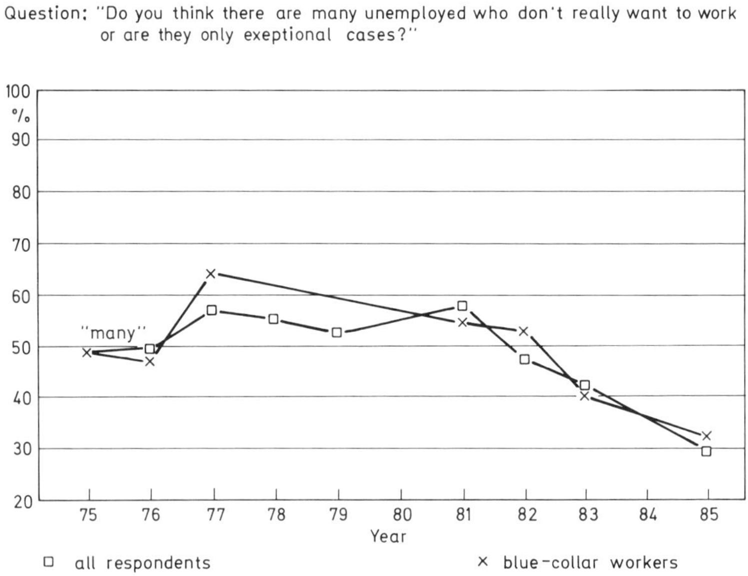

Chart 6 Unemployment and Attribution in Germany

Source: Institut für Demoskopie Allensbach.

German population toward the unemployed, as expressed through answers to the question: Are there many welfare chiselers among the unemployed? In 1975 when the time series begins, every second respondent expresses a critical attitude. Just recently had unemployment hit the one-million-mark. The increase in the proportion of "hard-liners" towards the end of the 1970s reflects the difficulties many Germans encountered in accepting the fact of persistent high rates of unemployment. But 1982 brought a turning point. The number of unemployed rose to about two million. The threat of becoming a victim grew real. At present, there is at least one member in every third German family who is unemployed or looks back on unemployment experience.

While the groups with higher socioeconomic status express less "backlash" and a more stable attitude, the overall oscillations are dominated by blue-collar workers (Chart 6). This segment is torn between two motives. First, they are overrepresented among the real or potential victims, liable to the risk of becoming unemployed themselves. Second, they are most intensively engaged in social comparisons with the unemployed. They are working hard, and they know it. As long as they believed they had secure jobs, they tended to be particularly suspicious of

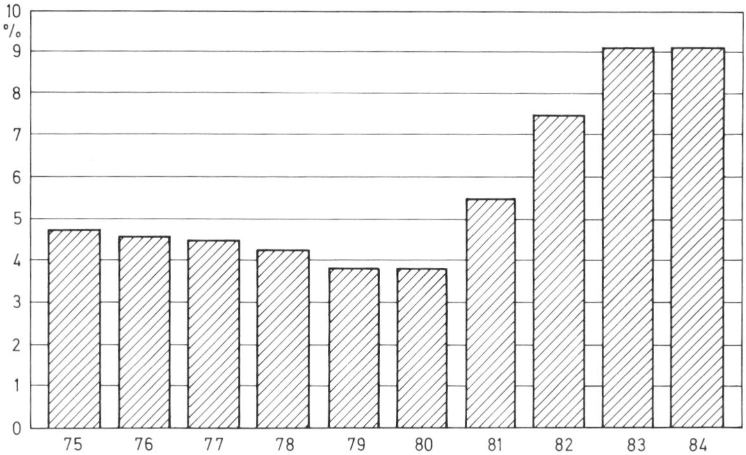

Chart 7 Rate of Unemployment in Germany

Source: Statistisches Bundesamt.

others who do not work regularly. Tolerance is a commodity in limited supply, precisely because, as the data discussed in the previous sections suggest, work is still largely perceived as drudgery rather than as a privilege.

How to Mobilize Solidarity?

The analysis up to this point has raised as many questions as it answered. Social science has not established a firm ground on which to build clear and conclusive predictions of the consequences of economic trends for social conflict. Yet some conclusions can be drawn from the data. There is less conflict potential in richer countries, particularly those having arrived at a more egalitarian income distribution. Second, the soil for discontent and protest is most fertile among younger workers with lower occupational status: it is here where the impact of recent economic trends is added to a quantum jump in aspirations which in turn is generated by the secularization of socialization experiences in times of affluence. Industrial societies have little familiarity or routine in dealing with demands that cannot be satisfied through the transfer of material resources. It took decades until Luddite-type violence against new machines by craftsmen fearing for their jobs had been replaced by collective bargaining. The evidence clearly points to a new prominence of non-material aspirations centering on a measure of autonomy and self-realization on the job, time flexibility, and, of course, labor force participation for those whose employment chances have been hurt most in recent years. Here is a potential hotbed of discontent; yet we are unable to tell if, when, in what way, and to what extent these new forms of discontent will become virulent so that they become a threat for the dominant economy and society.

Up to now, my perspective has been: how did the performance deficit of the economy affect social cohesion? I will now turn the sequence around: how can grass-root solidarity be mobilized to improve the seemingly intractable disease of our times, namely unemployment? There is a growing recognition that unemployment cannot be reduced to tolerable levels through aggregate strategies such as fiscal and monetary policies, e. g., stimulating investment and growth or deficit spending for large scale public employment programs. Then there are those strategies that Bolle and Greffe in their paper for this volume describe cavalierly as "social management of unemployment": the redistribution of work. Both sides in the debate persistently appeal to the public to be ready for sacrifices by consenting to "wage discipline" and to adapt flexibly to changing circumstances. On the one hand, wage discipline is demanded in order to allow for productive investment, while renouncing job security is demanded to increase employers' flexibility and room for maneuver. On the other hand, solidaric contributions of working time and income are required.

What are the chances for a large-scale popular act of solidarity with the unemployed? Lest this question sounds utopian, some historical episodes of solidarity may be recalled. The advent of the welfare state, an extended system of claims for income maintenance may be mentioned as well as the period of wage restraints of European workers in the two decades of reconstruction after World War II. Time and again, people and groups have contributed to a set of common goals extending beyond their individual calculus of utility maximization. Evidence for "sociotropic" civic behavior and opinion formation directed toward a perceived collective good, even at the expense of "pocketbook considerations" is ubiquitous (Hirschman 1982, Kinder 1982). We had better turn without further ado to the task of specifying the conditions under which certain forms of solidaristic behavior are generated, rather than take issue with those economists who try to explain collective behavior purely from the vantage point of the utility-maximizing individual (Frey 1977, Olson 1965). Again, I have to resort to German time series to demonstrate a positive predisposition toward wage discipline and restraint in the distributional arena by a large majority of the population in a more

Table 8 Wage Discipline in West Germany: Workers, 18 years and over

Question: "In the opinion of economists, business and the unemployment situation will improve only if workers this year settle for modest wage increase. Here are several views of this point. Which one would you agree with?"

	Unskilled blue-collar workers		Skilled blue-collar workers		Lower level white-collar workers		Upper level white-collar workers		Self-Empl.		Farmers		All workers	
	'75	'83	'75	'83	'75	'83	'75	'83	'75	'83	'75	'83	'75	'83
1	11%	14%	10%	15%	12%	30%	15%	37%	29%	54%	32%	34%	14%	28%
2	66	60	70	67	74	58	78	50	63	44	56	61	69	58
3	19	20	18	17	11	7	4	13	5	4	4	–	13	11
4	0	6	1	2	2	3	1	1	–	–	1	5	1	3
n =	270	69	285	139	374	220	117	84	111	48	82	19	1239	579

1. It would be allright if (year of survey) there would be no increase in wages and salaries.
2. I would favour increasing wages and salaries to compensate for rising prices.
3. I feel wages and salaries ought to be increased more than the rate of inflation.
4. none of the above.

Source: Institut für Demoskopie, Allensbach

affluent Western country. According to Table 8, Germans are basically inclined to tolerate stagnant real incomes. Only a small minority insists on real income increases, i.e., on a distribution of the annual productivity gains. Another minority that is willing to accept nominal stagnation, i.e., real income loss, has doubled in size from the middle of the 1970s to 1983.

There is no need to overinterpret the meaning of these popular declarations. At the most, the results point to a very general predisposition whose realization is contingent on many ifs and buts. Extensive narrative as well as standardized interviews with a cross-section of German respondents permit us to specify some of the hurdles many Germans perceive as blocking the realization of their generalized willingness to contribute their fair share to fighting unemployment. These are the obstacles:

- Doubts about the correspondence between people's sacrifice and employment creation. In particular, the market mechanism is not sufficiently trusted in its capacity to bring about the desired end. People are not sure that business will create jobs rather than just supplement its profits through the wages foregone.
- Dissenting views about side effects of employment creation. For

instance, many German respondents associate a stimulation of economic growth with negative consequences for the environment.

- Concern over the distributional consequences of wage discipline. Will others, in a similar position, contribute adequately? Do the unemployed deserve the sacrifices? Will third parties – business or the government bureaucracy – benefit from undeserved windfalls?

These thoughts have been extracted from extensive verbalized statements of German respondents from all walks of life (von Klipstein 1984). They suggest that a generalized spirit of solidarity leads a vulnerable existence. In order to come to full blossom in the reality of the économie problématique, this spirit has to be carefully nurtured in a congenial social environment. Prevailing notions of equity, the popular beliefs on how the economy functions, and dominant values and visions on the direction society ought to take have to be accommodated.

Quite consciously the entire discussion in this paper has embraced a naive model of policy making. It assumes a direct link between public opinion and policy. But the way in which individual wants or values are translated into collective decisions is obviously complex. The papers by Scharpf and Schmidt in this volume, therefore, consider the institutional structures that help to shape policy outcomes. The emphasis there switches from values to interests: from the balance of views to the balance of organized power in our societies (Klein 1981: 171).

References

Bell, D. (1975): The revolution of rising entitlements, *Fortune:* April: 98–103, 185, 187.

Daniel, W. W. (1981): Why is high unemployment still somehow acceptable? *New Society*, March.

Delaunay, Q. (1983): *Aspects économiques et sociaux du chômage*, Centre d'Études d'Emploi, Dossier de Recherche No. 7, Paris.

Eurobarometer (1977 and 1978): various issues

Frey, B. S. (1977): *Moderne politische Ökonomie*, München/Zürich.

Galland, O. and Louis, M.-V. (1981): Chômage et action collective, *Sociologie du travail*, 2.

Gehrmann, F. (Ed.) (1984): *Von der Anspruchs- zur Verzichtsgesellschaft?* Frankfurt/New York.

Hentschel, U. (1979): *Politische Einstellungen und Interessenorientierungen von Arbeitslosen*, ISO-Bericht, Köln.

Hirsch, F. (1976): *Social limits to growth*, Cambridge.

Hirschman, A. (1974): Exit, voice, and loalty.

Hirschman, A. (1982): Shifting involvements: private interest and public action, Princeton, N.J.

Inglehart, R. (1977): *The silent revolution*, Princeton.

Institut für Demoskopie Allensbach.
Katona, G. and Strümpel, B. (1978): *A new economic era*, New York.
Katona, G., Strümpel, B. and Zahn, E. (1970): *Aspirations and affluence: Comparative studies in the United States and Western Europe*, New York.
Kinder, D.R. (1982): *The political process and economic change*, New York.
Klein, R. (1981): Values, power and policies, in: OECD (Ed.), *The welfare state in crisis,* Paris.
Klipstein, M. v. (1984): Akzeptanzbedingungen einkommenssolidarischer Beschäftigungspolitik, in: Gehrmann, F. (Ed.): *Von der Anspruchs- zur Verzichtsgesellschaft?* Frankfurt/New York.
Klipstein, M. v. and Strümpel, B. (1984): *Der Überdruß am Überfluß – Die Deutschen nach dem Wirtschaftswunder*, München.
Noelle-Neumann, E. (1978): *Werden wir alle Proletarier?* Zürich.
OECD (Ed.) (1981): *The welfare state in crisis*, Paris.
Olson, M. (1965): *The logic of collective action.* Cambridge.
Pawlowsky, P. and Peter, M. (1984): The distribution of work quality in Germany – Contribution to the 1984 IAREP Annual in Conference in Tilburg, unpublished.
Poser, G. (1982): *Macro-economic implications of curtailment and life-style change*, San Francisco.
Schlozman, K.L. and Verba, S. (1979): *Injury to insult*, Cambridge, Mass., and London.
Statistisches Bundesamt (1980): *Budget Panel of Statistisches Bundesamt.*
Statistisches Bundesamt (1981): *Budget Panel of Statistisches Bundesamt.*
Strümpel, B. (Ed.) (1976): *Economic means for human needs: Social indicators of well-being and discontent*, Ann Arbor, Michigan.
Strümpel, B. (1983): Social Policy Evaluation and the Psychology of Stagnation, in: Spiro, R., Yuchtman-Yaar, E. (Eds.): *Evaluating the welfare state: social and political perspectives*, New York.
Thurow, L.C. (1980): *The zero-sum-society, distribution for economic change*, New York.
Yankelovich, D., Zetterberg, H., Strümpel, B., Shanks, M. (1985): *The world at work*, New York.
Yuchtman-Yaar, E. (1976): Effects of social psychological factors on subjective economic welfare, in: Strümpel, B. (Ed.): *Economic means for human needs: Social indicators of well-being and discontent*, Ann Arbor, Michigan, pp. 107–129.
Yuchtman-Yaar, E. (1983): Social welfare and entitlements, in: Spiro, R. and Yuchtman-Yaar, E. (Ed.): *Evaluating the welfare state: Social and political perspectives*, New York.

Time Use and Information Technology: Recent and Future Developments of Private Households

Ian Miles[*)]

Social Change and Ways of Life: An Analytic Approach

Chart 1 sets out a schematic model of relations between the formal and domestic economies. Households contribute labour and expenditure to the formal economy, from which they receive income, and goods and services. (For simplicity, we ignore exchanges between goods and services within the formal economy and are not representing money directly in the illustration[2]). Households' time is contributed to formal employment (or self-employment), to informal household work, and to consumption activities (mainly leisure and personal care).

Households consume final services, which may be purchased from the formal economy's private service industries, or delivered as social services from the formal economy's public service sectors. Or they may be produced using consumer goods in the household economy – although the person doing the servicing may not always be the person doing the consuming. There is not complete substitutability between the formal and informal modes of service provision, and their characteristics differ in important ways, but the trend toward self-servicing seems to vitiate much of the analysis of "post-industrial society" based on the hypothesis of a shift of consumer demand toward services[3]). There is change in the sorts of activities carried out in households, in the priorities for expenditure

---

*) The author works at the Science Policy Research Unit, University of Sussex.
The programme of work of the TASC group (Technology and Social Change) at SPRU (the Science Policy Research Unit) is described in Gershuny and Miles (1975). These authors were funded by the Joseph Rowntree Memorial Trust, to whom I would like to express my gratitude. My debt to my colleague Jay Gershuny will be obvious to readers. Costs of time budget data production and support for some analyses and validation work were forthcoming from the Economic and Social Research Council. To them, too, and to the co-workers who were thus funded (especially Graham Thomas and Sally Wyatt, whose contributions to this paper are also evident), further thanks are due.

2) Among the factors important in the growth of the service economy have been the rise of public services and the increasing importance of producer services.

3) Gershuny (1983), Gershuny and Miles (1983), Miles (1985a).

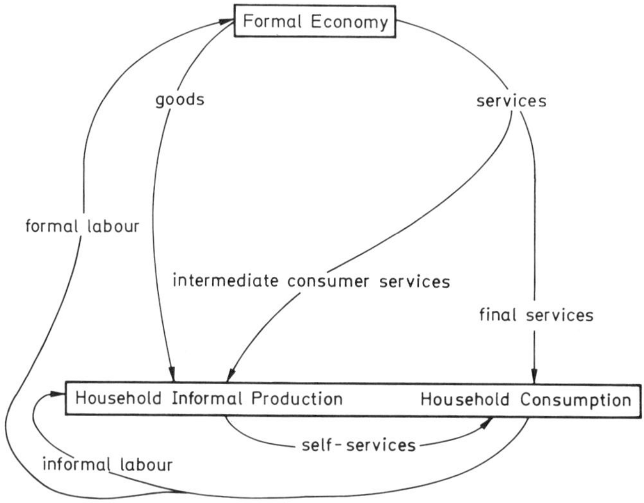

Note: money flows (income, expenditure) have been omitted from this diagram to avoid overloading it.

Chart 1 Relations Between the Formal and Household Economies

and time use: but this is more complicated than a simple evolution of demand toward "immaterial services". All household activities involve services, and most involve goods, too; whether these services are the ones supplied by the "service economy", or are household self-services, is a matter for empirical analysis.

The model highlights key relationships, whose evolution has significance for time use. First consider the time spent in consumption. Consumption requirements, other things being constant, can be expected to be related to household composition and demography – to such factors as the number of members of the household, their ages, their health status. Of course, other things are never constant; consumption requirements are liable to vary over time with changes in individual and collective values, aspiration levels and social comparisons, and the like. And the time available for consumption – which may play an important role in the changes in leisure/consumption activities that are often ascribed to "value change" – is determined by the commitments of each individual to engage in formal and informal work, as well as by biological and social requirements for sleep and other forms of personal care[4].

[4] Categories such as "personal care", "outdoor active leisure" and the like are based on standard time budget classifications; see Table 2 for the eight broad categories used in our studies.

The time of household members is also allocated to formal labour. (This is mainly time spent in employment and self-employment, exchanged for income. time spent in formal education, and in dealing with benefits authorities is also typically classed as formal work. Some income is distributed via welfare benefits and "rents" on capital.) The time allocated to formal work determines the time one has available for informal work and consumption; the income which is received determines funds available for household expenditure. Developments in the formal economy structure the working hours that are contributed, and the demand for different types of labour. Trends in working hours, unemployment, and the sexual division of formal labour are important factors. Income flows from the formal economy enable families and individuals to achieve particular standards in their housing environment and ownership of domestic equipment. The housing environment shapes the ease and quality of services that may be produced and consumed there: the number and size of rooms affects the scope for privacy or study at home, and different forms of housing tenure allow for varying amounts of do-it-yourself (DIY) activities.

Goods acquired by households are typically purchased from the formal economy (although there are some payments in kind and transfers across households), and include perishables, semi-durables, and durables. The household also acquires two types of services from the formal economy; it is not always easy to distinguish these in practice. Some are final services, they more or less directly enter into consumption, and are typically concerned with servicing human bodies and minds (e.g., catering, health, education, entertainment). Other service transfers from the formal economy, in contrast, enter into informal production. These "intermediate consumer services" include repairs of housing and private automobiles[5]. They are in practice often "mixed services" supplying inputs both to consumers and producers (e.g., garages, telecommunications). Devel-

[5] The distinction between intermediate and final services depends on that between formal services and self-services. Given that many formal services demand some input of informal labour (the "self-service cafe" is of course a case in point) and some home-based activities that substitute for formal services demand very little (e.g., turning on audio or video equipment), how is this to be done? The main issue would seem to be whether the activity is performed mainly with equipment or at a site that is owned or rented by the consumer/client. This would make TV broadcasting an intermediate service, then, although similar stage performances would be final services, and furthermore, more informal work is liable to be involved in getting to the theatre in the latter instance. However, this criterion should not be used too rigidly – what about home visits from a doctor or telephone consulting? In reality, the formal service vs. self-service dichotomy is shorthand for a complex of shifts among modes of provision differing in terms of site, equipment, property relations, and paid and unpaid labour inputs.

opments in organisation and technology in the formal economy affect not only employment, but also the relative productivity and costs of various goods and services. Trends in these factors are of interest, not least because a relative increase in the cost of services is one major factor leading households to undertake more "self-servicing".

Time is allocated, finally, to informal labour, mainly carried out to provide services for oneself or other household/family members. (Some labour goes into the informal production of goods with which self-services may later be produced. Some informal labour, furthermore, is voluntary or community work.) The household's allocation of informal labour to tasks is typically structured within the sexual division of informal labour and by household members' employment commitments.

We have presented a framework for identifying the interrelationships between different components of time use and developments in the formal economy. It directs our attention to a number of distinct developments: household characteristics and associated consumption requirements, together with the structures of individual responsibility for meeting these household requirements, the demand for particular sorts of work and entitlements to income from the formal economy, trends in the relative price and quality of goods and services, and developments in household circumstances and access to equipment. The next section of this paper describes major social changes (and continuities) relevant to these points, focusing on Britain in recent decades. Some pointers to international comparisons are indicated, but there is hardly space here to provide an adequate appraisal for a single country! We shall then consider how far the implications for time use are borne out by our time budget data; and, finally, consider broader implications for the social economy more generally, especially given the reorganisation of social life that is likely to be associated with new information technology.

Documenting Social Trends

Demographic Trends and Household Characteristics

Like other Western industrialised nations, Britain has displayed an ageing of its population, associated with the movement of the large birth cohort of the years after the first World War into retirement age, and a decline in fertility rates over the last few decades. Between 1961 and 1980 the number of Britons aged 65 or over grew from 6.2 million to 8.2 million, while the whole population grew only from c. 53 million to c. 56 million. In common with Denmark and Germany, the UK now has over 20% of its population aged 60 or more (and all EEC members are at 15% or more) (*Social Trends* 1984, 1986; Unless otherwise stated, statistics cited in this section derive from the most recent edition of *Social Trends*.)

Associated with this ageing process is a change in household composition. Average household size has been decreasing, from 3.1 per household in 1961 to 2.6 in 1984, for Great Britain. A major factor in this has been the growing number of single retired people living alone, reflecting not only population ageing but also a decreased tendency for parents and adult offspring to live together. The decrease in household size is also due to the falling birth rate, and the increased prevalence of divorce and single parenthood. Official projections suggest that smaller households will continue to constitute a growing share of British society.

What are the implications of these developments for the organisation of time use? A growth in the elderly population implies more need for social and health services relevant to these groups, whether supplied via formal public services, semi-formal voluntary organisations, or more informal patterns of neighbourhood or family care. The growing number of elderly people living alone makes family care less common, presumably increasing demand on other modes of service provision while freeing otherwise committed informal work time from (mainly women) family carers.

However, the elderly population is characterised by relatively low incomes; large numbers of older people live in officially defined poverty. This means that on the one hand there is less ability to purchase services, on the other that household equipment and housing circumstances tend to be below the national average. (A growing proportion of the population in such circumstances needs to be borne in mind in discussing general trends.)

Elderly peoples' consumption patterns may additionally be affected by the impact of reduced personal mobility on their activities. For example, while only around 10% of all adults have (or would have) physical difficulty using buses, almost 25% of those aged 75 or over are completely unable to use buses for this reason (*Social Trends* 1986: 150). Improvements in bus design to make access easier for elderly people have been introduced in a few areas, but the shift toward conductorless driver-only buses is widely reported to have made the use of public transport more difficult for all handicapped groups, and for those bearing large loads or young children. Of course, not all old people are infirm; even though the most rapid growth is in the population aged 75 and over, severe health problems are not the rule. In principle, there is considerable scope for these population groups to engage in voluntary work (for example, in supporting the less fortunate members of their cohorts).

The reduced number of children per household, associated with a lower fertility rate, also implies less informal labour in the household. However, against this general trend must be set the growth of single parent households: here there are again problems of poverty, and the lack of back-up for the parent (usually a woman) may make it more difficult to obtain formal employment. (School and childcare hours do not readily fit working hours, and there is no one to look after an ill child.) Though more grandparents may survive (and thus be available to help out), they may also be geographically distant or themselves working.

While the overall requirements for informal work per household may decline as a result of there being fewer family members and perhaps smaller living units, there may be losses of "economies of scale" here. We have seen some development of household technology to take account of the smaller household size, but the implications for time use are uncertain. The reduction in "economies of scale" may also apply to some purchased services, where bulk orders and the like are either ruled out or rendered more infrequent.

What of changes in household requirements associated with more sociological factors? Expenditure data for a number of Western European countries indicate that household expenditure has generally followed the "Engel's law"-like trend with a general decline in the proportions of expenditure devoted to food and shelter. Domestic functions showed a mixed pattern across countries; entertainment and transport expenditure grew absolutely and proportionally (Gershuny and Miles 1983). While official statistics tend to subsume activities like health and education as government expenditure, evidence is that private household expenditure related to these activities has also expanded. There thus seems to be an evolution of final demand toward more complex "luxury" activities.

Despite the current economic crisis, with its severe impacts upon many poorer social groups, living standards have continued to increase for the average UK household. This suggests a continuing shift in the consumption requirements of households towards more "sophisticated" luxury activities.

As well as a shift in demand across broad activity categories, there may have been evolution within these categories, also in the direction of increased "sophistication". Market researchers have suggested that meal preparation has become more like as hobby, with gourmet meals becoming a DIY activity. And improved household equipment has been associated with rising standards of domestic cleanliness – promoted in part by advertisers and manufacturers as well as by hygienists. It is difficult to generalise across all items of domestic equipment, but the demands for the technical quality of audio and video reproduction, of motor cars, and of various durables and semi-durables have increased, which affects their labour requirements as well as the service characteristics yielded. The allocation of time to an activity is thus decidedly not a simple function of the expenditure it receives: we cannot infer that time use patterns will directly follow demand shifts as reflected in household expenditure patterns, we need to take into account changes in household technology.

The Sexual Division of Domestic Responsibilities

Research concern with this topic – indeed, with housework in general – is a fairly recent development. Few time series data on beliefs and practices are available for the UK. The growth of the women's movement over the past fifteen years, with its questioning of received gender roles and promotion of new role models, has been a stimulus to research. It is also likely to have affected the field, undermining traditional attitudes to domestic responsibilities. In addition, attitudes are liable to be challenged by the growing female participation in the formal economy – which has no doubt fuelled the women's movement in turn.

However, recent surveys show that traditional gender stereotypes retain considerable influence in the UK. One study finds that 87% of married women and 75% of married men report that the female spouse is mainly responsible for care of the home and children. There is generally more disposition to say that an egalitarian distribution of housework "should" be the rule than there is of reports that it "is"; married people tend to be less egalitarian than others. Majorities' opinion that equality should prevail applies to household shopping, cleaning after the evening meal, and organising household money. Women are more often given responsibility for preparation of the evening meal, household cleaning, and, especially, washing and ironing clothes. The repair of household equipment is, however, most often seen as a job that men should do (Witherspoon 1985). Thus even if there has been a decrease in inequality (which would be anticipated on the grounds noted above), we can expect women still to put in the overwhelming majority of informal work on routine domestic tasks.

The Demand for Labour from the Formal Economy

General changes in the structure of employment are well documented. First are shifts in the occupational and industrial structure of the labour force, corresponding to the growth of the service sectors and the "tertiarisation" of industries in general. There seems to have been on the whole a marked upgrading of the types of job carried out, with increasing proportions of the workforce involved in professional and administrative work. These tends are broadly similar across a large number of Western countries (cf. Miles 1985b, for a review of the literature).

Second is the increased female participation in the labour force, again a common trend, and in large part related to the growth of service-type occupations, which have predominantly absorbed female labour. There has also been considerable growth of part-time employment for women in particular, reflecting laxer regulations on employment conditions for such work, the need to attract women with childcare responsibilities into employment, and firm strategies toward having "flexible workforces".

Third, there has typically been some reduction of working hours and increase in holiday entitlements for full-time workers. Fourth, there is some increase in shift working, and numerous initiatives around flexitime and similar innovations in managing formal working hours: while important for those concerned, these developments are probably not yet marked in statistical terms. Finally, the last decade has witnessed a major increase in unemployment, especially among young people, those ethnic minorities who contributed to the "peripheral", most flexible parts of the labour market, and ex-employees of declining industrial sectors ("deindustrialisation").

These five trends are common to most Western countries, though they have unfolded with somewhat different pace and timing. What are their implications for time use? Adult women are liable to be spending more time in formal work, adult men less (due to reduced working hours as well as to unemployment). This change in the volume of time available for informal work might constitute a pressure toward the equalisation of domestic work – perhaps, given the distribution of responsibilities noted earlier, by an overall reduction in domestic labour time rather than by more housework by men. Such a reduction might be achieved by lowering requirements (lowered standards, later and less childbearing, disengagement from responsibilities to care for the extended family), by improved domestic technology, or by the hiring in of domestic services.

Corresponding both to the peculiar demands of childcare, and the heavy attribution of responsibility for this to women, female labour force participation is very closely related to women's age and parental status (Table 1).

The relative inequality in wages and occupational attainment between men and women reflects the disruption of many women's careers by childcare responsibilities. Attitudes concerning the quality of male and female labour, conditioned by the expectations that this occasions, significantly restrict the training and promotion opportunities provided to women.

White (1986) reports that over the period 1971–1981 in the UK, however, there was a proportional shift of both men and women in

Table 1 Women's Economic Activity by Own Age and by Age of Youngest Child, Great Britain, 1980.

Economic Activity	Age of Youngest Child (none)	0–4	5–10	11–15	16+
Working full-time	78%	7%	16%	31%	32%
Working part-time	6	20	48	45	34
"Inactive"	7	69	32	19	29
	Women's Age (selected groups) 16–19	25–19	35–39	45–49	55–59
Working full-time	73%	31%	30%	35%	25%
Working part-time	1	18	37	38	28
"Inactive"	12	46	29	22	42

Note: full-time students excluded, and proportions unemployed not displayed: "inactive" thus largely "housewives".

Source: Martin and Roberts 1983, Tables 2.3, 2.5.

employment into occupations classified as falling into socioeconomic groups 1 and 2, though men continued to dominate. The proportion of working men in these groups rose from 23.1 % to 29.3 %, of women from 17.4% to 21.2%.

Several studies support the idea that the nature of one's work in the formal economy can have influence upon one's cognitive functioning, political attitudes, and leisure interests (e.g., Kohn and Schooler 1978). It would seem plausible to expect the documented changes in formal working life – even if occupational titles are imperfect indicators – to be reflected in value change. Market research oriented studies do claim to identify shifts away from "sustenance-driven" values to "inner-directed" ones in Wetern nations (MacNulty 1985; for a more academic presentation of similar ideas, see Inglehart 1977)[6]. This might lead to more differentiated life-styles, and more active leisure pursuits.

Finally, the growth of unemployment is often interpreted as freeing time for informal work and leisure. But many other commentators point out that the concept of "leisure" acquires its full meaning only when set against formal employment; and large proportions of unemployed people

[6] Value changes of these sorts may be related to other social trends, however, such as increased affluence (Ingleheart) or education levels, or even to mass media exposure.

do regard their daily lives as consisting of barren time rather than leisure. (Nevertheless their activities will be classified in time budgets and surveys of activity as leisure) (Miles 1983).

Be that as it may, it is tautologically evident that more time is available for production and consumption activities for unemployed people than their employed peers. There is evidence that this is associated with some growth of the "underground economy" – though on nothing like the scale alleged in some mass media and political bodies. The lack of expansion of the underground economy is not only due to the regulation of the activities of unemployed people by welfare officials. Employed people tend to be better equipped in marketable skills, and in access to markets and tools, than unemployed people. The lower-than-average occupational background of unemployed people and the loss of income associated with joblessness also mean that they are disadvantaged in terms of household equipment and disposable income. Thus purchase of goods and services is less available as an option, and unemployed people are likely to need to put in more domestic work to achieve the same outputs as others.

Furthermore, feelings of depression, low self-esteem, and reduced internal control/competence are common responses to job loss and prolonged unemployment (Jahoda 1982, Kelvin and Jarret 1985, Warr 1983). These would seem likely to lead to – and be reinforced by? – decreases in active pursuits and increases in passive leisure. (In other words, the converse of those suggested by theories of evolutionary value change.) Predictions as to time use are complicated, however, by the question as to whether these are absolute or relative increases and decreases, the influence of other family members, the availability of social facilities, and the possibility of qualitative variations within the time use categories. (E.g., reading newspapers and having conversations may be part of a search for jobs, a distraction from personal concerns, a way of informing oneself about current events... our diaries simply record the passage of time.)

Overall the consequences of unemployment – relatively marginal to the population averages, despite unemployment levels being well in excess of 10% of the working age population in several countries – seem likely to be: reduced time spent in expensive activities, more time spent in low-cost passive leisure activities (TV, radio), and more time spent in domestic work and in self-servicing, where there are apportunities for doing so which do not themselves require sophisticated equipment or high levels of expenditure.

Goods and Services

Many household requirements can be met in a variety of ways – for example, through the use of goods or the purchase of final services from the formal economy. The cost and quality of goods and services will bear on household choices. Trends in the prices of goods and services are easier to document than those in their quality. Over the years 1962–1983 the prices of services in Britain tended to increase, those of household durables to decrease, compared to the general cost of living index. Interestingly, official statistics indicate that the prices of very "basic" items – food, housing, fuel, and light – have grown rapidly (two of the three more so than most service prices); but the cost of household durables has decreased by about one third relative to other items (Thomas and Miles 1985). Shifts in the relative prices of goods and services thus seem to encourage household self-service provision. (This may be disguised in expenditure statistics since the price changes would give an increasing expenditure on services even if demand for goods and services moved in parallel.)

Comparisons can be made within activity categories. The 1986 edition of *Social Trends* contains statistics, for example, of the amount of paid work required in order to pay for various commodities[7]. The time-cost of petrol stayed relatively constant over the period 1971–1983; that of a motor car licence declined by almost a third; and that of a typical rail journey increased by over 25 %. The time-cost of a TV licence declined by around 25 % (radio services are now free of charge); that of an LP record by over 50 %; while that of cinema tickets rose by over 15 %.

In general, price comparisons suggest a favouring of goods as opposed to services (for example, over most of the period 1961–1984 the price of food has increased more slowly than that of meals bought and consumed outside the home (*Social Trends* 1986: 95)); similar developments seem to apply in other Western countries. (In addition, it is possible to identify some significant trends within services – for example, a decrease in telecommunications costs as opposed to conventional mail.)

What do these trends signify? A major factor would seem to be relatively slower growth of labour (and capital) productivity in most service industries (telecommunications may be an exception) than in manufacturing. Such a divergence in productivity has been used by conventional economists to account for the growth of the service economy, as an alternative to post-industrial theorists' invocation of a shift of consumer demand toward services. (For a review of these debates

[7] The data refers to the situation of a married man receiving the average male wage, with two children under 11, and a non-earning wife.

see Miles 1985b.) Post-industrial theory focused on demand shifts, while economists argued that the income elasticities of demand for goods and services were actually similar. The picture is more complicated. Gershuny and Miles (1983) documented a shift in expenditure by activities, as noted above; but *within* several activity categories – especially the "luxuries" – they document a shift from services to goods. In part, this shift must be a result of the relative cheapening of goods as opposed to services, in particular where they contribute to competing modes of provision of similar household requirements.

This implies an increase in the amount of time involved in self-service provision (e.g., driving cars, operating domestic equipment) and a decrease in time spent interacting with formal service providers (e.g., time travelling on public transport, liaising with personal and domestic services, etc.).

Statistics concerning the use of competing modes of provision other than time budget data themselves are not readily available in many cases. An exception is transport, where we can note that over the period 1961–1984 in the UK, while the number of passenger kilometres travelled by rail, buses, and coaches declined from 106 billion to 77 billion, those involved with private motor vehicles grew from 142 billion to 417 billion (*Social Trends* 1986: 187). Declines can be traced in the use and in the number of cinemas and theatres, laundries and launderettes, and even in pubs – while home entertainment and self-servicing equipment has diffused widely, as we shall see.

In addition to price, other features of the services and goods should also be taken into account. Appropriate relevant data are scattered. We need to discuss a number of points: the impacts of self-servicing on final service industries; the relative convenience and "personalisation" of different modes of service provision; and technological change in domestic equipment. We shall consider the latter in more detail in the next section.

The polemics about the desirability of economic growth that were influential in the early 1970s drew attention to the first of these points as one of the costs of growth. It was pointed out that increases in private affluence overall, for example, such that more private individuals possess motor cars, are liable to erode the demand for equivalent public services: so, in this instance, the provision of regular bus services may become uneconomic (without subsidy). To the extent that marketed services are curtailed due to a reduction in demand, a vicious circle is liable to be established, leading to further erosion of the service base. Urban design may actively contribute to this, by spacing out dwellings in such a way as to optimise car access while rendering traditional bus routing quite impractical. Other aspects of urban change are also significant: in the case of cinemas, theatres, and other public facilities, a decline in custom may be self-reinforcing owing to its contribution to growing fears of crime and environmental degradation. In the latter cases, television has become an almost universal alternative to what time budgets record as "away from home leisure"; in the case of transport and some other services, substantial groups remain who, because of poverty, age, infirmity, or other reasons, are forced to remain reliant on services that will deteriorate if left under the sole control of market forces.

Thus far, quality issues would seem to compound the shifts in time use projected from the discussion of price trends. It can also be argued that the shift from services to goods is liable to be enhanced by certain historical trends in the process and product of service and goods industries. Household equipment has not only proliferated, it has often become easier to use, and may free the owner from the demands of rigid timetables. In contrast, services have traditionally been produced and consumed in more or less the same moment, at the same place. The consumer or client has to adapt to the timing and convenience of the service provider, rather than set their own pace. Thus public transport usually adheres to fixed timetables, and like broadcasting, restaurants, shops, and banks tends to operate not at all or only at a minimal level through much of the night and on public holidays.

Efforts have been made by many service industries to limit the costs of their services - whether to stem the shift to self-servicing or to gain a competitive advantage over other firms in the same area. But the innovations that have been introduced here are typically mass production/mass consumption ones, and entail some reduction in service diversity. In some cases, this may increase consumer convenience (and thus lead to increased use of a service outlet – without, it should be noted, a necessary increase in time use around that service).

One example here is the concentration of shopping facilities in supermarkets and hypermarkets, with associated innovations in self-service shopping. These have proved popular facilities; the self-servicing that is involved takes place in public facilities rather than at home (and will not be distinguished in time budgets from other forms of "shopping"); however, the result would seem to be that the pattern of shopping changes, with the major (often car-based) expedition to the supermarket replacing a variety of shopping trips; perhaps increasing overall travel time while decreasing the total time spent in shopping-related activities. Another example of reduction in diversity, at least in the sense that the service product becomes standardised (although the range of items on the "menu" may increase) is the proliferation of chains of fast-food outlets; large numbers of consumers seem to value the predictable quality of these products.

The standardisation of a service may mean a reduction in diversity valued by some clients and consumers. We have noted that the shift to driver-only buses makes their use by various disadvantaged groups more difficult: the reduction of personal service in the person of the conductor, who can help one on and off buses, arrange for longer-than-normal stops, and provide information, saves costs, but limits service quality. Such trends in service innovation should promote more service use to the extent that they save on informal work time by decreasing unpredictability, and to the extent that they facilitate consumer choice; but they should decrease use to the extent that they fail to cater to the needs of substantial minorities.

A further set of changes involves the time-structuring of services. Over the post-war period, for example, there have been significant increases in the hours during which TV and radio broadcasts are available (and in the number of channels and presentational quality of broadcasts – e.g., colour TV, stereo radio), and some relaxation of regulations and informal agreements restricting the opening hours of pubs, shops, banks, etc. These developments have time implications for workers in the service industries, but they also mean more flexibility for service consumers. Where an activity like shopping is involved, there is presumably scope for change in the domestic division of labour: full-time employees become freer to carry out household shopping outside their working hours. Liberalised activities are liable to gain relative to those which are unchanged. However, we have little basis for identifying how far, for example, "temporal liberalisation" of different classes of leisure activity – pubs versus TV, for example – are liable to interact.

It is, in general, difficult to judge from published statistics how far each of the various quality trends has taken place across the broad range of services, and what their differential impacts are across population groups (some of whom may value the personal service traditions of small shops, pubs, etc.). In both cases, the specificities of particular services would need to be considered (e.g., monopolistic vs. competitive organisation of the service sectors; the role of public services and non-market forms of formal service provision; the role of infrastructure like urban form, roads, and telecommunications in changing accessibility to services; and demand for final service functions as a product of income differentials sind economic activities of different households). The general consequence of such changes, broadly, may have been some overall improvement in service quality for the more "luxury" activities. But is this enough to offset price trends where there is a choice between final service and self-service provision? There may well have been an overall decline in many services contributing to basic welfare (food, transport, housing) for poorer groups; these latter areas are ones where self-service provision requires more skill or costly investment than does entertainment.

These considerations again suggest a shift from final service consumption to time spent in self-service modes of provision. However, to assess this we also need to consider developments in domestic environments that affect the scope and efficiency of such provision.

Household Circumstances and Domestic Equipment

These have shifted considerably over the post-war period. There has been an increase in owner-occupation, from around 50% in the 1960s and early '70s to around 60% by 1983 in the UK, and a decline in local authority housing and cheap rented accomodation (Thomas and Miles 1985). While a steady increase in housing prices has made it more difficult for young families to acquire their own homes, the overall trend would support increases in work carried out on private accomodation – whether self-service of via purchased construction/decoration services. (Anecdotal evidence suggests that much of this work is carried out in the "underground economy".) On the one hand owner-occupation frees the tenant from restrictions imposed by landlords; on the other the increase in house prices (and the availability of subsidies from local authorities) has meant that the cost of improvements can usually be recouped on sale. We would thus anticipate an increase in DIY and related activities.

The complexity of some familiar improvement activities, such as central heating installation and the removal of structural walls to make large room areas, may work against this trend. But there has been considerable effort made to simplify the use of wallpaper, paint, plaster, glues, etc. for private use. (This may also help reduce the masculine mystique of these activities, such that we might expect greater female participation in them.) DIY shops have certainly proliferated in the UK over the last few decades: the DIY superstore is a feature of the outskirts of most medium sized towns and cities. This is a example of synergy among self-services; access to – and more importantly, transport of bulky materials from – these superstores requires private motor transport (or at least a driving licence so that one can hire transport on-site).

As for household equipment, the post-war economic boom was largely built upon the rapid diffusion of new mass consumer goods, items of domestic technology like motor cars, "white goods", and "brown goods". Ownership of such durables continued to increase over the more recent years of recession, with new goods such as video recorders, home computers, and microwave ovens rapidly diffusing. By the mid-80s, majorities of British households possessed such items as: refrigerators, freezers, washing machines, telephones, central heating, televisions, and motor cars (still owned by only around 60% of households). This continuing diffusion of equipment should be associated with a shift to modes of service provision associated with these items.

The full scale of this shift is unlikely to be visible in time use data, if technological improvements in household equipment over the decades do mean more efficiency in domestic work. But some informal work time may grow as a precondition for other activities' efficiency. (For example, more time may be spent in driving to the shops in order to make shopping itself easier; or to gain access to hypermarkets, or equipment to make DIY feasible.) And some public facilities used in self-servicing – e. g., the roads used by private cars – may become less efficient when there are higher volumes of use. In general, however, we expect less increase in the overall quantity of informal labour than would be expected from the growth of self-services.

As for leisure and consumption activities, the picture is even more complicated. The changed quality of the final service functions is liable to result in considerable change in consumption practices and thus in time use. TV does not deliver identical services to the theatre or cinema; it has new types of programme, and, given the minimal labour required to turn on the set it is much more prone to be used as a background or to be used on whim. This suggests that the growth of particular categories of consumption around new household technologies (and intermediate services) can be much more extensive than would have been projected around the traditional technologies. Ways of life are reshaped around greater physical mobility ready availability of mass entertainment, and increased convenience of final service activities. (Self-services are timed at one's own discretion; and the advent of cheap information storage devices like the video recorder makes time-shifting available.) We would anticipate a shift within leisure activities to those that have become more accessible in these ways; but this will be modified by changes in values and free time (making time-intensive pursuits like "outdoor leisure" more viable).

Trends in Time Use

Introduction

Time use data, coded into an enlarged form of the Szalai framework, are available for Britain back to the 1930s: but the first survey which provides a reasonably large sample for comparative purposes dates from the early 1960s. The most recent survey to which we have access is for 1983–1984[8]. Analyses of the most recent data are still in a relatively preliminary state, but already a number of conclusions bearing on the preceding sections' discussion are available[9]. Let us briefly recapitulate the main conclusions of this discussion – while reminding ourselves that the complexity of the various interacting factor means relatively few tendencies were not liable to be qualified by countertendencies.

The amount of time spent in formal work would be expected to decline on the average, although working hours for women in general should increase. Time spent in interacting with service agencies in the formal economy should decline relative to time spent in self-service provision, again with certain exceptions – especially elderly people. However, where self-service provision has always been a major component of final service provision, changes in domestic equipment may be expected to have reduced the overall volume of time occupied in the relevant tasks. We anticipate some relaxation of the traditional sexual division of domestic labour, perhaps involving reductions in housework time as much as men's sharing of the load. Time spent in leisure pursuits should have increased, but we can expect substantial changes within various categories of leisure activity.

Table 2 displays data over the period 1961–1984 on the overall pattern of time use – for an "average day" for people aged 15 or over (excluding those in full-time education)[10]. It displays a reduction in the overall time

---

[8] Gershuny, Jones, and Mullins (1985), Thomas, Wyatt, and Miles (1985) are the two main reports on the new survey to date; for a more accessible account, see Gershuny et al. (1986).

[9] Various caveats need to be entered about the data presented, though the results do not seem to be substantially distorted because of them. The recent data only concerns the autumn/winter season; there was a sample bias toward women (which has been compensated for where necessary); there was a low response rate but with the exception of the female bias the sample appears to be very representative.

[10] The comparison is for people not in full-time education aged 15 and over; the time period involved is 6.30 am to midnight in the earier surveys. For 1983/4 the equivalent amount of "personal care" has been deducted – deflating time spent in this activity and increasing that on others (especially home leisure and perhaps some domestic work). See Thomas, Wyatt, and Miles (1985) for further points relevant to the detailed interpretation of the data.

Table 2 Trends in Overall Time Use, 1961–1983/4, Britain

	1961	1974/5	1983/4	
Paid work	263	245	209	x
	66	72	58	%
	399	339	354	*
Domestic work	208	183	217	x
	95	97	98	%
	220	190	231	*
Personal care	268	268	247	x
	100	100	100	%
Civic activity	9	6	8	x
	26	22	19	%
	34	28	42	*
Outdoor leisure	24	33	45	x
	54	77	84	%
	44	44	53	*
Out of home indoor-leisure	43	74	51	x
	68	90	74	%
	63	82	68	*
Passive leisure	149	143	155	x
	98	97	98	%
	152	146	157	*
Other home leisure	86	98	119	x
	94	97	97	%
	92	101	122	*

x Minutes per average day (excluding midnight to 6 am)
% Participation rate (people aged 15+, excluding full-time students)
* Partipants' minutes per day

Source: Thomas et al. (1985).

spent in paid work by about an hour a day; a decrease followed by an increase in domestic work; a small decrease followed by a small increase in passive leisure; an increase and then decrease in "out-of-home indoor leisure"; and quite substantial increases in "other home leisure" and "outdoor leisure".

Such trends in aggregate time use do have implications for the take-up of goods and services from the formal economy. But an analysis of different population groups is required if we are to distinguish between the effects of the various socioeconomic trends discussed arlier. Chart 2 displays trends in the major categories of time use for major social groups. Over the period there is a substantial increase in their leisure time. This has much to do with decreases in formal work time. Informal work time, however, has not shown a consistent trend: in particular, men's informal work seems to have increased. Let us consider the various trends in a little more detail.

Formal and Informal Work

Conventional time budget diaries, for a variety of reasons, give inadequate information on the distribution of activities within formal employment, and (due in part to difficulties with work travel and breaks) tend to give higher estimates of time spent in paid work than do official sources (cf. Gershuny, Jones, and Mullins 1985). But it is clear from the comparisons of similar time budget instruments over time that the general trend does hold up: overall paid work in the population has been decreasing fairly regularly over the period. This is due both to a decline in the overall level of economic participation and to lower average working hours, but in our data neither component has a consistent trend (s. Table 2). In fact, employed men's working time has decreased, but women's has increased (Chart 2) – along with the female participation rate.

Men's informal working time, however, does seem to have increased, especially in the more recent period. This appears to apply to men with quite different economic locations, and is not simply a reflection of increased unemployment and retirement. Certainly unemployed men do more domestic work than others. (In terms of time, this is around three times as much on weekdays. But the efficiency of this work, given poverty-level domestic technology, is another matter; the wives of unemployed men appear to do less housework than those of employed men, but the total housework time in the former type of family is greater.) Employed men do display a clearcut trend in respect of domestic work over time.

Thus – although considerable inequality persists – there does seem to have been some decline in the rigid domestic division of labour by sex, associated initially with a reduction in women's workload and more recently by an increase in men's. The exception seems to be for employed men with non-working wives, who have not increased their share of domestic work. (Less than 20 %; as compared to 28 % for the employed husbands of part-time employed women – up from 22 % in 1975 – and 40 % for those of full-time employed women, up from 33 %.).

Women still do overwhelmingly more domestic work than men. What economies of scale there are in "living together" are typically distributed in favour of male partners. Wyatt (1988) compared "partnered" and

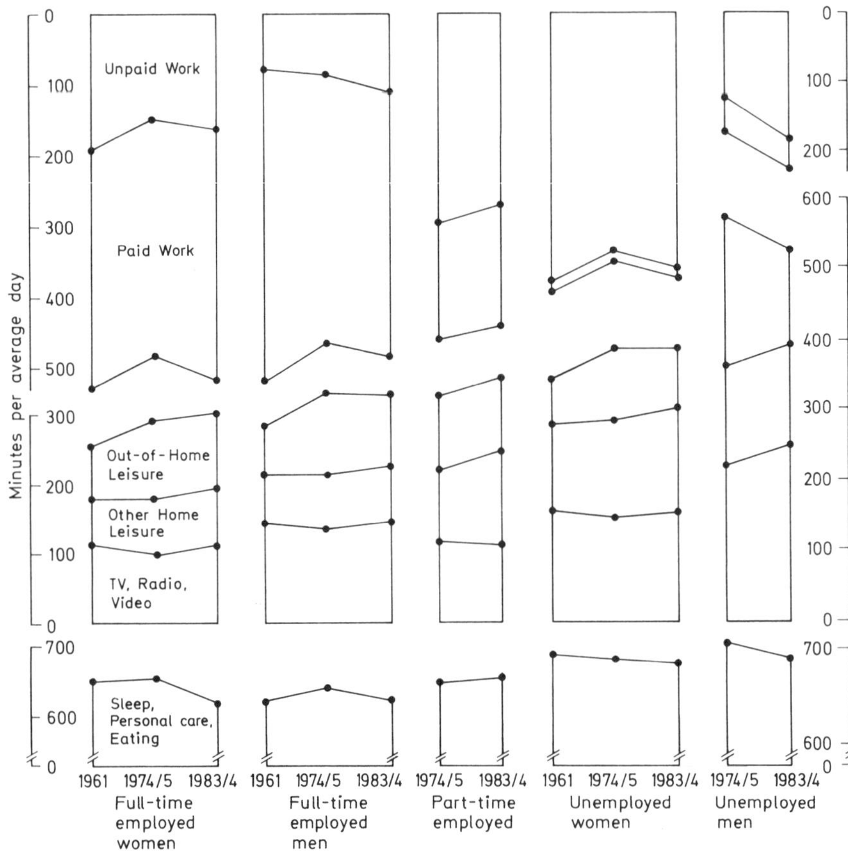

Chart 2 The Evolution of Time Use in Different Social Groups – Britain, 1961–1983/4

Source: Gershuny et al. (1986).

single women of three types. Single full-time employed women spend around 81 % of the time in domestic work as do their married counterparts; for employed women with children the ratio is 75 %; and for non-employed 78 %. Routine domestic work increases more than non-routine work. While living with a man increases women's workload by around a third, married men spend around 12 % less time doing domestic work than comparable single men (already lower than the level for single women) – although they actually do more non-routine domestic work (odd jobs and gardening), and thus an even greater reduction in routine

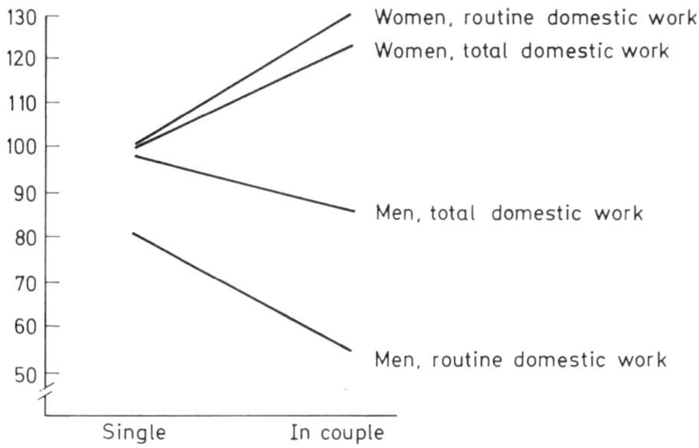

Chart 3 Effects of Marriage on Time Spent Doing Housework – Full-Time Employed Men and Women Without Children, Britain, 1983/4

Source: Wyatt (1988).

Table 3 Paid and Domestic Work Times of Couples – Men Working Full-Time, Women Under 60, Britain (Minutes per Average Day).

Wife's Economic Status		Activity Paid work	Domestic work routine	non-routine	Percentage of total work
Employed full-time men	○	387	39	61	48
	●	400	60	48	47
women	○	320	173	31	52
	●	353	175	32	53
Employed part-time men	○	404	35	47	50
	●	392	74	61	50
women	○	178	260	39	50
	●	174	282	55	50
Not employed men	○	375	39	57	53
	●	393	68	52	51
women	○	7	349	55	47
	●	9	370	84	49

Note: ○ = 1975, ● = 1983/4.

Source: Wyatt (1988).

chores is apparent (Chart 3). Men and women still specialise in activities which surveys suggested they "should" do. But the greates increases over time in men's domestic work seem to be in routine activities – especially cooking/washing up – rather than non-routine ones like gardening and DIY (Table 3).

Domestic work tends to be greatly increased by the presence of a child – and the division of labour is more pronounced in these circumstances, even where the woman is in full-time employment. (With both partners employed, housework tends to be shifted to the end of the week.) Thus some of the trends we have discussed may reflect the decline in childbearing; but we suspect that, in part at least, they do correspond to changed attitudes governing sexual inequalities. There is a tendency for couples of different types to achieve a rough equality in the total volume of work each partner carries out (see the last column in Table 3). The increase in men's domestic work has been offset by an increase in women's share of formal work, where the woman is employed. Perhaps it is the latter factor that is responsible for the shift in male activities.

Of course, economic and family circumstances are closely related to one's position in the life-cycle, and this is probably more evident for women than for men. Thus Martin and Roberts (1983; 186) noted

> a distinctive lifetime pattern of domestic work for women... Young women living at home with their parents have little domestic responsibility, but this increases dramatically as women set up their own households, usually on marriage. The main peak in domestic responsibility comes with young children; for some families there may be a second peak if they take on the regular care of an elderly or sick relative; while the small minority of people who care for example, for a permanently handicapped child have a considerably increased amount of domestic work.

This pattern is mirrored in the time budget results: there is a remarkably linear trade-off between paid and unpaid work for employed women through the life-cycle, with the exception of women in young middle age, who shoulder a particularly heavy dual burden (Chart 4; compare Table 1). With women returning to work more rapidly after childbirth, this may become more common, and comparative analysis of earlier surveys will be valuable.

How do the various trends correspond to shifts between self-servicing and the purchase of services? Consider Table 3. For couples who are both in full-time employment, we note little change in overall work time, with a increase in non-routine domestic work largely compensating for a decline in formal work. This is a group that may have relatively high quantities of disposable income and time due to low childcare responsibilities; their use of marketed services (as leisure, and as an alternative to routine domestic

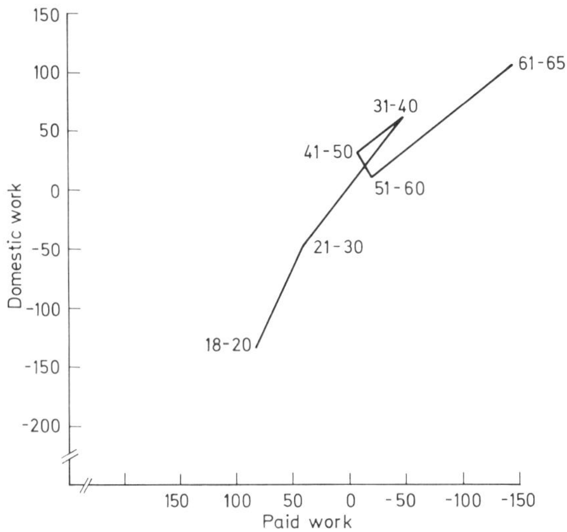

Chart 4 Age-Related Trends in Employed Women's Paid and Unpaid Work (Deviations From Means for All Employed Women)

Source: Gershuny et al., 1986

work) may remain high. Other couples with working men display increases in domestic work time, suggesting greater reliance on self-servicing in general, for both routine and non-routine household activities. (To the extent that increases in childcare are involved, this may be a compositional effect, reflecting the increasing tendency of women to engage in formal work, moderated partly but decreasingly by their having young children). Examining the data in more detail, it is interesting to note that this is not matched by an increase in shopping time.

Leisure Activities

We have noted a fairly general increase in leisure time across the last few decades. For employed people, however, the greater part of this came in the 1960s. There have been rather different patterns of evolution of specific leisure activities over the period.

Active outdoor leisure appears to have grown continuously. This includes a range of pursuits, some with little demand upon formal services (e.g. country walks, although even these may be in parkland or other sites that require care from workers who may be designated as agricultural or construction workers in employment statistics.) Other active outdoor pursuits, such as organised sports, may well require support from trained service staff – as trainers and supervisors of activities as well as servicing its physical infrastructure.

"Away-from-home leisure" – use of pubs, cinemas, etc. – is another matter. This category increased over the 1960s and subsequently declined. "Passive home leisure" – TV watching in large part – showed the reverse trend. This looks like the temporal unfolding of competition between different modes of service provision. First increased disposable income and leisure time are oriented to material services; over the more recent period, cost considerations and the increased quality of some self-service modes of provision (longer broadcasting hours, video recorders, better reception) may have been important. For the population at large, the increased proportion of elderly people is also likely to have led to increased home leisure, which increases quite markedly with age – especially for men (Chart 5).

The changes are multiplied; for example, among the factors in the earlier period contributing to "away-from-home leisure" seems to have been the increased use of pubs by younger women (Gershuny and Thomas 1980, Miles 1984.) Another important trend over the earlier period actually represents the growth of a "self-servicing" activity: there was considerable increase in visiting and preparing meals for friends. Despite the uneven development of passive leisure, home-based leisure taken as a whole does seem to have increased over the whole period 1961–1984 for most groups. Overall, then, these developments provide little evidence of growing demand for the traditional final service products of the formal economy; in contrast, demand for goods (e.g., records) and services (e.g., broadcasts) that can be used with one's own equipment seem to be growing.

Retirement and unemployment both promote major increases in passive and "other home" leisure. Unemployed men also engage in considerably more of other types of leisure activity on weekdays than do employed men; however, much of this is not service-intensive. For example, a great deal of their "outdoor active leisure" is simply time spent walking around to avoid staying sitting in the house. Financial restrictions evidently limit the consumption of formal services by unemployed and retired groups.

Finally, we should note that leisure activities display quite varied types of time structuring. Gershuny has recently been assessing the "elasticity" of various categories of informal work and leisure. He is using these data to assess the degree to which these activities "enter" the time that is available for those with lower hours of formal work on the day in question, and finding quite striking regularities over time and across countries. A reduction in working time could be achieved in various ways,

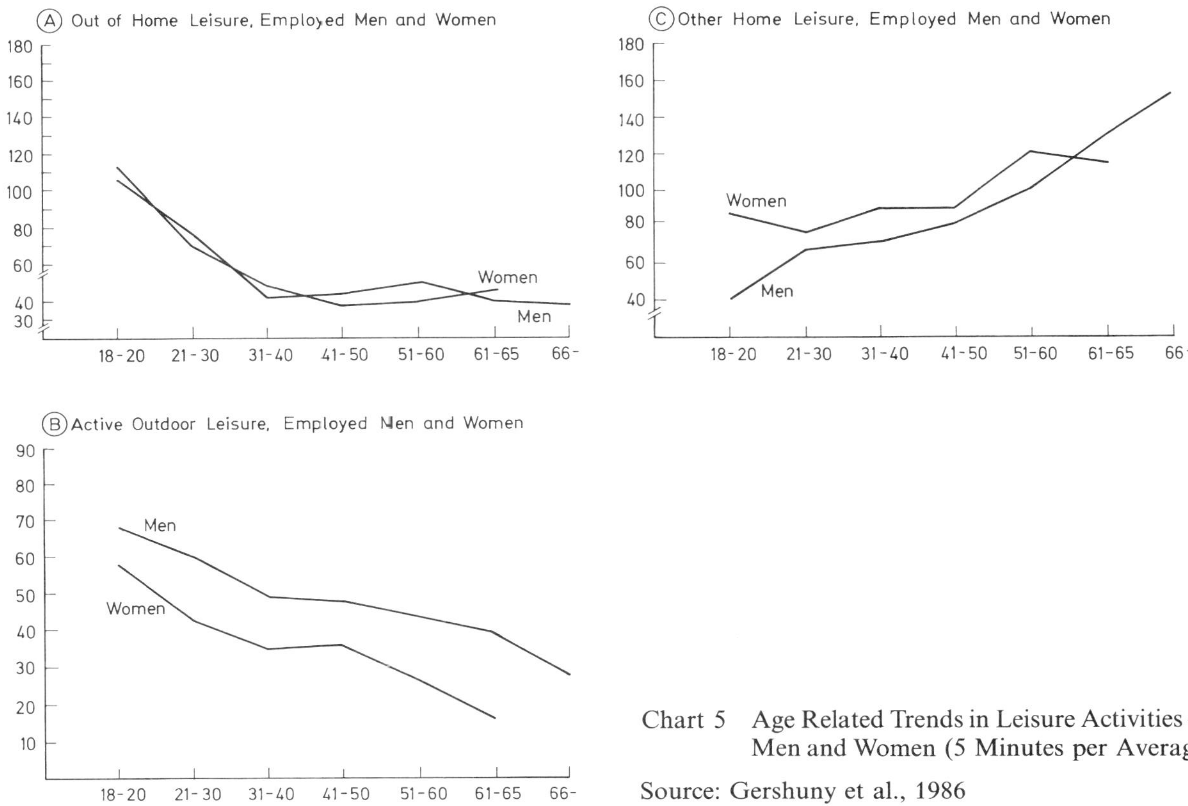

Chart 5 Age Related Trends in Leisure Activities – Employed Men and Women (5 Minutes per Average Day)

Source: Gershuny et al., 1986

with distinctive implications for leisure pursuits. Active outdoor pursuits tend to be carried out on weekends or other free days, rather than in the hours left over on working days. Gershuny and Thomas (1985), for example, have shown that countryside leisure activities increase more rapidly in holidays than do other forms of leisure. A sophisticated analysis of different methods of organising time spent in formal work is required in order to estimate the potential impacts of changes in working time on leisure activities – and thus on patterns of demand from the formal economy.

Technological Change and Future Patterns of Time Use

Introduction

Time budget analysis reveals a complex pattern of change in ways of life, but one which in many respects bears out the expectations that we developed earlier. But as the previous paragraph suggested, our focus on predicting time use from socioeconomic trends should not blind us to the likelihood that different patterns of time use have substantial implications for the formation of demands that are placed on the formal economy; demands concerning working hours, and demand for goods and services.

Chart 1 provided a framework for analysing changes within, and in the relation between, formal and informal economies, which has proved useful for discussing time use and socioeconomic trends. Many questions are left unanswered, although some of them can be tackled by further, more sophisticated, use of the time budget data along the directions suggested.

Even without moving on to this, it is possible to consider likely patterns of development of time use and formal/informal economic relations. While a forecasting exercise would probably require extrapolations of the demographic and economic developments discussed in section 2, the technological revolution associated with information technology (IT) suggests that other types of analysis are also necessary. Despite the "hype" put out by prophets of "information society", it does seem very likely that IT will be associated with profound changes in our ways of life – and thus with major shifts in some aspects of time use (Gershuny and Miles 1983, NEDO 1985).

Some of these issues identified in our initial discussion have indirect links with IT-related change: for example, changes in the sexual division of formal labour are likely to be reflected in changes in household income levels and in the division of responsibilities within households. Others have more direct linkages: there is liable to be considerable shift in the pattern and even the level of demand for formal labour – and an overall reduction in working hours, say, has considerable implications for services and self-services, although these depend very much on the precise mechanisms for the distribution of work. Likewise, a growth in teleworking would give people more free time at home, due to the reduction in travel requirements. As we do not have space here to undertake this complete re-examination, let us focus on the goods/services topic. This has been rather neglected in the "information society" literature, preoccupied as it is by the debate concerning the implications of IT for formal labour. Much of the controversy has been technologically determinist, with IT seen as inevitably displacing (and often deskilling) labour via rationalisation, or as inevitably upgrading working conditions and leading to an expansion of demand for cheaper and new IT-based goods and services.

An appraisal of the factors that may or may not lead to final demand being generated for old and new goods and services is required for a more adequate approach to forecasting. The future pattern of choice between services and self-services is part of this appraisal.

IT and Final Services in the Formal Economy

Service industries are often capital-intensive, but much of their capital is plant – buildings – rather than equipment – machinery. They have lagged in technological innovation, partly because much of their activity involves the processing of information and the application of knowledge. IT offers the prospect of a technological revolution in services comparable to that observed in manufacturing in the nineteenth century; and a shift in investment in marketed services from plant to equipment is now visible in the UK (Barras 1984).

This seems to undermine the historical trends in the relative price of goods and services. Through processes of rationalisation and capital-intensification, services could even be cheapened relative to goods, reversing some past trends in consumer choice. There are suggestions that this may already be apparent in the case of "fast food", although the technological and organisational innovations here are not IT-based (information-handling is a small part of catering, which is essentially a service-based production and delivery of customised foodstuffs within a compatible environment) – and that they rest also on low labour costs.

However, two points need to be borne in mind. The first is that these rationalisation processes are liable to be at best a holding measure in employment terms, bringing "jobless growth" to service sectors. Demand is increased to the extent that it does not involve increases in the workforce. IT does in practice already seem to make such "jobless growth" possible in both public and private services.[11] Second is the entrance of a number of low-wage countries into consumer goods manufacturing. There are indications that in some instances IT can help offset the labour cost advantages of these countries by permitting economies of scope in manufacturing, enabling First World producers with better market intelligence and more innovative designs to recapture domestic markets. These instances may well be limited to areas like textiles and garments where there is currently rather restricted self-service provision for routine requirements. In consumer electronics the future may be more evident in the practice of firms who contract out production and assembly to Third World countries. The upshot would be that even if services can offset unfortunate price trends vis-à-vis goods produced in the First World, they may still face stiffer competition from the world market.[12]

A number of other IT-related innovations in final services in the formal economy also need to be considered. A range of improvements are possible in such services, indeed, many are already being employed in some instances (Miles et al. 1988). These include:

- Telebooking and information services. Information can be provided electronically at the point of service delivery (e.g., bus stops) or at the users' homes (e.g., viewdata on transport service timing and availability), increasing the convenience of the service and the confidence with which it can be used. It is a small step on for the customer to avoid queuing and delays by remote purchasing of tickets – and to use Electronic Funds Transfer to save problems with change, etc. A somewhat larger step is to move these services on to a more client-centred basis.
- Client-centred-services and services with customer design facilities. Much service innovation to date has involved standardisation of mass production/mass consumption services; however, IT permits economies of scope in services as well as manufacturing. In the transport example the step would be for the VDU at the bus stop, or the terminal in the home, to allow for dial-a-ride or similar systems, with flexible rerouting of public transport to meet the pattern of demand that is thus expressed. There are many other instances where scheduling and use of resources can similarly be brought more into line with customer requirements: at present queuing and delays deter use of

[11] On "jobless growth" in services, see Gershuny and Miles (1983).

[12] The rising interest in deregulating services trade in GATT and elsewhere should also be noted here. The message of this paragraph is decidedly *not* that First World countries should adopt protectionist measures against the NICs.

many public and private services. Education and information-based services can be programmed more flexibly to meet individual aptitudes and interests; Computer-Aided Design can be used to increase client design choice and involvement in the decision-making process – tailoring not only clothes, but also equipment, menus, health care regimes, etc.

- Self-service and simplification. Although involving informal work inputs, self-servicing has proved popular due to the opportunity to exercise choice at one's own pace; automation of many existing services involves some self-servicing, and also relaxes the time-structuring of shopping, banking, and information services. Often this can be associated with a shift to teleservices, such as teleshopping and telebanking, which save travel time – although they may involve formal work of new types in delivery as well as in programming and updating of information. The use of expert system-type facilities may allow both for self-servicing and for the greater support of scarce professionals by, for example, paramedics, who can engage in routine assessments of client needs and the like.
- New services. A wide range of new IT-based services are currently emerging. These include: emergency and alarm services for elderly and handicapped people; viewdata-based information services such as electronic newspapers, new types of personal contact; tele-gaming and -entertainment of new sorts, using home computers and public telecommunication systems. While many new services can operate quite adequately on existing telecommunication facilities, it is likely that major improvements in channel capacity (e.g., a broadband network) as well as in software (currently cumbersome) and peripherals (cheap printers, better-quality VDUs) is required for many others.

Many formal services may display product as well as process innovation. These may in part reduce the tendency for self-services to substitute for services in the formal economy. How far they actually take place will be determined by several key factors: provision of the appropriate infrastructure, organisational dynamics of services (the typically small scale of many service firms may slow innovation, especially those that demand some coordination – such as Electronic Funds Transfer) and the policies of national governments towards public services (cost-cutting rationalisation, or efforts to increase the scope and adequacy of services).[13)]

[13)] Miles et al. (1988).

IT and Self-Services

Many prospective innovations in formally provided services imply more home-based interaction (using domestic IT goods) with service providers. Many of the innovations also involve an increasing role for self-service in which the consumer/client is more active in formal service production, less a passive recipient of delivered services. (There are alternatives to home-based systems, such as the VDU at the bus stop, the community centre, and library with terminals installed, the viewdata booth; these may be important innovations. But given the low cost and convenience of equipment, they are likely in the long term to be complementary facilities, used when away from home or for specific purposes.) Thus formal service organisations may actually themselves promote some capital-intensification of households and increase in self-servicing.

But self-servicing also comprises an alternative to many formal services, and innovations in domestic equipment may have an important role to play here. These prospective innovations constitute change in the household that is perhaps as radical as that associated with the diffusion of white goods during the post-war boom.[14] Already there has been considerable substitution of microelectronic controls and displays for conventional electromechanical ones, and much packaging together of different items of equipment; however, so far these are mostly gimmicks, or at best, poor indications of future change. Among the important developments are:

- The controllability of equipment. Devices are becoming capable of being controlled remotely (by infrared, wireless, etc.) and the possibilities for telecontrol (e.g., to be able to instruct equipment by phone) are emerging. Controls and feedback from equipment are becoming more "user-friendly", with voice control and voice synthesis, WIMPS, more realistic and informative output displays. Likewise, they are more programmable, offering more options tailoring operations to user requirements. And they are more "informed", taking account of previous choices and results, and of environmental conditions.
- The physical features of equipment are also changing. New safety features are being installed, new types of breakdown feature (including auto-diagnostics and easier repair), and equipment is geared to greater power conservation. Devices are more portable, and permit greater mobility; and the variety of different designs for specific user groups is increasing. Major improvements in quality in audio reproduction and, even more so, in video are under development; apart from digital reproduction technologies, we can expect to see wide-screen, flat-

[14] Miles (1988).

screen, high-definition TV displays, for example, serving as "electronic wallpaper" and communications devices as well as media for broadcast entertainment.

- Integration. Perhaps the most significant developments are those around the integration of different items of domestic equipment into "Interactive Home Systems". Led in the first instance by the integration of energy-controlling devices (central heating, ventilation, metering, and tariff-regulated operation of domestic euqipment) and alarm systems (fire, smoke, intruder, and health emergency devices), eventually Small Area Networks for homes will be capable of carrying high quality video and audio data as well (but this may lie some decades away).

Taken together, these developments would seem to constitute a powerful impetus for self-service activities in the home. The ease and convenience of many forms of informal work is liable to be increased, along with the quality of the final service that is produced. It is difficult to compare the implications of developments in formal services and in self-services; the pace of development in each sphere would need to be assessed, along with the specificities of demand for particular final service functions. But there is clearly little room for complacency on the part of final service organisations; their innovative skills are liable to be taxed to the full by the challenge from the informal economy.

Implications for Time Use and Ways of Life

Our assumptions concerning the long-term consequences of IT-related innovation are as follows. First, there will continue to be a reduction in the time allocated for formal work, and some reduction in work-related activities like travel. However, there may well be a major increase in vocational training and retraining; indeed, this would be important in facilitating more benign directions of technological development. The disturbation of what working time there is is a matter of government policy and firm strategy.

One scenario involves a much more dualistic society, divided between individuals (and households) working in the formal economy and those that are "clients" of social services (and, presumably, other government services, such as law and order). A scenario that is much more challenging in terms of short-term policymaking, but is perhaps more viable in the long term, is one that involves considerable redistribution of formal working time – so that the typical working week and lifetime would be well below current levels.[15] Policy efforts directed against gender

[15] See the survey of expert opinion on these topics by NEDO (1986); see also Miles (1985a) on dualism.

inequality and especially the deleterious effects of childcare on women's careers could form part of a more egalitarian scenario; however, it is quite conceivable that a redistribution of work among men could be accompanied by some intensification of the sexual division of domestic labour (although trend extrapolation would suggest some move toward greater efforts to reduce gender inequality). In any case, it is not IT itself driving the developments along: in many respects IT mitigates against conventional gender demarcations, turning many manual jobs into "feminine" keyboarding, much housework and service work into "masculine" gadget-manipulation.

Given a "surprise-free" (and therefore improbable) scenario, with no major policy shifts either way, and only a partial effort made to redistribute working time, what implications follow? Continued female participation in the formal economy is liable to mean continuing reductions in gender inequality in domestic work. We would also anticipate further shifts toward self-servicing, although the role of formal service organisations – especially public services – could be very important here. It is likely that new areas of demand will be generated around existing activities – just as the advent of the automobile has been associated with a considerable increase in "requirements" for travel, so new IT equipment may well interact with the shifts in consumer priorities towards areas like health and education. (This is quite possibly critically influenced by the pace of development of new telecommunications infrastructure.) Although it may be difficult to envisage the growth of new markets in such areas providing a basis for renewed economic growth, a combination of factors converge to make such expansion quite plausible.[16)]

As with the post-war boom's growth paradigm, this may well provide much greater freedom to the average consumer – while creating problems of declining services and a "privatisation" of individual life. Again the active intervention of public services into the innovation process is likely to be a key factor in determining the eventual role of these changes. It is a priority for these service organisations to engage in social experiments and other means of exploring the potential of new technologies for meeting the social needs of the 1980s and beyond, rather than simply using them to rationalise the provision of services designed in the 1960s.

---

16) Miles (1985c).

References

Barras, R. (1984): *Growth and technical change in the UK service sector*, London: Technical Change Centre.

Gershuny, J. (1983): *Social innovation and the division of labour*, London: Oxford University Press.

Gershuny, J. (1986): Time use, technology, and the future of work, *Journal of the Market Research Society*, 26, 4.

Gershuny, J. and Miles, I. (1983): *The new service economy*, London: Frances Pinter.

Gershuny, J. and Miles, I. (1985): Toward a new social economics, In: B. Roberts, R. Finnegan, and D. Gallie (Eds.): *New approaches to economic life*, Manchester: Manchester University Press.

Gershuny, J. and Thomas, G. (1980): *Changing Patterns of Time Use*, Falmer, Brighton: SPRU (occasional paper series).

Gershuny, J. and Thomas, G. (1985): *Countryside recreation in daily life*, Battleby, Perth: Countryside Commission for Scotland (Scottish Leisure Survex Report no. 3).

Gershuny, J., Jones, S. and Mullins, C. (1985): *Evaluation of the 1983/4 ESRC time budget survey*, mimeo, University of Bath, report to the ESRC.

Gershuny, J., Miles I., Jones, S., Mullins, C. Thomas, G. and Wyatt, S. (1986): Preliminary analyses of the 1983-4 ESRC time budget survey, *Quarterly Journal of Social Affairs*, 2 (1): 13–39.

Inglehart, R. (1977): *The silent revolution*, Princeton, N.J.: Princeton University Press.

Jahoda, M. (1982): *Employment and unemployment: a social psychological analysis*, Cambridge: Cambridge University Press.

Kelvin, R. and Jarret, J. (1985): *Unemployment*, Cambridge: Cambridge University Press.

Kohn, M.C. and Schooler, C. (1978): The reciprocal effects of the substantive complexity of work and intellectual flexibility, *American Journal of Sociology*, 84 (1): 24–52.

MacNulty, W.K. (1985): UK social change through a wide angle lens, *Futures*, 17,4: 331 337.

Martin, J. and Roberts, C. (1983): *Women and employment: a lifetime perspective*, London: H.M.S.O. (Department of Employment/OPCS).

Miles, I. (1983): *Adaptation to Unemployment?* Falmer, Brighton: SPRU Occasonal Paper Series.

Miles, I. (1984): *Work, non-work and ageing*, mimeo: SPRU, report to the ESRC.

Miles, I. (1985a): The new post-industrial state, *Futures*, 17 (6): 588–617.

Miles, I. (1985b): I servizi nell'era informazione, Journal: *L'Impresa*, Sommario 5/85; 15–24.

Miles, I. (1985c): Social forecasting and information technology, mimeo, Science Policy Research Unit; paper presented to Nordic Summer School workshop on Social Innovation, December .

Miles, I. (1986): The tertiary sector in socioeconomic development, mimeo: SPRU prepared for UNCTAD workshop on Service Sector.

Miles, I. (1988): *Home Informatics*, London: Pinter.

Miles, I., Rush, H., Bessant, J. and Turner, K. (1988): *Information Horizons*, Aldeshot: Edward Elgar.

NEDO (IT EDC) (1985): *IT Futures*, London: National Economic Development Office.

NEDO (IT EDC) (1986): *IT Futures Surveyed*, London: National Economic Development Office.

Szalai, A. (Ed.) (1972): *The use of time*, The Hague: Mouton.

Thomas, G. and Miles, I. (1985): *Technology and changes in the provision of services to households*, Brussels: FAST Programme of the European Communities, Fol no. 90.

Thomas, G., Wyatt, S. and Miles, I. (1985): *Preliminary analyses of the ESRC time budget data*, mimeo, report to the ESRC, SPRU.

Warr, P. (1983): Job Loss, unemployment and Psychological Well-Being, In: E. van de Vliert and V. Allen (Eds.): *Role transitions*, New York: Plenum.

White, M. (1986): IT and the changing structure of employment, London: Policy Studies Institute, Mimeo (prepared for (and available from) National Economic Development Office, IT EDC, Long Term Perspectives Sub-Committee).

Witherspoon, S. (1985): Sex roles and gender issues, In: Jowell, R.; Witherspoon, S. (Eds.): *British social attitudes: The 1985 report*, Aldershot: Gower Publishing.

Wyatt, S. (1988): Timing housework: Gains and losses for women, Falmer: Science Policy Research Unit, mimeo.

D. Changing Sources of Sustenance

Changing Patterns of Small Entrepreneurship

Vittorio Capecchi

The attention focused on the factors involved in the development of entrepreneurship in the European Economic Community can be traced to two important concerns:

a) In Europe the number of unemployed (especially young people and adult women) is increasing, and the trend is brought about not only by difficult circumstances and recession, but also by the introduction of new technologies in the factory and the office.
b) In the race to develop new technologies and the ability to use them, Europe is seen to be lagging behind the United States and Japan.

The European press speaks of the "collapse" and "deep-seated crisis of the old world." In virtually all European countries these observations and assessments have prompted a critical appraisal of the traditional economic policy of channeling most of a government's support to the major national groupings of the country (or the multinational firms operating on its territory), which are regarded as the driving force behind the entire economy.

There is an awareness of the fact that even if the large firms present on the national territory are healthy, they do not solve the problems of unemployment, developing less favored regions, or educating people about new technologies. One alternative economic policy now emerging therefore represents an attempt to allow the full exploitation of all the human, cultural, and physical resources of a given region, without giving large firms sole responsibility for its socioeconomic development. This approach has aroused substantial interest in smaller forms of enterprise. This chapter analyzes various types of smaller-scale entrepreneurial activities that are currently regarded as most representative of the situation in Europe and, in order to make it possible to compare them, uses examples drawn from one region of Italy in which such types of activity are widespread, Emilia-Romagna.[1)]

---

1) In this analysis of Emilia-Romagna I have utilized especially the following Italian contributions: Becattini (1979, 1987), Bianco and Luciano (1982), Brusco (1980), Capecchi (1978, 1981, 1982, 1983), Capecchi and Pesce (1983, 1986), Fuà and Zacchia

For a definition of entrepreneurship, I turn to Joseph Schumpeter (1947), for whom the entrepreneur is someone who does something new or does something old in a new way. He distinguishes between periods of routine and upheaval confronting entrepreneurs who have to struggle against workers' resistance to new methods, consumers' resistance to new products, and other obstacles. As he wrote in 1947 in "The Creative Response in Economic History," innovation tends to coincide with the "creative response" as opposed to the "adaptive response". Entrepreneurial activity is therefore depicted as a "deviant" function that can last for only a limited period, even if the person having discharged that function remains responsible for the enterprise.

Later in the post-war period criticisms were leveled at this type of analysis, primarily by those who were promoting an economic analysis focusing exclusively on development based on mass production. In 1951, for example, C. Shaw Solo wrote that innovation is a normal part of owning a firm, while Galbraith, In *American Capitalism* (1952), stated that the introduction of innovation depended exclusively on large firms with a predominantly monopolistic character. The various phases in the innovation process had become so complex, and science-based technology so pervasive, that it was no longer possible for an individual inventor or a small firm to innovate. The concept of the "technostructure" developed by Galbraith in *New Industrial State* (1967) attests to the change of times. Innovation was part of the normal activities' range of the large firms. We have come a long way from the "deviant" and "creative" figure that the entrepreneur cut in Schumpeter's analysis. Interest in Schumpeter's theories revived in the early sixties, when economists began to realize that the innovation process was much more uncertain and unpredictable than was thought in Galbraith's early works.

A great deal of research demonstrated that a large number of inventions and innovations were produced by small firms and individual inventors. Given my interest in entrepreneurial figures outside the large firm, a definition like Schumpeter's is acceptable in the present context. This poses the questions of the extent to which "small entrepreneurs," a group that will be identified historically, can be classified as innovative and deviant, and, on the other hand, the extent to which they can be associated with routine or a spirit of "adaptiveness."

In Capecchi and Pesce (1986) movements into and out of entrepreneurship in Italy were gathered on two generations (see Figures 1 and 2),

---

(1983). I also have considered certain European and American point of view: Greffe (1984), Keeble and Wever (1985), Noble (1984), Pahl (1984), Piore and Sabel (1984), Sabel and Zeitlin (1985), Wilkinson (1981).

(namely, the one of people who were between twenty and thirty years old in the 1950s, and the one of people between twenty and thirty years in the 1980s). The data were then related to the set of opportunities and barriers that have an origin in the distant past, and to the opportunities and the barriers that characterize the time when these generations were working. It had to be kept in mind, however, that "barriers", such as difficulty in finding occupation as a dependent employee, provided stimuli for entrepreneurship. Transitions into and out of entrepreneurship within the same family have been taken into account. A distinction was made between those mobility patterns that take place within the official economy and those that take place within informal economy. (A broad discussion of this and related topics can be found in Capecchi and Pesce 1983.) The "Ford type of industrialization" was distinguished from the "type of industrialization characterized by flexible specialization" according to Sabel and Zeitlin (1985).

The Transition to Small Entrepreneurship for Poorly-Educated Males

The 20 years represented in Figure 1 constitute the period during which the development of small enterprise in Emilia-Romagna was greatest: the fifties and sixties. The generation of people in question was between 20 and 30 years of age in 1950 and had experienced the Second World War and the partisan resistance to the fascists. The prototypical figure was a very poorly educated young man belonging to a farming family. His active involvement in agriculture was declining: between 1950 and 1970, the proportion of the workforce employed in agriculture in Emilia-Romagna dropped from 52% to 20%. He encountered a set of opportunities and barriers associated with the training system, the market, the type of industrialization, the relationships between the various economies, his relationships with his own firm, family, and national and local government.

Some of the main opportunities for or barriers to social mobility were rooted in the cultural tradition of the region and the potential entrepreneur's family background. Bearing in mind that most small enterprises were to develop in the industrial sector (particularly the field of mechanical engineering), one can distinguish between three categories of opportunities: specific agricultural structures favoring the acquisition of entrepreneurial skills, proto-industrial activities in agriculture, and proto-industrial and industrial activities in urban centers.

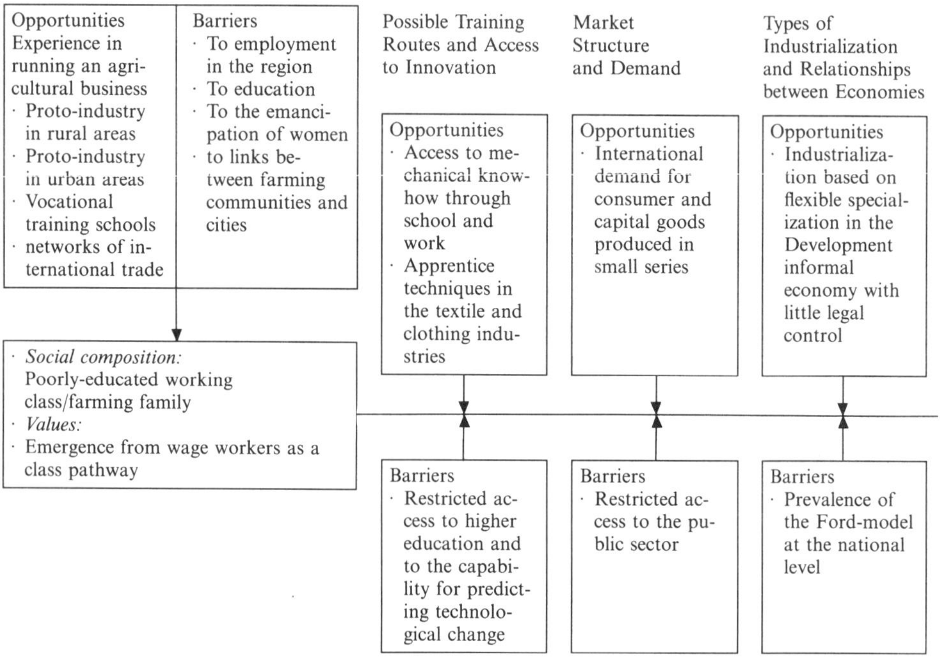

Figure 1 Transition to small entrepreneurship in Emilia Romagna for men

To understand the development of entrepreneurial activity in a period like the one considered in this chapter, it is important to determine how the transition was made from agriculture to industry. It is often forgotten that managing a farm can also provide various types of important experience in entrepreneurship.

In Emilia-Romagna and similar regions capital investment in farming was characterized at the beginning of the century by share-farming contracts. The share farmer and his family yielded part of the harvest to the owner in exchange for the use of the land together with extensive provisions governing such things as the purchase of machinery and farm improvements. Around the turn of the century this type of contract was so widespread that only 40 % of those employed in agriculture were farm laborers and employees, with 35 % of the farm population being share farmers; 17 %, owner-occupiers; and 7 %, tenants. Some 60 % of all people working the land were therefore directly involved in the management of the holding. Since share farmers learned how to keep accounts, to invest, and to make a host of other decisions, they often acquired genuine entrepreneurial training through share-farming con-

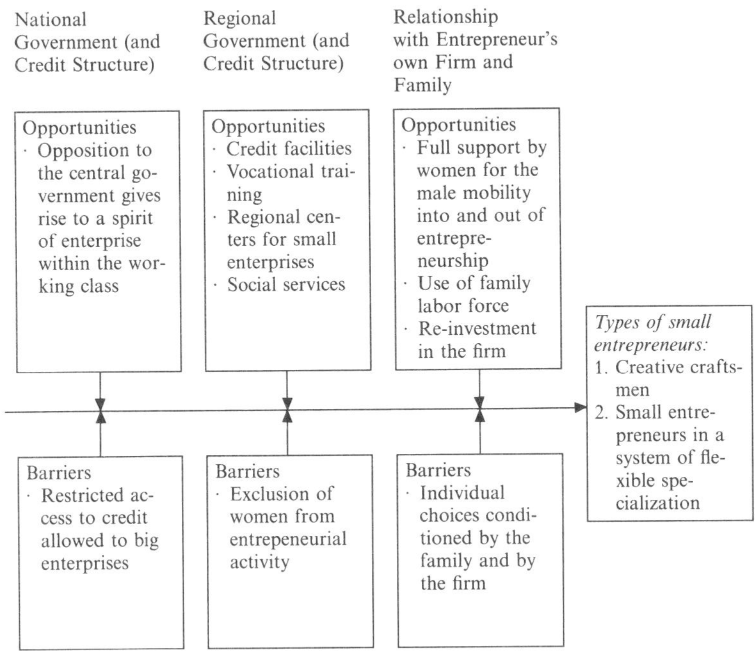

between 20 and 30 years of age in 1950

tracts. The first half of the twentieth century in rural areas also saw the spread of agricultural workers' cooperatives and the mutual aid and cultural cooperatives set up by the socialists, which helped to create an alternative to the transition experienced in other agricultural regions, where extremely poor and highly specialized farming (such as the cultivation of tomatoes in many southern regions), the excessive subdivision of land into many small holdings, the absence of many managerial responsibility, and the lack of participation in cooperative schemes were factors that discouraged entrepreneurial activity.

Proto-industrial experience was therefore being gained in Emilia-Romagna within farming families, in particular those engaged in share farming. As Poni's studies (1982) have shown, "the looms were weaving and the spinning wheels were spinning" during the winter months, when the families were not busy working in the fields, and for these proto-industrial activities to take place in the farming communities, three conditions had to be met:

1) The agrarian structures had to favor industrial activity by those working the land. (In certain areas, for example, vineyards required

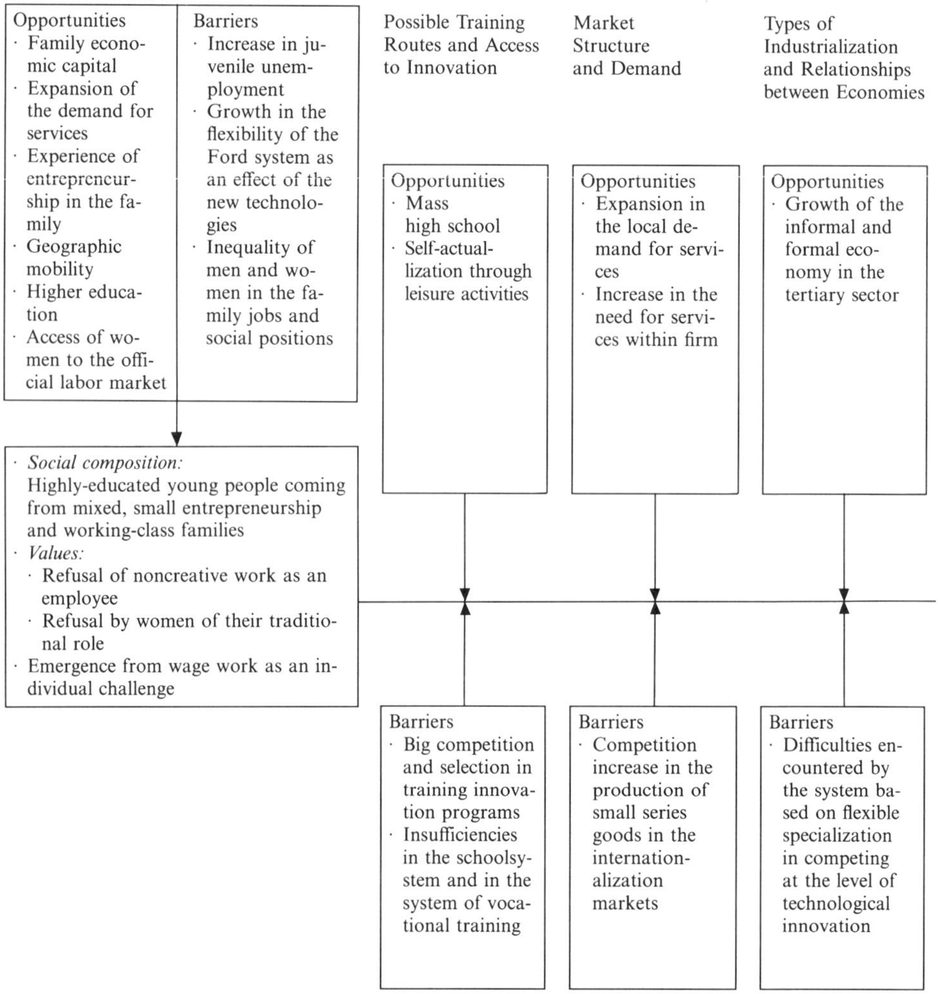

Figure 2 Transition to small entrepreneurship in Emilia Romagna for people

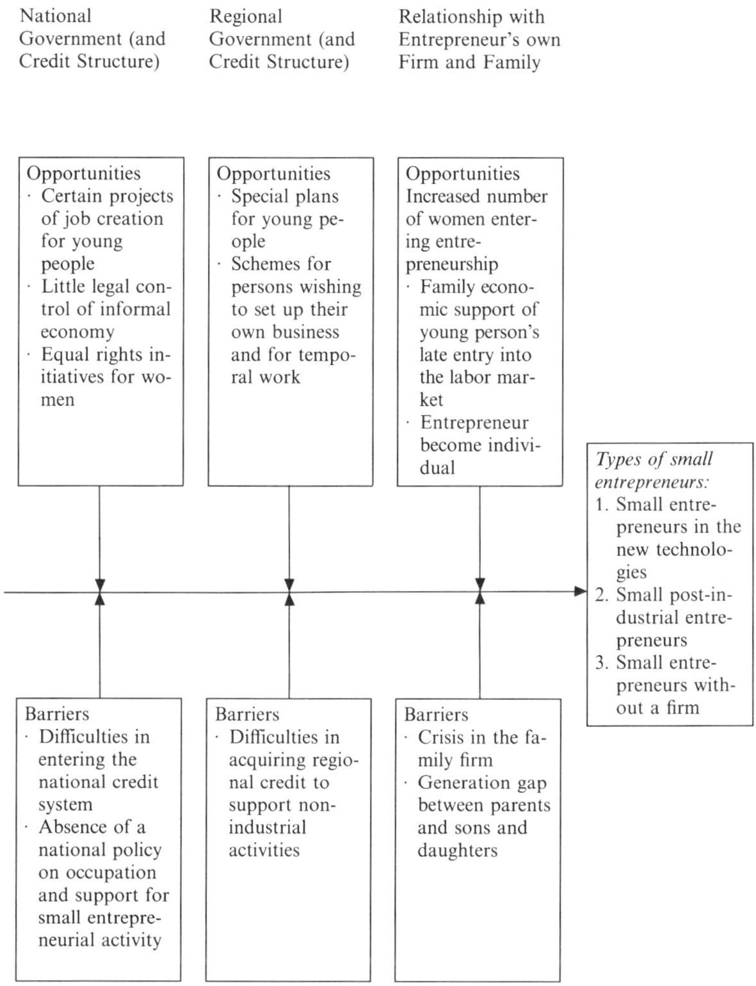

between 20 and 30 years of age in 1980

continuous attention, even during the winter months, or there may not have been enough space to carry out such activities.)

2) The power of the traditional urban corporations and guilds had to have diminished enough to allow the emergence of industrial competitors in rural areas and the use of urban capital there.
3) External demand had to emerge alongside a national (and often even international) market for the products manufactured by these farming communities.

Variations in these conditions between agricultural regions made for important differences.

Another category of such opportunities offered by the regional tradition and family culture consisted of all the proto-industrial and industrial activities carried out in urban centers during the period leading up to the fifties. A census does not necessarily reveal historical traces of such activities, which require specialized research. Research of this type has demonstrated, for example, that Bologna in the sixteenth century had extensive experience with industrial activity because that city was one of the main centers of silk production. There was an enormous number of silk factories operated by wheels driven by a system of waterways that covered the entire city. Bologna was not the only city in the region where industrial activities flourished. At Carpi (in the province of Modena), which is today one of the most important centers of knitwear production, an industry for straw hats developed in the sixteenth century and became so important by the beginning of the twentieth century that Carpi had an international sales network with subsidiaries in Paris, New York, London, Manila, and Tientsin. Clearly such industrial activities, together with crafts and commerce, contribute to propagating the commercial and industrial experience that is completely absent in many of the regions of southern Italy.

A crucial role in this category of opportunities was played by the schools and vocational training institutes for craftsmen and skilled workers that were founded in Bologna towards the middle of the nineteenth century. Specific research[2)] on this topic has demonstrated how Bologna's industrial decline following the crisis in the silk industry prompted two intellectuals, Aldini and Valeriani, to undertake a fact-finding journey at the end of the eighteenth century in order to acquaint themselves with the state of technology in other European countries, in particular England. After their return they introduced the most modern mechanical innovations in Bologna by setting up a craftschool equipped with modern teaching aids. This establishment subsequently became an

---

2) Comune di Bologna (1980).

undergraduate school for technicians, but it attached considerable importance to theoretical subjects such as mechanical drawing and provided broad training that was to prepare skilled workers for innovation.

With regard to this set of opportunities, it has often been discussed which of the two avenues to entrepreneurial activity has been more important in the regions of central Italy: that passing through agriculture or that having a predominantly urban origin. The answer probably depends on the resulting type of enterprise. The urban background has probably more importance in machine building, whereas small enterprise in the textiles and clothing sector may have been influenced mainly by rural background combined with proto-industrial experience, geared in rural areas. The importance of such entrepreneurial tradition is evident in both cases.

In the family tradition behind many of the actors from a working-class or farming background, the first barrier to private enterprise throughout the first half of the twentieth century was the lack of full employment. Despite work in farming, land reclamation, the crafts, and industrial enterprises, the supply of labor exceeded demand in Emilia-Romagna and throughout the first half of the twentieth century, it was a poor region from which 350,000 people emigrated between 1901 and 1936.

In addition to these obstacles, there were barriers to the spread of education in rural areas. Commenting publicly on education at the end of the nineteenth century, the Agricultural Society of the Province of Bologna wrote:

> When it is not proportionate to social conditions and intelligence, education does not develop moral fiber; more than anything else, it develops greed together with the brutality to satisfy it; it creates dissenters.[3)]

There was thus a barrier to mass education and, in rural areas, a further barrier to the professional advancement of women. When farming became mechanized, women were excluded from training courses in how to use tractors and new machinery. The alternatives open to a working-class woman in the first half of the nineteenth century were work in the fields, the least skilled public-sector jobs, the factories in which unskilled labor was also used, or middle-class households.

All in all, the greatest barriers were those preventing families living in rural areas approaching the cities. The isolated farmhouses built in the middle of the fields had been put there deliberately by the landowners who entrusted the holdings to share farmers. While this type of contract

[3)] Bergonsini (1966).

probably exerted a favorable influence on the subsequent acquisition of entrepreneurial skills through the experience it gave in managing the farm on a relatively independent basis, it also reinforced the share farmers' isolation and exclusion from education.

Furthermore, fascism did everything possible to pit share farmers against farm laborers and the few skilled workers against manual laborers, and it was only in the struggle against fascism that solidarity was forged between these sections of the proletariat. At the end of the war, Emilia-Romagna was the region of Italy in which the highest proportion of the electorate voted for the Communist and Socialist parties. The expectations of these voters for more fundamental changes in society were disappointed, though, and the generation that was between 20 and 30 years of age in 1950 found itself in a region with a left wing government in a country governed by center-right politicians. There was, therefore, a sharp contrast between the policies pursued by the national and the regional government, a situation that produced the powerful system of opportunities and barriers described here.

The economic policy pursued by the Christian Democratic central government in the post-war period particularly favored the development of the large manufacturing industries based in northern Italy (especially those in Milan and Turin), thus creating one of the country's largest waves of migration from the south to the north. As far as Emilia-Romagna was concerned, the government, as documented in Melossi (1977), saw to it that virtually all the funds made available by the Marshall Plan for the purchase of machinery in the area of the dollar at the end of 1951 went to Piemont and Lombardy, while Emilia-Romagna received only 0.7%. Furthermore, the central government, which administered the funds for the machine building industry, decided to dismantle the few large factories in Emilia-Romagna that still produced arms. The Officine Reggiane in Reggio Emilia, which expanded its workforce to 12,000 during the war, was dismantled thereafter, making way for a new factory employing only 700. The workforce at the Ducati factory in Bologna shrunk from between 6,000 and 7,000 to 1,300 in 1954; that at the Calzoni factory in Bologna, from 1,600 to 130; and at the Cogne firm in Imola, from 2,400 to 600. Clearly, the dismantling of this industry had released a fairly large number of skilled workers, who, in effect, found themselves barred from work as employees in large factories. They could either follow those emigrating from the south to the cities of the north or look for new opportunities in private enterprises in their own region.

The regional government acted differently by immediately declaring its support for small enterprise and doing all within its power to facilitate the creation of a credit structure geared to industrial investment and the financing of small firms. The regional government pursued a policy of equipping areas for small industry and craftwork and set up region-wide social services that increased the material well-being of farming and working-class families. This encouragement was – and still is – one of the features distinguishing Emilia-Romagna from the regional governments in southern Italy. Regional government officials and local authorities developed the skill making the most of the funds made available at the central government and European levels (such as EEC funds for vocational training), the result being that a network of entrepreneurial skills grew out of an awareness of being politically at odds with the central government.

Another important point was that a person could complete part of the transition to entrepreneurship within the informal economy (that is, without legal controls and without payment of taxes). Even today within the clothing and textile sectors, outwork is generally just a start towards small entrepreneurship. Only after a phase of unregulated labor does a small craft firm enter the official economy. In machine building the transition to entrepreneurship includes the informal employment of women as accountants and as office employees, while the small firm can continue with the help of informally paid employees from outside the family. These opportunities and the barriers to white-collar jobs created an inducement that met with the features of the type of industrialization and of the connections between the various economies which are important to examine in detail, specifying the differences with the Ford pattern of development.

The Ford pattern, based on Taylorist principles for organizing work in the mass-production of products in large enterprises, makes assumptions not only about the internal organization of work, by drawing an extremely sharp distinction between manual and white-collar workers and, within the white-collar category, by separating the executive and managerial levels. The Ford system also makes assumptions about the consumer. As Ford himself said, the customer could choose any color he wished for his car, as long as it was black.

This assumption concerning the uniformity of the consumer wishes was challenged even before any discussion of the internal organization of work. Once individuals were able to afford more than the bare necessities, the development of industrial societies, the distinctions between social classes, and the individualistic forces acting within each social class led to an ever-increasing demand for highly individualized consumer and capital goods. Ever wider markets opened up for consumer durables and capital goods produced in small series, and these markets stimulated the creation (in both Europe and the United States, according to Sabel and Zeitlin) of small firms geared to producing customized capital and consumer goods. At the same time that mass production was developing in large textile and machine-building factories, a specialized but flexible type of production was also developing in groups of small textile and mechanical workshops.

An example of such small enterprises with flexible specialization in Emilia-Romagna is the manufacture of packaging and wrapping machines in Bologna. This small branch (which today provides work for 10,000–15,000 employees) emerged in 1924, when the first factory ACMA (Anonima Costruzione Macchine Automatiche) was built in the sector on the basis of an idea by Commendatore Barbieri. In the course of his activities in the paper and cardboard industry, Barbieri was in contact with Cavaliere Gazzoni, who manufactured "Idrolitina," a powder for making sparkling water. Gazzoni asked Barbieri to provide a machine for packaging this powder, and this gave rise to a large enterprise specialized in the construction of this type of machinery. This factory developed the necessary technologies. The work, in turn, gave birth to nine other factories as well as a medium-sized offshoot that, using similar technology, won a national competition for cigarette-manufacturing machines.

The process whereby this industrial subsystem spread involved three mechanisms:

1) The sector expanded through imitation and/or complementary products. When engineers and technicians left the "parent" factory to set up new enterprises, they almost never began competing directly with the products manufactured by the former. If the first factory produced machines for packaging foodstuffs, the second one would make machines for wrapping cigarettes, the third for packaging medicines, the fourth for bottling liquids, and so on.
2) Machines initially manufactured entirely by the same firm (early industrial firms in Bologna even had their own foundries on their premises) were subdivided into components, and entrepreneurial activity developed through a decentralization process. A multitude of processes were thus decentralized and carried out by still smaller firms, with the result that the firms decentralizing the work remained small or medium-sized (between 200 and 300 employees on average, and even fewer in certain cases).
3) Many small firms became specialized in carrying out certain processes and manufacturing certain components of machines. Such specialization made these firms much more independent since they worked for more than one firm on the same type or with similar characteristics.

The outcome of this process was a subsystem of small enterprises where there was no leading firm. Today, too, an enterprise that produces the finished product cannot be the center of the subsystem, since it is usually equipped only to assemble the parts produced by other enterprises: the production of some of these parts may be so important that the enterprises producing them are in a position to impose their own prices. This subsystem therefore constitutes a network of firms whose relationship is completely different from that between large firms operating on the Ford pattern and small enterprises. The large Ford-type factory may subcontract processes or components of the finished product to small firms, but the small firms are always dependent on the large ones. In the subsystem featuring flexible specialization, on the other hand, there are many small firms. Those firms producing the finished product and those manufacturing particular components or carrying out special processes are relatively independent.

Flexible specialization in this industrial system differs from the Ford-inspired system in six ways.

a) The production of such equipment as automatic packaging and wrapping machines is based on approximately 300 small firms employing a total workforce of between 10,000 and 15,000. The workforce cannot be quantified with certainty, for some of the firms also work for factories in other subsectors.
b) The firms are located in a particular area (in the case just described, in the province of Bologna); each province of Emilia-Romagna has areas that are specialized in a given type of product.
c) The products are generally consumer or capital goods manufactured in small series for specific clients. The production is therefore specialized but flexible, and the goods are sold on international markets.
d) The relative independence of firms is widespread, because their products complement rather than compete with each other. This facilitates agreements on such things as the purchase of raw materials, the setting-up of sales, and back-up networks in foreign countries.
e) Workers in this type of firm are much more highly skilled than those in a large factory operating on the Ford pattern. First, a system of small complementary factories facilitates the dissemination of skills and decision-making abilities in the workshop. Second, it is very easy to encourage the acquisition of relevant skills in small factories that produce components or products in small series, because the worker is a jack-of-all-trades and knows all the phases involved in the production process in that particular plant.
f) The system enables workers to learn how the subsystem works, acquire broad skills, and then use them after deciding, for example, to set up on their own as entrepreneurs to sell a complete machine (using components produced by other small entrepreneurs), produce a component for the machine, or carry out a specific, promising manufacturing process.

The example given concerns an internationally successful product that has so far encountered very few competitors. The underlying logic is, however, extremely similar not only for the production of other types of mechanical instruments (such as machinery for woodworking, agriculture, metal processing) but also of textiles, clothing, and footwear. This type of flexible specialization is widespread throughout central Italy and the Veneto region, and the comments made about this type of production apply beyond machine building in Emilia-Romagna.

The development of subsystems consisting of small enterprise based on flexible specialization exemplify entrepreneurship as Schumpeter defined it. First, the distinctive functional feature of these enterprises is that they bring together, at least during the initial phase, a given type of production with the purpose of exploiting new international market opportunities (the demand for consumer goods and instrumental goods manufactured in small series). From an internal standpoint, a technological innovation is adaptive to major technological innovations, but is undoubtedly creative, all of which is achieved by the figure of a specialized worker who proved that he was capable of being an entrepreneur even when still an employee and then made a step upwards in the social class by setting up his own firm.

Second, the social background of craftsmen (small entrepreneurs employing fewer than 20 people) is similar to that of blue-collar workers, as both come from farming families (see Capecchi 1982).

Schumpeter's definition of entrepreneurship is supported by this information on the class background of this group of small entrepreneurs, for these entrepreneurs are both creative and adaptive in their use of technology. Their work histories deviate from those of employed workers but they remain leftist militants and deviate against the center-right wing national government. Their values are those described by Schumpeter: a non-rational attachment to their firm, the search for well-being for their families, and a "deviant" attitude.

This transition to entrepreneurship is, however, strewn with barriers (even within the same family), and it is not by chance that this type of entrepreneurial activity is described as masculine in this chapter. Wives have played a crucial, but always subordinate, role in this development, even when (as in the case of small craft enterprises in the textiles sector) the business grew mainly as a result of the women's experience in working at home. The ownership of these small craft and industrial enterprises remains in the hands of the men, even though increased levels of income and active participation in the husband's work have enabled wives in farming or working-class families in the Emilia-Romagna region to emancipate themselves. This situation has changed, to a certain extent in recent generations, as will be shown below.

Entrepreneurial Career Paths for Highly Educated Young Men and Women

As Figure 1 has shown, the crafts are not the only path to small entrepreneurship. A new one has developed to allow workers (mostly male) to move towards an industrial activity within a system of economic development based on flexible specialization (see Figure 1). There is quite a different set of barriers and opportunities for the generation of workers in Emilia-Romagna who were twenty to thirty years old in 1980, accompanied by equally different types of small entrepreneurship (see Figure 2). The reasons are to be found in technological changes (changes in the relations between systems of industrialization) and the changes that took place in the level of education, values, and other domains within the new generations. The spread of the new electronic and computer technologies introduced flexibility into the large Ford-style firm. Large firms now began to produce small and medium series and were competitive in the market with the products produced by the industrial subsystems based on the flexible specialization considered in the previous section of this chapter. In order for a type of industrialization based on flexible specialization to be competitive, it is evident that electronics and computers must be introduced into its production processes. This step is clearly difficult in a system based on flexible specialization, because it requires a degree of coordination that the system does not possess. The strategy chosen in Emilia-Romagna was therefore to further broaden the production base with the growth of small electronics and computing consultancy firms, often operating in the informal economy. Many of them have managed to incorporate electronics into the machines they produce. The entire packaging and wrapping machines sector, for example, has carried out this transformation without compromising its competitive position on international markets. Even so, some firms have had difficulty, blame for which has fallen on the regional government, which has adopted a policy of granting technological assistance to firms and gradually modernizing vocational training courses.

The market, too, has had an active role in creating opportunities and barriers. In the 1950s the market stimulated private enterprise by providing the demand for small series machines needed in industry and agriculture. At the present time, however, a large proportion of industrial production at an international level is being geared to market outlets no longer in industry or agriculture, but in all the different branches of the tertiary sector. Equipment is needed in hospitals, educational establishments, banks, the insurance sector, and commerce, for example. The problem facing the industrial system is then, that new market outlets must be found through innovation within a given product category. Indeed, innovation must address the very nature of the product itself, and this is no easy matter for a group of small entrepreneurs.

New generations, therefore, face a situation very different from that which confronted the generation of those who were 20 to 30 years old in the 1950s. Industry can no longer be considered the only road to small entrepreneurship. The growing importance of the tertiary sector not only concerns labor; it becomes more and more the pivotal point for activities of small entrepreneurship. These transformations in the productive system and the services correspond to deep transformation in social composition and in values within the generation of those young people who were 20 to 30 years old in 1980.

The most visible transformation has taken place in education. Since the region was still mostly agricultural in 1950, the parents of the 1980 generation received a fairly low level of education. Almost all young males and females in the succeeding generation have a high school diploma and in many cases, a higher degree. Their values and attitudes towards study and work have changed accordingly. Young women of the 1980s, for example, are seeking jobs in the official labor market and refuse to perform woman's traditional role of supporting the male entrepreneurial careers. Moreover, men and women of the 1980 generation refuse to accept unqualified paid labor for their entire working lives.

This refusal might be due to the increased economic well-being of their families and to the growth of individual expertise. Let us then compare Figures 1 and 2 for the main changes in the opportunities and barriers influencing the transition to small entrepreneurship. As far as training opportunities and access to innovation are concerned, the generation of workers who were 20 to 30 years old in the 1950s had male-dominated access to mechanical know-how through school and work. The system of industrialization based on flexible specialization permitted one to acquire an advanced training even if one started out as an unskilled worker. At the same time, technical schools were educating skilled workers, who were eventually able to start their own private activities. During the 50s, however, the general level of education was very low, and most learning occurred on the job. People between 20 and 30 years old in the 1980s can attend the university, acquire experience and expertise in the new technologies, and assimilate knowledge during their leisure time. Their training options are much broader than those available in 1950s. Because of the backwardness of the Italian educational system, though, this increase of opportunities is still no guarantee that a person will acquire the expertise necessary to cope with today's processes of transformation. Since it is hard to get qualified jobs, families enjoying a relatively high standard of living continue to lend financial support to their young men and women as they seek a job that will satisfy their expectations.

The structure of the market, the demand for goods and services, and the relations between the different economies and the different systems of industrialization have changed as well. During the 1950s the Ford-style system did not compete with the system based on flexible specialization, for small series production and the production of instrumental goods did not compete with large series production by large firms. The industrial system was the center of all production activities. In the 1980s the Ford-style system has begun to compete with the system based on flexible specialization, and the outcome is what now is called a process of "tertiarization": a growth in the demand for household and personal services and a growth in the demand for services supporting industrial, agricultural, and productive activities in general. The increased number of people working in the tertiary sector is multiplying, as is the demand for industrial production requested by hospitals, schools, banks, and other institutions. These profound changes open up new opportunities to enter the tertiary and the advanced tertiary sector while making it more difficult to continue the more traditional family style of small firm based on electrical and mechanical know-how.

Even the roles of national and regional government have changed. During the 1950s small entrepreneurs from the Emilia Romagna, mostly of a peasant/working-class family, felt little allegiance to the Christian-Democratic central government. They saw themselves as part of the working class. The situation is more complicated today. Small entrepreneurs radically changed their class identification, even though their political behavior towards the political left has not changed. The leftist regional government in Emilia Romagna still offers more entrepreneurial opportunities than either the National government or most other Italian regions. The leftist regional government is finding it increasingly difficult to respond to an ever greater array of clientele.

Furthermore, both the regional government and the regional and national credit system direct their help mostly to industrial craft firms; it is increasingly difficult to receive support for a post-industrial type of entrepreneurship. Within the prevailing system of family firms during the 1950s, all members of the family cooperated to make their business succeed; whereas young people today are being supported by their families, though their careers have become self-oriented. They aspire to careers that are very different from the ones of their parents. In order to maintain a position within the industrial system, they must learn new technologies unknown to their parents. If they leave industry, they enter into sectors that had never been considered by their parents, thereby broadening the choice of paths leading to small entrepreneurship. Three types of small entrepreneurs can be identified within the Region:

1) Some people of the new generation, especially men, are trained in new

electronic and computer technologies and enter entrepreneurship with modalities different from those of their fathers. These young people thoroughly understand that the diffusion of the new technologies brings in large firms as strong competitors. Their choices lead in three directions:

a) to an organization based on flexible specialization is maintained while the system is modernized by the introduction of electronics and computers through process and product innovation;
b) to new enterprises introduced, as consulting centers (in an area of electronics and computers); and
c) to a new way of entrepreneurship based on the collaboration with the university to produce prototypes or specialized products at a high technological level.

These entrepreneurs might be called "small entrepreneurs for the new technologies". This avenue is reserved primarily for men, but young women, although excluded from high level technology, are frequently engaged in the small firms of their fathers and become computer consultants dealing with problems of administration and management for the small craft firm.

2) Other members of this new generation, men and women alike, frequently refuse to work in the firms run by their fathers, even when the father (seldom the mother) has become a small entrepreneur. These young people consider this type of labor as restrictive industrial manual labor, fatiguing and monotonous in terms of time and pace. This group of young people of the 80s faces a general crisis of unemployment, but refuses to view work as a unique and absolute value in life.
We must also take into account the fact that a strong expansion of the demand for services was influenced by a consistent level of wealth in the Emilia-Romagna Region following World War II. Other forms of entrepreneurship developed then outside of the industrial sector and of a different sort with respect to the traditional small firms: cooperative companies in the area of services (food and nutrition, health, body care, etc.), of cultural activities, companies aiming at reviving traditional arts and craft (musical instruments, gold work, and jewelry), or small size agricultural work in the country (agricultural cooperative companies of a new form, agricultural-tourism, etc.), leisure time activities (sport, photography, music, audiovisuals, etc.) transformed into entrepreneurial activities.
It is very interesting to notice an autonomous participation of women in the new type of entrepreneurship, because women are searching for individual self-realization within their professions and are refusing the

traditional division of male and female roles. This second sort of entrepreneur might be named "small post-industrial entrepreneur".

3) The majority of people belonging to this new generation (both males and females) have families with a lower level of social, cultural, and economic capital, and they aim at self-employment and at small entrepreneurship but cannot find the right pathway towards its realization. The objective and generalized narrowing of the range of employment within the labor market of the official economy goes together with the subjective refusal of unqualified and uncreative employed labor. As a mediation between two contrasting trends these young people accept unqualified and precarious or unprotected employment, but only as a transitory activity even for a long term. The fact of so many possibilities, however, produces a strange category of young people who are entrepreneurs in their "spirit" but cannot realize their aim in reality. People belonging to this category could be called "small entrepreneurs without a firm".

Notes for a European Policy of Small Entrepreneurship

The different types of small entrepreneurs that the present study has identified within an Italian region most likely represent a typology common to other European nations or regions (and a comparative analysis would be welcome). This sort of research is useful not only in describing an important social phenomenon but also in guiding national or EEC action in the social area under discussion.

The results of the study show that "support of small firms" is strictly limited in various ways.

1) The label "small firm" subsumes very different types of activity. A small firm performing executive tasks for large Ford-style firms is very different from small firms in a subsystem featuring flexible specialization and from "small entrepreneurs for new technology" who produce services for industries, prototypes, etc. There is a variety of situations that cannot be unified under the characteristic of "small firms", and it is important that the different types of small entrepreneurship be helped in an adequate way (for example by a Technological Park).
2) It is important to change the traditional bias favoring industry into an attitude that also supports transitions to post-industrial entrepreneurship.
3) A widespread problem concerns "small entrepreneurs without a firm", those young people who have at least a high school education and who

desire autonomous work and/or make the transition to small entrepreneurship. Attention paid to this category of people could stimulate the establishment of centers that give professional support through counselling, continuing education, and other services.

References

Becattini, G. (1979): Dal settore industriale al distretto industriale. Alcune considerazioni sull'unità di indagine, *Rivista di economia e politica industriale*, n. 1.

Becattini, G. (Ed.) (1987): *Mercato e forze locali: il distretto industriale*, Bologna: Il Mulino.

Bergonsini, L. (1966): L'analfabetismo nell' Emilia Romagna nel primo secolo dell' Unità, *STatistica*, n. 2.

Bianco, M. L. and Luciano, A. (1982): *La sindrome di Archimede*, Bologna: Il Mulino.

Brusco, S. (1980): Il modello Emilia: disintegrazione produttiva e integrazione sociale, *Problemi della transizione*, n. 5.

Capecchi, V. (1982): Classe operaia e cultura borghese, In: AA.VV. *Famiglia operaia, mutamenti culturali, 150 ore*, Bologna: Il Mulino.

Capecchi, V. (1983): La economia sumergida in Italia, *Sociologia del Trabajo*, n. 9.

Capecchi, V. and Pesce, A. (1983): Se la diversità é un valore, *Inchiesta*, n. 59–60.

Capecchi, V. and Pesce, A. (1986): *Vivero lo spazio e il tempo*, Bologna: Comune di Bologna.

Capecchi, V. ed al. (1978): *La piccola impresa nell'economia italiana*, Bari: De Donato.

Capecchi, V., Enrietii, A. and Rollier, M. (Eds.) (1981): *Innovazione e ristrutturazione nel settore delle macchine utensili*, Milano: F. Angeli.

Comune di Bologna (1980): *Macchine, scuola industria*, Bologna: Il Mulino.

Fuà, G. and Zacchia, C. (Eds.) (1983): *Industrializzazione senza fratture*, Bologna: Il Mulino.

Galbraith, J. K. (1952): *American capitalism*, Boston: Houghton Mifflin.

Galbraith, J. K. (1967): *New industrial state*, Boston: Houghton Mifflin.

Greffe, X. (Ed.) (1984): *Les P. M. E. creent-elles des empois?* Paris: Economica.

Keeble, D. and Wever, E. (Eds.) (1985): *New firms and regional development in Europe*, London: Croom Helm.

Melossi, D. (1977): Lotta di classe nel piano di lavoro, In: AAVV *Restaurazione capitalistica e piano del lavoro*, Roma: Editrice Sindicale Italiana.

Noble, D. F. (1984): *Forces of production*, New York: Alfred A. Knopf.

Pahl, R. E. (1984): *Divisions of labour*, London: Basil Blackwell.

Piore, M. J. and Sabel, C. (1984): *The second industrial divide*, New York: Basic Books.

Poni, C. (1982): *Fossi e cavedagne benedicon le campagne*, Bologna: Il Mulino.

Sabel, C. and Zeitlin, J. (1985): Historical alternatives to mass production: politics, markets and technology in nineteenth century industrialization, *Past and Present*, n. 108.

Schumpeter, J. (1947): The creative response in economic history, *Journal of Economic History*, November.
Solo, C. S. (1951): Innovation in the capitalistic process: A critic of Schumpeterian theory, *Quarterly Journal of Economics*, August.
Wilkinson, F. (Ed.) (1981): *The dynamics of labour market segmentation*, London: Academic Press.

Forms of Work and the Role of Self-Provisioning

R. E. Pahl

It has now become a commonplace to observe that employment in the formal economy is only one form of work. However, it is equally important to understand that it is inappropriate to subsume all other forms of work under some catch-all concept such as "the informal economy". Forms of work may differ substantially depending on the social relations in which they are embedded. A focus on the interconnections between technology, capital, and labour has to recognise that the social relations of "the workplace" may be as much a product of the domestic circumstances of household members as the more conventionally understood relations of factory or office. Furthermore, the notion of "the workplace" has to be extended.

During the last five years there has been considerable interest in the social science community in "work outside employment", and many conferences and seminars have been held, bringing together information and ideas from different European countries.[1] This was what might be termed the "natural history" period in the development of the subject when researchers brought back beautiful specimens from the field or urban jungle and it became more generally recognised that previous taxonomies, if not theoretical assumptions, had to be modified.

It is ironic that just at the time when the uncounted work outside the formal economy has become recognised, there are clear signs that certain forms of informal work are likely to be declining. Work which is largely defined in terms of its illegality – "off the books", "on the side", "for cash", and so on – may be more closely tied to levels of growth in the formal, counted sphere than is generally realised. In two recent elegant contributions O'Higgins casts serious doubt on the contention that the "unobserved economy" is in some way an alternative to the formal economy (O'Higgins 1984a, 1984b). Rather, he asserts, when the formal economy declines, so, too, does the informal. Some attention has been

[1] For example, the Consiglio Italiano per le Scienze Sociale (CISS) held a conference at Frascati, near Rome, from November 25–28, 1982. Bibliographic surveys of work in France, Germany, Italy, Britain, and other countries were presented.

given to the possible reasons for this putative decline in informal paid work outside the household (Pahl 1984: 91–98, Wallace and Pahl 1986), but this is not the central concern of this present paper. Here the focus is on the form of work done by household members with their own land, labour, and capital equipment, in their own time for their own or members of their family's benefit. This is the work which is termed self-provisioning.

The Growth of Self-Provisioning: The Example of Britain

There are indications that from around 1973 there was a substantial increase in certain forms of self-provisioning among British households. A substantial amount of production once again took place in the home by household members, which earlier in the century might have been done by employing another individual or firm. Table 1 provides an assessment of the growth of self-provisioning based on trade figures.[2]

A number of reasons were adduced for this substantial increase in domestic work. First, the sale of local authority houses and the encouragement of owner-occupation by the Conservative government, which came into office in 1979, helped to maintain demand; second, middle-class home owners found that the combination of lower disposable incomes and higher labour costs squeezed them into doing more work for themselves; third, both manual and non-manual workers were reducing their hours in employment, thus giving them more time for other activities.[3]

The growth in this particular area of self-provisioning is obviously related to a number of factors not all operating together. To begin with, new tools and cheap, readily available materials encouraged experimentation in providing domestic comforts and improvements, such as draught exclusion and the like. Later, as inflation rapidly grew in the early 1970s, people saw the advantage of improving what was their strongest hedge against inflation; and, since the cost of labour for building and services was also escalating, it seemed good sense for people to paint their own

---

[2] In the assessment of the DIY trade at the end of the 1970s, it was seen to be "one of the most profitable in the retail sector". The research organisation Euromonitor suggested that the market would amount to £4,500 million in retail price terms by 1981.

[3] As the authors of the Report cited in Table 1 suggest, "many in the trade believe that the home improvement, as opposed to DIY, boom is only now beginning in this country" (Earnshaw, Hayes and Sons, *Report on DIY/Home Improvement*, Eurometer Publications, London, 1980, p. 5).

Table 1 Indicators of the Growth of Various Forms of Self-Provisioning 1974–1980 (Trade in £ Million)

	1974	1976	1978	1979	1980*)
DIY repairs and improvements	96	142	205	256	325
Tools etc. and wood products	232	351	571	703	890
Home decorating	483	608	775	866	1,035
Total	811	1,101	1,551	1,825	2,250
Gardening equipment	235	289	399	460	600
Car maintenance	374	490	670	820	950
All of above	1,420	1,880	2,620	3,105	3,800
Deflator (1975 = 100), all consumer prices	80.9	115.6	145.0	163.4	189.5
All self-provisioning expenditure at 1975 prices	1,755	1,626	1,807	1,900	2,004

*) Estimates

Overall expenditure shows a 14 per cent growth 1974–80 whereas final expenditure and GDP grew by 8 per cent over that period. DIY, tools and home decorating shows a 19 per cent growth over the period. The deflator is for all consumer prices. The particular items on the table probably had a slower than average growth so the estimates are likely to underestimate the growth in consumption of these categories.

Source: Euromonitor Publications 1980: 6. The deflator was kindly worked out by Dr. J.I. Gershuny.

houses and even to attempt more ambitious work. The political impetus to increased home ownership has already been noted, and many local authorities began to encourage tenants to maintain their own homes after 1979 as they reduced their direct labour operations. Finally, the growth of unemployment and perhaps an increasing awareness that whom you know was coming to matter more than what you know contributed to a tendency for people to move house less frequently; whatever the reason, between 1980 and 1981 there was a reduction of 7% in households moving from one area of the country to another.[4]

Furthermore, according to market research data, women were said to be increasing their share of such work. It was suggested that married women working part-time in the service sector, often in pleasant, well-decorated surroundings, would adopt a more critical approach to their own domestic environment. In a September 1980 survey of women aged

[4] OPCS *Monitor*, MN 82/3, Office of Population Censuses and Surveys, London, 1982.

Table 2 Division of Labour in Domestic Improvement Work, by Region (Percentages)

Home improvement work done by:	North	Midlands	South	All*)
Husband only	2	1	9	4
Husband mainly	26	34	43	34
Husband and wife together	60	45	39	49
Wife mainly	11	16	8	11
Wife only	1	4	1	2
				100

*) N = 481

Source: Taylor Nelson and Associates Ltd. *Survey for Polycell*, September 1980.

between 16 and 45 who were first-time home owners, who had been living in their first home for less than five years, and who had undertaken at least one DIY (Do-It-Yourself) task in the past twelve months, 77 % claimed that they would consider doing home improvement jobs themselves before seeking professional help; 84 % said that they enjoyed working on home improvements and felt quite capable of tackling wallpapering and painting; the same proportion claimed that they were involved in planning DIY work, no doubt largely owing to the need to agree on style and colour schemes; and 80 % said that they were planning further improvements, despite having already done substantial amounts. It is interesting that much of this DIY work is done by the man and wife jointly.[5] This applies particularly to painting and papering, but about a fifth of the wives also claimed to be able to do plastering. The division of labour in domestic improvement work by region is given in Table 2.

When the women were asked (not as rigorously as one would have liked) about their attitudes to this work, 64 % agreed that they liked to share the work as much as possible, but the same proportion also said that they had to prod their husbands before they would do DIY work around the house. Interestingly, 59 % of the women felt that they could do jobs

[5] "IPC found that in 69 % of cases women were the main decision makers in both selection and purchase. Only 25 % of husbands claimed to be the predominant influence ... in general product lines it is estimated that within five years the number of women doing DIY jobs around the house will have risen to 48 %" (Earnshaw, Hayes *Report on DIY*, p. 9).

themselves just as well as their husbands, and only 21 % said they would rather get someone professional in to do the job.[6)]

It is evidently extremely difficult to get a precise measure of this form of self-provisioning, and even within the trade estimates differ substantially.[7)] However, it does seem clear that the work is becoming more specialised. Thus, the DIY market for wood board and laminates in 1980 was estimated at £ 240 million at retail prices, and the growth of DIY timber has compensated for the decline in demand from the building industry. Ordinary householders are attempting more than putting up simple shelving, and the demand for moulded wood is growing. Similarly, in double glazing, 40 % of secondary installations are done by DIY.[8)]

There seems little doubt that from the middle 1950s to the early 1980s there has been a substantial increase of work done by household members on the maintenance and improvement of their dwellings, stimulated and encouraged by the development of new products[9)] and the spread of power tools (almost 60 % of households owned a power drill in 1981). This expansion must have been limited by the fact that only since the late 1970s have more than half the households owned their own dwellings, an increasing proportion of which have relatively modest incomes. While all the data provided by the DIY industry should be viewed with caution, if not scepticism, Table 3 suggests that a truly remarkable amount of work goes on in the dwelling.

It is important to recognise that the sale of DIY equipment and materials obviously appears in the national accounts, so there is no question of including this in any other hidden or informal "economy". What is not formally assessed in the national accounts is the unpaid labour of household members, except insofar as that is reflected in the increased capital value of the domestic property in which their labour is invested. Clearly, it would be misguided to assume that this self-provisioning was anything more subtle than substituting unpaid for paid labour. Documentation of the growth of garden centres and of the domestic maintenance of cars and other equipment would show the same trend towards more household work.

This activity may enable households to live more comfortably than they might otherwise be able to do, and it is hard to sustain a view that all this work is a form "sweat equity" imposed on those who would be unable to afford to maintain their own dwellings if they were dependent on the

---

6) Polycell, *The Polycell Report on the DIY Market*, Paragon Communications, London, 1981.

7) Ibid., pp. 12–13.

8) Ibid., pp. 14–15.

9) Polyfilla was introduced in 1956.

Table 3 DIY Jobs Done in Britain over a Twelve-Month Period

Task	% of adults aged 25 and over
Painted interior woodwork	84
Filled cracks and holes	72
Hung wallpaper	70
Painted internal walls	68
Painted exterior woodwork	45
Put up shelves	40
Put up tiles on walls	37
Regrouted tiles	30
Plastered	28
Painted exterior walls	21
Put up ceiling tiles	16
Installed some form of heat installation	13

Source: Gordon Simmons Research Ltd., reported in *The 1981 Polycell Report on the DIY Market.* From the context it would appear that the information in this table relates to 1980.

wage labour of others. Certainly, some self-provisioning is a coping response for those with insufficient financial resources to hire labour in the market; but it also provides aesthetic satisfaction, pride in workmanship, and a sense of domestic solidarity. It is also expensive and a product of affluence, not poverty. Indeed, work in and on the domestic dwellings by men and women may do as much to develop their broader political consciousness as their experience of employment.

Self-Provisioning and Household Work Strategies

It might be assumed that this growth in self-provisioning is a response to current economic change and the unemployed are the best placed to take advantage of their own "free" time to work for themselves. Evidence from Britain and France makes it clear that this assumption is false (Foudi, Stankiewicz, and Vaneecloo 1981, Pahl 1984, Wallace and Pahl 1986). The unemployed are less likely to engage in informal work in and outside the home compared with those in full-time employment. There is not a time/money trade-off as some had assumed to be the case.

In an attempt to discover precisely which households engaged in what forms of work, a detailed 1 in 9 sample survey of all households on the Isle of Sheppey in Kent was undertaken in 1981, yielding a sample of 730 with a response rate of 79% (SCPR 1981). Full details of the context of this study are reported elsewhere (Pahl 1984). Here some of the more salient findings are reviewed and discussed.

Gathering information on forms of labour is fairly straightforward. Collecting employment characteristics presents relatively little difficulty: questions on the nature of the present occupation of respondent and partner elicited data that could be readily classified into the Registrar General's socioeconomic groups, which were later collapsed into class categories. Information was also gathered about other earners in the household and about household income. All these data enabled households to be precisely categorised in relation to their involvement in formal labour. Other questions were designed to draw on all the other work that respondents did for employers or for any other person or institution outside the household, whether or not they were paid. Inevitably, such questions had to be phrased more and more generally in order to encompass all the possible tasks and activities that respondents could do. Unfortunately, respondents did not always remember or did not always think certain tasks worth mentioning. However, these questions did provide excellent data on occupation, income, and a range of informal work.

A further set of questions explored the sources of labour that households used to get forty-one distinctive tasks done. Broadly, sources of labour were provided either formally, through the market (for example, garages), state services (for example, the home help service) or members of the household themselves, or through informal sources (friends, neighbours, relatives or others "working off the books"), which might have been paid or unpaid. These tasks were carefully selected after two years of ethnographic work in the area, and they reflect the nature and range of tasks likely to be undertaken by households on the Island (see Appendix I).

When exploring the question of self-provisioning, we wanted to know whether those households who, say, do their own home decorating also, perhaps, fix their own cars, make jam, and also grow their own vegetables. Is there a cumulation of self-provisioning, or do some households specialise in decorating for themselves, whereas others specialise in other spheres and use the formal market provision of services for those spheres in which they do not have competence? In order to answer such questions, a scale of measurement was devised.

The self-provisioning scale (self-prov) measures the spread of activity that given households do using the labour of members of the households themselves: that is, not simply the number of tasks, but rather the range of tasks that are done using the labour of household members. Each household gets a score from 0 to 6 depending on the use of its labour over a carefully selected range of possible tasks.

The scale does not show whether a household is able to do its own plastering *and* painting *and* glazing, but whether it has actually done *one* of these activities *as well as* vegetable growing and a car maintenance task, and so on. The six-point scale was based on distinct spheres of household or domestic tasks that could be bought in the market. People can buy vegetables, cakes, and jerseys; they do not have to dig, bake, and knit. Indeed, jerseys bought in shops, in the market, or at a bring-and-buy sale may well be substantially cheaper than those made at home. The tasks for the six-point self-prov scale were then arranged so that households could score one point if they did just one task within each cluster. Tasks of a fairly routine nature were included in the self-prov scale (SPS) only if they were performed with some frequency, but the larger tasks were included if they were performed at any time at all. The clusters of tasks for the self-provisioning scale are, therefore, as follows:

SPS 1: Vegetable growing at any time.
SPS 2: Either painting or plastering or mending a broken window in the last year.
SPS 3: Either checking the oil level or tuning the engine or doing the work on the brakes of a car at any time.
SPS 4: Either putting in an RSJ (rolled steel joist) or double glazing or central heating or building a bathroom or an extension or converting an attic at any time.
SPS 5: Either making jam or beer or wine regularly.
SPS 6: Making or knitting clothes at any time.

Why do some households do more work for themselves than others? Do they choose to do it as a form of self-expression, or are they almost compelled to do it by the lack of other resources, because they have no money to buy services formally and no other resources to repay informal labour reciprocally? We may expect that those households based on couples including a number of young children require more tasks to be done and, because of a reduction of income per head owing to the number of dependants in the household, are obliged to do more tasks for themselves. These arguments might apply *a fortiori* to households headed by a manual worker, who is likely to have a lower individual income than a middle-class earner but where both partners are, perhaps, more likely to have skills to do self-provisioning work than are middle-class couples, less well-trained in manual skills. In this way, perhaps, differences in levels of living between the two classes are reduced. Furthermore, it is likely that such high self-provisioners would own their own homes, be inward-looking, privatised, and perhaps also more likely to vote Conservative. There might be a secondary peak of self-provisioning at a later stage of the

Table 4 Household Type, by Self-Provisioning Scale (Percentages*))

Self-prov. scale	Couple households	Male-headed non-couple households	Female headed non-couple households	All
1	–	–	–	–
2	3	13	31	10
3	13	37	31	19
4	28	30	28	28
5	40	17	9	32
6	16	3	1	11
Total (*N*)	526	40	164	730

*) Percentates in tables do not always add to 100 because of rounding.

life cycle, in the years before retirement after children have left home, when there is time and energy to devote to domestic tasks as a way of demonstrating a particular style of life.

Certainly, it is quite clear that couple households do score more highly on the self-prov scale, as Table 4, relating to the sample as a whole, indicates. If the self-prov. scale is dichotomised into low (scores 2–4) and high (scores 5–6), then over half the couples score in the high category. This is a better basis for the assertion that substantial domestic work by households takes place, since it avoids the problems posed by certain tasks being appropriate only at certain stages of the life cycle. Particular individual circumstances are thus reduced by using the scale.

For ease of analysis, the dichotomised self-prov scale is used to illustrate some important differences. Selecting only those households where the male is in full-time employment, high self-prov scores are the more likely the greater the involvement of his partner in formal employment. Thus, where both partners are in full-time employment, 65 % of households score high on the self-prov scale, whereas when the female partner is retired the high proportion falls to 50 %. Taking the 65 households with more than two earners, 69 % scored high on the self-prov scale. Finally, selecting those households where both partners were in full-time employment, but at least one of them was on shift work, the proportion scoring high on the self-prov scale rose to as much as 74 %. Yet, when male shiftworkers had as a partner a non-employed full-time housewife, the proportion scoring high dropped to 43 %.

These findings are unequivocal: employment and self-provisioning go together, rather than one being a substitute for another. Furthermore, despite what was initially expected, class did not make a substantial difference: indeed, counter to the initial hypothesis, the proportion scoring high on the self-prov scale ranged from 64 % in Class 1 through 59 % in Class 2 to 50 % for Class 3. Evidently, this result is partly the consequence of more frequent car and home ownership in the higher classes, but it still does not follow that households should, apparently, choose to do so many tasks with their own labour.

Some interesting intra-class variations appear when the combined household class classification is used. Thus, when Class 1 males are married to Class 3 females, the proportion scoring high on the self-prov scale rises to 70 % as against 64 % for Class 1 as a whole. Similarly, when Class 3 males are married to higher-status females, their scores are substantially above the rate for the class as a whole. This suggests, perhaps, that status inconsistency between partners is a source of tension or of complex feelings of guilt, which generates a distinct dynamic element in the household work strategy. Lower-status men and women may compensate to their partners by doing more conventionally gender-linked tasks. So lower-status men may do more decorating or car maintenance and lower-status women more of the female-type tasks. Thus the internal dynamics of the couple modify what would otherwise seem to be a direct linear relationship between higher class and higher rating on the self-prov scale.

Childcare work does not appear on the self-prov scale, yet couples with children were overall more likely to score higher than couples with no children (60 % compared with 47 %). However, the very highest score (79 %) is for couples having their youngest child aged between 5 and 15 with the wife or partner over 35 years of age; where there are also older children or other adults in the same household the proportion of high scorers on the self-prov scale is 67 %. These latter may, therefore, be contributing not only extra money but also extra working capacity to the household. Analysis showed that level of income on its own was less important as a factor affecting levels of self-provisioning, which, it must be remembered, relate to a range of tasks done by different household members in and around the home. For this reason it is perhaps less surprising that the more adults there are in the household the higher the score.

Households, then, do more activities with their own labour if they have a larger gender-divided pool of hands and access to land and capital. Growing their own vegetables requires access to land, whether a garden or an allotment, and owning a house or car requires capital. However, the land and capital by themselves do not necessarily encourage the use of the household's own labour. Ownership of property does not mechanistically determine behaviour: there is not a direct linear correlation between household work practices and household income.

Higher income is a necessary but not a sufficient condition for higher rating on the self-prov scale. A process of polarization has developed on the Island: this produces at one end busy households with many workers, some of whom are in employment, in which a wide range of domestic tasks get done by household members; at the other end are the households with only one or two earners, without a car and probably not owning their own homes or, if they do, having sufficient energy or strength and also insufficient resources to be able to maintain them adequately.

The emphasis so far has been largely on range and not depth of sources of labour for clusters of tasks. In order to compensate for this bias, we devised a new DIY scale, where we put together all the ten domestic repair and maintenance tasks into one scale and households scored if they had done one or more of these tasks by using the labour of a member of the household:

1. Painting
2. Plastering
3. Mending a broken window
4. Putting in a rolled steel joist
5. Putting in double glazing
6. Putting in a new bathroom
7. Building a garage
8. Building an extension to the home
9. Converting an attic
10. Putting in central heating.

Table 5 Age of Respondents in Couple Households, by DIY Scale

DIY scale	Age of Respondents (%) 30 or under	31–50	51–64	65+	Total N	%
0	17	31	9	43	42	8
1	19	42	20	18	187	35
2	21	43	23	13	150	28
3	13	63	18	5	84	16
4	–	75	25	–	38	7
5	20	50	20	10	8	2
6	–	–	–	–	10	2
7	–	–	–	–	6	1
8	–	–	–	–	2	–
					527*)	100

*) The total is aberrant since one household could not be classified in all the other couple tables for lack of information but the age of the respondent is known.

Table 6 Economic Activity of Females in Selected Couple Households Where the Male Partner is in Full-Time Employment, by DIY Scale (Percentages)

DIY scale	Female partner is: full-time empl.	part-time empl.	full-time h'wife
0	9	6	2
1	33	30	23
2	30	28	14
3	17	17	11
4	6	9	5
5+	3	4	4
Total (N)	102	99	167

We limited analysis to couple households. Table 5 shows the DIY scale by age of respondent. The dominance of those in middle life is clear: again, it is households in this age range with children that dominate. Among those who did not score, 69% were couples without children as against 31% with children. By point 4 on the scale these positions were reversed – 29% of childless couples reached this score against 66% of couples with children.

More DIY is done in working-class households with multiple earners. The relationship between the employment status of the couple and the DIY scale is set out in Table 6. The remarkable conclusion illustrated by this table is that those couples where both partners are employed do more of such activity than in households where the female partner is a full-time housewife. The DIY scale underlines in a most emphatic fashion the conclusions derived from analysis of the self-prov scale. Economic activity and high levels of the use of household labour for self-provisioning go together. Those most committed to the labour market are also the most committed to using their own labour in their own time for their own purposes.

Forms of Work and Sources of Labour

So far in this paper, discussion has focused on but one form of work, namely self-provisioning. All forms of work and sources of labour can be illustrated by the following matrix (Table 7). The particular pattern or mix of forms of work and sources of labour is a household work strategy which is generally not self-consciously planned but may be so under certain circumstances.

Table 7 Forms of Work and Sources of Labour

Form of work of Household Member	Sources of Labour for Household Tasks			
Senior female	House-hold member	Informal paid	Informal unpaid	Formal or Institu-tion
Formal				
Informal paid				
Informal unpaid				
Self-provisioning				
Senior male				
Formal				
Informal paid				
Informal unpaid				
Self-provisioning				
As above for all other household members who have left full-time education				

It is highly significant that the Sheppey Survey (SCPR 1981) shows that involvement in formal employment and self-provisioning are directly related. The polarisation process whereby some households engage in all forms of work and others without employment are unable to engage in either self-provisioning or informal paid or unpaid work in the locality is highly significant (Miles 1983). This evidence from Britain shows clearly that self-provisioning and other forms of informal work are not available as survival strategies for the poor and the unemployed. This is a counter-intuitive conclusion with clear policy implications. However, this is not to say that in other European countries informalisation may not be part of the coping mechanism of poor or marginalised populations (Bagnasco, Brusco, and Capecchi 1982, Mingione 1983). Similarly, the British data could not support the thesis put forward in Germany that informal work can in some way serve as a substitute for the State provision of welfare services (Heinze and Olk 1982). Finally, research in a number of localities in France has produced very diverse results (Gaudin and Schiray 1982) in impressive empirical detail.[10]

This very diversity in European studies on forms of informal work may itself be a conclusion of very great significance: diversity in ways of getting by may be a new feature in European economics, and understanding at the level of the national society may have to be refocused. Increasingly, the local arena has come to be seen as the most salient social world for all forms of work outside employment. Once the point is made, the reasons become self-evident: informal work is exchanged between households in a particular locality where whom one knows matters more than what one knows. If one of the key mainsprings for social and political action is shifting to this very local context – if, indeed, it has ever been anywhere else – then a greater concern with the processes at work in such arenas will be necessary. One conclusion does stand out from the studies in the various countries: informal work is spread very unevenly between households and between localities. Furthermore, the categories most involved in various forms of informal work are not necessarily those that government departments and other official bodies believe to be so. Thus, the process of polarisation described for households on the Isle of Sheppey in Kent raises the following practical problems for social policy:

1) Those most in need of informal sources of labour, namely single-parent households and the elderly, are the least able to reciprocate in kind or in cash.
2) Those most eligible to engage in various forms of "community work" in the eyes of official bodies, namely married women free from the responsibility of children, are most likely to be full-time or part-time employed and also heavily engaged in self-provisioning for their own households. Hence the care of the elderly, the mentally handicapped, and other categories of people who are being "de-institutionalised" into the community may become a serious social issue.

---

[10] It is unfortunate that this research is still little known outside France. This is partly because many of the results appear in mimeographed form and reflect the work of a team of researchers. One of the best of such studies was produced in 1982 by the University of Lille *Travail Noir, Productions Domestiques et Entraide – Approches économique, juridique, sociologique de l'Economie Informelle et de ses transformations*, pp. 369. Another study from a team of researchers at Toulouse *Le systeme des Activités des Menages au Mirail – changement de la famille, changement par la famille?* was published in 1980. Other studies have been published in the *Cahiers de l'Observation du Changement Social* (éditions du CNRS). There has also been some interesting work on time budgets and some attempts to measure more rigorously work done by women in the household (see A. Fouquet and A. Chateau *Le Travail Domestique: essai de quantification*, Archives et Documents No. 32 (INSEE August 1981)).

3) Those most able and willing to engage in informal work, namely the unemployed with skills, are those who, at present, are most highly penalised by fiscal, social, and psychological sanctions or burdens. There is a strong fiscal disincentive in Britain for wives of unemployed males to remain in employment, and such households may find themselves in a state-induced cycle of deprivation so that those most in need of helping themselves are most restricted in being able to do so.
4) As a result of the unequal distribution of opportunities for gaining informal work outside the household, which has been extensively documented in both Britain and France, communities are increasingly divided amongst themselves. The fear of being informed on to the authorities is a considerable disincentive to work informally for others, whether or not such work is remunerated. Hence at a time when "the crisis of the welfare state" is encouraging governments to devolve more responsibility to the locality, the social strengths that may have resided there are being undermined.

These are but four instances of the way the balance of different forms of work between different social categories has direct practical implications for public policy. There is an urgent need for more comparative research relating the household work strategies of different social categories to the different forms of welfare provision in member states of the European community.

Forms of Work and Technological Change

In the interests of generating discussion and debate, I turn now to a line of thought which has already received some attention by scholars in a number of countries in order to offer some critical comments.

This position is based on the assumption that a combination of technological innovation in manufacturing industry and social innovation in households' behaviour, particularly in the way goods and services are produced inside the household, generates tendencies that result in a qualitatively different kind of society. More work is done in households as members use their own labour and their own capital equipment to produce goods and services for themselves. The logic of economic development, which moves away from primary production through manufacturing to the provision of services, is halted. Accelerating productivity in manufacturing industry, relative to that of the final service industry, means that goods get cheaper relative to final services. Hence, households buy manufactured goods that enable them to produce more services for themselves. Essentially, such a line of thought is based on the efficiency and innovative capacity of capitalism and on a value system that supports and approves innovative patterns of household consumption. The way people spend their time and money itself generates an economic response in the balance and content of goods and services.

Such a line of thought has been developed over the years by Jonathan Gershuny, and I will use his work to elaborate on it more fully.[11] Gershuny does not discuss either capitalism or class in his account of the development of a kind of self-service economy; he assumes that it is a net social benefit for the labour and some of the capital costs of the provision of services to be shifted to the household. Goods and services become cheaper, better, and more convenient. Such factors implicitly offset costs in time and any redistribution of work within the household.[12] Social innovation, for Gershuny, involves both technological development of process innovation at the workplace and a similar process centred on the household. He foresees a matching of a new wave of technological innovation – microprocessors, information storage devices, and new information-transmission infrastructure – with a new demand for home-centred services:

> In domestic services we can construct systems for automatic centralised monitoring and control of a range of household functions (heating, lighting, safety), and these household systems can themselves be linked to local security or safety services. In addition, we might imagine information packages giving advice on household operations.[13]

Unfortunately, the distributional consequences of this line of thought are not considered by Gershuny. He simply asserts that in the past "the poor got richer over time"[14] and claims that in the future the process he describes as "social innovation" will do two things:

> It increases the demand for labour, in the formal economy, by establishing new markets for the new products used in the "innovative modes of production", and

---

[11] See J. Gershuny's recent book, *Social Innovation and the Divisions of Labour*, Oxford University Press, 1983, for the most fully worked out statement of his position.

[12] The farmers of East Kent have shifted much of the costs of distribution of fruit to the consumer. Not only are we encouraged to pick our own soft fruit in season, but out of season we serve ourselves to apples in "farm shops". The farmer leaves a supply of apples, scales, and a tin with money in it in a farm building. The customer serves himself with fruit, leaves the money (taking change if necessary), and drives himself away in his own car. The farmer replenishes the stock of apples from his cold store and takes out money at intervals. Even if all the available takings are stolen – in practice unlikely on a regular basis – the farmer is still better off than he would be hiring even the cheapest labour.

[13] Gershuny, *Social Innovation*, p. 166.

[14] Ibid., p. 14.

also in the informal sector. And it reduces the supply of labour to the money economy.[15]

He goes on to say:

We must recognise that trends of events are in part determined by a logic that is internal to our social institutions and material environment, and quite out of our control [although the future course of development] is to some extent malleable.[16]

Yet, even in his most optimistic view of future economic and political developments, Gershuny admits that any new demand for labour will be for the skilled and not for the unskilled, and that the growth of informal production is more likely to reduce women's paid work disproportionately.[17] In the face of such apparently inherent inequalities, he seems helpless to effect any change. For example, he remarks that the absence of "sexual equity" is the result of unprogressive social attitudes:

Despite recent and quite substantial changes in publicly expressible attitudes, domestic work is still regarded as chiefly women's work. The fact of their perceived responsibility for domestic work reduces the amount of time women have available for paid work, *which places them at a disadvantage in the wage labour market.* And here is the inequality: precisely *because* similar sorts of men and women, *because* husbands and wives may be expected to want to work similar lengths of time, while women maintain their special responsibility for housework, women are more likely to take on part-time jobs (which are generally of inferior status), they have less energy to concentrate on their jobs, less flexibility to work longer hours when they are needed, so they cannot compete on equal terms with men.[18]

Evidently, Gershuny does not condone such attitudes, but he describes them in such a way as to imply that they are inevitable. So, these two interactive processes of innovation in technology and household behaviour produce new mixes of work for different social categories. Manual workers decline relative to "knowledge" workers, and new work is done by household members.

Gershuny mentions in passing a point that I consider to be outstandingly important, namely, that

households increasingly acquire their services by a combination of unpaid work with capital goods and materials purchased with money earned in paid employment. Households without formal employment may therefore find that

[15] Ibid., p. 177.
[16] Ibid., p. 177.
[17] Ibid., p. 183.
[18] Ibid., p. 153 (Gershuny's emphasis).

their abilities to engage in informal production activities are also impaired. And the more that a particular society provides its final services on an informal rather than a formal basis, the more expensive are its formal services. So, the process of "informalisation" of production does not necessarily alleviate the burden of unemployment.[19]

Gershuny recognises such inequalities and patterns of polarisation, but he does not address them as a central part of his argument. His analysis of the way time and money interact in the development of a self-service society to produce a diminishing marginal utility of income is important, as long as it is not forgotten that households still need substantial amounts of money in order to engage in selfservice activity.

However imaginative Gershuny's work is,[20] one must read between the lines of his book to discover the new patterns of inequality that are being generated and indeed emphasised by the processes of social innovation he describes. By under-emphasising the distributional consequences, and by inferring that what people do is what they actually want to do, those who adopt this line of thinking may be unwittingly closing options and ignoring potential political reactions of a conventional or unconventional kind. Nevertheless, this line of thinking is valuable and provides a distinct and rigorous approach to the connections between household work and society.

Conclusions and Recommendations

The task of bringing together what is known about work outside employment in individual member states of the European Community has largely been accomplished, with the conference arranged in Frascati in November 1982 playing an important part in this. However, there is now a danger that each national group will talk past the other, since there have been almost no comparative studies, and evidently conditions between member states vary substantially. This could lead to considerable confusion if results relating to, say, the Isle of Sheppey are uncritically compared with results from Lille, Naples, or wherever.

It is evident that the production and consumption of goods and services through work outside employment is an essential element in the economic life of the European Community member states. Research is now needed

[19] Ibid., p. 48.

[20] I readily acknowledge that I have been continuously stimulated and helped by his work for the last seven years.

which relates changes in the pattern of forms of work and sources of labour for different categories of households to distinctive social, economic, and political contexts. A state of the art survey which attempted to draw generalities out of disparate studies in disparate contexts would be misleading and counter-productive. Those who have attempted to make international comparisons, based on evidence that was not intended to have comparative significance, have acknowledged the danger and ineffectiveness of the enterprise (Redclift and Mingione 1985). Domestic production in Italy is quite a different social phenomenon from domestic production in Britain. The concentration of capital in the two countries is obviously very different as, too, is the role of the state and the nature of the social and economic infrastructure. Similarly, the domestic social relations in, say, southern Italy are different from those one might expect in Denmark.

Thus, at a time when there are attempts to achieve greater political and economic integration within the European Community, social diversity (disintegration would be too strong a word) may well be increasing. Clearly, the social processes in different member states may be similar in certain respects – but the differences and variations may be more significant. Hence, there is a clear need to build on research already done by the various teams in the different countries. Studies which have had a nation-specific orientation need to be reassessed in a wider context. In particular, the following themes need to be addressed:

1) What are the most effective household units for getting by in the last years of the twentieth century? Are multiple-earner households more adaptable and effective than single-earner households? Are the effective households (however designated) expanding at the expense of the less effective? This will involve analysis at a national level, possibly involving the re-tabulation of existing data on the structure and economic circumstances of households.
2) What are the state policies in relation to welfare and employment conditions which, intentionally or unintentionally, create distinctive household work strategies? How do these vary between EC member states, and how may they be comparatively evaluated?
3) What are the distributional consequences of the changing nature of work outside employment within and between households? This may be effectively illuminated through comparative analysis.
4) How far have technological developments encouraged self-provisioning amongst certain households and thus underlined a process of social polarisation which might have serious and deleterious unintended consequences?
5) How far do the domestic relations of production and consumption modify or engender social and political consciousness? How far,

- indeed, are the politics of the kitchen replacing the politics of the factory or office? The pattern of women's employment and its relation to all forms of work may be a more dynamic force in many contemporary European societies than the growth of a so-called service society or one based on the products of high technology.

The need for these and other questions to be faced and reformulated in a broader theoretical context is urgent. However, equally important is that they be faced in the context of detailed empirical studies of the forms of work and sources of labour which household members engage in or use. Information on actual household work practices involves research which is both expensive and time consuming. The changing nature of work cannot be completely understood by consulting national statistics in libraries. Yet it is well understood that the changing divisions of labour are a central component in understanding contemporary European societies. Understanding the processes which create and are created by distinctive household work strategies is an incredibly difficult and complex task. That is no reason for not attempting such a task and, as this paper indicates, a start has been made in most of the EEC member states.

Appendix Sheppey Survey Work Tasks

1) House maintenance (3)
    1 Indoor painting
    2 Plastering
    3 Mending a broken window
2) Home improvement and decoration (7)
    4 Double glazing
    5 Putting in a bathroom
    6 Building a garage
    7 Building an extension
    8 Converting an attic to living space
    9 Putting in a rolled steel joist (RSJ)
    10 Putting in central heating
3) Routine housework (12)
    11 Washing up
    12 Tidying house or flat
    13 Hoovering or brushing carpets
    14 Cleaning outside windows
    15 Cooking family meals
    16 Making a packed lunch
    17 Getting a take-away meal
    18 Shopping
    19 Washing clothes

20 Washing sheets
21 Ironing clothes
22 Ironing sheets

4) Domestic production (8)
23 Baking a cake
24 Making clothes
25 Knitting
26 Repairing clothes
27 Growing vegetables
28 Making jam
29 Making bread
30 Making beer or wine

5) Car maintenance (4)
31 Washing the car
32 Checking the oil
33 Tuning the engine
34 Repairing or checking the brakes

6) Childcare (7)
35 Bathing child
36 Changing nappies
37 Looking after a sick child
38 Collecting child from school
39 Seeing schoolteacher about child
40 Taking child to doctor
41 Getting child's hair cut

References

Bagnasco, A., Brusco, S., and Capecchi, V. (1982): Economia sommersa a tematiche emergenti sulla società italiana. Paper prepared for the CISS Conference on The Informal Economy, Social Conflicts and the Future of Industrial society, Frascati (Rome) November 25–28.

Euromonitor Publications (1980): *Report on DIY/Home Improvement*, London: Eurometer Publications (privately published by Earnshaw, Hayes & Sons).

Foudi, R., Stankiewicz, F., and Vaneecloo, N. (1981): Les chomers et l'economie informelle. Mimeo, University of Lille.

Gaudin, J. and Schiray, M. (1982): L'Economie cachée: Taxonomie – lecture française des usages des mots et des notions. Paper prepared for the CISS Conference on The Informal Economy, Social Conflicts and the Future of Industrial Society, Frascati (Rome) November 25–28.

Gershuny, J. (1983): *Social innovation and the division of labour*, Oxford University Press.

Heinze, R. and Olk, T. (1982): Development of the informal economy, *Futures*, (June): 189–204.
Miles, I. (1983): *Adaptation to unemployment*, SPRU, Occasional Paper No. 20 University of Sussex.
Mingione, E. (1983): Informalization, re-structuring and the survival strategies of the working class, *International Journal of Urban and Regional Research*, 7 (3): 311–339.
Mingione, E. (1984): Informalization and restructuring: The family and the state, In: A.J. Scott and M. Storper (Eds.): *Production, work, territory*.
O'Higgins, M. (1984a): The Relationship between the formal and hidden economies: An explanatory analysis for four countries, In: A. Wenig and W. Gaertner (Eds.): *The economics of the shadow economy*. Heidelberg: Springer.
O'Higgins, M. (1984b): Assessing the unobserved economy in the United Kingdom. In: Feigen, E. (Ed.) *The Unobserved Economy*, Cambridge University Press.
Pahl, R.E. (1984): *Divisions of labour*, Oxford: Blackwell.
Polycell (1981): *The Polycell Report on the DIY Market*, London: Paragon Publications.
Redclift, N. and Mingione, E. (Eds.) (1985): *Beyond employment: household, gender and subsistence*, Oxford: Blackwell.
SCPR (1981): *Isle of Sheppey study*, Technical Report P. 631. 30 Northampton Square, London EC1 VOAX.
Wallace, C.D. and Pahl, R.E. (1986): Polarisation, unemployment and all forms of work, In: S. Allen et al. (Eds.): *The experience of unemployment*. The Macmillan Press: Basingstoke.

A Comparison of the Resource Potential of Different Social Networks

Martin Pfaff and Klaus Deimer

Aims and Objectives[1]

Since the crisis of economic growth brought on in almost all Western industrialized countries by the world-wide recession of 1974/75, there has been increasing pressure on the programs for the delivery of service to people in need of personal care. These systems have been criticized not only for their excessive expense at a time of mounting fiscal difficulties but also for their presumed lack of effectiveness in attaining their underlying goals. Increasingly, attention has been focused on intermediary and small networks and particular types of new social initiatives as a complement to or even substitute for the existing types of collective networks of care. According to the principle of subsidiarity, primary responsibility for care should rest with the family, the neighborhood, and with small networks; intermediary and large networks should be called upon to provide services and care only if the family, the neighborhood, and small networks are unable to cope with the problem. In any case, the principle holds that individual and social initiatives and self-help groups should be integrated more effectively into the overall system of care than is presently the case.

Against the background of the ongoing debate, this chapter represents an attempt to compare different types of social networks dispassionately in terms of their strengths and weaknesses in delivering desired "goods and services." Answers to the following questions are sought:

1) How large is the scope of, and potential for, voluntary social services that could complement existing systems for the delivery of professional services? Can this potential be found equally across the various strata of society?
2) What types of social resources (information, services, and goods, for

[1] The authors wish to acknowledge the support of the Deutsche Forschungsgemeinschaft (German Research Foundation) for a project entitled "Comparative Evaluation of Different Forms of Institutional Arrangements of Types of Social Services." This paper is based on the ongoing project work.

example) can be provided or exchanged particularly well through small, self-organized, and thus voluntary types of social networks? According to which principle is the resource potential of these small social networks to be integrated within the overall welfare mix?

3) Turning to a specific case exemplifying more novel approaches to a welfare mix:
   - Are organizations like KISS (Contact and Information Facility for Self-Help Groups – Kontakt- und Informationsstelle für Selbsthilfegruppen) and SEKIS (Self-Help Contact and Information Facility – Selbsthilfe Kontakt- und Informationsstelle) suitable for integrating the new social initiatives into the existing system of care?
   - How can this type of organizational innovation be improved in order to mobilize the dormant resource potential?

Estimating the Potential for Voluntary Social Services

Before turning to questions of the structure and quality of new social initiatives, we first attempt to make some broad estimates of their overall level or volume. Furthermore, we focus on their relationship to the system of social stratification.

Voluntary Behavior and Voluntary Potential

How large is the scope and potential for voluntary social services that could complement existing systems for the delivery of professional services? This seemingly straightforward question is far more difficult to answer than to ask. The level of estimated voluntary social services depends largely upon the definition of the term, which has many layers of meaning.[2] Some benchmark figures may be provided for three countries. Nonetheless,

1) in the United States recent surveys have shown that voluntary services are being provided by roughly 30% of the population (see Gallup Report 1985: 25);
2) when related to the economically active population, voluntary and gratuitous work was estimated to range from 5.5% to 20% in Austria,

[2] In this chapter the term self-help is understood to mean not only specific activities of "in groups" geared to the internal solution of a single problem (for example, rheumatic illness) but also voluntary action in the field of social services and neighborhood-help. Thus, we mean not only self-help in the narrow sense of the word but also mutual aid and voluntary services granted to others. See Deimer and Jaufmann (1983: 71).

Table 1 Social Services Actually Rendered on a Voluntary Basis and Preparedness to Grant Social Services on a Voluntary and Gratuitous Basis (Percent)[1)]

Level of education	Age									
	16–39 years		40–54 years		55–64 years		above 65 years		Total	
	a*)	b*)	a	b	a	b	a	b	a	b
Secondary school without apprenticeship	9		7		6		4		6	
		6		5		3		2		4
	91	28	92	22	94	14	96	7	94	17
		55		65		75		85		71
Secondary school with apprenticeship	11		12		11		6		10	
		7		6		6		2		5
	89	31	88	23	89	12	94	9	89	23
		49		58		71		83		60
Intermediate-level high school	13		17		14		11		13	
		9		9		8		1		8
	87	31	83	21	86	21	89	10	86	25
		46		51		56		77		52
High school/ university	22		27		14		18		22	
		13		7		6		2		10
	77	35	72	32	86	25	82	12	78	32
		27		30		54		67		33
Total	13		13		10		6		11	
		8		6		5		2		6
	86	31	87	23	90	15	93	8	88	23
		45		56		68		81		57

1) The following questions were asked:

a) "There are voluntary and gratuitous activities carried out in the social field in addition to one's regular activities which are not considered to be one's direct work, such as care of others, activities in associations, looking after babies or school children (except for one's own). Do you carry out such added tasks from time to time?"

b) "Would you be willing to carry out such tasks?" (Only asked of persons who answered "no" to question a))

*) Legend:

a	b
yes	
	yes
no	depends
no	

Source: Deimer et al. (1984): 186.

depending upon the frequency and regularity of the work being considered (Badelt 1985; 180); and

3) in the Federal Republic of Germany estimates vary widely depending upon the definition of voluntary and gratuitous work being employed. The range stretches from 1 % to 22 %.[3)]

As noted, including neighborhood help, in Table 1, 11 % of the persons we surveyed indicated that they had actually rendered social services as volunteers. Beyond the actual level of social services, there is a potential that may be developed in the pursuit of a new welfare mix. Table 1 also shows that a further 29 % of the persons interviewed, as part of work on our project, would be willing to provide added social services and that 6 % of those people would be prepared to provide such services. The remaining 23 % would make their voluntary effort dependent upon specific conditions tied to the context or the content of the service to be provided. From these rather broad estimates we may conclude that any new design of the welfare mix could count at most upon roughly a third of the population to provide voluntary social services.

The Social Group Orientation of the Potential for Voluntary Social Service

Can this potential for voluntary social services be found equally across the various strata of society? The data in Table 1 reveal patterns of the actual and potential commitment of social groups to voluntary service. Most strikingly, that commitment increases with the level of education and decreases with age. The implications of this tendency for the design of the welfare mix come readily to mind. Relatively educated and young people are more likely than the less educated and the elderly to accept voluntary social services as part and parcel of a new welfare mix. And relatively educated and young people are more likely than the less educated and the elderly to participate actively in a system that would integrate voluntary social services within existing broader networks of care.

A similar pattern emerges when the sex and the professional status of the persons interviewed is considered in addition to their age and level of education. The actual and potential activity is greater for civil servants and white-collar workers than for the self-employed and for blue-collar workers (see Fig. 1). Other studies indicate that the willingness to provide

---

3) The estimate of 1 % relates solely to self-help in the health field. The estimated 22 % relates to the whole range of voluntary action, including environmental action groups or unpaid work in sports associations (as training staff, for instance), see Estorff (1985).

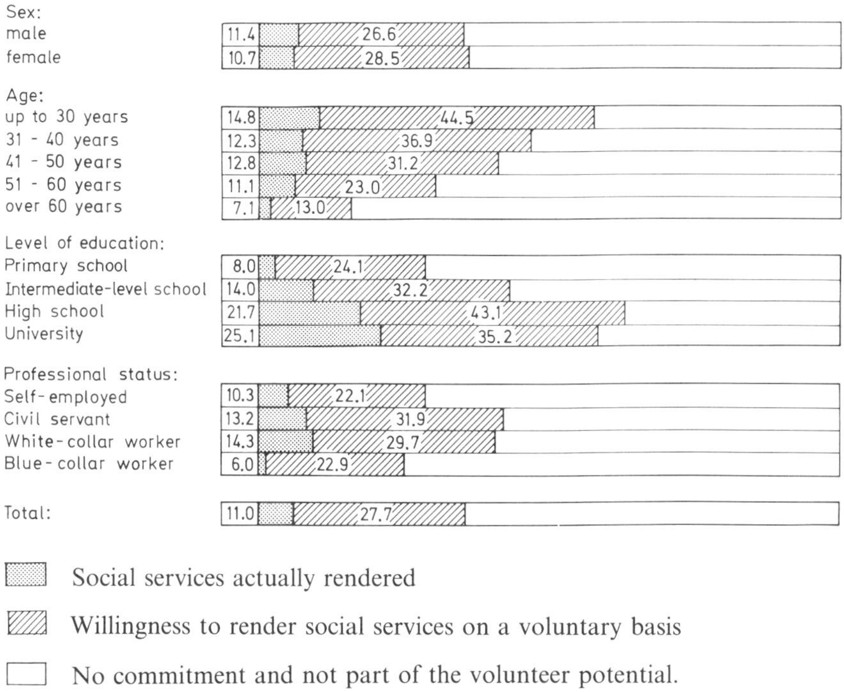

Figure 1 Social Services Actually Rendered and Willingness to Render Social Services, By Socio-Demographic Status, in Percent

Source: Own computaions based on Infratest, Bürger und Sozialstaat 1983; n = 6533.

voluntary social services increases with income (Badelt 1980: 124 and his sources). The "middle-class bias" of self-help and self-organization appears evident from surveys undertaken in several countries (see, for example, The Gallup Report 1985; 26; Wolfenden Committee 1978: 56).

Types of Resources Granted or Exchanged in Different Social Networks

Given this overall scope and the previously cited limitations on voluntary social services, we turn to their structure and content, focusing first on the types of resources that can be granted or exchanged and, secondly, on the principles for integrating them into different types of networks.

Theoretical Foundations

What types of social resources can be granted or exchanged particularly well via small, self-organized, and thus voluntary types of social networks? In order to answer this question, we draw on a particular approach to the social psychology of behavior associated with the term "resource theory of social exchange" as formulated by E. and U. Foa (1976: 99). Accordingly, particular forms of behavior are undertaken if they are considered, or expected, to yield material or non-material rewards taking the form of particular social resources: money, goods, services, love, status, and information. Each of these classes of generalized resources encompasses a range of particular resources. Love consists of emotional affinity, warmth, well-being, and proximity; status of prestige, respect, and attention; information of opinions, instructions, and advice; money of all types of media of exchange; goods of all tangible products and materials; and services of all actions undertaken to benefit a person's body or property. Voluntary social services encompass the grant of each of these resource classes from one individual to another, or from one individual to a group of others (see Pfaff et al. forthcoming; 138). These resources, then, represent the content or the particular "quality" that is transmitted in a social network from the grantor to the recipient.

Foa and Foa distinguish between universalistic and particularistic types of resources. The partners in an interaction involving universalistic resources (money, goods, and information) can be exchanged more readily without undue loss of the quality of the resource being transmitted than is the case with particularistic types of resources. For the latter, services, status and love, Foa and Foa postulate that a more affective type of relationship exists between the interacting persons, making an exchange of persons more difficult or outright impossible. We may apply the resource theory of social exchange to the interactions taking place in particular types of networks, thus identifying their relative strengths and weaknesses as social arrangements for the grant or exchange of particular social resources.

Empirical Evidence

In the process of interaction several social resources generally are granted or exchanged simultaneously. Thus, a profile of resource flows can be pieced together on the basis of survey evidence gathered through interviews with the suppliers of social services. From this profile we can then identify the dominant resource(s) characteristic of a particular type of network, as is evident from Figure 2.

- The large-scale or collective networks characteristic of public delivery systems generally transmit "information" as a dominant resource, with

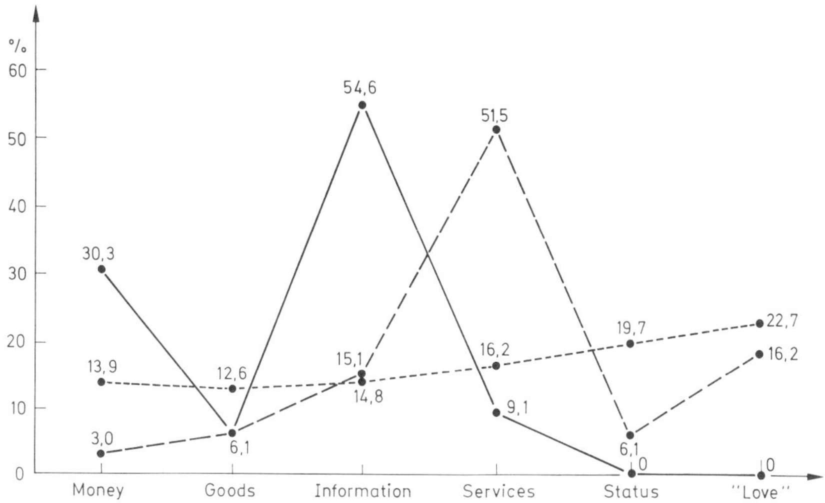

— Large networks (public institutions at different levels); n = 12 (multiple response)

--- Intermediary Institutions; n = 17 (multiple response)

..... Self-help (members of voluntary social action groups); n = 64 (multiple response).

Figure 2 Relative Importance of the Social Resources Transmitted by Different Types of Networks as Reflected in Supplier Perceptions (in Percent).

Source: Authors' data (1983/84).

"money" being less central. "Services" and "goods" are considered to play a subordinate role. "Status" and "love" are not generally considered to be part of the social resource flows emanating from collective networks.

- For intermediary networks "services" play a dominant role, but other types of resource come into the picture as well. While "money" and "information" lose in importance, "love" plays an increasingly important role.
- Primary or small networks have a more balanced resource profile in which all six types of resources are present and in which particularistic types of resources play a more dominant role than the universalistic types of resources do.

In terms of what beneficiaries expect of social services, the resource flows that Foa and Foa associate with particular types of resources have the patterns depicted in Table 2.

Table 2 Expectations of Beneficiaries Regarding Dominant Resource Flows Associated with Different Types of Networks

Social resource	Type of Network		
	Large network (public institutions at different levels)	Intermediary institutions	Self-help groups
Love	0.4	15.2	40.4
Status	1.7	1.5	4.9
Information	21.0	20.9	31.3
Money	40.4	1.5	0.4
Goods	20.5	12.6	2.3
Services	16.0	48.4	20.7

Source: Author's data (1985), n = 507.

- The resource of "money" is most frequently associated with large networks and least frequently associated with very small intermediary networks and self-help groups.
- The association of "information" as a resource with all three levels is more balanced than is the case with "money". "Information" is expected most of self-help groups.
- The particularistic resource of "services" is also associated with all three levels but most strikingly with the intermediary networks.
- "Status" plays a minor role in the relationship between beneficiaries and networks, although its value is slightly higher in the case of self-help groups.
- Interestingly, the patterns associated with "goods" differ from those associated with "money". Large networks generally are associated with the transfer of goods, while intermediary networks play a lesser – and small networks a fairly negligible – role in this regard.
- Last but not least, the resource "love" is associated mainly with self-help groups, and to a far lesser extent with intemediary institutions.

Comparative Advantages of Different Networks

According to which principle is the resource potential of smaller networks to be integrated within the overall welfare mix? From the empirical patterns outlined above, it is clear that smaller networks have an advantage over intermediary and large networks in the transmission of particularistic resources. However, the dominant resources associated with intermediary networks differed from those of small networks in a far less predictable way.

Judging by dominant resource profiles, we may thus conclude that certain types of networks are better suited to transmitting certain types of resources than other types of networks and that these comparative advantages should and could perhaps be used in designing a welfare mix that enhances the effective and efficient transmission of particular social resources. Furthermore, given the relative advantage of each level of social networks, and given the range of resources needed by individuals, cooperation between all three levels of networks appears to be called for.

The necessity for improved integration of all levels of social networks is increasingly being recognized by representatives of each level in the Federal Republic of Germany. This development was by no means always self-evident. In the not-too-distant past relations between particular representatives of the three levels of networks were characterized more by competition than by cooperation. And the process of change in the awareness of the potential for further integration has only just begun (see, for example, Niedrig 1985). Nonetheless, specific steps have been taken to promote this process of integration by mobilizing the resource potential inherent in the domain of self-help and neighborhood-help and by attempting to provide the support of larger networks that often appears to be necessary if such processes of integration are to be effective.

Two Case Studies: KISS (Hamburg) and SEKIS (Berlin)

In September 1985 there were no fewer than seventy-eight local and regional self-help contact and information facilities and similar types of organizations in the Federal Republic of Germany, twelve of which had been set up between December 1984 and September 1985 alone (Deutsche Arbeitsgemeinschaft 1984: 31, and 1985). These organizations can be found throughout the Federal Republic, including West Berlin, generally in urban agglomerations. Even though all of these facilities have been organized with the aim of providing counsel and support to self-help groups, the way they are run varies considerably depending on their organizational sponsorship and the associated financial support. The operations range from a local health-insurance fund to a true self-managed form of social initiative. Out of this broad range of organizations for aiding and encouraging self-help groups and other types of novel initiatives, we focus on two: KISS (Kontakt- und Informationsstelle für Selbsthilfegruppen, or "Contact and Information Facility for Self-Help Groups") and SEKIS (Selbsthilfe Informations- und Kontaktstelle, or "Self-Help Information and Contact Facility") and ask whether such organizations are suitable for integrating the new social initiatives into the existing system of care.

Aims and Mode of Operation

KISS was originally set up in Hamburg in 1981 in the context of a research project dealing with self-help groups in the health field and carried out in the field of medical sociology at the University Hamburg-Eppendorf (Estorff 1985: 171). It has since become independent from the research project and is being financed by the city government of Hamburg (DM 197,000 in 1986). It defines its own function as that of acting as a hub for all health-related self-help activities within the Hamburg region (see Estorff 1985: 174).

KISS orients its activities to private citizens, professional helpers, and self-help groups needing support. Its central aim is to address persons who have thus far not been active in self-help groups and encourage them to engage in such activities. It also assists self-help groups by supplying them with information, advice, and supporting materials. Additionally, KISS is engaged in an active public relations program designed to promote the concept of self-help networks.

SEKIS is sponsored by the Deutscher Paritätischer Wohlfahrtsverband (DPWV), but its principial funding comes from the city government of West Berlin, the Senate (Fink 1983: 8). The Senate intends to use SEKIS as a hub for its model program of supporting and aiding self-help groups. The use of DPWV as an orgnizational sponsor resulted from a compromise between the Senate and the self-help groups of Berlin. However, the long-term aim is to provide SEKIS with its own organizational framework (Deutsche Arbeitsgemeinschaft Selbsthilfegruppen 1984; 5).

The central aim of SEKIS is roughly parallel to that of KISS. However, its stronger financial basis allows for an infrastructure (meeting rooms and technical aids, for example) that is more extensive than that of KISS. In order to mobilize the latent potential for self-help and volunteer service, SEKIS has broadened its overall aim to encompass the entire field of social services: "SEKIS attempts to act as a point of contact for all those who wish to find or found a self-help group in the fields of health or social affairs" (DPWV 1985: 8). By thus broadening the scope of its activities, SEKIS has a better chance than KISS to develop the potential for neighborhood-help and to integrate self-help groups within the broad networks of care.

Successes and Failures

Evidence available to date indicates that the work of the contact facilities has been quite successful, less in terms of mobilizing the latent potential (of about 23 % of the persons interviewed in our study mentioned before) than in furthering the idea of interlocking networks of self-help organizations and in lending support to such organizations. Thus, they have started to develop the sure potential (about 6 % of the West German population). SEKIS was able to provide service facilities in the broad social context as well. In 1984 it was able to provide counsel to 1,350 cases in the field of health and to another 1,121 cases in all other social services. In 2,575 additional cases, SEKIS represented the interests of a great part of the self-help sector by providing financial counselling or other support in conflicts with the Senate, regional offices, other administrative units, and research facilities (author's calculation based on DPWV 1985: 18).

On the other hand, the "SEKIS solution" was criticized strongly by a segment of the alternative movement. It was seen as a competitive screening authority that was intended to create "the ideal applicant for public support" and that would tend "to institutionalize the division of the alternative sector into useful and non-useful projects" (Kück 1983). Despite, or rather because of, the nonprofit and public character of the sponsoring organization (DPWV), fears about bureaucratic red tape abound. It is feared that continued financial support will be lost if the recipient groups are not "well behaved." The health-oriented self-help groups often are especially afraid of "being used" for political and strategic purposes.

When both successes and "failures" are weighed, it appears evident that the character of the project as a model should be replaced by an instrument that would be effective in mobilizing an even greater number of the potential volunteers.

Possible Improvements

Can the organizational mechanism of care-giving networks as realized particularly through SEKIS be developed further? We postulate four theses in this regard.

1) If a broad voluntary potential is to be realized, the infrastructure supporting self-help initiatives must not be limited to the health field and to "in-groups." The support must be also given, for example, to initiatives in neighborhood-help and self-help in the cultural field.
2) The independence of these types of organizations must be promoted, with independence relating not only to political or conceptual issues but to financial ones as well. This means that activities should not be

limited to counselling self-help groups and organizations. A facility like SEKIS should act as a representative of the interests of self-help groups vis-à-vis the city, the state, and the federal government, not only as an instrument of these political bodies in dealing with self-help groups.

3) It is no doubt idealistic to expect a facility like SEKIS to serve in the capacity just mentioned. At a minimum, however, a mixed financing system should be instituted to make sure that the influence of any particular sponsor is kept within bounds.
4) In many cases cooperation between professionals, semiprofessionals, and volunteers (including self-help groups) can be advantageous to social policy. A counselling and contact facility of the type described in this chapter can be useful as a hub for the intertwining of different social networks. However, to sound a note of caution again, such a facility must not be "used" by the cities and intermediate-level welfare organizations solely to recruit volunteers to help pursue their organization's specific aims. These networks of volunteers must act in partnership with the larger networks.

Some Conclusions

How can this type of organizational innovation be improved in order to yield the realization of the dormant resource potential? When summarizing the various points touched on in the process of reasoning, the following conclusions can be arrived at:

a) In the Federal Republic of Germany there is potential for voluntary social service. It could indeed serve as a basis of a "new welfare mix" founded on self-help and new social initiatives.
b) For each of the three levels of social networks – the large networks of the public sector, the intermediary institutions, and self-help groups – there are particular types of social resources for whose transmission it is better suited than the other levels. Each level has its comparative advantages.
c) The "instrument" of coordination that could conceivably help to develop this potential and that could thus achieve a multiplier-effect could indeed consist in the new self-help contact and information facilities.

   At the same time, we have attempted to identify those factors that would threaten such development:

a) Current volunteer services and the potential for further volunteer service exhibit a "middle-class bias." Groups most needy of self-help and mutual help are underrepresented in the pool of potential volunteers.

b) In practical politics the need for a "resource mix" that combines the comparative advantages of all three levels of social networks is not generally recognized yet. Through the principle of subsidiarity, cutbacks of public services are often made without sufficient attention to the question of whether the intermediate level and self-help groups can fill the vacuum thus created. In fact, such a response is generally and tacitly expected.

c) Contact and information facilities of the type described in this chapter are highly promising but still experimental. The large number of such facilities alone cannot hide the fact that their scope of the potential realized is still far too limited. Facilities like KISS and SEKIS thus represent an exception to the rule.

A concept of social policy aimed at eliminating the constraints currently being experienced in the transfer of services and at designing a more rational welfare mix might stand a better chance than the present concept does of providing for the types of benefit touched on in the beginning of this section. If such a concept cannot be realized, the withdrawal of the welfare state from several fields of social service can be expected to continue as it has in recent years. Let it not be forgotten, in any case, that the principle of subsidiarity also requires solidarity.[4)]

References

Badelt, C. (1980): *Sozioökonomie der Selbstorganization*, Frankfurt am Main and New York.

Badelt, C. (1985): *Politische Ökonomie der Freiwilligenarbeit*, Frankfurt am Main and New York.

Deimer, K. and Jaufmann, D. (1983): Soziale Selbsthilfegruppen: Bestandsaufnahme und Potentialabschätzungen in unterschiedlich strukturierten Raumeinheiten, In: *Soziale Selbsthilfegruppen in der Bundesrepublik Deutschland*, (Eds.) W.H. Asam and M. Heck, Munich.

Deimer, K.; Kistler, E.; Pfaff, M.; and Theis, A. (1984): *Berücksichtigung von Verbraucherinteressen bei staatlichen Anbietern*, Frankfurt am Main and New York.

Deutsche Arbeitsgemeinschaft Selbsthilfegruppen e.V., (Ed.) (1984): *Selbsthilfe-Kontaktstellen*, Gießen.

idem, (1985): *Liste von Selbsthilfe-Kontaktstellen*, Gießen.

DPWV-Gesamtverband e.V., (Ed.) (1985): *SEKIS-Selbsthilfe Kontakt- und Informationsstelle, Annual Report 1984*, Berlin.

---

4) Nell-Breuning (1976): 7–8, Evangelisches Soziallexikon (1969): 667.

Estorff, A. (1985): Unterstützung von Selbsthilfegruppen durch lokale Kontakt- und Informationsstellen – Beispiel: Hamburg, In: *Subsidiarität und Selbsthilfegruppe*, (Eds.) W.H. Asam and M. Heck, Munich.

idem, (1985): Zielsetzungen, Funktionsweise und Erfahrungen mit örtlichen Informations- und Kontaktstellen für Selbsthilfegruppen und sozial- und gesundheitspolitische Konsequenzen; Paper prepared for the Workshop discussion of The Federal Ministry for Youth, Family Affairs, and Health on the topic of "Infrastructure Support for Self-Help," 12. December 1985.

Evangelisches Soziallexikon, 6th ed. (1969): S. v. "Katholische Soziallehre," by F. Karrenberg

Fink, U. (1983): *Zwischenbericht des Senators für Gesundheit, Soziales und Familie zum Thema: Förderung von Selbsthilfegruppen*, Berlin.

Foa, E.B. and Foa, U.G. (1976): Resource Theory of Social Exchange, In: *Contemporary Topics in Social Psychology*, (Eds.): J.W. Thibaut, J.T. Spence, and R.C. Carson, Morristown, N.J.

Gallup Report (1985): No. 234, Princeton, NJ.

Infratest (1983): *Bürger und Sozialstaat*, Untersuchungsbericht, München.

Kück, M. (1983): Ist die Autonomie flöten gegangen? Erfahrungen mit dem Berliner Förderungsprogramm für den Selbsthilfe- und Alternativsektor, *Die Tageszeitung*, 7 October 1983.

v. Nell-Breuning, O. (1976): Das Subsidiaritätsprinzip, *Theorie und Praxis der sozialen Arbeit*, 27: 7–8.

Niedrig, H. (1985): Daten und Tendenzen der freien Wohlfahrtspflege, *Theorie und Praxis der sozialen Arbeit*, 2:

Pfaff, M.; Deimer, K.; Jaufmann, D.; and Kistler, E. (forthcoming): *Gesellschaftliche Ressourcen und Transaktionen in sozialen Netzen.*

Wolfenden Committee (1978): *The Future of Voluntary Organizations*, London.

Concluding Essay

Tanks and Bicycles – Two Scenarios for Europe

Martin Jänicke

Prognoses show that the future of Western Europe up to 1990 seems to be relatively clear. The growth of the GNP is expected to be high in absolute terms, but low in relative terms, that is, not high enough to solve such important problems as mass unemployment and public deficits (see Pfeiffer 1986). The unemployment rate will stay high in many countries of the European Communities, and public deficits will be recalcitrant. In most European countries a large part of the additional demand will be financed by public debt. In 1990 even the Federal Republic of Germany will look back upon two decades of continuous deficit spending. Countries such as Ireland, Italy, and Belgium have a financial future that is even worse.

In the international arena the tendency toward protectionism will be strong. And the debt problem of the Third World, the United States, and many other countries will remain a continuing threat to the world economy. Even under the somewhat unrealistic assumption of high economic growth and no recession, the United States will not solve the problem of deficits before 1991. In other words, the present problems will more or less persist until 1990. Actually, there is little disagreement about this between economic forecasters (Jänicke 1986a).

Two Possibilities

But what about the 1990s? Usually, two scenarios are discussed, the "pessimistic" and the "optimistic," that of near stagnation and that of a long-term revival of the economy. The pessimistic one is paralleled by visions of Mancur Olson (1982). The optimistic scenario is generally inspired by Kondratiev's or Schumpeter's theory of "long waves" (see Futures 1981, Jänicke 1985).

Maybe the best long-term prognosis to be ventured is that both possibilities are real. SHELL forecasters have been saying this for several years. Their scenario of "disharmonies" leads to near stagnation. The happier scenario is that of "structural change" (Löw 1985). The World

Table 1 Two Scenarios

Stagnation	Innovation
1. Tank syndrome/rigidity	1. Bicycle syndrome/flexibiliy
2. Super-industrialism	2. Post-industrialism
3. Quantitative growth; high-volume production; long-term limits to growth	3. Qualitative growth; high-value production; growth of limits
4. Centralization of capital and power by the successful branches of the post-war cycle	4. Decentralization; strong influence of economic newcomers and innovative minorities
5. Dominance of the world market and the super powers	5. Regionalization, nationally and internationally
6. Laissez-faire strategies; market failure combined with government failure; bureaucratic repair strategies	6. Preventive political policy, cooperative long-term planning
7. Externalization; high social costs; evironmental and social risks	7. Internalization; appropriate technology; low-risk forms of production
8. Income and jobs as privilege	8. Effective mechanisms of redistribution
9. Problems of legitimation, acceptance, and motivation; high level of social and economic conflicts	9. Motivation by participation; a consensus-oriented political culture

Bank offers two similar paths for the industrialized countries, the only difference being that the assumed growth rates are higher (World Bank 1986).

I do not believe that differences in economic growth are a good basis for "optimism" or "pessimism." The problem-solving capacity of a rapid expansion of production should not be overestimated, especially in times that need structural change. Therefore, I speak about a scenario of innovation and a scenario of stagnation by rigidity, or, metaphorically, about bicycles and tanks (see Table 1).

The driver of a tank may be intelligent, but not necessarily so. He can easily be blind and stupid. The consequences of errors or mistakes tend to be "externalized" to the social and physical environment. The bicyclist, however, must anticipate all eventualities because they may become seriously "internal" for him. He must be intelligent, preventive, and flexible, making the most of his eyes and ears so that he causes no damage to the social and physical environment.

The "tank syndrome" describes a deadly privilege of power. It may be an advantage for a long time. But at some time or other the tank will be stopped by lack of fuel or a large obstacle. This may cause a deep "crisis" for the driver, whereas the bicyclist is doing well.

Most Western European countries – partly in contrast to Scandinavian countries or Japan – suffer from a combination of market failure and government failure. This phenomenon seems to be recognized when the OECD speaks of "socioeconomic rigidities" (including "the rigidifying effects of lumpy, capital-intensive technology") (OECD 1983) or when the term "Eurosclerosis" (Giersch) is used. In most cases, however, this line of argument is directed against the welfare state or the role of trade unions. But lower wages and poorer people do not solve the deep-rooted problem of innovation and adaption, that is, of overcoming the tank syndrome.

The Scenario of Stagnation

Innovation is a useful prerequisite for power, but power is no useful prerequisite for innovation. One reason for this is long-term political business cycles. In an early stage of a long wave innovators may be successful with new products or new ideas. In the next stage they accumulate capital and market power that make them successful even if they are not innovative. In the third stage former innovators – such as a company or a whole industry – may accumulate political lobbying power. In addition to their market power this gives them the chance to succeed by using the state and its budgets, not so much by coming up with good ideas and products.

In my opinion, the term "Eurosclerosis" can derive its justification from the fact, that too many Western European enterprises and industries have reached this third stage of market power combined with political power. Eurosclerosis is also characterized by the stability of this economic power structure. We can study this by looking at the European automobile industry and its low standard of pollution control. In the warm climate of political non-intervention and laissez-faire policies, there has been no strong incentive for innovation, say, in the direction of cleaner engines. The same can be said about the electricity power industry in many European countries and its lack of interest in alternative energy and energy conservation. Agribusiness is another example; so is the construction industry, which still draws heavily on public budgets; and so is the military-industrial complex. (According to one study, high military expenditures were related to low growth in productivity between 1960 and 1980) (see Wirtschaftswoche 1985).

In general, hierarchical power (i.e., power of and within large organizations) can be defined by three privileges: the privilege of low pressure to learn (K. Deutsch); the privilege of low pressure to adapt and cooperate (M. Weber); and the privilege to externalize and to redistribute (K.W. Kapp). All this undermines the motivation to innovate and to adapt.

The tank syndrome has still other characteristics that cause problems with innovation. In addition to the aforementioned privileges, there are special myths.

1) The myth of high growth rates and their problem-solving capacity. National economics that are unable to solve problems like mass unemployment and the public debt through structural change will tend to concentrate all hopes on higher growth and will tend to pay too high a price for stimulating that growth.
2) The myth of laissez-faire. It is, among other things, the defense formula of privileged societal oligarchies that want to be left in peace. But preventive action in such fields as energy or environmental policy can stimulate technical innovations.
3) The myth of industry. Many developed countries of the world have had to learn that industry is not the only source of wealth. The Eastern European countries, although suffering from severe disadvantages of "over-industrialization", have not yet learned this lesson. Many Western European political economists, too, still tend to disregard the economic potential of services and information. All member countries of the European Community promote information technologies, but what about information itself? The United States has, for instance, four times as many economic data banks than Western and Northern Europe combined (see Wirtschaftswoche 1986). The myth of industry is strong even in the European Community's economic statistics, which are mainly a compilation of data form the manufacturing sector, although in many countries about 60% of the gross national product is produced in the service sector.

   According to the tank syndrome, then, the scenario of stagnation will be characterized by: overly powerful industries that have seen their more innovative days; an overly weak position of the state within that economic power structure, leading to a low capacity for preventive and regulative action; and an overly high level of external or social costs and remedial bureaucratic activities of all kinds.

Stagnation is associated with a socioeconomic structure that tends to generate social, economic, fiscal, and/or environmental crises. The term describes an economic system whose traditional industries absorb too large a proportion of the available macroeconomic ressources. Not even the Schumpeterian crisis mechanisms of "productive destruction" are sufficiently effective to stimulate innovation (or if they do work, they come too late). I disagree with Mancur Olson (1982) mainly on one point: It is not the age of democratic institutions that causes the problem. Rather, it is the age of a special economic (and bureaucratic) power structure that tends to ignore challenges of innovation and political reform.

The Scenario of Innovation

The scenario of innovation will work only under two conditions. First, the just mentioned restrictions of traditional power and privilege structures must be overcome. Second, and more important, the process of innovation must be conceived in a comprehensive way. It is not only a question of hardware but of several levels of techniques. I distinguish three levels of techniques (see Gottl-Ottlilienfeld 1931, Mannheim 1940):

1. "hard" techniques (Realtechnik): making use of raw materials and energies on the basis of inventions;
2. social techniques (Sozialtechnik): organizing human behavior (including human self-organization) on the basis of inventions; and
3. intellectual techniques (Intellektualtechnik): organizing information on the basis of inventions.

The scenario of innovation includes all three levels. The "long waves" of Kondratiev or Schumpeter were accompanied not only by innovations such as steam engines or automobiles but also by social innovations such as the institutional achievements of the American and French revolutions, the Bismarckian social reforms of the 1880s, and the welfare state and Keynesian economic policy at the beginning of the post-war cycle. Such social innovations as quality circles, self-help groups, and participatory mechanisms in planning are more recent examples.

Intellectual techniques range, for instance, from computer software to brainstorming. They have relevance in theory and methodology. Their main innovation task is to systematize new questions and organize information patterns for new answers in a time of radical change. This includes techniques to "ignore" or "forget" the immense amount of old and irrelevant information (stored, for instance, in libraries) causing a huge information overload. It also includes the need for informational autonomy, that is, independence from one-sided information by vested interests.

The level of social techniques is the most important (Meden 1984). And the most important social innovation is the development and implementation of institutions for cooperative and long-term planning based on consensus. Who has the best techniques for realizing a commonly shared, long-term perspective? Japan and the South Asian "mini-Japans" all have institutions for long-term planning. The same is true of Sweden and Norway. In the European Communities, however, the myth of laissez-faire politics is relatively strong. Will this promote successful competition in the world arena?

There are two potential long-term steering mechanisms: the crisis mechanisms of the "laissez-faire" concept and the political mechanism of cooperative (not bureaucratic) planning. The laissez-faire concept will lose out in the competition with cooperative planning. The crisis mechanism comes too late and costs too much.

The second area of social innovation is the field of decentralization. Here it is important at the same time to create better central mechanisms for coordination or redistribution.

The third arena of social innovation is that of stimulating new types of economies and shifting macroeconomic resource to new fields. Old industries that pay relatively low taxes but receive relatively broad support from the state budget must lose their privileges.

Political action is especially important in those fields where the existing structure creates obstacles to keep newcomers from developing, as is for instance the case when alternative ways of producing electricity are involved. Such action presupposes more autonomy and a broader political basis for government policy.

The fourth area of social innovation is the service and information economy. The service sector is creating nearly all the new jobs, 22.4 million of them in the United States between 1970 and 1984, whereas the contribution of the industrial sector to job creation was zero (Kemp Shelp 1985). The service sector is also a key source of exports (Feketekuty and Hausen 1985). Contrary to myth, it plays an increasingly important role for the productivity of a developed economy. This function is important for the industrial and agricultural sector, but it is also important for the service economy itself. The service economy raises its productivity by means of production that is itself highly service intensive. But the service economy's labor force, too, is becoming increasingly dependent on services, requiring, for example, an exceedingly high level of education. The service sector can also raise its own productivity through intelligent organizational services, such as by redirecting improperly utilized or wasted resources of the universities (Riddle 1987).

A fifth area is the production of relevant information by such new disciplines as future studies, environmental studies, epidemiology, and social innovation research. The most important research field is the one dealing with with the complexities and problemprone relationships that are neglected by the process of specialization.

To avoid any misunderstanding it must be stressed that "bicycle" scenarios as outlined above it not oriented to the bureaucratic planning of every detail of the economy. The government cannot prescribe the most appropriate technology, but it should, for instance, be able to impose taxes on technologies that have proven to be dangerous or deleterious to welfare or the long-term bases of survival. The scenario of innovation is oriented to a long-term perspective shared by all relevant actors, including the innovative newcomers. It stresses high-value forms of production (Reich 1983). It aims at institutional innovations that stimulate motivation, efficiency, and effectiveness (such as by introducing new mechanisms of decentralization and co-ordination). It overcomes the neglect of the service and information economy, a type of production for which the countries of the European Community seem to be well suited. It is a scenario in which the decentral units – being nearer to the motivation and experience of people are at least strong enough to counterbalance the hierarchical centralism of economic, bureaucratic, or military power. It is a scenario of regionalization, both nationally and internationally.

The British and the Scandinavian Experience

So far, I have discussed two scenarios or ideal types of development (in the sense of Max Weber). I am now turning to real cases.

At the Free University of Berlin, research has been conducted on structural change in thirty-one industrialized countries, including those in Eastern Europe (Jänicke 1986 b). On the basis of indicators such as energy consumption, steel consumption, or the weight of transported goods, the degree of change away from "high-volume" types of production has been ascertained. There were almost no signs of such changes in the countries of both eastern and southern Europe between 1973 and 1983 (the German Democratic Republic and Italy being somewhat deviant cases). Most Southern European countries experienced traditional industrial growth coupled with decreasing or low employment and increasing "structural" environmental pollution. A radical structural change in relative terms (relative decline of the high-volume indicators to the growth of the GNP) was found in Japan and Norway. A radical change in absolute terms was registered in Sweden and, to a lesser degree, in the United Kingdom.

On the whole, the results of this research suggests a distinction between four types of economic development in Europe:

1) the Eastern European type of unchanged traditional high-volume production with poor technical innovation and rising structural environmental problems;

2) the somewhat similar Southern European type of traditional industrialism, which is marked by a low and/or decreasing level of employment;
3) the British type of structural change by crisis, which involves the demise of powerful old industries, that have been politically stabilized for too long, and which features a critical decline of employment; and
4) the Scandinavian type of structural change, typified by an active and more consensual role of the government and by a high and/or rising level of employment (Jänicke 1988).

The British type of structural change will be found in other regions of the EC as well, Belgium being an example. But the United Kingdom itself seems to be a country in which nearly every macroeconomic actor, including the present prime minister, follows the tank syndrome – traditionalism, rigidity, egocentrism, and a high level of internal and external conflict to the bitter end. The story of British economic failure seems to be the story of an economic power and structure of privilege that is too rigid, of the shortcomings of the laissez-faire approach, of the neglect of political prevention, economic cooperation, and political consensus. Mechanisms for creating consensus are important for the process of innovation, because this is the most promising way to include the minority of innovators in the debates and decisions on long-term developments. This lesson can also be learned from the Japanese example.

Sweden was going through an even more radical structural change of the economy than Great Britain. Swedish consumption of crude steel declined by 40% between 1973 and 1983. The weight of transported goods declined by 29%, and primary energy consumption stagnated. The Swedish industrial labour force shrank by 15% from 1975 to 1983. However, Sweden has a rising level of employment, the highest today in the Western world. (And it has a better environment because of structural change). Given the burden of high public debt, the Swedish case cannot be taken too lightly. But in Norway structural change was accompanied by a sounder financial situation. There civilian employment increased by 18.5% between 1973 and 1983. Denmark completed structural change as the world champion of energy conservation (consumption declined by 15% within ten years). Though the unemployment rate increased, the employment level remained high, as in the other four Scandinavian countries (and Japan).

Such an international comparison should not be misunderstood as a kind of idealization. Many details must be examined. Success is only relative. And the structural problems common to all industrialized countries may be more important than their differences. But the political steering mechanisms of the Scandinavian states (or such different countries as Japan, Austria, and Switzerland) seem to provide a clearer basis for the elaboration of a long-term perspective for Europe as compared to countries where laissez-faire for tanks is the predominant philosophy.

References

Feketekuty, G. and Hauser, K. (1985): Information Technology and Trade in Services, *Economic Impact*, 52: 22.

Futures (August 1981), 4.

Gottl-Ottlilienfeld, F. von (1931): *Wirtschaft und Wissenschaft*, 2 vols, Jena: Verlag Gustav Fischer.

Jänicke, M. (Ed.) (1985): *Vor uns die goldenen neunziger Jahre? Langzeitprognosen auf dem Prüfstand*, München: Piper.

Jänicke, M. (1986a): *Staatsversagen. Die Ohnmacht der Politik in der Industriegesellschaft*, München: Piper.

Jänicke, M.; Mönch, H.; and Ranneberg, T. (1986b): Umweltentlastung durch Strukturwandel, Wissenschaftszentrum Berlin, discussion paper, IIUG dp 86–1 (available in english under the title: Struktural Change and Environmental Impact, dp 88–402).

Jänicke, M.; Mönch, H. (1988): Ökologischer und wirtschaftlicher Wandel im Industrievergleich, *Politische Vierteljahresschrift*, Special Edition 19/1988, ed. by M. Schmidt.

Kemp Shelp, R. (1985): Service Technology and Economic Development, *Economic Impact*, 52: 18.

Löw, A. (1985): Stagnierender Energiebedarf auch bei wachsender Wirtschaft – Ergebnisse der SHELL-Szenarien für die Bundesrepublik bis zum Jahr 2000, *Zeitschrift für Energiewirtschaft*, 2: 85–94.

Mannheim, K. (1940): *Man and Society in an Age of Reconstruction*, Part V, London: F. Routledge and Kegan.

Meden, C.G. and King, A. (Eds.) (1984): *Social Innovations for Development*, Oxford: Pergamon Press.

OECD (1983): *Positive Adjustment Policies – Managing Structural Change*, Paris: OECD, p. 7.

Olson, M. (1982): *The Rise and Decline of Nations – Economic Growth, Stagflation and Social Rigidities*, New Haven and London: Yale University Press.

Pfeiffer, A. (1986): Die Strategie der Gemeinschaft zum Abbau der Arbeitslosigkeit, *EG Magazin*, 15 (February): 1–8.

Reich, R.B. (1983): *The Next American Frontier*, Washington, D.C.: Times Books.

Riddle, D.I. (1987): Serviceled Growth, New York: Praeger Publishers.

Wirtschaftswoche (1985):Militärische Last und Produktivität, 20 September.

Wirtschaftswoche (1986): Spitzenreiter Amerika, 31 January: 88.

The World Bank (1986): *World Development Report 1986*, Washington D.C.: Oxford University Press.